READING IN THE PRESENCE OF CHRIST

T&T Clark New Studies in Bonhoeffer's Theology and Ethics

Series editors
Jennifer McBride
Michael Mawson
Philip G. Ziegler

READING IN THE PRESENCE OF CHRIST

A Study of Dietrich Bonhoeffer's Bibliology and Exegesis

Joel Banman

LONDON • NEW YORK • OXFORD • NEW DELHI • SYDNEY

T&T CLARK
Bloomsbury Publishing Plc
50 Bedford Square, London, WC1B 3DP, UK
1385 Broadway, New York, NY 10018, USA
29 Earlsfort Terrace, Dublin 2, Ireland

BLOOMSBURY, T&T CLARK and the T&T Clark logo are trademarks of
Bloomsbury Publishing Plc

First published in Great Britain 2021
This paperback edition published 2022

Copyright © Joel Banman, 2021

Joel Banman has asserted his right under the Copyright, Designs and Patents Act,
1988, to be identified as Author of this work.

For legal purposes the Acknowledgements on p. x constitute an extension of this copyright page.

Cover design: Terry Woodley
Cover image © bpk / Rotraut Forberg

All rights reserved. No part of this publication may be reproduced or
transmitted in any form or by any means, electronic or mechanical, including
photocopying, recording, or any information storage or retrieval system,
without prior permission in writing from the publishers.

Bloomsbury Publishing Plc does not have any control over, or responsibility for,
any third-party websites referred to or in this book. All internet addresses given
in this book were correct at the time of going to press. The author and publisher regret
any inconvenience caused if addresses have changed or sites have ceased
to exist, but can accept no responsibility for any such changes.

A catalogue record for this book is available from the British Library.

A catalog record for this book is available from the Library of Congress.

ISBN: HB: 978-0-5676-9859-9
       PB: 978-0-5676-9926-8
       ePDF: 978-0-5676-9860-5
       eBook: 978-0-5676-9862-9

Series: T&T Clark New Studies in Bonhoeffer's Theology and Ethics

Typeset by Integra Software Services Pvt. Ltd.

To find out more about our authors and books visit www.bloomsbury.com
and sign up for our newsletters.

For Rebekah

CONTENTS

Acknowledgements x
Abbreviations xi

Chapter 1
    BONHOEFFER AS A SCRIPTURAL THEOLOGIAN 1
    Bonhoeffer and the Bible 3
    On bibliology 5
    Summary of chapters 8

Part I
BIBLIOLOGY

Chapter 2
    THEOLOGIAN OF GOD'S WORD 15
    The Barthian challenge to liberal theology 16
    Bonhoeffer and the dialectical movement 20
    Bonhoeffer's early bibliology 26
    Conclusion 31

Chapter 3
    REVELATION AS *CHRISTUS PRAESENS* 33
    Revelation as the ground of ecclesiology 33
    Ecclesiology as the ground of epistemology 38
    The Bible in Bonhoeffer's academic theology 45
    An occasionalist bibliology 48

Chapter 4
    THE PRESENT LOGOS 53
    Bonhoeffer's Christological revision 55
        The transcendent Christ 56
        The present Christ 58
        The whole Christ 60
    Bonhoeffer's theology of the word 63
        Intelligibility 64
        Embodiment 65
        Spirit 67
    Conclusion 69

Chapter 5
THE WORD'S COMING TO WORD — 71
The present Christ as the word of proclamation — 71
The present Christ as the word of Scripture — 76
Scripture as witness and word — 83
The exegetical 'who' question — 86

Part II
EXEGESIS

Chapter 6
PRAYING THE PSALMS — 93
Whose prayers are they anyway? — 94
Psalm 42 as the prayer of the church — 100
Praying Psalm 90 with the saints — 102
Psalm 58 as the prayer of Christ — 106
Conclusion — 108

Chapter 7
MEDITATING ON THE WORD — 111
Praying Psalm 119 — 112
   The 'way' of God's word — 112
   Learning to love God's law — 113
   Praying with the psalmist — 115
Meditation vs exegesis — 117
   Silence and speech — 118
   Solitude and community — 119
   Stillness and action — 121
The transforming presence of Christ — 123
Conclusion — 126

Chapter 8
READING IN THE PRESENT TENSE — 127
The reconstruction of Jerusalem — 128
Baumgärtel's critique — 132
The present-tense character of revelation — 135
Reading out of context — 139
Conclusion — 145

Chapter 9
THE CALL OF THE PRESENT LORD — 149
Discipleship and revelation — 150
The Sermon on the Mount — 154
The cruciform shape of discipleship — 157
The church and discipleship — 161
Conclusion — 163

Chapter 10
    DOING THE TRUTH   165
    Revelation, reality and good   166
    The path according to Scripture   172
    The place of Scripture in *Ethics*   176
        'God's Love and the Disintegration of the World'   177
        'Natural Life'   181
    Conclusion   183

Chapter 11
    THE WORD FOR OTHERS   185
    Revelation in a religionless age   185
    Bonhoeffer and the Bible in prison   190
    Polyphonic exegesis   196

Chapter 12
    CONCLUSION   201
    Reading in the presence of Christ   201
        What is Scripture?   203
        What does God do with Scripture?   204
        What should we do with Scripture?   205
    Reading Scripture with Bonhoeffer   208
        A sacramental reading of Scripture   208
        A creedal reading of Scripture   209
        A narrative reading of Scripture   212
    Conclusion   215

Bibliography   217
Index   225

ACKNOWLEDGEMENTS

This book began as a doctoral dissertation at the University of Otago, New Zealand. My first thanks goes out to my primary supervisor, Christopher Holmes, who offered his expertise and guidance throughout this project with honesty, patience, and (as was often necessary) pastoral sensitivity. Additional thanks to my secondary supervisor, Murray Rae, and to my examination committee, Michael Mawson, Stephen Plant, and Philip Ziegler, each of whom offered astute judgements and invaluable suggestions that greatly improved the final form of this project.

I gratefully acknowledge the University of Otago's Division of Humanities and Graduate Research School for providing me with the opportunity and resources to complete this project. I am especially thankful for their award of a doctoral scholarship, without which I could not have pursued this research.

Thanks to everyone at the University of Otago who contributed to the discussions following my seminar presentations, and to my colleagues who helpfully commented on chapter drafts and conference papers as this research was taking shape. Cameron Coombe deserves special mention for taking on the unenviable task of reviewing a complete draft of my dissertation. The Otago scholarly community was truly remarkable. Collegiality grew into friendship, and I am grateful to everyone who took time in their busy schedules to have lunch together or to share drinks after a long week of writing.

Thanks to the editors of this series, Jennifer McBride, Michael Mawson, and Philip Ziegler, for inviting me to contribute this volume. Thanks also to the editorial team at T&T Clark and to the anonymous reviewers of this manuscript, all of whom have helped make this book better than it otherwise would have been.

Finally, I could not have completed this book without the tireless support of my friends and family. My parents, Steve and Sandra, have been an endless source of love and support, not least by providing a home for us during an unexpectedly complicated transition back to life in Canada. My children, Nathaniel and Lucy, continue to astound me with their unconditional love and patience. My wife, Rebekah, has selflessly shared in all the trials and joys that accompanied this work, and I cannot imagine having done it without her. This one is for her.

A portion of CHAPTER 4 originally appeared in Joel Banman, 'The Word of the Church to the World: Bonhoeffer's Concept of the Logos and the Bilingual Character of Public Theology', *The Bonhoeffer Legacy: An International Journal* 5 (2018): 47–62. An abridged and modified version of CHAPTER 9 originally appeared in Joel Banman, 'Discipleship as a "Who" Question: Bonhoeffer on Reading Scripture as the Call of the Present Christ', *Stimulus: The New Zealand Journal of Christian Thought and Practice* 26 (2019): 18–23. My thanks for their permission to reproduce material here.

ABBREVIATIONS

CD Karl Barth, *Church Dogmatics*, ed. Thomas F. Torrance and Geoffrey W. Bromiley, 4 vols. (Edinburgh: T&T Clark, 1956–1975)

DB-ER Eberhard Bethge, *Dietrich Bonhoeffer: A Biography*, rev. ed., ed. and trans. Victoria J. Barnett (Minneapolis: Fortress, 2000)

DBW Dietrich Bonhoeffer, *Dietrich Bonhoeffer Werke*, ed. Eberhard Bethge, 17 vols. (Gütersloh: Chr. Kaiser, 1986–1999)

DBWE Dietrich Bonhoeffer, *Dietrich Bonhoeffer Works*, ed. Victoria J. Barnett, Wayne Whitson Floyd Jr. and Barbara Wojhoski, 17 vols. (Minneapolis: Fortress, 1996–2014)

LW Martin Luther, *Luther's Works*, American ed., ed. Jaroslav Pelikan and Helmut T. Lehman, 55 vols. (St. Louis: Concordia/Philadelphia: Fortress, 1955–1976)

1

BONHOEFFER AS A SCRIPTURAL THEOLOGIAN

Dietrich Bonhoeffer, in a 1936 letter to his brother-in-law, wrote, 'Let me first admit quite simply: I believe that the Bible alone is the answer to all our questions, and that we merely need ask perpetually and with a bit of humility in order to get the answer from it. One cannot simply *read* the Bible like other books.'[1] With a statement like this, he was directly contradicting the proposal of Benjamin Jowett, who wrote in 1860 that Scripture should in fact be interpreted '*like any other book*'.[2] And indeed it was that throughout the eighteenth and nineteenth centuries scholars approached the Bible with the same kinds of methods and critiques that might be applied to any other ancient text.[3] Whatever else this might have meant, it certainly meant that questions of 'contemporary import' were, at best, secondary to questions of what the biblical texts meant 'back then' in their own original context. This approach was not limited to the academy. The triumph of historical-critical methods trickled down into the pulpit, so that even now it is common to hear sermons begin by emphasizing the profound distance (as Gotthold Lessing puts it, the 'ugly, broad ditch') between the biblical world and our own.[4] The preacher's job is to bridge this gap and thereby to show how some treasures might be smuggled in from this ancient text, right over Lessing's unsuspecting head.

The outlook of this study is that a certain kind of Christological reading of Christian Scripture does not have to contend with this gap – at least not in the same way. If Christ is the content of Scripture, the word within the words, then the ugly, broad ditch between the ancient text and the contemporary hearer is a modernist fiction. For, the Christ who is risen (and the church knows of no other 'Christ') is the present Christ, and therefore Scripture is by virtue of its subject

---

1. DBWE 14, 167; DBW 14, 144–5.
2. Benjamin Jowett, 'On the Interpretation of Scripture', in *Essays and Reviews*, 10th ed. (London: Longman, Green, Longman, and Roberts, 1862), 458.
3. For the history of these developments, see Hans W. Frei, *The Eclipse of Biblical Narrative: A Study in Eighteenth and Nineteenth Century Hermeneutics* (New Haven/London: Yale University Press, 1974).
4. Gotthold E. Lessing, *Lessing's Theological Writings*, ed. and trans. Henry Chadwick (Stanford, CA: Stanford University Press, 1957), 55.

matter a present word.⁵ The church's exegetical task, then, is not about learning to bridge contexts or come up with contemporary 'applications'. The church's reading and proclamation of Scripture ought to discern the presence of the one who really encounters us in and as God's word.

That, in any case, is the wager on which this book is staked. My argument is that Dietrich Bonhoeffer read and preached Scripture in just this way. Bonhoeffer's theology of Scripture and his legacy as an exegete have been open questions from the earliest days of his reception. Over fifty years ago, Old Testament scholar Walter Harrelson concluded that 'Bonhoeffer's greatest contributions to Christian theology do not lie in the area of biblical exegesis. The greatness of Bonhoeffer is to be found in his work on ethics, Christology, and the relation of Christian faith to contemporary society'.⁶ Harrelson recognizes the importance of Scripture in Bonhoeffer's own theological work, conceding that Bonhoeffer could not have made his greatest contributions apart from his 'profound wrestling with the Bible'. Therefore, Harrelson concludes, although Bonhoeffer cannot teach us how to read the Bible, he can 'teach us to learn to live and die with the biblical Word in our hands'.⁷ This deeply ambivalent conclusion about Bonhoeffer's value as an interpreter of Scripture is not uncommon. Many others have admired his theology while maintaining critical reservations about his approach to scriptural interpretation.⁸

Some of this ambivalence may simply be attributed to the persistently uneasy relationship between biblical studies and dogmatic theology. However, I suspect another reason might be a methodological tendency to focus studies of Bonhoeffer's biblical interpretation strictly on his exegetical writings. The attempt to extract a consistent, repeatable hermeneutical method from examples of his biblical interpretation often yields mixed results. I intend to come at the question from a

---

5. The influence of Hans Frei will be obvious here, specifically his book, *The Identity of Jesus Christ: The Hermeneutical Bases of Dogmatic Theology* (Philadelphia: Fortress, 1975). I will return in this book's conclusion to the potential dialogue between Frei and Bonhoeffer.

6. Walter Harrelson, 'Bonhoeffer and the Bible', in *The Place of Bonhoeffer: Problems and Possibilities in His Thought*, ed. Martin E. Marty (London: SCM, 1963), 138–9.

7. Ibid., 139.

8. This is especially prominent in the earlier literature, before theological interpretation of Scripture gained legitimacy as an academic discipline. Alongside ibid., 115–42, see also John A. Phillips, *The Form of Christ in the World: A Study of Bonhoeffer's Christology* (London: Collins, 1967), 84–94; Martin Kuske, *The Old Testament as the Book of Christ: An Appraisal of Bonhoeffer's Interpretation*, trans. S. T. Kimbrough Jr (Philadelphia: Westminster, 1976), 81–4; Ernst Georg Wendel, *Studien zur Homiletik Dietrich Bonhoeffers: Predigt – Hermeneutik – Sprache*, Hermeneutische Untersuchungen zur Theologie 21 (Tübingen: J. C. B. Mohr, 1985), 100–2 and even DB-ER, 526–9. The target of several of these critiques is Bonhoeffer's study of Ezra-Nehemiah, which I discuss at length in CHAPTER 8. A charitable assessment of Bonhoeffer's Old Testament interpretation is found in Barry Harvey, *Taking Hold of the Real: Dietrich Bonhoeffer and the Profound Worldliness of Christianity* (Cambridge: James Clarke & Co., 2015), 209–33.

somewhat different angle. Following John Webster's logic that 'bibliology is prior to hermeneutics',[9] my operating assumption is that Bonhoeffer's interpretation of Scripture is driven by his theology of Scripture. Accordingly, the first half of this study is an enquiry into Bonhoeffer's *bibliology*. I will define the task of bibliology in more detail below, but broadly speaking, bibliology is a theological account of what Scripture *is* and, correspondingly, what God *does* with Scripture. I make the case that Bonhoeffer's bibliology, which is often implicit, can be seen at work throughout his exegetical writings. An analysis of the relationship between Bonhoeffer's bibliology and his exegesis illuminates the character of both, enabling a more thorough assessment of Bonhoeffer's legacy as a theological interpreter of Scripture. My approach in this book is to study Bonhoeffer as a scriptural theologian through the lens of his theology *of* Scripture.

Bonhoeffer and the Bible

Although the Bible can be found in a prominent place throughout his writings, it was never more central to his academic and personal life than during the so-called middle years of his theological development.[10] His well-known 'turn from the phraseological to the real' in the early 1930s corresponds to an increasing emphasis on scriptural exegesis in his writings.[11] Three of his published books written during this period – *Creation and Fall*, *Discipleship* and *Prayerbook of the Bible* – are essentially exegetical works, and the fourth – *Life Together* – makes constant reference to Scripture, depicting the Bible and especially the Psalter as central to Christian community. Bonhoeffer's 'transition from theologian to Christian', as Bethge describes it, was a quiet and unspoken change, but noticeable

---

9. John Webster, *The Domain of the Word: Scripture and Theological Reason* (London: T&T Clark, 2012), 4.

10. Bonhoeffer's life and theology can be usefully organized into three general periods: his early 'academic' years (1927–33), his middle 'pastoral' years (1933–40) and his later 'political' years (1940–5). This is Bethge's schema, which he puts forth in Eberhard Bethge, 'The Challenge of Dietrich Bonhoeffer's Life and Theology', in *World Come of Age: A Symposium on Dietrich Bonhoeffer*, ed. Ronald Gregor Smith (London: Collins, 1967), 22–88. I should state at the outset that these divisions are intended to provide a useful organizing principle for discussing Bonhoeffer's theological development. There are no hard and fast divisions between these periods, and, as will become clear throughout, I regard Bonhoeffer's corpus as far more united than divided across these periods.

11. Bonhoeffer describes it this way to Bethge: 'There are people who change, and many who can hardly change at all. I don't think I have ever changed much, except perhaps at the time of my first impressions abroad, and under the first conscious influence of Papa's personality. It was then that a turning from the phraseological to the real ensued.' DBWE 8, 358; DBW 8, 397.

to those who knew him before and after.¹² His 1936 letter to Elisabeth Zinn shows that his 'turn' coincided with a new regard for Scripture:

> I threw myself into my work in an extremely un-Christian and not at all humble fashion ... But then something different came, something that has changed and transformed my life to this very day. For the first time, I came to the Bible ... I had often preached, I had seen a great deal of the church, had spoken and written about it – and yet I was not yet a Christian but rather in an utterly wild and uncontrolled fashion my own master ... The Bible, especially the Sermon on the Mount, freed me from all this. Since then everything has changed.¹³

This change, including his newfound appreciation for Scripture, was infectious to those around him, not least his students at Finkenwalde. In a circular letter, the Finkenwaldians wrote, 'The Bible stands at the center of our work. It has once again become the point of departure and the center of our theological work and of all our Christian activity. Here we have learned once again how to read the Bible prayerfully.'¹⁴ Thus their community was defined not just by the centrality of Scripture but also by the prayerful character of their reading. In another letter, they report, 'By avoiding exegesis [that is, of the historical-critical kind] in our evening devotional each day, Pastor Bonhoeffer made the biblical word even more precious to us in its objectivity.'¹⁵ Nevertheless, by early 1941, Bonhoeffer's daily practice of reading Scripture was waning. In a 31 January 1941 letter, he reflects, 'Sometimes there are weeks in which I read very little of the Bible. Something prevents me from doing so. Then one day I pick it up again, and suddenly everything is so much more powerful, and I can't let go of it at all.'¹⁶ And a year and a half later, in a 25 June 1942 letter, he writes,

> I am amazed that I am living, and can live, for days without the Bible ... When I then open the Bible again, it is new and delightful to me as never before, and I only wish I could preach again. I know that I only need to open my own books to hear all that can be said against this.¹⁷

Although the importance of Scripture to Bonhoeffer leaps off the page in these passages, it is nonetheless significant that scriptural meditation was no longer part of his daily routine in the early 1940s.¹⁸ His imprisonment, however, would

---

12. DB-ER, 202–6.
13. DBWE 14, 134; DBW 14, 112–13.
14. DBWE 14, 111; DBW 14, 91.
15. DBWE 14, 90; DBW 14, 72.
16. DBWE 16, 133; DBW 16, 122.
17. DBWE 16, 329; DBW 16, 325.
18. It is noteworthy that in the 25 June 1942 letter to Bethge, Bonhoeffer continues his reflections with statements about his 'instinctive revulsion' and growing 'opposition to all that is "religious"', connected with his sense that he was 'on the verge of some kind of breakthrough' (DBWE 16, 329; DBW 16, 325). The conceptual antecedents to his prison letters are clear in this passage.

give him the time to focus once again on regular Scripture reading. He writes to Bethge on 18 November 1943 of his 'daily Bible study', noting, 'I have read the Old Testament two and a half times through and have learned a great deal.'[19] Some weeks later, he writes again of his increasing appreciation of the Old Testament.[20]

Bonhoeffer's relationship to the Bible underwent several changes during his life, but the Finkenwalde years are particularly rich. This is the time when he was training future pastors how to do their own exegesis and preaching of Scripture, supported by a regular practice of prayerful meditation. It is the time when his writings are most overtly and consistently 'biblical', in both form and content.[21] Indeed, Bonhoeffer produced enough scriptural exegesis during this period to tip the balance of his writings overall; thus, it is largely on account of the voluminous Finkenwalde material that Ernst Georg Wendel can say that 'the majority of Bonhoeffer's work is biblical exposition'.[22] This is why the second part of this book, which undertakes a series of studies of Bonhoeffer's exegetical writings, is disproportionally weighted towards this phase of his development.

On bibliology

The heart of this study is an analysis of Bonhoeffer's bibliology, so a few introductory words about bibliology are in order. I take it as axiomatic that in the field of Christian dogmatics there is such a thing as Holy Scripture, and moreover that this thing called Holy Scripture can be described theologically in terms of its ontology and its place in the divine economy.[23] The pursuit of such a description is the task of bibliology. As such, bibliology aims to address two distinct but interrelated questions: (1) What is Holy Scripture? (2) What does God do with Holy Scripture? In what follows, I expound Bonhoeffer's bibliology by attending

---

19. DBWE 8, 181; DBW 8, 188.

20. In an oft-quoted passage, Bonhoeffer says, 'By the way, I notice more and more how much I am thinking and perceiving things in line with the Old Testament; thus in recent months I have been reading much more the Old than the New Testament. Only when one knows that the name of God may not be uttered may one sometimes speak the name of Jesus Christ. Only when one loves life and the earth so much that with it everything seems to be lost and at its end may one believe in the resurrection of the dead and a new world. Only when one accepts the law of God as binding for oneself may one perhaps sometimes speak of grace. And only when the wrath and vengeance of God against God's enemies are allowed to stand can something of forgiveness and the love of enemies touch our hearts. Whoever wishes to be and perceive things too quickly and too directly in the New Testament ways is to my mind no Christian' (DBWE 8, 213; DBW 8, 226).

21. This is not to deny the scriptural basis of his later writings, especially his *Ethics*. I will argue for this in CHAPTER 10.

22. Wendel, *Studien zur Homiletik Dietrich Bonhoeffers*, 68.

23. John Webster, *Holy Scripture: A Dogmatic Sketch* (Cambridge: Cambridge University Press, 2003), 1.

to the development of his theology of revelation, and drawing out the implications of these developments for his ontology of Scripture and his account of Scripture's role in God's revelatory activity.

To focus my discussion from the beginning, I add three delimitations to my undertaking of the bibliological task. Firstly, I take it that Christian bibliology is concerned with the canonical collection of texts that comprises the Old and New Testaments of the Christian Scriptures. To put it baldly, bibliology is about that book called the *Bible*. Christian bibliological ontology must deal with the reality of these particular texts and what, if anything, they have to do with God. Of course, whatever one might say theologically about the Bible, there is plenty that can be said non-theologically. In its present form, the Bible is the product of the work of human editors, translators, printers, distributors and countless others. Therefore, a second delimitation: Christian bibliology acknowledges a degree of human agency in the existence of the canonical texts that it seeks to describe theologically. Christian theological interest in Holy Scripture usually focuses on the role that these ostensibly human texts occupy in the course of divine revelation. My interest is the same, which leads to the third delimitation: bibliology is inseparable from and derivative of the theology of revelation. Bibliology explicates how and to what extent biblical writings function in the economy of God's self-revealing activity in and for humankind. In sum, bibliology is an account of the Bible as God's word.

In order to parse the relationship between revelation and Scripture in Bonhoeffer's thought, I have attended carefully to the place and character of revelation in his theological development, from his earliest essay in systematics leading up to his Finkenwalde years. Although my study is not comprehensive in this regard, I have endeavoured to establish with the greatest possible clarity the centrality of revelation throughout his writings.[24] After his encounter with Karl Barth's theology, Bonhoeffer wholeheartedly affirmed that God's absolute transcendence negates the possibility of speaking truthfully about God apart from God's own self-revealing speech. Bonhoeffer took up the dialectical problem of how God could remain God in revelation, which is to say, how God could remain

---

24. This topic is often discussed in the context of Bonhoeffer's theological relationship to Karl Barth. Some excellent monographs have been published in recent years: Michael P. DeJonge, *Bonhoeffer's Theological Formation: Berlin, Barth, and Protestant Theology* (Oxford: Oxford University Press, 2012); Edward van 't Slot, *Negativism of Revelation?: Bonhoeffer and Barth on Faith and Actualism*, Dogmatik in der Moderne 12 (Tübingen: Mohr Siebeck, 2015). Slightly older but still valuable is Andreas Pangritz, *Karl Barth in the Theology of Dietrich Bonhoeffer*, trans. Barbara Rumscheidt and Martin Rumscheidt (Grand Rapids: Eerdmans, 2000). On Bonhoeffer's theology of the word, see Frits de Lange, *Waiting for the Word: Dietrich Bonhoeffer on Speaking about God*, trans. Martin N. Walton (Grand Rapids: Eerdmans, 2000); Philip G. Ziegler, 'Dietrich Bonhoeffer: A Theologian of the Word of God', in *Bonhoeffer, Christ and Culture*, ed. Keith L. Johnson (Downers Grove, IL: IVP Academic, 2013), 17–37.

fully transcendent even in the event of becoming immanently available. This was, for the young Bonhoeffer, *the* theological problem, and his dissertations represent his early attempts to address it. It was through his wrestling with the Barthian problem that he developed ways of thinking about revelation that he would carry with him for the rest of his life. I will set out this case in detail in the first half of this study; suffice it here to say that Bonhoeffer's theology of revelation became the backbone of his bibliology.

Despite Bonhoeffer's fixation on the Bible during the mid-1930s, there has been relatively little scholarship devoted to his theology of Holy Scripture, and only slightly more to his biblical interpretation.[25] In what follows, I trace the contours of a bibliology grounded in his early theology of revelation and reconfigured through his 1933 Christology. One of my central claims is that Bonhoeffer's treatment of Holy Scripture in the 1930s represents a consistent application of his bibliology, and therefore much of what seems odd or

---

25. John Godsey devotes a significant portion of his study to Bonhoeffer's theological exegesis, but it is expository rather than evaluative in nature (*The Theology of Dietrich Bonhoeffer* [London: SCM, 1960], 119–94). When Godsey does offer an assessment of Bonhoeffer's theology as a whole, he is far more concerned with Bonhoeffer's later developments than his Finkenwalde exegetical material. Ernst Feil, *The Theology of Dietrich Bonhoeffer*, trans. Martin Rumscheidt (Minneapolis: Fortress, 2007), 3–55 spends an entire section on Bonhoeffer's 'hermeneutical point of departure', but hardly acknowledges, much less analyses, the place of Scripture in Bonhoeffer's theological method. John W. de Gruchy, ed., *The Cambridge Companion to Dietrich Bonhoeffer* (Cambridge: Cambridge University Press, 1999) contains no entry on Bonhoeffer and Scripture. Fortunately, Michael Mawson and Philip G. Ziegler, eds, *The Oxford Handbook of Dietrich Bonhoeffer* (Oxford: Oxford University Press, 2019) corrects this oversight. Charles Marsh, *Reclaiming Dietrich Bonhoeffer: The Promise of His Theology* (New York: Oxford University Press, 1994) offers a philosophically sophisticated rendering of Bonhoeffer's thought, but in his efforts to ensure that the 1930s Bonhoeffer does not come across as 'pietistic and naive', he downplays the biblical simplicity and immediacy that characterize Bonhoeffer's Finkenwalde writings. For other studies of Bonhoeffer's scriptural exegesis, see Kuske, *The Old Testament as the Book of Christ*; Martin Hohmann, *Die Korrelation von Altem und Neuem Bund (Innerbiblische Korrelation statt Kontrastkorrelation)* (Berlin: Evangelische Verlagsanstalt, 1978); Wendel, *Studien zur Homiletik Dietrich Bonhoeffers*; Stephen J. Plant, 'Uses of the Bible in the "Ethics" of Dietrich Bonhoeffer' (PhD thesis, University of Cambridge, 1993); Ralf K. Wüstenberg and Jens Zimmermann, eds, *God Speaks to Us: Dietrich Bonhoeffer's Biblical Hermeneutics*, International Bonhoeffer Interpretations 5 (Frankfurt am Main: Peter Lang, 2013); Stephen J. Plant, *Taking Stock of Bonhoeffer: Studies in Biblical Interpretation and Ethics* (Surrey: Ashgate, 2014); Nadine Hamilton, *Dietrich Bonhoeffers Hermeneutik der Responsivität: Ein Kapitel Schriftlehre im Anschluss an Schöpfung und Fall*, Forschungen zur systematischen und ökumenischen Theologie 155 (Göttingen: Vandenhoeck & Ruprecht, 2016); Jens Zimmermann, *Dietrich Bonhoeffer's Christian Humanism* (Oxford: Oxford University Press, 2019), 236–90.

incongruous in his Finkenwalde exegetical writings can be understood as an extension of his most basic theological insights. By attending to the centrality and the character of his theology of revelation, along with its practical outworking in his biblical exegesis, I offer a portrait of Bonhoeffer as a theologian of the word of God.[26]

Summary of chapters

My aims in what follows are, first, to articulate Bonhoeffer's bibliology in such a way that its systematic relationship to the wider scope of his theology becomes clear and, second, to demonstrate his bibliology in practice, showing how his exegesis of Scripture is consistent with his bibliology, and, conversely, how his bibliology entails certain kinds of exegetical decisions. Thus, I follow John Webster's logic that bibliology precedes exegesis, and my study is structured accordingly.

PART I covers the topic of Bonhoeffer's bibliology, beginning with two chapters devoted to his theology of revelation. In CHAPTER 2, I establish the centrality of God's word in Bonhoeffer's theological imagination. Much of this chapter is familiar territory, as I seek to place Bonhoeffer in the context of early dialectical theology, but I do so with the particular aim of establishing his lifelong commitment to the word of God as the 'first principle' of theology. By Bonhoeffer's own account of twentieth-century Protestant theology, Karl Barth marked the decisive turning point away from modern liberalism, reorienting theology as discourse about *God* rather than the history of religions or human religious experience. Bonhoeffer's allegiance to the dialectical school shows itself in his adherence to revelation as the *petitio principii* of theology. In CHAPTER 3, I examine the distinctive character of Bonhoeffer's early theology of revelation. In his dissertations, *Sanctorum Communio* and *Act and Being*, he develops a concept of revelation grounded in Christ's personal and historical presence *in* and *as* the church: 'Christ existing as community'. I argue, however, that Bonhoeffer's ecclesiological interpretation of Christ's presence is insufficient to ground anything but an occasionalist ontology of Scripture.

I argue over the next two chapters that Bonhoeffer's revised account of *Christus praesens* offers firmer ground for a robust ontology of Scripture. Notwithstanding the centrality of revelation in Bonhoeffer's thought during his early academic years, he does not come into his own as a *scriptural* theologian until the mid-1930s. In CHAPTER 4, I argue that his 1933 Christology lectures establish the theological groundwork for this development. In his Christology lectures, he resituates his account of *Christus praesens* within the structure of his Christology. It is by virtue of Christ's eternal promeity that Christ is present as word, sacrament and church-community. Bonhoeffer's Finkenwalde homiletics makes it clear that, because

---

26. Here I am following the lead and extending the argument of Ziegler, 'Dietrich Bonhoeffer: A Theologian of the Word of God', 17–37.

Christ is inherently the present one, he is present wherever the word is present. Accordingly, in CHAPTER 5, I examine the homiletical material from Finkenwalde, which exhibits the indissoluble connection that Bonhoeffer makes between Christ's speaking and Christ's presence. Moreover, I clarify how and why the nature of Scripture as a *witness* to God's word entails its treatment as the very word of God. The words that God speaks in testimony to himself, the word that is personally present in its being spoken, simply are the words of Scripture. It is not through a quality inherent in the words themselves, but strictly in their being spoken by the Spirit that they make Christ present. The exegetical question, appropriately, is always a 'who' question. It is not: what does this text mean for us today? But rather: *who* is speaking these words to us today?

In PART II of this study, I examine a selection of Bonhoeffer's exegetical writings, beginning with two chapters on the Psalms. In CHAPTER 6, I show that Bonhoeffer's prayerful approach to the Psalter is in keeping with his bibliology. Attending to Christ's presence in the Psalms is a matter of learning to pray these ancient words in Christ's name today. In light of his bibliology, I consider his controversial statement: 'Because Christ was in David, Christ speaks in the Psalms.' It is the way he relates revelation and Scripture under the category of witness that makes sense of his Christological reading of the Psalms. I argue that his Christological exegetical lens has an expansive rather than a reductive effect; it is not something he pulls out of the text, but rather something that pulls him more deeply into it. I analyse three of his sermons from the Psalter in defence of this point.

Then, in CHAPTER 7, I demonstrate that Bonhoeffer's account of Christ's presence in Scripture includes the process of formation. Christ's presence is not something that we can take or leave; Christ's presence is a transforming presence. Bonhoeffer endorses scriptural meditation as a distinct Christian discipline, through which human beings assume an intentionally receptive posture towards God's word. It is the process by which we move from hearing to understanding, and from understanding to love. Bonhoeffer's incomplete reflections on Psalm 119 both teach and exemplify this meditative approach to Scripture. God's word in Scripture, therefore, is not just how God encounters us from the outside, but also how God transforms us from the inside.

In CHAPTER 8, I analyse Bonhoeffer's exegesis of Ezra-Nehemiah and reconsider the historical-critical critiques that have been levelled against it. I make the case that Bonhoeffer's exegetical moves are defensible in light of his bibliology. Specifically, I emphasize the present-tense character of divine and human speech in his thought. For Bonhoeffer, exegesis is not the task of establishing the one true meaning of the text, nor does it aim at producing an authoritative, standalone 'interpretation'. Exegesis means prayerfully discerning the 'right word' for the present and aims at a present-tense act of 'telling the truth' about Scripture. Bonhoeffer's exegesis of Ezra-Nehemiah therefore represents a consistent application of his bibliology.

In CHAPTER 9, I look at his most extensive published piece of biblical exegesis, *Discipleship*. This book is perhaps the best example of Bonhoeffer's exegetical 'who' question in action. *Discipleship* represents Bonhoeffer's concern to unfold the commandments of the Sermon on the Mount as the words of Jesus who is present as the *Lord*. The Lord who commands is the incarnate, crucified and risen one, and he alone is the giver and fulfilment of the law. Accordingly, Bonhoeffer prioritizes hearing and obeying over interpreting, and pays special attention to the cruciform shape of discipleship. *Discipleship* asks what it means to be in the presence of the Lord, the one who commands and whose presence as the commanding Lord entails a decision.

The place of Scripture in Bonhoeffer's ethical thought is an important question, and so I continue this discussion in CHAPTER 10. *Ethics* contains relatively little exegetical material, but I argue that the connection between ethics and Scripture for Bonhoeffer lies in the question of *reality*. Bonhoeffer speaks of reality as the reality of *revelation*, and where Bonhoeffer speaks of revelation, it is appropriate to speak of God's self-revealing address in the words of Scripture. But Bonhoeffer makes an important distinction: Scripture does not tell human beings what to do; it testifies to Christ, thereby teaching the reality of revelation. It is in knowing reality as it is in Christ that human beings can venture concrete decisions in history. Bonhoeffer's use of 'scriptural evidence' throughout *Ethics* bolsters *doctrinal* rather than ethical arguments, which become the framework for responsible ethical discourse. In Bonhoeffer's thinking, we go to Scripture not to find out what to do, but simply to learn revelation. Doctrinal theology concerns the truth of revelation, and ethics means 'doing the truth'.

Finally, in CHAPTER 11, I consider the relationship between Bonhoeffer's bibliology and the 'nonreligious interpretation of biblical concepts'. I show that Bonhoeffer's critique of religion and of Barth's 'positivism of revelation' was grounded in his theology of revelation-as-*Christus-praesens*, and that his interpretation of Scripture in prison represents both continuity with and development beyond his earlier exegetical writings. I conclude by remarking on the exegetical implications of his prison theology, arguing that nonreligious exegesis is fundamentally about learning to read Scripture in a polyphonic way as God's word-for-others.

My aim in CHAPTER 12 is to flesh out my conclusions about Bonhoeffer's bibliology and exegesis in conversation with more recent scholarship on theological interpretation. With reference to Hans Boersma's *Scripture as Real Presence*, I show how Bonhoeffer's programme can be viewed as a *ressourcement* of patristic exegesis. Then, I draw on Robert Jenson and Hans Frei to explore the possibility of bringing more methodological precision to Bonhoeffer's project. Each of them affirms a version of *Christus praesens*, which gives their proposals potential to complement or correct Bonhoeffer's, even as Bonhoeffer helps to fill in some of the gaps in theirs.

Readers will find a central claim recurring throughout this book: if Jesus Christ is the Word of God, then he is present wherever God's word is present. This proposition defines Dietrich Bonhoeffer's theology of revelation, his bibliology and ultimately his approach to biblical exegesis. As God's chosen and elected witness to his word in Christ, Holy Scripture is where Christ himself speaks by the Spirit, and Christ is wholly present as the content and agent of this divine speech. God's self-revelation is his personal presence in Christ by the Spirit's ongoing ministry of the Word. An encounter with the word of Scripture, therefore, is an encounter with God's Word in person.

Following Bonhoeffer, I suggest, does not mean adhering to his every interpretive move and exegetical decision; it means following his exegetical trajectory from the written word to the living and present Jesus Christ. From his academic dissertations to his prison letters, Bonhoeffer's interpretation of divine revelation as Christ's real presence can be traced as one of his most consistent and central theological commitments. His theology of revelation-as-*Christus-praesens* is the thread I trace in this study of Bonhoeffer's theology and exegesis of Holy Scripture, and the lens through which I will view Bonhoeffer's theology as a whole. Of course, this is not the only lens through which to view Bonhoeffer's corpus, nor is it the only unifying feature of his thought. But it is a central theme for him and, in my view, has not received sufficient attention. Christ's presence lies at the heart of Bonhoeffer's bibliology and informs his exegesis in identifiable ways. For Bonhoeffer, Christ is really present wherever God's word is spoken. If God speaks in the word of Scripture, then Christ is fully there. We cannot come to terms with Bonhoeffer's exegesis until we have come to terms with this remarkable claim.

Part I

BIBLIOLOGY

2

THEOLOGIAN OF GOD'S WORD

Writing from prison in 1944, in the correspondence that includes his famous 'Outline for a Book', Bonhoeffer reflects on the kinds of questions that the church must be asking, and the kind of person needed to answer them. He writes, 'As a "modern" theologian who has nevertheless inherited the legacy of liberal theology, I feel responsible to address these questions. There are probably not many among the younger generation who combine these two elements.'[1] It is remarkable that even at this late stage of Bonhoeffer's life, he would see himself as uniquely positioned between 'modern' and liberal theology. It is, after all, this very same tension between the liberal theology of his Berlin professors and the 'modern' theology inaugurated by Karl Barth and the dialectical movement that defined Bonhoeffer's theological development from the outset.[2]

This context is not just a matter of general interest for Bonhoeffer's theology; it is critical for understanding his theology of revelation, his bibliology and the way he interprets Scripture. Moreover, the same tension that Bonhoeffer experienced in Berlin can be felt in the academy today, since we have yet to find widespread agreement on how historical criticism can peacefully coexist with theological interpretation, much less how they might be mutually beneficial. Bonhoeffer was on the frontier of these kinds of discussions, which had been set in motion by the publication of Karl Barth's *The Epistle to the Romans* in 1918. As Bonhoeffer navigated his own way through this academic gauntlet, he consistently sided with Barth and the dialectical movement, even as he found some of their

---

1. DBWE 8, 498; DBW 8, 555.
2. See Michael Mawson, *Christ Existing as Community: Bonhoeffer's Ecclesiology* (Oxford: Oxford University Press, 2018), 13–35; DeJonge, *Bonhoeffer's Theological Formation*, 1–14; Slot, *Negativism of Revelation*, 35–55; Pangritz, *Karl Barth in the Theology of Dietrich Bonhoeffer*.

proposals lacking.³ In this chapter, I examine Bonhoeffer's relationship with the dialectical movement, arguing that he was, from his earliest encounter with Barth's writings, a theologian of the word of God. The centrality of revelation in Bonhoeffer's thought is perhaps his most consistent trait throughout his theological development. This chapter concludes with an examination of Bonhoeffer's 1925 essay on scriptural interpretation, which both provides initial support for my portrait of Bonhoeffer as a theologian of God's word and details his earliest attempt at (what I identify as) a 'bibliology'. In the wider scope of this study, my aim in this chapter is to establish the basic framework for evaluating Bonhoeffer's later theology of Scripture and exegetical writings. As I will show in later chapters, many of his striking assertions about Scripture as well as his seemingly strange exegetical decisions can be better understood in the context of his ongoing attempt to speak of God on the basis of God's word alone. This chapter establishes that context.

The Barthian challenge to liberal theology

The history and significance of the dialectical movement in 1920s Germany have been detailed many times, and I will not rehearse the details here.⁴ My interest lies in Bonhoeffer's own understanding of the movement and how he positioned himself in relation to it. This requires only a brief review of Bonhoeffer's academic context, which I will provide largely with reference to his own interpretation of this context in his 1931–2 lecture course on the history of twentieth-century systematic theology.⁵ The broad shape of Bonhoeffer's presentation reflects his perception of which people and movements had been most significant in driving the theological issues of his day. He perceived at the heart of twentieth-century theology an ongoing debate over the place of revelation in theology and how to interpret Scripture rightly, and he consistently portrays Barth as the pivotal figure in this history. The central question, as he saw it, was this: how is it possible for human beings to speak of God?

---

3. Although the focus of this chapter is the influence of Karl Barth and the dialectical movement on Bonhoeffer's theology of revelation, one can hardly overestimate the importance of Martin Luther and the Protestant doctrine of *sola scriptura* when evaluating Bonhoeffer as a scriptural theologian. For more on Luther's influence on Bonhoeffer, see Michael P. DeJonge, *Bonhoeffer's Reception of Luther* (Oxford: Oxford University Press, 2017) and DeJonge, *Bonhoeffer's Theological Formation*.

4. For such an account, see Bruce L. McCormack, *Karl Barth's Critically Realistic Dialectical Theology: Its Genesis and Development 1909–1936* (Oxford: Clarendon, 1995) and, more recently, David W. Congdon, *The Mission of Demythologizing: Rudolf Bultmann's Dialectical Theology* (Minneapolis: Fortress, 2015).

5. DBWE 11, 177–244; DBW 11, 139–213.

Kant's critiques had rendered all claims to metaphysical truth unreliable and untenable, which led to an increasing interest in Christianity as a historical religion or as human piety, which, unlike God, could be subjected to acceptably scientific scrutiny. The rise of the natural sciences and empiricism had pressured theology to strive for scientific objectivity in its findings. It was held that, because metaphysical claims are inaccessible to scientific enquiry, theologians ought to focus on empirically verifiable and universally accessible truth. 'Religion as historical and piety as psychological fact are accessible to precise research',[6] Bonhoeffer explains, which is why historical and psychological research dominated the period. For theologians who took this view, the subject matter of theology was not God, but religion. It no longer made sense to ask whether or not Christianity was true, because Christianity was no longer viewed as a collection of dogmas but rather as a historical religion.

By Bonhoeffer's time, the history-of-religions school (*Religionsgeschichtlicheschule*) had a firm hold in Berlin. Ernst Troeltsch (1865–1923) had died shortly before Bonhoeffer began his studies, but his legacy lived on. Throughout Bonhoeffer's lectures, Troeltsch emerges as the foremost representative of the history-of-religions school. Troeltsch had moved the attention away from the *truth* of Christianity and instead enquired into its validity or absoluteness. As Bonhoeffer puts it, '[It was] a goal of the history-of-religions [school] to determine dogmatically that Christianity has the highest validity for our culture.'[7] Troeltsch had insisted that theology be grounded in a robust philosophy of religion and that the claims of Christianity be evaluated from a history-of-religions perspective. In his historical study, *The Absoluteness of Christianity*, Troeltsch had concluded that 'Christianity is the pinnacle of all religious development thus far and the basis and presupposition for every distinct and meaningful development in man's religious life in the future. There is no probability that it will ever be surpassed or cut off from its historical foundations as far as our historical vision can reach.'[8] For Troeltsch, the only valid starting point for theology is the '*normative* knowledge acquired through the scientific study of religion'.[9] Religion, not revelation, was Troeltsch's point of departure, and with that, Troeltsch intentionally restricted himself from making any attempt or claim to speak God's word. For him, as with Feuerbach, theology is anthropology.[10]

---

6. DBWE 11, 184; DBW 11, 146.

7. DBWE 11, 206; DBW 11, 172.

8. Ernst Troeltsch, *The Absoluteness of Christianity and the History of Religions*, trans. David Reid (London: SCM, 1972), 131.

9. Ibid., 25.

10. Ludwig Feuerbach, *The Essence of Christianity*, trans. George Eliot (New York: Harper & Brothers, 1957), xxxvii.

Adolf von Harnack (1851–1930) was the most prominent theologian and church historian in Berlin when Bonhoeffer studied there. He was also a neighbour and a friend of the Bonhoeffer family in Grunewald. Although Bonhoeffer departed from Harnack theologically, he never lost respect or admiration for his former teacher.[11] Harnack employed historical methods to relate Christianity as a historical religion to the piety of the contemporary believers. His goal was 'to express Christianity so that it simply stands there as timeless truth'.[12] Harnack took the 'philosophical premises' developed by Troeltsch and attempted 'to reconcile history and faith'.[13] Like Troeltsch, Harnack wanted to get behind the historical husk of Christianity to reveal its timeless kernel of truth. One of Harnack's main contributions was what is now called the Hellenization thesis; his *History of Dogma* is the 'history of the assimilation of the gospel with the Greek spirit'.[14] For Harnack, it was only in the Reformation that the 'pure gospel' began to be rediscovered. With respect to the Bible, Harnack argued that the New Testament has two distinct layers: (1) early Christian preaching and (2) Jesus's own preaching. Both layers must be mined in order to excavate the timeless truth beneath. Under these layers, he found the supposed essence of Jesus as 'a devout Israelite who lives by doing God's will'.[15] Harnack viewed the message of Jesus as a message about God the Father only, not a message about Jesus as God's Son. The Reformers were the first to begin untangling this pure gospel from the Greek metaphysical thought forms that developed around its early Christian proclamation. But, according to Harnack, even Luther, the great Reformer, granted Christ too central a role in his theology; Jesus was nothing but an example of pure devotion to God and obedience to God's will. The end result was a purely ethical interpretation of Christianity. Harnack judged that in its pure ethical form, Christianity is not just *a* religion but *the* religion, religion *per se*. His entire analysis was governed by a foundational assumption: 'What proves to be timeless is that which has proved to be generally valid to this day.'[16]

---

11. 'Harnack has great inner warmth and true striving for the truth' (DBWE 11, 203; DBW 11, 169). In Bonhoeffer's last recorded correspondence with Harnack, he warmly reflects, 'That you were our teacher for so many sessions is now past; but that we are permitted to call ourselves your students will remain' (DBWE 10, 195; DBW 10, 158). Harnack replied, 'I have the utmost confidence in your work and your progress along the right path' (DBWE 10, 197; DBW 10, 160-1). Finally, Bonhoeffer's heartfelt 'Eulogy for Adolf von Harnack' (DBWE 10, 379-81; DBW 10, 346-9) reasserts the deep respect Bonhoeffer held for his illustrious teacher.
12. DBWE 11, 199; DBW 11, 164.
13. DBWE 11, 200; DBW 11, 165. Bonhoeffer notes, however, that Harnack wanted to distance himself from the history-of-religions school, under the influence of his teacher, Albrecht Ritschl, from whom he also departed significantly.
14. DBWE 11, 202; DBW 11, 167.
15. DBWE 11, 202; DBW 11, 168.
16. DBWE 11, 202; DBW 11, 168.

Bonhoeffer rejected Harnack's project in principle. Universal truth, for Harnack, could not be tied to any historical particularities. A purely ethical doctrine can be proclaimed without dependence on or reference to the person of Christ. This may have been a boon to Harnack's project, but it signalled failure to Bonhoeffer. The true essence of Christianity, for Bonhoeffer, cannot be purely ethical or religious. All religion, even the Christian religion, is simply the human attempt to approach God. The essence of Christianity is the message of God approaching humanity in Christ. 'Christ is not the bringer of a new religion, but the bringer of God.'[17] An ethicist or religious leader presents ideas or practices that one may choose to adopt to whatever extent is deemed suitable; Christ, on the other hand, presents himself as the revelation of God, which makes an ultimate demand on every person who encounters him. That is why, for Bonhoeffer, 'absoluteness is [grounded] not in a religious experience but rather in the word of God, in its identity'.[18] Christianity is 'absolute' not because it conforms to an ethical or a religious standard that we already have at our disposal, but rather because the *word* of God is the word of *God*.

This was the basic insight of Karl Barth. In Bonhoeffer's account, Barth marks the truly decisive turn away from the liberal occupation with religion as the object of theology. For Barth, theology must be concerned with right speech about God, and for this reason its object must be God's word. Barth staunchly refused to conflate questions of religion with questions of God. He insisted that it is God and God alone who can speak truly about God, and that God irrupts into the present ever and again to speak in the freedom of divine grace. Because religion turns God into an object, it is always in danger of idolatry, which is why 'Barth opposes religion in the name of God.'[19] In his effort to safeguard the freedom of God in revelation, Barth maintained that God can never become an object to us, even though God's word always comes to us objectively in history: 'The historicity … of God's word is its objectivity. The divinity of God's word is its nonobjectivity.'[20] God can never become an object for us; yet, God's word comes to us only in objective (historical) form. This is why Barth endorses dialectical speech as appropriate for theological discourse. Dialectics prevents human words about God from calcifying into universal propositions or timeless truths. The attempt to measure theology by a predetermined standard of truth betrays a fundamental misunderstanding of the theological task. The subject-matter of theology is *God*, and there is nothing that exists alongside or external to God by which statements about God might be measured.

Barth's theology, as Bonhoeffer portrays it, is more alive, more present than what Troeltsch and Harnack were offering. It is a theology of the *speaking* God.

---

17. DBWE 10, 358; DBW 10, 321.
18. DBWE 11, 209; DBW 11, 175 (brackets in original).
19. DBWE 11, 229; DBW 11, 197.
20. DBWE 11, 233; DBW 11, 202.

Accordingly, his theology is directed towards the Christian task of preaching.[21] To preach, for Barth, is to speak the word of God, but this is only possible as God speaks. The preacher cannot control this, but must wait for it, expect it. The hearing of this word depends on the act of the Holy Spirit: 'The Holy Spirit allows human beings to believe and to hear that the righteousness of humankind lies entirely in Christ.'[22] All preaching, then, is 'Advent speech', speech that is oriented to the future, which is 'in every case Christ himself, as the absolute One who is outside us'.[23] The eschatological character of God's word that Bonhoeffer found in Barth would orient his approach to the problem of Christ's presence in preaching.[24]

Barth set theology on a new course by identifying its object as the word of God rather than religion. Theologians who followed in his footsteps no longer occupied themselves with questions of religion or piety, but concerned themselves solely with the word of God. In Bonhoeffer's words, 'One can only have God by expecting God. Instead of beginning with religion, theology should begin by speaking from the word of God.'[25] Only God can speak God's word, and God's freedom means that this word can never come under human control. Thus Bonhoeffer affirms: '*Deus dixit* – to accept this is the beginning of all genuine theological thinking, to allow space for the freedom of the living God.'[26]

Bonhoeffer and the dialectical movement

As far as Bonhoeffer was concerned, Karl Barth was dialectical theology's 'founder and most original thinker'.[27] Of those associated with that movement, Barth would always be his most constant theological conversation partner, and I will consider a key aspect of this one-sided conversation in CHAPTER 3. But Bonhoeffer made sure to read the works of the other major contributors to that new movement, including Eduard Thurneysen, Friedrich Gogarten, Emil Brunner and Rudolf Bultmann.

His references to Eduard Thurneysen (1888–1974) are rare. He was fond of Thurneysen's image of walking across a river on moving blocks of ice, which he found in 'Schrift und Offenbarung': 'Historical concern about the Bible is like a man walking on ice floes, jumping from one verse to the next, knowing that one

---

21. 'Barth's theology comes from preaching; this is his only concern' (DBWE 11, 227; DBW 11, 195).
22. DBWE 11, 239; DBW 11, 209.
23. DBWE 11, 239; DBW 11, 209.
24. I will discuss this at length in CHAPTER 5.
25. DBWE 11, 230; DBW 11, 198.
26. DBWE 11, 231; DBW 11, 199.
27. DBWE 10, 462; DBW 10, 434–5.

will really reach the promised shore.'²⁸ There is also evidence that he continued to read Thurneysen at least until his years at Finkenwalde.²⁹ Despite the relative paucity of direct citations, Bonhoeffer recognized Thurneysen's importance in the dialectical movement. In 1931, after seeing Barth in Bonn and then Gogarten in Berlin, he commented that 'only Thurneysen is missing in the list of Olympians'.³⁰

Bonhoeffer saw Friedrich Gogarten (1887–1967) lecture in Berlin in October 1931, but he was less impressed with him personally than he had been with Barth.³¹ Personal impressions aside, Bonhoeffer welcomed Gogarten's theological appropriation of German personalist philosophy, especially that of Eberhard Grisebach. Bonhoeffer took Grisebach's anthropological 'I-You' relation as the antidote to idealist attempts to address the problem of transcendence. Although Bonhoeffer tends to cite Grisebach, Bethge suggests that Bonhoeffer probably discovered Grisebach in Gogarten's writings.³² In any case, Bonhoeffer himself identified the theological appropriation of the I-You relation as 'Gogarten's service to theology'.³³

Emil Brunner (1889–1966) was another theologian in Barth's circle who embraced a version of personalist philosophy. But he comes off rather less favourably in Bonhoeffer's writings than other dialectical theologians. Bonhoeffer was generally underwhelmed by Brunner's books. His impression of *The Mediator* was 'that he simply "dashed the book off" without any kind of polishing or revising',³⁴ and *The Divine Imperative* 'had been done somewhat too hastily'.³⁵ Despite these misgivings, Bonhoeffer does appreciate some of Brunner's contributions. He identifies *The Divine Imperative* as the 'first comprehensive ethical work of dialectical theology',³⁶ and there are some features of this work that overlap with Bonhoeffer's ethical writings. On the whole, however, it appears that Brunner was not a significant influence on Bonhoeffer's thought.

---

28. From Hans Pfeifer's notes on the Christology lectures in DBWE 12, 331 ed. n. 78; DBW 12, 314 ed. n. 65; cf. DBWE 9, 297; DBW 9, 320; DBWE 11, 439; DBW 11, 422. This image is in Eduard Thurneysen, 'Schrift und Offenbarung', in *Das Wort Gottes und die Kirche: Aufsätze und Vorträge*, ed. Ernst Wolf, Theologishe Bücherei: Neudrucke und Berichte aus dem 20. Jahrhundert 44 (München: Chr. Kaiser, 1971), 60.

29. The editors of Bonhoeffer's Finkenwalde writings link two statements from Bonhoeffer's lectures on pastoral care to Thurneysen's essay, 'Rechtfertigung und Seelsorge', namely, that pastoral care is proclamation and that it is prayer. As proclamation, DBWE 14, 560 ed. n. 3; DBW 14, 555 ed. n. 3; as prayer, DBWE 14, 567 ed. n. 24; DBW 14, 562 ed. n. 24.

30. DBWE 11, 49; DBW 11, 27.

31. He remarked in a letter, 'I wouldn't feel at all especially attracted to Breslau, while I would go to Bonn again in a minute' (DBWE 11, 49; DBW 11, 28). Gogarten taught in Breslau from 1931 to 1935.

32. DB-ER, 83.

33. DBWE 12, 200; DBW 12, 163.

34. DBWE 10, 136; DBW 17, 81–2.

35. DBWE 11, 121; DBW 11, 89.

36. DBWE 12, 209; DBW 12, 173.

Bonhoeffer's friend Erwin Sutz had introduced him to Brunner in 1932, and Bonhoeffer thanked him for the opportunity. Meanwhile, Bonhoeffer had been urging their mutual friend, Paul Lehmann, not to study under Brunner, but to choose Barth or Bultmann instead.[37]

Bonhoeffer's most substantive early engagement with Rudolf Bultmann (1884–1976) appears in *Act and Being*, in which he draws on several of Bultmann's essays of the 1920s.[38] The 1925 essay, 'What Does It Mean to Speak of God?', addresses the same basic paradox that drives Bonhoeffer's work in *Act and Being*, namely, how to coordinate the transcendent reality of God with the human act of comprehending God in revelation. Bultmann argues that if speaking of God means speaking *about* God, it is by definition impossible, because 'every "speaking *about*" presupposes a standpoint external to that which is being talked about'.[39] But no such standpoint exists, neither external to God nor external to ourselves. These are points that Bonhoeffer affirms, although he does not go along with Bultmann in saying that talk of God 'is only possible as talk of ourselves'[40] or that 'to apprehend our existence means to apprehend God'.[41] Years later, Bonhoeffer would write to Bethge that Bultmann's work on demythologizing did not go '"too far," as most people thought, but rather not far enough'.[42] Evidently he never left Bultmann entirely behind.

Certainly there is more that could be said about Bonhoeffer's theological relationship to these and other figures in the dialectical movement, but Barth would always be the key player for Bonhoeffer. It was Barth who levelled the first attack against liberalism with his theology of revelation. In this regard, Bonhoeffer thought, 'In all of recent literature no one is seriously the equal of Barth.'[43] Bonhoeffer recognized and respected Thurneysen's contribution to this movement, but does not seem to have read him widely nor ascribe much significance to him. Gogarten likely gave him an important early philosophical key in the personalism of Grisebach, but Bonhoeffer's explicit use of I–You philosophy quickly wanes after his academic years. Brunner seems to have had made less of an impression, although Bonhoeffer followed his career longer than that of others. Bultmann eventually emerges as a dialectical alternative to Barth,

---

37. DBWE 11, 124; DBW 17, 107–8.

38. DBWE 2, 77 n. 89; 95–101; DBW 2, 71 n. 89; 90–7. Bonhoeffer's other references to Bultmann essentially rehearse the stance he had taken in *Act and Being*: DBWE 10, 402; DBW 10, 371–2; DBWE 12, 221; DBW 12, 186.

39. Rudolf Bultmann, 'What Does It Mean to Speak of God?', in *Faith and Understanding: Collected Essays*, ed. Robert W. Funk, trans. Louise Pettibone Smith, The Library of Philosophy and Theology (London: SCM, 1969), 53.

40. Ibid., 61.

41. Ibid., 63.

42. DBWE 8, 372; DBW 8, 414.

43. DBWE 11, 241; DBW 11, 211.

most prominently in *Letters and Papers from Prison* and as early as *Act and Being*. Yet even Bultmann would remain 'one of the pawns, not the knights or castles, on his chessboard'.[44]

I do not have space to examine historically the emergence, development and eventual break-up of the dialectical movement.[45] Historically speaking, Bonhoeffer was at most a follower, never a leader of this movement. Even the label, 'dialectical', is contestable, and I will not address its adequacy to unite the theological projects of Barth, Bultmann, Gogarten, Brunner and others.[46] The label does, however, evoke that particular group of thinkers, and I use it strictly for that purpose. To ask whether Bonhoeffer was a dialectical theologian, then, is not necessarily to enquire about his theological method, his doctrinal commitments or his attitude towards philosophy. The question is twofold. Firstly, what, from his perspective, united the dialectical theologians, so that, despite their differences, they each rightly qualify to be classified under that label? Secondly, does Bonhoeffer share in that same uniting principle?

Firstly, what did Bonhoeffer think it meant to be 'dialectical'? Here an important distinction must be made between the dialectical method and the dialectical movement.[47] Bonhoeffer does refer to the dialectical method as a characteristic of Barth's theology.[48] Because God can never be locked into static propositional

---

44. This expression comes from a correspondence between Barth and Bethge, after Barth had read Bethge's biography of Bonhoeffer: 'Until now I have always thought of myself as one of the pawns, not the knights or castles, on his chessboard.' Karl Barth, *Letters 1961-1968*, trans. Geoffrey W. Bromiley (Grand Rapids: Eerdmans, 1981), 251.

45. See McCormack's account of 'the break-up of the dialectical theologians' in *Karl Barth's Critically Realistic Dialectical Theology*, 391-411.

46. Bonhoeffer labelled this movement 'the theology of crisis' in his seminar presentation in New York (DBWE 10, 462-76; DBW 10, 434-76).

47. At this point, one thinks of Michael Beintker's distinction between four kinds of dialectics operating in Barth's 1922 *Römerbrief*. See Michael Beintker, *Die Dialektik in der 'dialektischen Theologie' Karl Barths: Studien zur Entwicklung der Barthschen Theologie und zur Vorgeschichte der 'Kirchlichen Dogmatik'* (Munich: Chr. Kaiser, 1987), 25-31. McCormack cites this as Beintker's 'major contribution' to the study of Barth's early theological development (*Karl Barth's Critically Realistic Dialectical Theology*, 11). DeJonge, *Bonhoeffer's Theological Formation*, 38-9, taking his cue from McCormack, follows Beintker's distinction between a dialectic in reality (*Realdialektik*) and a dialectical form of thought (*Denkform*), arguing that Bonhoeffer takes the latter, not the former, as a defining characteristic of Barth's theology. But it should be emphasized that Bonhoeffer's early views on this are not entirely consistent. In *Act and Being*, he says: 'The proviso made by dialectical theology is not a logical one that might be canceled by the opposite but, in view of predestination, a real one in each case' (DBWE 2, 86; DBW 2, 80). But this is a contradiction of his ninth graduation thesis: 'The dialectic of the so-called dialectical theology bears logical, not real character and is in danger of neglecting the historicity of Jesus' (DBWE 9, 441; DBW 9, 478).

48. DBWE 11, 233; DBW 11, 202; DBWE 2, 85-7; DBW 2, 79-81.

statements, every thesis must be countered by an antithesis. To say 'God' is to say 'not-God'. Nevertheless, for Bonhoeffer, it was not the dialectical *method* that united the dialectical movement; it was, rather, their shared affirmation of 'the word of God as the task of theology'.[49] Bonhoeffer expressly refutes the idea that 'Barth's critical proviso [i.e. dialectics] constitutes his systematic method'.[50] Dialectics as a method is appropriate to the freedom of God's word of self-revelation, and so is a fitting method for theologians of the dialectical movement. But one can never be assured of speaking rightly of God by adhering to a particular method. The broader task of the dialectical movement was to make human speech correspond to God's speech.

For Bonhoeffer, Barth is the undisputed champion of this movement. He belongs with Paul, Luther and Kierkegaard 'in the tradition of genuine Christian thinking', because Barth's thinking is always guided by 'the premise of the revelation of God in Christ'.[51] Barth's assault on post-Schleiermacherian liberalism arose from his steadfast commitment to 'the category of the word of God, of the revelation straight from above, from *outside* of man, according to the justification of the sinner by grace'.[52] The 'theological premise of justification by faith'[53] is the interpretive framework for all properly 'Barthian' thinking.[54] And this theological premise, in Bonhoeffer's view, is what united the dialectical movement against the reigning paradigms of German liberalism. Recall that Bonhoeffer's early criticism of Gogarten was that he interpreted the I–You relation apart from revelation. Similarly, Bonhoeffer rebukes Bultmann for implying that the direction of revelation might be reversed, from human beings to God rather than from God to human beings. The issue in both cases is that these 'dialectical' theologians do not adhere closely enough to the *petitio principii* of dialectical theology: God must be the one to speak God's word. The dialectical movement presented a (more or less) united front against liberal theology by asserting that the topic of theology can only be the word of God.

Therefore, whatever might be said about the unity of the dialectical theologians in terms of a shared theological method or style of discourse, Bonhoeffer found the essence of their unity in their dogged commitment to God's revelation. Did Bonhoeffer share this same commitment? I will argue throughout this study that he did, and that this basic commitment to revelation as the *petitio principii*

---

49. This is the title of Barth's 1922 essay. See Karl Barth, 'The Word of God as the Task of Theology', in *The Word of God and Theology*, trans. Amy Marga (London: T&T Clark, 2011), 171–98.
50. DBWE 2, 86 n. 11; DBW 2, 80 n. 11.
51. DBWE 10, 463; DBW 10, 435.
52. DBWE 10, 467; DBW 10, 440.
53. DBWE 10, 476; DBW 10, 449.
54. It is worth noting that *sola fide* was something that Bonhoeffer had received early on from Holl's interpretation of Luther. See DeJonge, *Bonhoeffer's Reception of Luther*, 16–41.

of theology can be traced throughout his works, beginning with his early academic writings. Part of the work of the following chapters will be to trace this commitment, but it is worth noting up front that Bonhoeffer counted himself among the dialectical school. In a 1936 letter to Barth, he makes an admission:

> I must also tell you something that I have not told anyone else, namely, that I felt somewhat excluded from your circle because I was not included as a contributor to your Festschrift. I really would have liked to contribute an article for you, but please do not misunderstand. I simply understood it as an objective judgment that I was not counted among the theologians associated with you. That made me sorry because I know it to be inaccurate.[55]

The theologians associated with Barth diverged in many ways, but, in Bonhoeffer's view, the group was united positively in its point of departure in God's word and negatively in its critique of liberalism. Barth had initiated this movement, but the others could agree at least to that much. Bultmann, for example, insisted, 'The subject of theology is *God*, and the chief charge to be brought against liberal theology is that it has dealt not with God but with man.'[56] Similarly, Gogarten stated, 'We are so deeply immersed in humanity that we have lost God ... None of our thoughts reach beyond the human sphere.'[57] And even after the dissolution of *Zwischen den Zeiten*, Brunner reflected, 'To-day we struggle no longer, as we did fifteen years ago, concerning "religion," but concerning the "Word of God".'[58] Each reflects a common cause, membership in a rebellion led by Barth against the core tenets of the sort of liberal theology practised and defended in Berlin. And Bonhoeffer was as ardent a rebel in this cause as any of them. Even when Bonhoeffer was critical of Barth, 'Bonhoeffer viewed these criticisms as coming

---

55. DBWE 14, 253; DBW 14, 236. The Festschrift in question was published as Ernst Wolf, ed., *Theologische Aufsätze: Karl Barth zum 50. Geburtstag* (Munich: Chr. Kaiser, 1936). Bultmann and Thurneysen were among the contributors. According to Eberhard Busch, *Karl Barth: His Life from Letters and Autobiographical Texts*, trans. John Bowden (Grand Rapids: Eerdmans, 1994), 276, 'Bonhoeffer was missing because of an oversight', not because he was intentionally excluded.

56. Rudolf Bultmann, 'Liberal Theology and the Latest Theological Movement', in *Faith and Understanding: Collected Essays*, ed. Robert W. Funk, trans. Louise Pettibone Smith, The Library of Philosophy and Theology (London: SCM, 1969), 29.

57. Friedrich Gogarten, 'Between the Times', in *The Beginnings of Dialectical Theology*, trans. Keith R. Crim and Louis De Grazia (Richmond, VA: John Knox, 1968), 279.

58. Emil Brunner, 'Nature and Grace', in *Natural Theology*, trans. Peter Fraenkel (London: Centenary, 1946), 17.

from within, not without, the Barthian movement'.[59] In the next section, I will demonstrate what Bonhoeffer's commitment to the dialectical first principle of revelation entailed for his early theology of Scripture.

Bonhoeffer's early bibliology

In the summer semester of 1925, Bonhoeffer enrolled in Reinhold Seeberg's seminar in systematics. He had already impressed the likes of Adolf von Harnack and Karl Holl with his aptitude for historical theology,[60] but his first foray into systematics would not be so warmly received. The topic of his seminar paper was the relationship between historical and spiritual exegesis, a topic he was enthusiastic about.[61] Seeberg, however, was less than enthusiastic about the result, denouncing it as 'a disturbing exercise in Barthianism'.[62] Disturbing or not, it certainly was an exercise in Barthianism, announcing Bonhoeffer's close – if not quite total – allegiance to Barth and the dialectical school. This paper is important in light of my present topic because it demonstrates his early commitment to a 'dialectical' (in the sense described above) theology in the context of scriptural interpretation. Here we see a young theologian, enthusiastic about Barth's revolution, making a first attempt to coordinate God's speech with the scriptural word, and in such a way as to avoid the cardinal sin of theological discourse: the objectification of God's word. This, as I will show in later chapters, is a perennial concern for Bonhoeffer.

---

59. DB-ER, 178. Bonhoeffer held a lifelong respect for certain liberal theologians, notably Harnack. As for Seeberg's 'influence' on Bonhoeffer, Martin Rumscheidt has argued persuasively that, although Bonhoeffer drew on Seeberg in the preparation of *Sanctorum Communio*, and to a lesser extent, *Act and Being*, Seeberg did not exercise much longstanding influence over Bonhoeffer. Rumscheidt distinguishes between genuine influence and 'the use of intellectual resources'. While Bonhoeffer made use of Seeberg's volunteerism and emphasis on sociality in his academic theology, there is no indication of the sort of theological and personal 'influence' that can be perceived, for example, in Bonhoeffer's regard for Harnack. See Martin Rumscheidt, 'The Significance of Adolf von Harnack and Reinhold Seeberg for Dietrich Bonhoeffer', in *Bonhoeffer's Intellectual Formation*, ed. Peter Frick (Tübingen: Mohr Siebeck, 2008), 201–24.

60. See, for example, Bonhoeffer's seminar paper on 1 Clement, written for Harnack (DBWE 9, 216–56; DBW 9, 220–71), and his seminar paper on Luther's later feelings about his work, written for Holl (DBWE 9, 257–84; DBW 9, 271–305). Both papers received grades of 'very good'.

61. See Bonhoeffer's May 1925 letter to Walter Dreß, where he says that Holl's sole 'church-historical' focus in his Luther seminar is 'not very stimulating', whereas the upcoming 'paper on "Historical and Pneumatic Exegesis" for Seeberg interests me very much' (DBWE 9, 145; DBW 17, 20).

62. DB-ER, 79.

The opening statement of Bonhoeffer's essay expresses his motivating concern: 'Christian religion stands or falls with the belief in a historical and perceptibly real divine revelation.'[63] It is precisely the location of revelation in real human history that raises the question of 'the relationship of history and the Spirit'.[64] Bonhoeffer has no interest in dodging the historical nature of revelation, asserting, as strongly as any historical critic, that the Bible is a human book and can be studied as such. In keeping with its methods, historical and textual critics of the Bible rightly distinguish sources, analyse forms and evaluate the historicity of its contents. The problem, Bonhoeffer alleges, is not with these critical tools but with their result: 'After this total disintegration of the texts, historical criticism leaves the field of battle. Debris and fragments are left behind. Its work is apparently finished.'[65] In Bonhoeffer's account, historical critics are interested only in taking the text apart, levelling it or relativizing it. He does grant that the best of them are nevertheless able to recognize something of the Bible's uniqueness or inner-logic, but none can access the text as God's word with historical methods alone. Seeberg does not mask his vexation at Bonhoeffer's unflattering portrait of historical criticism.[66] Himself an accomplished historical critic, Seeberg placed great value on critical methods, convinced that such work could bear theological fruit. He argued, for example, that 'we believe in the divinity of Christ in its specific and ancient sense, not because it is "prescribed," but because our modern methodological consideration of history and religious psychological analysis leads us to this result'.[67] One can hear echoes of Seeberg's present and former Berlin colleagues in this statement.[68]

As critical as he was of purely historical exegesis, Bonhoeffer finds at least as much fault with a particular kind of 'spiritual' exegesis. His main target, strikingly, is the early church and its dependence on the *regula fidei*. He regards the rule of faith as an external standard imposed on Scripture, which early

---

63. DBWE 9, 285; DBW 9, 305.
64. DBWE 9, 285; DBW 9, 306.
65. DBWE 9, 286; DBW 9, 307. Seeberg notes at this point, 'But it is only preliminary work for history' (DBWE 9, 286 ed. n. 13; DBW 9, 307 ed. n. 13). The editors point out that the language of 'fragments' and 'field of ruins' occurs in Thurneysen's 'Schrift und Offenbarung'.
66. See, for example, DBWE 9, 286 ed. n. 14; 287 ed. n. 19; DBW 9, 307 ed. n. 14; 308 ed. n. 19.
67. Reinhold Seeberg, *Die Kirche Deutschlands im neunzehnten Jahrhundert: eine Einführung in die religiösen, theologischen und kirchlichen Fragen der Gegenwart*, 3rd ed. (Leipzig: Deichert, 1910), 307, citation and translation in DBWE 9, 286 ed. n. 14; DBW 9, 307 ed. n. 14.
68. As discussed above, Troeltsch and Harnack had each in their own way sought to ground the Christian religion in purely historical study. See Troeltsch, *The Absoluteness of Christianity* and Adolf von Harnack, *What Is Christianity?* 2nd ed., trans. Thomas Bailey Saunders (New York: G. P. Putnam's Sons, 1903). Seeberg also takes issue with Bonhoeffer's critique of Troeltsch in DBWE 9, 176; DBW 9, 176.

orthodox Christianity used to 'verify' revelation in Scripture and thereby 'prove' the canonicity of each book. This, he contends, was a fundamental misstep, the foundation of all attempts 'to tie down revelation as scripture'.[69] He identifies the root of this error as 'a lack of insight into the relationship of revelation and scripture'.[70] Here he takes aim at a certain view of biblical canonicity. It is telling that this is the one place in the essay where Barth becomes a target of critique, as the Lutheran Bonhoeffer takes issue with the Reformed Barth's high regard for the canon.[71] Bonhoeffer wants to say, with Luther, that the standard of Scripture is 'what promotes Christ [*was Christus treibet*]'.[72] This is not to say that the concept of the canon carries no weight for Bonhoeffer at this time. For him, 'the canon comprises only the highly striking evidence of the deep insight by which the significant writings were chosen from the great amount of literature of that time'.[73] In other words, the canon proves itself by doing what Scripture does: promoting Christ. Whatever does not have this as its content of revelation, Bonhoeffer ventures, 'is not canonical', and therefore the canon in principle 'must be regarded as open'.[74]

Why does Bonhoeffer affirm an open canon, at least in principle? Edward van 't Slot argues that Bonhoeffer gradually moves away from this early account of an

---

69. DBWE 9, 288; DBW 9, 309.

70. DBWE 9, 287; DBW 9, 308.

71. In phrasing it this way, I only intend to draw attention to the confessional difference that emerges on this particular topic at this particular time. Although confessional differences can help to account for some of the key differences between Barth and Bonhoeffer, their own denominational commitments are far from unambiguous and it would simply be untrue to say that Barth generally follows Calvin where Bonhoeffer follows Luther. I would more cautiously suggest that in those places where Bonhoeffer most explicitly and resolutely departs from Barth, it tends to be in places where Barth is departing from Luther. See also the nuanced discussion in DeJonge, *Bonhoeffer's Theological Formation*, 101–14.

72. DBWE 9, 297; DBW 9, 320–1; DBW 9, 320–1. Bonhoeffer cites Luther's preface to James: 'Now it is the office of a true apostle to preach of the Passion and resurrection and office of Christ, and to lay the foundation for faith in him, as Christ himself says in John 15[:27], "You shall bear witness to me." All the genuine sacred books agree in this, that all of them preach and [promote] [*treiben*] Christ. And that is the true test by which to judge all books, when we see whether or not they promote Christ ... Whatever does not teach Christ is not yet apostolic, even though St. Peter or St. Paul does the teaching. Again, whatever preaches Christ would be apostolic, even if Judas, Annas, Pilate, and Herod were doing it' (LW 35, 396; translation modified).

73. DBWE 9, 297; DBW 9, 321.

74. DBWE 9, 297; DBW 9, 321; cf. DBW 9, 320–1. The English translation in DBWE 9 is less than felicitous here: 'What the content of revelation does not have is not canonical' (DBWE 9, 297). The German original is 'was diesen Offenbarungsinhalt nicht hat, ist unkanonisch' (DBW 9, 321), which should be rendered as 'what does not have this content of revelation is not canonical'.

essentially open canon and that his later affirmation of the wholeness of Scripture requires a functionally closed canon.[75] For Barth the canon is a fixed point of reference, because it is through *these* texts that God freely reveals himself, whereas for Bonhoeffer a text is confirmed as canonical when and where it 'promotes Christ'. At this early phase, Slot contends, Bonhoeffer endorses Luther's principle in order to maintain the *freedom* of God in biblical revelation, but in later phases of development Bonhoeffer had to modify this view, not least because of the difficulties it presents for Christology. To wit: If we know the canon based on 'whatever promotes Christ', how do we come to know *Christ*? Is it not on the basis of the canonical biblical testimony? Or is it on some other basis? Slot's concern (and he believes that Bonhoeffer began to have the same misgivings) is that the content of Christology exercises control over the biblical canon, rather than the reverse. As Bonhoeffer begins to affirm the *whole* of Scripture as the witness to Christ, he must attribute a larger degree of priority and fixity to the canon. The wholeness of Scripture becomes the presupposition that justifies a Christological hermeneutic, rather than a Christological hermeneutic leading to conclusions about what is or is not 'canonical'. Slot is right to observe that Bonhoeffer's concern here as well as later in life is essentially Barthian. He wants to affirm God's freedom in revelation, which means that 'God, in revealing himself, is in no way bound by any human tradition, and surely not to a list of books, composed by confused human beings, containing a contingent set of frozen truths'.[76] Thus, throughout this early essay on pneumatological interpretation, Bonhoeffer is working out how a Barthian emphasis on God's freedom might feed into a non-Barthian account of the Christian canon. He resists all attempts to verify revelation by anything outside of revelation itself. Nothing – neither canonicity, nor accordance with the *regula fidei*, nor the doctrine of verbal inspiration – can provide 'evidence' of revelation in Scripture. Revelation in Scripture is God's speaking God's word through it, and this word always 'promotes Christ'.

What about inspiration? Although Bonhoeffer rejects the doctrine of verbal inspiration here and throughout his life, he does affirm a certain kind of inspiration at work in Scripture. Inspiration, Bonhoeffer argues in this context, is the revelatory event wherein God *communicates* God's word to humankind. The biblical authors were 'inspired' insofar as they were 'those to whom the Spirit had disclosed that revelation could be found precisely in this historical person, Jesus – fully human, appearing completely in the framework of ordinary events'.[77] That is, they were not given words to write down; they became witnesses to Jesus Christ, either as prophets or as apostles, in whom, they believed, revelation was to be found. The

---

75. Edward van 't Slot, 'The Freedom of Scripture: Bonhoeffer's Changing View of Biblical Canonicity', in *God Speaks to Us: Dietrich Bonhoeffer's Biblical Hermeneutics*, ed. Ralf K. Wüstenberg and Jens Zimmermann, International Bonhoeffer Interpretations 5 (Frankfurt am Main: Peter Lang, 2013), 101–22.
76. Ibid., 109–10.
77. DBWE 9, 293; DBW 9, 316.

words they recorded are not only 'of the Spirit' but also 'an incarnate image of the person of Jesus Christ himself'.[78] These words do not thereby lose their historical character, but are 'incarnate images' precisely in their historical aspect.

Scripture is not identical with revelation. Scripture 'belongs to a great complex of revelation as a *document that gives witness*'.[79] Bonhoeffer thus follows Barth in asserting that Scripture is the witness to revelation. He wants to separate Scripture from revelation[80] so he can sort out their proper relationship, which he regards as the key to a proper understanding of Scripture and interpretation. The reason historical criticism presented such a challenge to theology was its challenge to the supposed 'infallibility' of Scripture. The Bible and revelation must be carefully distinguished. If revelation simply *is* the biblical text, then textual or historical criticism is tantamount to criticism of revelation itself. On the contrary, he asserts, 'it is absolutely necessary that we assure ourselves of the fallibility of these texts so that we can recognize the miracle that we really do hear God's words in human words'.[81] Revelation, he argues, is a historical event, which God undertakes as subject and object. God not only speaks the word, but also 'hears in us'.[82] This occurs 'in certain indescribable and undetermined moments and words'.[83] This perspective is at some distance from what Bonhoeffer will espouse in *Act and Being*, where Bonhoeffer criticizes Barth on precisely this point. But he remains committed to saying, with the rest of the historical-critical guild, that nothing in or of the text is irrefutably of divine origin. The Bible is human all the way down.

To return to the central question of Bonhoeffer's essay, what is the relationship between historical and spiritual interpretation? If revelation is only accessible in Scripture, then the spiritual exegete is no less bound to the human text than the historical critic. The biblical text is their shared starting point. They diverge only after their preliminary textual work is complete, the historian to history, the theologian to revelation. Thus could Bonhoeffer conclude: 'Scripture is only a *source* for history. For spiritual interpretation, scripture is a *witness*.'[84] In the final analysis, Bonhoeffer posits an asymmetrical relationship between the two methods. Spiritual interpretation is what safeguards dogmatics from becoming merely 'the presentation of New Testament piety', whereas historical-critical exegesis helps to clarify the historical character of revelation. The former is essential, but the

---

78. DBWE 9, 294; DBW 9, 316.
79. DBWE 9, 289; DBW 9, 311.
80. This is confirmed by Bonhoeffer's own outline of the contents of this essay, which frames his approach to pneumatological interpretation as 'Scripture and revelation separated' (DBWE 9, 299; DBW 9, 323).
81. DBWE 9, 297; DBW 9, 320.
82. DBWE 9, 293; DBW 9, 316.
83. DBWE 9, 290; DBW 9, 312.
84. DBWE 9, 296; DBW 9, 320.

latter is not.⁸⁵ This was a bold position to take in Berlin at the time, where the historical-critical method was regarded as an absolute necessity for the credibility of any biblically grounded theological proposal. 'Historical knowledge and critical reflection', Harnack insisted, 'are indispensable if we are to avoid naive biblicism'.⁸⁶ Bonhoeffer, under Barth's influence, disagreed, saying that 'the attempt to speak God's word with human words … will never go beyond the stage of experiment if God does not assent to it … Every attempt at pneumatological interpretation is a prayer, a plea for the Holy Spirit'.⁸⁷

Conclusion

This early essay demonstrates what would be a perennial concern for Bonhoeffer, to work out 'the relationship of history and the Spirit' under the conviction that Christianity must be grounded in 'a historical and perceptibly real divine revelation'.⁸⁸ Relating history and the Spirit in the Bible means drawing a careful distinction between the biblical text and divine revelation. And the latter comes from God alone. It is also significant that Bonhoeffer's pledge of allegiance to the dialectical movement took up the topic of biblical interpretation. As he would demonstrate in his dissertations, he is quite capable of sustaining lengthy theological discussions about revelation and the word of God without making much reference to Scripture. There is no clear explanation why. It may be that Seeberg's negative response to this paper, a reflection of the overall animosity of the Berlin faculty towards the dialectical school, dissuaded Bonhoeffer from defending the Barthian

---

85. DBWE 9, 297–8; DBW 9, 321. One can hear clear echoes of Karl Barth, *The Epistle to the Romans*, 6th ed., trans. Edwin C. Hoskins (London: Oxford University Press, 1933), 6: 'I have nothing whatever to say against historical criticism … My complaint is that recent commentators confine themselves to an interpretation of the text which seems to me to be no commentary at all, but merely the first step towards a commentary.' By this, Barth means that 'recent commentators' do not go far enough to wrestle seriously with the text, confining themselves instead to textual reconstruction, religious history and psychological analysis. When, for example, Paul's doctrines or statements are too difficult to appropriate to their contemporary context, they are quick to set them aside as mere quirks of his personality or his first-century context. For Barth, by contrast, the interpretive task remains unfinished until the exegete has reached a genuine understanding, until the modern interpreter actually hears what Paul says. Thus, in his well-known statement, 'the critical historian needs to be more critical' (ibid., 8).

86. Translation in George Hunsinger, 'The Harnack/Barth Correspondence: A Paraphrase with Comments', in *Disruptive Grace: Studies in the Theology of Karl Barth* (Grand Rapids: Eerdmans, 2000), 321.

87. DBWE 9, 298; DBW 9, 322.

88. DBWE 9, 285; DBW 9, 305.

movement from this angle. And other angles were available. After all, the hallmark of the 'new theology' was, in Bonhoeffer's view, its grounding in the word of God, not the Bible as such.

I conclude that Bonhoeffer was, from his earliest encounter with Barth's writings, a theologian of revelation. And if the dialectical movement was defined by its commitment to the word of God as the theme of theology, then Bonhoeffer ought to be counted among its most ardent supporters. Barth had provided the young Bonhoeffer with a point of departure, setting him down a theological path that he would follow, like the others in that movement, to a distinct end. Along this path, Thurneysen, Brunner and Gogarten would fade into the background, while Barth would persist as an ever-present conversation partner, and Bultmann would recur at significant moments. But at no point along this path did Bonhoeffer abandon what set him along that path in the first place: '*Deus dixit* – to accept this is the beginning of all genuine theological thinking, to allow space for the freedom of the living God.'[89] By including Bonhoeffer within the dialectical circle, I am not making a claim about his methodological commitments or his historical importance in that movement. My claim is, rather, that Bonhoeffer was a theologian of the word of God.[90] As a theologian of God's word, Bonhoeffer held Scripture in a particularly high regard, and the important questions he first raised in his earliest essay on 'pneumatological interpretation' would recur throughout his life. It would, however, be some years before he would revisit the topic of scriptural interpretation with this kind of direct, extended treatment. Nevertheless, he would continue to develop as a theologian of God's word in his academic theological writings. In the next chapter, I will explore his distinctive account of revelation as he develops it in his dissertations, *Sanctorum Communio* and *Act and Being*.

---

89. DBWE 11, 231; DBW 11, 199.
90. See Ziegler, 'Dietrich Bonhoeffer: A Theologian of the Word of God', 17–37. For more on the theme of *Deus dixit* in Bonhoeffer's thought, see Lange, *Waiting for the Word*, 63–85.

3

REVELATION AS *CHRISTUS PRAESENS*

Theology must be grounded in God's self-revelation. On this basis alone is it possible for human words to correspond to God's word. Bonhoeffer's unswerving commitment to this point of departure associates him with the dialectical movement and classifies him as a theologian of God's word. But what *is* revelation? Where is it found? How do human beings come to know God in God's revelation? These are the questions that any theologian of God's word must answer.

In this chapter, I argue that Bonhoeffer's answer comes by way of an interpretation of *Christ's presence*. To this end, I look to his dissertations, *Sanctorum Communio* and *Act and Being*, in order to identify the place and character of revelation in each. In both works, I contend, Bonhoeffer operates as a theologian of God's word, firmly committed to revelation as the *petitio principii* of theology, and yet in a way that leaves the place of Scripture somewhat underdetermined. Bonhoeffer's critical reception of Barth is particularly illuminating, because it shows just how far he was – and was not – willing to go with Barth. My principal aim in this chapter is to establish that Bonhoeffer's theology of revelation was grounded in an account of Christ's presence. The meaning of revelation is *Christus praesens*. Indeed, revelation *is* the present Christ. In his dissertations, he pursues this claim with a distinctively social-ecclesiological interpretation of Christ's presence, 'Christ existing as church-community'. This innovative approach enabled him to address the basic paradox of revelation. Nevertheless, I will argue, in its purely ecclesial form, revelation-as-*Christus-praesens* entails an (effectively) occasionalist bibliology.

Revelation as the ground of ecclesiology

The stated theme of Bonhoeffer's first dissertation, *Sanctorum Communio*, is ecclesiology, and it has rightly been studied as such. Other scholars have noted the importance of its theological anthropology, its use of sociology and its relation to

Bonhoeffer's ethics – to name a few.[1] But what is often missed is the degree to which all of these themes revolve around the question of revelation. Bonhoeffer refuses to treat the topic of the church in isolation either from revelation or from the concrete human community.[2] Although his references to Barth in *Sanctorum Communio* are relatively few, Barth presides over the whole endeavour. Hans Christoph von Hase, Bonhoeffer's cousin and fellow disciple of Barth, clearly perceived this: 'There will not be many who really understand [*Sanctorum Communio*], the Barthians won't because of the sociology, and the sociologists won't because of Barth.'[3] Here, Bonhoeffer sets out for the first time what will become one of his most consistent theological convictions: the word of God is the presence of Jesus Christ. If the church-community really is the present Christ, then the theology of revelation is at the root of ecclesiology. The question Bonhoeffer seeks to answer here concerns revelation's 'concrete locus within the reality of the world'.[4]

In the course of Bonhoeffer's argument, the concept of revelation recurs precisely where he wants to emphasize the theological character of his study and resist the reductive attempt to explain the reality of the church on the basis of sociology alone. This is where revelation becomes central to his argument: '*The reality of the church is a reality of revelation, a reality that essentially must be* either believed or denied.'[5] Asserting the connection even more forcefully, he says, '*Only the concept of revelation can lead to the Christian concept of the*

---

1. See, for example, Mawson, *Christ Existing as Community*; Christiane Tietz, 'Bonhoeffer on the Ontological Structure of the Church', in *Ontology and Ethics: Bonhoeffer and Contemporary Scholarship*, ed. Adam C. Clark and Michael Mawson (Eugene, OR: Pickwick, 2013), 32–46; Clifford J. Green, *Bonhoeffer: A Theology of Sociality*, 2nd ed. (Grand Rapids: Eerdmans, 1999), 19–65; Peter Berger, 'The Social Character of the Question Concerning Jesus Christ: Sociology and Ecclesiology', in *The Place of Bonhoeffer: Problems and Possibilities in His Thought*, ed. Martin E. Marty (London: SCM, 1963), 53–79.

2. The connection between revelation and ecclesiology appears on the first page: 'The more this investigation has considered the significance of the sociological category for theology, the more clearly has emerged the social intention of all the basic Christian concepts. "Person," "primal state," "sin," and "revelation" can be fully comprehended only in reference to sociality' (DBWE 1, 21; DBW 1, 13). These four key concepts correspond to the structure of his dissertation, which devotes one chapter each to 'The Christian Concept of Person', 'The Primal State and the Problem of Community', 'Sin and Broken Community' and 'Sanctorum Communio'. That his treatment of revelation *is* ecclesiology indicates that, for Bonhoeffer at this time, they are essentially the same topic.

3. Unpublished letter of 13 October 1930, quoted in DB-ER, 83. Hase apparently sensed the audacity of Bonhoeffer's project, and facetiously offered to describe *Sanctorum Communio* in his own doctoral dissertation as a 'noteworthy, promising attempt from one of our young, as yet unknown theological hotheads' (DBWE 10, 253–4; DBW 10, 208–9).

4. Joachim von Soosten, 'Editor's Afterword to the German Edition', in DBWE 1.

5. DBWE 1, 127; DBW 1, 80.

church.'⁶ Later, he states, 'With regard to content, the church's structure is based on the Christian idea of revelation.'⁷ This passage occurs in his discussion of the church's place within his sociological typology, where he argues for the church 'as a distinct sociological type'.⁸ The particular type of community that the church is, he argues, is based on its unique character as a divinely instituted reality that exists in historical, human form. No other community, religious or otherwise, has this unique character, which suggests that the church ought to be described according to a unique sociological type. These types follow from various distinctions: some types of communities are compulsory, others voluntary; some are longstanding, others spontaneous; some gather based on rule, others based on free association; some are oriented towards a particular goal, others an end in themselves. These distinctions imply distinct sociological categories, and Bonhoeffer wants to say that the church is '*a form of community sui generis, namely community of Spirit [Geistgemeinschaft] as community of love [Liebesgemeinschaft]*',⁹ which transcends and combines various sociological types. Yet he also wants to reassert that 'this distinctive sociological structure can be understood only theologically, and not in morphological and sociological terms alone'.¹⁰ As a sociological type, the church 'is dependent upon the Word of God, and it alone'.¹¹ Because the church is established and sustained by God's word, proclaimed in sermon and sacrament, 'it is present within every historical form in which the word is preached'.¹² In order to retain the theological character of his sociological analysis, he refers the morphological description of the church to its basis in revelation.

Throughout this discussion, the young Bonhoeffer is wrestling with the question of the concrete form of God's revelation in history. As Hase puts it, Bonhoeffer insists 'that the reality of revelation could be discovered only in the actual existing congregation, and that Christ must be comprehended as "existing as church-community"'.¹³ The idea that the church cannot be reduced to sociological description was a direct affront to the history-of-religions school represented in Berlin. With Barth (and Kierkegaard), Bonhoeffer wants to maintain the 'infinite

---

6. DBWE 1, 134; DBW 1, 84.
7. DBWE 1, 264; DBW 1, 183.
8. DBWE 1, 252; DBW 1, 173.
9. DBWE 1, 266; DBW 1, 183.
10. DBWE 1, 264; DBW 1, 183.
11. DBWE 1, 270–1; DBW 1, 188.
12. DBWE 1, 271; DBW 1, 188. Bonhoeffer wants to include the Roman Catholic church in this distinctly Protestant ecclesiology: 'Based on the efficacy of the word, we must believe the sanctorum communio to be present even within the sociologically unique type of the Roman Catholic church' (DBWE 1, 271; DBW 1, 188).
13. Hans Christoph von Hase, '"Turning Away from the Phraseological to the Real": A Personal Recollection', in DBWE 10, 597; DBW 10, 594.

qualitative distinction' between God and human beings,[14] but in a way that takes the historical form of revelation seriously. It becomes clear that Bonhoeffer has not given up the question that drove his 1925 paper on scriptural interpretation: 'Christian religion stands or falls with the belief in a historical and perceptibly real divine revelation, a revelation that those who have eyes to see can see and those who have ears to hear can hear.'[15] This assertion applies, *mutatis mutandis*, to ecclesiology.

The concept of revelation appears at these critical moments in *Sanctorum Communio* as Bonhoeffer's way to maintain the theological character of his work, a bulwark to ward off any suggestion that the genuine reality of the church could be described in purely sociological terms. Nevertheless, because 'God's revelation actually takes place in history',[16] its historical form must be taken with the utmost seriousness. Therein lies the tension between sociological and theological enquiry, between the 'empirical' and the 'essential' church. The degree of Bonhoeffer's success in navigating between these poles is beside the point. What matters is the importance he placed on the need to interpret the 'reality of revelation' according to its concrete, historical form without reducing it to the historical form. Bonhoeffer's claim in *Sanctorum Communio* that the concrete form of Christ in the world *is* the church-community cannot be reversed, as Bethge rightly observes.[17] 'Christ existing as church-community' does not mean that the church-community just *is* Christ without remainder. The historical form Christ takes is this community, but this historical community is not Christ. This is how Bonhoeffer addresses the (Barthian) question of revelation throughout *Sanctorum Communio*.

---

14. Barth, *The Epistle to the Romans*, 10. In context, Barth says, 'If I have a system, it is limited to a recognition of what Kierkegaard called the "infinite qualitative distinction" between time and eternity, and to my regarding this as possessing negative as well as positive significance: "God is in heaven, and thou art on earth." The relation between such a God and such a man, and the relation between such a man and such a God, is for me the theme of the Bible and the essence of philosophy.'

15. DBWE 9, 285; DBW 9, 305–6.

16. DBWE 1, 222; DBW 1, 151.

17. 'Bonhoeffer never regarded his formula of "Christ existing as church-community" as being true in reverse' (DB-ER, 84). Bethge credits this observation to Regin Prenter. With reference to 'Christ existing as community', Ernst Feil argues that Bonhoeffer's concern 'was not so much the concrete Christ who entered history as it was the concept of the church as collective person' (Feil, *The Theology of Dietrich Bonhoeffer*, 63). Feil claims that *Sanctorum Communio* effectively collapses Christology into ecclesiology. Michael Mawson, however, argues for a greater degree of Christological sophistication in *Sanctorum Communio* than Feil allows. Mawson argues that Bonhoeffer carefully distinguishes between Christ, the Holy Spirit and the concrete church-community, and that his formula, 'Christ existing as community', is how he describes the mediatorial work of Christ in history. Mawson, *Christ Existing as Community*, 144–9.

For my present purposes, the most significant aspect of Bonhoeffer's early theology of revelation is its *social* character. In the preface to *Sanctorum Communio*, Bonhoeffer asserts that 'all the basic Christian concepts ... can be fully comprehended only in reference to sociality'.[18] Clifford Green has argued that this statement is programmatic for the whole of his early theology. When considering Bonhoeffer's treatment of revelation in *Sanctorum Communio*, Green says, 'Revelation, that is, the person of Christ, exists in *social form*: the church. Revelation is not an idea, a past historical happening, a doctrine, or an entity. It is a *person*, and since person and community are inseparable, the revelation of Christ is present in a personal-communal form: "Christus als Gemeinde existierend".'[19] Green draws attention to two important features of Bonhoeffer's theology of revelation: that revelation is the *person* of Christ and that this person exists in a particular historical form, namely, the church-community. The young Bonhoeffer spoke of revelation as a social reality, because the present Christ is present as the collective-person of the church-community. As a result, Bonhoeffer made little use of 'revelation' as an 'abstract noun' and generally preferred the verbal form to describe 'personal *self-giving*'.[20] This act, in order to be a genuine *revealing* of one person to another, must transcend the boundary between I and You. Genuine sociality cannot occur unless there is a genuine *boundary* that separates persons. Bonhoeffer locates this boundary in the ethical sphere, that is, in the personal will. Only the will of the other poses an absolute limit to the self. Transcending this boundary is only possible in the church-community; the new way of being-together in Christ is vicarious-representative action (*Stellvertretung*). That is why revelation 'is' and 'occurs' only in the church-community.

Bonhoeffer's social interpretation of revelation offers a distinctive account of transcendence. 'Transcendence in Bonhoeffer's theology of sociality', Green argues, 'is *socio-ethical transcendence*'.[21] Even the transcendence of God is not a function of God's being divine but of his being *person*. In *Act and Being*, Bonhoeffer employs his social interpretation of personhood more explicitly to address the problem of divine transcendence and historical continuity in revelation. Says Green, 'Since the revealing Christ is present in the personal form of the social community of faith, revelation has both a transcendence and continuity of being'; this is how Bonhoeffer 'is able to present a dialectical integration of act and being in the interpretation of revelation'.[22] Green argues that this socio-ethical interpretation of transcendence and historical continuity demonstrates Bonhoeffer's continued theology of sociality, which revolves around anthropological and soteriological questions. I would only add that Bonhoeffer's continued 'theology of sociality' in his early years, and his corresponding interest in anthropology and soteriology, emerges from his basic 'dialectical' concern that theology can only proceed on the

---

18. DBWE 1, 21; DBW 1, 13.
19. Green, *A Theology of Sociality*, 53.
20. Ibid., 56.
21. Ibid., 64.
22. Ibid., 89.

basis of revelation.²³ Determining precisely how divine revelation relates to human history, then, is a crucial question for any theology of revelation. *Sanctorum Communio* and *Act and Being* represent Bonhoeffer's early attempt to answer this question with reference to the sociality of the church. Whereas in *Sanctorum Communio*, the dialectical first principle of revelation is more implicit, in *Act and Being*, he takes up the topic of revelation more directly.

Ecclesiology as the ground of epistemology

Bonhoeffer completed *Act and Being* in 1930 as his *Habilitationschrift*, one of the requirements to qualify as a university lecturer. Like *Sanctorum Communio*, it is a dense and ambitious work. In recent years, several excellent studies of *Act and Being* have been published, particularly with reference to its critical dialogue with Karl Barth and its significance for Bonhoeffer's theology of revelation.²⁴ My interest concerns what *Act and Being* contributes to our understanding of Bonhoeffer's theology of revelation and his use (or neglect) of Scripture at the time.

Bonhoeffer presents his book as a contribution to the problem of act and being, but the nature of the problem is not entirely clear. Michael DeJonge, in his fine study of *Act and Being*, has noted that 'despite repeated references to the problem of act and being, Bonhoeffer never precisely formulates its nature or succinctly indicates the criteria for its solution'.²⁵ The work's subtitle gives readers a clue: 'transcendental philosophy and ontology in systematic theology'. In the first part of the book, Bonhoeffer carries on a critical dialogue with modern German philosophy under those two broad categories. Transcendental philosophy corresponds to 'act', ontology to 'being'. The basic orientation of these two forms of thought suggests that the problem of act and being is the problem of whether epistemology ought to take its beginning from the act of knowing or the reality of the thing known. Bonhoeffer argues that neither approach fully accounts for the unity of the knowing subject and the object of knowledge. But his concern is not limited to the general problem of transcendence in epistemology. His aim throughout is to assess the value of various epistemologies for the theology of

---

23. In this, I agree with Mawson that Green overestimates the systematic function of the concept of person in *Sanctorum Communio*. Bonhoeffer is putting sociological concepts in the service of theology, as he himself says in the first sentence of his preface (DBWE 1, 21; DBW 1, 13). Thus, his treatments of creation, sin and revelation determine how he speaks of the concept of person, rather than the reverse. Against Green, Mawson argues that there is no stable anthropological concept that grounds Bonhoeffer's systematic accounts of creation, sin and revelation. See Mawson, *Christ Existing as Community*, 66–73.
24. DeJonge, *Bonhoeffer's Theological Formation*; Slot, *Negativism of Revelation*.
25. DeJonge, *Bonhoeffer's Theological Formation*, 15.

revelation. The theological problem of act and being is 'the issue of determining the relationship between "the being of God" and the mental act which grasps that being'.[26]

The basic paradox – the *aporia* – of the theology of revelation is its claim that the unknowable God becomes known. To say that God is known is to say that God is the object of human consciousness, but an object immanent in human knowledge cannot be the transcendent God. To express it in the terms Bonhoeffer uses, in revelation, the transcendent God enters into the structurally closed circle of human consciousness. How can one speak of this state of affairs? Should revelation be interpreted in terms of act, that is, in terms that emphasize the absolute transcendence of God over against the human knower? Or is it best articulated in terms of being, which prioritizes the objectivity of the reality of God in revelation? In this question, Bonhoeffer thought that Barth had levelled a decisive critique against any theology of revelation grounded in being, since any existing thing to which human beings have unfettered access is by definition not transcendent. If God is to remain God in revelation, God must never become an object of knowledge. God must remain the Lord. But as much as Bonhoeffer agreed with Barth's thoroughgoing attack on the objectification of God, he remained sceptical of Barth's alternative. Although Bonhoeffer raises questions about Barth's dependence on transcendental philosophy, his real concern is that Barth has not dealt with the fundamental difficulty facing the theology of revelation. In order to speak of a *revelation* of God that is also revelation of *God*, one must account for both the objectivity and the non-objectivity of God's self-disclosure. Bonhoeffer thinks that Barth has failed to describe God's objectivity in revelation, thereby rendering God as eternally beyond human grasp.

Bonhoeffer's theology of revelation addresses three important questions. Firstly, what 'is' revelation? Secondly, what is the nature and meaning of 'knowledge' in revelation? And thirdly, what is the nature and meaning of the human being who receives or knows revelation? In other words, the concept of revelation has implications for theology proper, for epistemology and for theological anthropology. In Bonhoeffer's judgement, an interpretation of revelation that begins in *act* is unsatisfactory on all three fronts. Karl Barth is the paradigmatic act-theologian, although he is not its sole practitioner. But Bonhoeffer names Barth more than any other as his main interlocutor.

Firstly, what is revelation? What is revelation's mode of being? How do we interpret 'the being of God in revelation'? For Barth, the 'mode of being' of revelation is act. As God's act, 'revelation is an event that has its basis in the freedom of God'.[27] The ground of God's action is God's freedom. But how should God's freedom be understood? Bonhoeffer argues that Barth relies on a 'formalistic-actualistic understanding of the freedom and contingency of God in revelation'.[28]

---

26. DBWE 2, 27; DBW 2, 22.
27. DBWE 2, 82; DBW 2, 76.
28. DBWE 2, 90; DBW 2, 85.

A 'formal' concept of freedom lacks material content. It says nothing except that God is free *from* all external constraints; it says nothing about what God's freedom is *for*. This is a problem for Bonhoeffer. As the basis of God's act of self-revelation, a formal concept of freedom means that 'God is bound to nothing, not even the "existing," "historical" Word'.[29] Barth wants to affirm the *finitum incapax infiniti* by denying that God in revelation could ever be identified with a historical means of revelation – even if this historical means is the humanity of Jesus.[30] But if God is free even from historical revelation, then what ground is left for the theologian to stand on? Theological and profane thinking both stand under the judgement or the blessing of God's word. For Bonhoeffer, Barth's dialectic 'means that I always counter a judgment of knowing with one of not-knowing, and that any attempt to constrain God is itself limited by God's freedom … In other words, I introduce a factor into my thinking that renders it *a priori* uncertain'.[31] And Bonhoeffer cannot accept this, because if 'we are truly to speak of *revelation*, it must somehow be manifest to human beings and knowable by them'.[32] A beginning in God's act,

---

29. DBWE 2, 82; DBW 2, 76.

30. In 1924, Barth wrote that he wanted to avoid 'the exclusive "Jesus Christ"-pit of the Lutherans', that he sought instead 'a Trinity of *being*, not just an economic Trinity!' (Eduard Thurneysen, ed., *Karl Barth–Eduard Thurneysen: Briefswechel, 1921–1930* [Zurich: TVZ, 1974], 245; quoted in McCormack, *Karl Barth's Critically Realistic Dialectical Theology*, 351). According to McCormack, Barth's concern here was to 'oppose a concept of revelation which was guilty of a deification of the creature – even if the creature in question was named Jesus of Nazareth' (ibid., 351). In Barth's 1927 dogmatics, he says that the statement, *finitum non capax infiniti*, 'takes care of all trinitarian heresies with one strike' (Karl Barth, *Die christliche Dogmatik im Entwurf 1 – Die Lehre vom Worte Gottes: Prolegomena zur christlichen Dogmatik* [Munich: Chr. Kaiser, 1927], 188). The *incapax* applies to the humanity of Jesus no less than to any other finite reality. For Barth, according to McCormack, to say that Jesus is God is not to conflate the human and divine natures of Jesus, but rather to affirm that 'God is the revealing Subject in the human Jesus' (McCormack, *Karl Barth's Critically Realistic Dialectical Theology*, 356). Bonhoeffer is more willing than Barth to say, *finitum capax infiniti*, but it is worth noting that he affirms 'the old maxim finitum incapax infiniti' in DBWE 9, 289; DBW 9, 310.

31. DBWE 2, 124; DBW 2, 121. Bonhoeffer recognizes Barth's dialectical method as his attempt to honour the freedom of God by placing all human speech under a 'critical proviso' (DBWE 2, 86 n. 11; DBW 2, 80 n. 11). Barth's theological dialectic differs from philosophical dialectic because Barth refuses to synthesize thesis and antithesis into a *tertium* (Karl Barth, 'Fate and Idea in Theology', in *The Way of Theology in Karl Barth: Essays and Comments*, ed. Martin Rumscheidt, trans. George Hunsinger [Eugene, OR: Pickwick, 1986], 53). Theology grounded in God's word must honour the freedom of God in revelation, for 'God's Word is not bound, nor ever will be bound' (ibid., 59). Even a self-critical dialectic is no way to guarantee fidelity to God's word. For Barth, 'the unity of reality and truth occurs in and only in God's Word' (ibid., 58). And God's word is grounded in God's freedom.

32. DBWE 2, 92; DBW 2, 86.

grounded in a formal account of God's freedom, ends with God remaining outside the human sphere. 'God remains always the Lord, always subject, so that whoever claims to have God as an object no longer has *God*; God is always the God who "comes" and never the God who "is there".'[33]

For God to be God in revelation, 'God can never become the object of consciousness'.[34] But what then can it mean to have knowledge of God? For Barth, the only ground for knowing God is God's self-knowledge. God as the subject of revelation means that God is also 'the subject of the cognition of revelation'.[35] Knowing God never means that God has become an object of knowledge. It means that God has acted by the Holy Spirit to effect human faith in Christ. But Bonhoeffer thinks that Barth is unclear about 'how the religious act of human beings and God's action in faith are to be thought, without dividing them into two – by nature different – spheres'.[36] What the human being experiences as 'faith' cannot be identified with God's act of effecting human faith. Human beings cannot know that God is enacting faith in them any more than they can know God directly. Here again, Bonhoeffer thinks that Barth is unable to make a meaningful distinction between theological and profane thought, between belief and unbelief. For all theological questions, Barth leads to the conclusion that 'human knowing is not-knowing'.[37]

Finally, what does Barth's doctrine of revelation require on the level of theological anthropology? As Barth puts it, 'The human being to whom God reveals himself is the very one to whom God cannot be revealed.'[38] The problem is how the self-knowing and self-revealing God might break into the closed circle of human knowledge without becoming enclosed in it. For Barth, this act 'can only break apart the human subject'.[39] It is of crucial importance that 'God is kept in view as subject' in revelation and that 'the subject of understanding is God as Holy Spirit'.[40] If the subject who believes in revelation is the Holy Spirit, then God as the 'believing I' transcends the human subject no less than God as the content of revelation itself. One can never rest in one's knowledge of God, either in revelation or in any experience of belief, past or present. All knowledge of God is at once

---

33. DBWE 2, 85; DBW 2, 79. Bonhoeffer attributes this paraphrase to Barth in parentheses, but does not offer any direct citations. The editors cite Barth, 'Fate and Idea', 39ff, where Barth suggests that the 'hesitation necessary toward theological realism' is that it ends up 'with the idea of a God whose being is merely there instead of a God who comes' (ibid., 42).
34. DBWE 2, 92; DBW 2, 86.
35. DBWE 2, 92; DBW 2, 86.
36. DBWE 2, 93; DBW 2, 88.
37. DBWE 2, 124; DBW 2, 121. Bonhoeffer is citing Barth, *Die christliche Dogmatik*, 61.
38. Barth, *Die christliche Dogmatik*, 287. Bonhoeffer quotes from this passage in DBWE 2, 99; DBW 2, 94.
39. Barth, *Die christliche Dogmatik*, 287.
40. DBWE 2, 92; DBW 2, 86–7.

judged as being knowledge of not-God. The 'I' who believes is at once confronted with the judgement of being 'not-I'.

It is for these reasons that Bonhoeffer regards Barth's view of revelation as tantamount to 'nonrevelation'.[41] He thinks that Barth operates with too radical a break between the being of God in revelation and the cognitive act directed towards God in revelation, between knowing and not-knowing, between the believing and non-believing human subject. God remains God. The 'believing I' remains a 'heavenly double' of the 'unbelieving I'.[42] Unable to maintain the continuity of the human subject, Barth cannot account for how the existence of the human being is encountered in revelation. If the new human holds no continuity with the old, then the old has not really been affected. If there is no way to identify the sinful person in continuity with the redeemed, then God has not actually come to sinful humanity. God has not actually been revealed.

Bonhoeffer's critical reservations about Barth do not negate the theological affinity between them.[43] He stands closer to Barth than any other twentieth-century theologian in the pages of *Act and Being*. He wants to affirm with Barth and the dialectical school that God remains God in revelation, that God can never be delivered into human ways of knowing. But, as already noted, he thinks that a point of departure in act-thinking fails to account for the genuine encounter with God in revelation such that the human being is really affected.[44] As an alternative, Bonhoeffer proposes a theology of revelation with its starting point in the *church*. In this, he is intentionally building on the ecclesiology of *Sanctorum Communio*. The church, he had argued, is the concrete form of Christ's presence in the world. For this reason, Bonhoeffer thinks, it must be the basis for thinking about revelation. Thereby the ecclesiological interpretation of revelation in *Sanctorum Communio* becomes the ground for theological epistemology in *Act and Being*.

---

41. DBWE 2, 99; DBW 2, 95.

42. DBWE 2, 99; DBW 2, 95. Bonhoeffer first uses this expression in connection with Barth's theology in his seminar paper, 'Luther's Views of the Holy Spirit': 'It is after all not the Holy Spirit in *me* but instead a second self that has been separated off, and this one lives in heaven far away from here. It is a "heavenly double" of my earthly self!' (DBWE 9, 343; DBW 9, 377). In both contexts, Bonhoeffer is criticizing what he regards as an unacceptable rift in Barth's thought between the sinful and the redeemed human being.

43. Andreas Pangritz rightly notes that 'precisely because he feels close to him ... Bonhoeffer endeavours to work out as clearly as possible the differences which nevertheless exist between them' (Pangritz, *Karl Barth in the Theology of Dietrich Bonhoeffer*, 29).

44. An analysis of Bonhoeffer's evaluation of 'being-theology' falls beyond the scope of this chapter. Suffice it to say that a point of departure in God's *being* in revelation would be theologically disastrous for reasons already hinted at earlier in this section. Being-theology construes God's being in revelation according to some already-existing and humanly accessible reality. God's objectivity thereby reduces to the objectification of God. See DBWE 2, 103–9; DBW 2, 99–105. See also DeJonge, *Bonhoeffer's Theological Formation*, 115–28.

3. Revelation as Christus Praesens

The 'being of revelation' is not 'an existing thing' or a 'nonobjective act', but rather is 'the being of the community of persons that is constituted and formed by the person of Christ'.[45] For Bonhoeffer, the church is simultaneously the historical fellowship of human beings and the presence of the risen Christ. He minces no words about it: 'The church *is* the present Christ, "Christ existing as community [Gemeinde]"'.[46] The form of the present Christ is the historical church-community. Christ is present in person as the collective-person of the church. The mode of being of revelation is Christ's personal ecclesial presence.

What does this say about God's freedom in revelation? Bonhoeffer had viewed Barth's concept of freedom as 'formal' and lacking substantive content. His own view was that God's freedom should be interpreted by God's free act of self-limitation rather than by the 'possibility' that God could have acted otherwise:

> In revelation it is not so much a question of the freedom of God – eternally remaining within the divine self, aseity – on the other side of revelation, as it is of God's coming out of God's own self in revelation. It is a matter of God's *given* Word, the covenant in which God is bound by God's own action. It is a question of the freedom of God, which finds its strongest evidence precisely in that God freely chose to be bound to historical human beings and to be placed at the disposal of human beings. God is free not from human beings but for them. Christ is the word of God's freedom. God *is* present, that is, not in eternal nonobjectivity but … 'haveable', graspable in the Word within the church. Here the formal understanding of God's freedom is countered by a substantial one.[47]

---

45. DBWE 2, 113; DBW 2, 110. Although Bonhoeffer interprets the church through sociological categories, he carefully avoids conflating Christ's presence with the empirical community. The church is 'not a human community [Gemeinschaft] to which Christ then comes or not, nor is it a gathering of those who (as individuals) seek Christ … The church is rather the community of faith created by and founded upon Christ, in which Christ is revealed … as the new human, or rather, as the new humanity itself' (DBWE 2, 112; DBW 2, 109).

46. DBWE 2, 111, my emphasis; DBW 2, 108. Bonhoeffer's programmatic definition of the church as 'Christus als Gemeinde existierend' is translated throughout DBWE 1 as 'Christ existing as church-community', and in DBWE 2 as 'Christ existing as community'. While the latter is a more literal rendering of the German, the former better captures its ecclesiological and sociological intent. This formulation is Bonhoeffer's Christological modification of Hegel's 'Gott als Gemeinde existierend', which, as Wayne Whitson Floyd suggests, Bonhoeffer likely found in Reinhold Seeberg's *Dogmatik* (Wayne Whitson Floyd Jr, 'Encounter with an Other: Immanuel Kant and G. W. F. Hegel in the Theology of Dietrich Bonhoeffer', in *Bonhoeffer's Intellectual Formation*, ed. Peter Frick [Tübingen: Mohr Siebeck, 2008], 98 n. 7).

47. DBWE 2, 90–1; DBW 2, 85.

The meaning of God's freedom is in the free act itself, not in the precondition of choice. God's freedom, in other words, inheres not in what God *can* do, but in what God actually *does*.

If the being of revelation is the personal presence of 'Christ existing as church-community', how should we speak about knowledge? Bonhoeffer proposes an account of what he calls '*ecclesial knowing*'.[48] For the Protestant Bonhoeffer, the church comes into being through the present proclamation of Christ in word and sacrament. This means that theology is bound to preaching. To be sure, preaching was also Barth's point of departure, but his emphasis was on the mystery and expectation of human words speaking God's word.[49] For Bonhoeffer, the word that gathers the church-community is the word through which and by which Christ is present in person. Theology as a churchly discipline means theology in the presence of Christ: 'Because theology turns revelation into something that exists, it may be practiced only where the living person of Christ is itself present and can destroy this existing thing or acknowledge it.'[50] This continual subjection of theological statements to divine judgement differs from the thesis–antithesis of Barth's dialectical method, because dialectics is essentially individualistic, whereas Bonhoeffer's ecclesial method must be practised in the church-community.[51] Because revelation is not an idea but the person of Jesus Christ, speech in accordance with revelation must be practised in the presence of Christ. When theology is undertaken in the service and under the judgement of the church of Christ, it holds the promise in and for that community of speaking rightly of God.

Bonhoeffer's ecclesiological approach has anthropological implications. Barth's dialectic of belief–unbelief had ended up with a believing 'heavenly double' that bears no continuity with the earthly self. But to begin with continuity is no better, because if the 'believing I' is simply identical with the 'unbelieving I', then the human being has not been encountered in revelation. The solution? Human beings must be understood only in their relatedness to others. The being of the individual is inseparable from his or her being-in-community. To be in the church-community is to have one's being-in-Christ, even if one never sheds one's being-in-Adam. In Adam, the individual in the church is always the 'unbelieving I' assailed by sin and death. Yet sin and death are borne not by each individual, but by the community of faith, that is, by the collective-person of Christ.

---

48. DBWE 2, 126; DBW 2, 123.

49. See esp. Karl Barth, 'The Need and Promise of Christian Proclamation', in *The Word of God and Theology*, trans. Amy Marga (London: T&T Clark, 2011), 101–30.

50. DBWE 2, 131; DBW 2, 129.

51. Lest there be any misunderstanding, Barth had clearly stated that the proper locus of theology is the church. He understood theology as 'that discipline of the church ... oriented toward God as the object of its proclamation' (Barth, 'Fate and Idea', 26).

Like Barth, Bonhoeffer interprets human knowledge of God in terms of God's self-knowledge, but rather than pointing to the inner-trinitarian relations of Father, Son and Holy Spirit, Bonhoeffer refers this question to the person of Christ as the believing subject of the church-community. This is how he maintains that the content of revelation is identical with God himself. The problem, Bonhoeffer suggests, was Barth's attempt to secure this continuity individualistically, in abstraction from the church-community. It is not the individual, but the church as a whole who 'knows' God in revelation. This knowledge cannot be secured by the individual; it must be encountered in the community, which is the present Christ himself. So, Bonhoeffer says, 'God gives the divine self in Christ to the community of faith and to every individual as members of this community of faith. This happens in such a way that the acting subject in the community of faith, proclaiming and believing, is Christ.'[52] This is how Bonhoeffer distinguishes profane from theological thought. It is the ecclesial form of knowing that is directed to the word of the church in sermon and sacrament, through which Christ speaks his word and gathers his community. But because this human word is the word of Christ, it stands under Christ's judgement.

The Bible in Bonhoeffer's academic theology

Eberhard Jüngel once made the incisive observation that Barth's doctrine of the Trinity and Bultmann's programme of demythologizing both perform the same function in their respective theological projects. Their shared concern is 'for appropriate speech about God', which is 'fulfilled in not objectifying God or letting him be objectified as an It or He' but rather 'in bringing him to speech as Thou'.[53] In my estimation, Bonhoeffer's account of *Christus praesens* fulfils the same function in his theology. In *Sanctorum Communio* as well as *Act and Being*, he is attempting to provide his own distinct way of 'bringing God to speech as Thou'. In these works, *Christus praesens* essentially means 'Christ existing as community'. Christ's presence is his presence as church. As genuine human community, the church can be described empirically in sociological terms. But as genuine revelation, the essence of the church can never be reduced to its sociological description, because the essence of the church is not 'community' but 'Christ existing as community'. Although he later moves away from this ecclesiocentric view,[54] he never abandons his conviction that revelation is the concrete form of Christ's presence in the world.

---

52. DBWE 2, 112; DBW 2, 109.
53. Eberhard Jüngel, *God's Being Is in Becoming: The Trinitarian Being of God in the Theology of Karl Barth*, trans. John Webster (Edinburgh: T&T Clark, 2001), 34.
54. So Bethge: 'Ecclesiology dominated Bonhoeffer's theology in its early stages, absorbing the Christology. Later the reverse became true' (DB-ER, 84).

Bonhoeffer's social-ecclesiological interpretation of Christ's presence solves many of the problems he found in the act- and being-theologies of his contemporaries, but it resulted in a somewhat uneven treatment of Holy Scripture. This presents itself in a peculiar lacuna in Bonhoeffer's treatment of Barth, namely, his reception of Barth's doctrine of the threefold form of the word. Given Bonhoeffer's attention to Barth's doctrine of revelation in *Act and Being*, it is remarkable that he makes no mention of Barth's account of the threefold form of the word of God.[55] The threefold form, after all, is central to the substance and the structure of *Die christliche Dogmatik*, one of Bonhoeffer's primary sources in his interpretation of Barth in *Act and Being*. Why does Bonhoeffer not engage with this aspect of Barth's theology?

Barth had developed the doctrine of the threefold form in Göttingen and reaffirmed it in *Die christliche Dogmatik*.[56] The word of God, Barth says, occurs in the threefold form of revelation (Christologically understood), Scripture and proclamation. As immediate revelation, God's word transcends history. It is 'spoken immediately and exclusively in history, but at the boundary of history, in prehistory [Urgeschichte]'.[57] This is the first form of God's word. From this first form comes a second: God's word as the written testimony of the prophets and apostles. Holy Scripture belongs to history as the historical witness to God's immediate revelation. And as to how this word comes into the present, Barth describes its third and final form: church proclamation is the present witness to God's immediate revelation attested in Scripture. In its first form, God's word does not belong to history, although it occurs historically; in its second form, it belongs to history as our past; in its third form, it belongs to history as our present. But God's word can never be reduced to a single, historical form. Barth is careful to say that it is *one* word of God in this threefold form, and that only in the unity of this threefold form does God's word come to human beings in the present. The word is thereby unidirectional; it is always the way of God to humanity, never the human way to God. In its threefold form, the word of God comes to human beings in the church in the form of proclamation, insofar as it is grounded in Holy Scripture, which is the written witness to God's word revealed in Jesus Christ.

Bonhoeffer would have been familiar with Barth's doctrine of the threefold form, and there is evidence that Bonhoeffer had engaged directly with this section of *Die christliche Dogmatik* prior to his work on *Act and Being*.

---

55. Barth, *Die christliche Dogmatik*, 37–47.

56. Of course, after Bonhoeffer finished with *Act and Being*, Barth continued to develop his doctrine of the threefold form in *Church Dogmatics*.

57. Barth, *Die christliche Dogmatik*, 46. Torrance notes that '*Urgeschichte* means for Barth that the Revelation of God enters into our actual history and meets us within it … but in such a way that Revelation is not tied to history or resolved into it' (Thomas F. Torrance, *Karl Barth: An Introduction to His Early Theology, 1910–1931* [London: SCM, 1962], 109–10).

Barth's 1927 dogmatics appeared too late for Bonhoeffer to incorporate it into his work on *Sanctorum Communio*, completed in mid-1927, but when Bonhoeffer revised his manuscript for publication in 1930, he was able to add a new section on 'authority and freedom in the empirical church'.[58] This section contains Bonhoeffer's only direct citation of *Die christliche Dogmatik* in *Sanctorum Communio*. He begins: 'The church rests upon the word', citing §§21–22 of *Die christliche Dogmatik* in support.[59] The nature of the discussion that follows suggests that Bonhoeffer's new section was meant to engage with Barth's account of 'the authority of the church' (§21) and 'the freedom of conscience' (§22).[60] In Barth's dogmatics, these sections appear in the chapter on *Holy Scripture*. Barth's concern in these sections is to account for the objectivity of God in revelation through Scripture. He argues that in an indirect, a relative and a formal sense, the hearing of God's word in Scripture is determined objectively by the authority of the church, and subjectively by the freedom of the conscience. But in both cases Barth reminds his readers that 'direct, absolute, and material authority remains exclusively reserved for Scripture as the Word of God itself'.[61] Bonhoeffer's treatment, by contrast, does not exhibit the same emphasis. He was more interested in parsing the relationship between church authority and the freedom of those within the church. Displaced from its origin in Barth's doctrine of Holy Scripture, Bonhoeffer's use of Barth's distinction between absolute and relative authority and freedom acquires a different character. Although he says, with Barth, that the church's authority and the freedom of the individual in relation to it derive from the word, he never clarifies the connection of this word to the Bible. It is the word of God in the church, namely, *proclamation*.[62] Apart from a single passing reference, the Bible is conspicuously absent in this discussion.[63]

---

58. The differences between Bonhoeffer's original dissertation manuscript (1927) and the published version (1930) are substantial, not least because the published version excised 20–25 per cent of the material from the original. However, as in the case of the section presently under consideration, Bonhoeffer had also added some new content to his work prior to publication. For a detailed history of the text, see DBWE 1, 9–13.
59. DBWE 1, 250–2; DBW 1, 172–3.
60. Barth, *Die christliche Dogmatik*, 362–410.
61. Barth, *Die christliche Dogmatik*, 362; cf. 388–9.
62. Accordingly, when Mawson discusses the place of God's word in Bonhoeffer's ecclesiology, he notes that 'Bonhoeffer is adamant that this word which constitutes the church is the word found in preaching and the sacraments' (Mawson, *Christ Existing as Community*, 161).
63. The passing reference is this: 'The councils and synods ... ought to state plainly and clearly where they stand with regard to the Bible, doctrine, the creed, and Christian teaching' (DBWE 1, 251; DBW 1, 173). But this on its own does not indicate that the Bible might occupy a special place in relation to doctrine, the creed or Christian teaching.

Why does Bonhoeffer not discuss Barth's doctrine of the threefold form in *Act and Being*?[64] Part of the reason is simply that Barth is not the direct, exclusive target of Bonhoeffer's indictment of 'act-theology'. He is interested in Barth's theology insofar as it represents the category of 'act' thinking. The doctrine of the threefold form does not fit neatly into this category, because it actually encourages talk of revelation in its historical objectivity. Arguably, Barth's doctrine of the threefold form challenges Bonhoeffer's argument that Barth describes revelation in purely non-objective terms. Furthermore, the evidence suggests that Bonhoeffer was far more interested in working out revelation's relationship to proclamation than its connection to Scripture. Barth's account of the threefold form, by contrast, makes Holy Scripture a central topic. For Barth, there is no way to speak of revelation that does not include the biblical testimony. If Bonhoeffer were to have adopted Barth's threefold form directly, he would have had to pay much more attention to the interplay between each of the three forms. As it happens, Bonhoeffer was much more concerned with the first and the third, and as a result, Scripture does not often become a direct object of theological reflection. In Bonhoeffer's earliest bibliology, I will now conclude, Scripture was the *occasion* for God's word, but not, strictly speaking, God's word itself.

An occasionalist bibliology

The question at hand is what Bonhoeffer's theology of revelation entails for his doctrine of Holy Scripture. Revelation is the presence of Christ, and in Bonhoeffer's early theology, this always means the presence of the *church-community*. The relationship of Holy Scripture to revelation is thereby governed by its role in constituting and upholding this community, which is fulfilled primarily in the event of proclamation. This has implications for the ways in which Bonhoeffer employs Scripture during this period.

In *Act and Being*, references to Scripture are few, and most take aim against the doctrine of 'verbal inspiration'.[65] This is not to suggest that Bonhoeffer viewed

---

64. It appears that a version of Barth's threefold form is affirmed in Bonhoeffer's 1930 examination paper, 'The Meaning and Choice of a Biblical Text for the Sermon in the Worship of the Congregation', likely dated 5 July 1930, just months after his submission of *Act and Being*. His rationale for Christian preachers' exclusive use of the Bible follows a Barthian threefold logic (DBWE 10, 382; DBW 10, 350). It is possible, therefore, that some version of Barth's doctrine of the threefold form of God's word stands behind or alongside Bonhoeffer's ecclesiocentric approach in his early academic theology. But if this is the case, then it is all the more striking that Scripture receives so little treatment throughout his dissertations – especially *Act and Being*, in which the doctrine of revelation is a central topic.

65. See DBWE 2, 92, 104, 108.

the Bible negatively in *Act and Being*, only that he focused his attention more on denouncing what he perceived as a misguided view of the Bible than on proposing a constructive alternative. Bonhoeffer's criticisms of the doctrine of verbal inspiration fall under the category of the theology of *being*. Verbal inspiration posits a direct identity between revelation and the biblical text. Identifying revelation with the Bible makes the same mistake of all being-oriented thought: it puts God 'at the disposal of human beings'.[66] If revelation were identical with the Bible as such, it would simply be another object there for assimilation into the closed circle of human knowing. The human being would not be encountered by the transcendent.

Bonhoeffer's doctrine of revelation, as analysed above, constitutes the framework for his theology of Holy Scripture. If revelation is *Christus praesens*, and if *Christus praesens* is 'Christ existing as community', the following question suggests itself: What is the relationship between revelation in Scripture and revelation as 'Christ existing as church-community'? In *Sanctorum Communio*, Bonhoeffer argues in good Protestant fashion that 'a Christian church-community ... is held together by its *assembling around the word*'.[67] This has two implications. Firstly, there can be no genuine hearing of the word in isolation from the assembled community. And secondly, there can be no genuine proclamation of the word in isolation from the office of preaching. Assembly and office must be held together in the church. If the value of the assembly is determined on the basis of its potential value to the individual, its significance has already been surrendered. If the need for preaching is judged by its usefulness to the congregation, it has already been misunderstood. Individualism is the culprit in both cases. Individualist approaches to Scripture tend to trade on being-concepts of revelation, on the idea that revelation is just 'there' in the Bible for each person to know and to communicate. On the contrary, Bonhoeffer argues,

> The word is the word preached by the church-community. Is it not the Bible, then? Yes, it is the Bible also, but only in the church-community. Does this mean then that the Bible becomes the "word" only through the church-community? That is indeed true, namely as the church-community is created only through the word and sustained by it. The question as to what was first, the word or the church-community, is meaningless because the word inspired by the Spirit exists only where human beings hear it, so that the *church-community makes the word the word, as the word constitutes the church-community as church.* The Bible is the word only in the church-community ... The word, to be specific, is present in the church-community as the word of scripture and of preaching – essentially as the latter.[68]

---

66. DBWE 2, 104; DBW 2, 101.
67. DBWE 1, 226; DBW 1, 154.
68. DBWE 1, 232; DBW 1, 159.

On this account, the Bible *as such* occupies no constitutive role in the church. Its presence in the church is justified on the basis of what it *becomes* in the church. And although Bonhoeffer avoids prioritizing either word or church-community, he is happy to say that preaching, not Scripture, is the essential form of the word in the church.[69] The Bible is decidedly subordinate not only to the broader doctrine of God's word and revelation, but to God's word in the specific form of preaching. This distinguishes Bonhoeffer from Barth, for whom the word of God comes in the threefold form of revelation, Scripture and preaching. In effect if not intention, Bonhoeffer treats Scripture – the written form of the word – as theologically secondary to the preached form of the word. I contend that this is a consequence of Bonhoeffer's sociological-ecclesiological point of departure. If the church is a social reality constituted by God's word, it is fitting that preference be given to the social form of the word, that is, the form that *occurs* in the present and thereby *gathers* the community. The Bible, by comparison, is inert and lifeless as mere text – at least until it is put in the service of proclamation.

The lone constructive reference to Scripture in *Act and Being* occurs in the discussion of 'theological knowing'. Bonhoeffer says that 'theology is the memory of the church' and that it 'helps the church to understand the presuppositions of Christian preaching'. The object of theological knowledge 'is all the happenings held in remembrance in the Christian community of faith; in the Bible; in preaching and sacrament, prayer, confession; in the word of the person of Christ, which is preserved as something that exists in the historical church'.[70] As far as 'theological knowing' is concerned, the Bible falls within the catalogue of ecclesial memory. Theology proceeds on the basis of not only Scripture, but also past preaching, prayer, sacrament and confession. *Act and Being* contains no direct explanation of how or even if Holy Scripture holds a unique place in the practice of theology.

In certain respects, Bonhoeffer's way of relating theology and Scripture to church proclamation tracks closely with Barth. Barth opens *Die christliche Dogmatik* by saying, 'There is Christian dogmatics because there is Christian speech'.[71] And in his 1922 essay, 'The Need and Promise of Christian Proclamation', Barth describes the basic standpoint of his theology as that of 'the man in the pulpit, before whom stands the mysterious Bible and the mysterious minds of his more or less numerous listeners. Indeed, which one is more mysterious? In any case, the question is: "*What now?*"'[72] But unlike the early Barth, Bonhoeffer placed

---

69. It is significant that this discussion occurs under the heading, 'The sanctorum communio as the bearer of the "office"'. Bonhoeffer consistently affirms the *office* of preaching prior to the individual preacher, which is how he maintains a communal interpretation of preaching, even when directing advice to individual preachers. See DBWE 14, 488–90; DBW 14, 479–81.

70. DBWE 2, 130; DBW 2, 128.

71. Barth, *Die christliche Dogmatik*, 1.

72. Barth, 'The Need and Promise of Christian Proclamation', 108.

greater emphasis on the meaning of preaching in and for the *community* of faith. It is not the preacher who bears the weight of the expectation that God will speak, but the preaching office. Likewise, it is not the individual who waits to hear God's word from the pulpit, but the assembled Christian community. Bonhoeffer was suspicious of any traces of individualism that might be lurking in the doctrine of revelation. He thought that many false starts could be avoided simply by beginning with a communal rather than an individual account of revelation. This helps to explain his emphasis on the ecclesial use of Scripture, both in liturgy (e.g. public reading, prayer, song) and in proclamation.

Proclamation in particular takes centre stage in Bonhoeffer's early theology of revelation. The proclaimed word of God, after all, is inherently communal. The sermon cannot be reduced simply to its impact on the preacher or the individual hearer. It ought to be understood as something that happens in and for the church. Outside of its ecclesial context, the Bible might be misappropriated in various ways. It might be erroneously identified as revelation via the doctrine of verbal inspiration. It might be disregarded as an irrelevant, if interesting, historical artefact. It might be used as a source for religious studies. But in its proper theological use as Holy Scripture, the Bible cannot be regarded as something at the disposal of the individual human interpreter. By locating the Bible dogmatically in ecclesiology, he was able to affirm the transcendence of revelation in Holy Scripture.

Yet for all its merits, Bonhoeffer's early theology of revelation resulted in an effectively occasionalist ontology of Scripture. His account of revelation as Christ's *ecclesial* presence, while it offers a creative solution to the basic problem of revelation (i.e. God's objectivity and non-objectivity), does not afford much importance to direct theological reflection on the nature of Scripture. If God reveals himself in the historical form of the church-community, then Scripture's relationship to revelation is essentially its relationship to ecclesiology. The result is that Scripture, as the ground of the church's preaching and sacraments, is the occasion for God's word, but is not God's word itself. Barth had found a way to speak of Scripture as God's word in his doctrine of the threefold form. Whatever Bonhoeffer finally thought of Barth's doctrine, he does not seem to have accepted it wholesale, but neither did he propose an alternative. In CHAPTER 4, I will show how his revised account of Christ's presence in his 1933 Christology lectures becomes the ground of a genuine alternative.

4

THE PRESENT LOGOS

When Bonhoeffer lectured on the topic of creation and sin in Berlin, he could have chosen to address the subject systematically. Instead, he decided to frame the lecture course as a theological exposition of Genesis 1-3, undoubtedly to the surprise (and perhaps chagrin) of some of his colleagues. The lectures were a success with his students, and at their insistence he published his lectures in 1933 as *Creation and Fall: A Theological Exposition of Genesis 1-3*. In the introduction to the published version, Bonhoeffer sets out what appears to be a programmatic statement about his approach to theological exegesis:

> The church of Holy Scripture – and there is no other 'church' – lives from the end. Therefore it reads the whole of Holy Scripture as the book of the end, of the new [vom Neuen], of Christ ... The Bible is after all nothing other than the book of the church. It *is* this in its very essence, or it is nothing. It therefore needs to be read and proclaimed wholly from the viewpoint of the end.[1]

Bonhoeffer continues, commenting on the 'method' this entails:

> Theological exposition takes the Bible as the book of the church and interprets it as such. This is its presupposition and this presupposition constitutes its method; its method is a continual returning from the text (as determined by all the methods of philological and historical research) to this presupposition. That is the objectivity [Sachlichkeit] in the method of theological exposition. And on this objectivity alone does it base its claim to have the nature of a science [Wissenschaftlichkeit].[2]

Thus, in his introduction, which has every appearance of a methodological prolegomenon, Bonhoeffer indicates three criteria for theological exegesis:

---

1. DBWE 3, 22; DBW 3, 22.
2. DBWE 3, 22–3; DBW 3, 22.

ecclesiology, Christology and eschatology.³ In CHAPTER 3, I concluded that the bibliology entailed by Bonhoeffer's ecclesiocentric account of Christ's presence was, effectively, occasionalist. In *Creation and Fall*, he is already showing signs of moving beyond this position.

I will not be engaging with *Creation and Fall* in as much detail as might be expected in a study of Bonhoeffer's exegesis.⁴ Although *Creation and Fall* has been cited as a programmatic introduction to Bonhoeffer's theological exegesis of Scripture,⁵ its usefulness in evaluating his later exegetical material is somewhat limited. In *Creation and Fall*, Bonhoeffer is still working with a fundamentally ecclesiocentric bibliology, a point made clear when he says that the Bible is the book of the church 'in its very essence'. He likewise anchors the objectivity (Sachlichkeit) of exegesis in the *church*, describing exegesis as an ongoing dialogue between the biblical text and that text's function in the life of the church-community. At Finkenwalde, without rejecting his earlier formulation, he works with a more explicitly Christocentric bibliology. For example, in his 1935 essay, 'Vergegenwärtigung neutestamentlicher Texte' (Making New Testament Texts Present), he states: 'Holy Scripture is ... as a whole *the witness* of God in Christ, and in every passage the point is to make the character of this word as a witness audible.'⁶ Accordingly, he speaks of the objectivity (Sachlichkeit) of exegesis in terms of Scripture's *substance* (Sache), namely the crucified and risen Lord Jesus. *Creation and Fall*, therefore, is rightly regarded as a transitional work.⁷ In many ways, it is more useful as a window into his earlier academic theology (specifically with its emphasis on theological anthropology) than into his later exegetical works.⁸

---

3. Marie Theres Igrec, 'Bonhoeffer's "Theological Interpretation" of the Biblical Narrative of the "Creation and Fall" of Man', in *God Speaks to Us: Dietrich Bonhoeffer's Biblical Hermeneutics*, ed. Ralf K. Wüstenberg and Jens Zimmermann, International Bonhoeffer Interpretations 5 (Frankfurt am Main: Peter Lang, 2013), 150.

4. For a thorough study, see Hamilton, *Dietrich Bonhoeffers Hermeneutik der Responsivität*.

5. Kuske, *The Old Testament as the Book of Christ*, 28–31. Moreover, the title of Kuske's book is adapted from the introduction, which I quoted above. The church reads 'the whole of Holy Scripture as the book ... of Christ' (DBWE 3, 22), which, as Kuske argues, must include the Old Testament (Kuske, *The Old Testament as the Book of Christ*, 32).

6. DBWE 14, 421; DBW 14, 408. I discuss this essay in greater detail, including my translation of *Vergegenwärtigung*, in CHAPTER 5.

7. John de Gruchy argues this point in his introduction to *Creation and Fall*, in DBWE 3, 5–12. See also Igrec, 'Bonhoeffer's "Theological Interpretation"', 141; Kuske, *The Old Testament as the Book of Christ*, 35.

8. The focus of *Creation and Fall*, as de Gruchy says, 'is still on questions of human identity and sociality. Indeed in many respects *Creation and Fall* is an exposition of Bonhoeffer's earlier "theology of sociality" ... in a more accessible form' (in DBWE 3, 10). See also Green, *A Theology of Sociality*, 186–206.

I am not suggesting that Bonhoeffer's earlier ecclesiological bibliology is incompatible with his later Christological bibliology. The change I am discerning is subtler. In this chapter, I argue that Bonhoeffer's 1933 Christology lectures inaugurate a gradual but thoroughgoing, systematic restructuring of his theology. Bethge perceived this shift: 'Ecclesiology dominated Bonhoeffer's theology in its early stages, absorbing the Christology. Later the reverse became true.'[9] While it would be overstating the case to say that Bonhoeffer made a radical break with his early ecclesiology, Christology does indeed overtake ecclesiology in Bonhoeffer's middle- and late-period writings. Where he had previously worked out theological questions with reference to the church-community, by the mid-1930s he is doing so with reference to the person and work of Jesus Christ. In the matter of bibliology, this systematic reconfiguration provides the basis for a non-occasionalist ontology of Scripture. I begin by showing how in his 1933 lectures he addresses the aporia of theology (discussed in CHAPTER 3) within the structure of Christology rather than with reference to the sociality of the church. Then I outline his theology of the word, wherein he makes the vital connection between Christ's speech and Christ's presence. This will constitute the ground for an ontology of Scripture that transcends the occasionalism of his earlier writings. Because Christ speaks the words of Scripture, it is proper to say that Scripture is the word of God.

Bonhoeffer's Christological revision

Bonhoeffer's 1933 lectures on Christology in Berlin mark a pivotal development in his thought. According to Bethge, Bonhoeffer 'considered these two-hour lectures more difficult than anything he had done … because he had to bring together all of his thoughts, statements, and experiments and test their validity and foundation'.[10] As Larry Rasmussen rightly notes, 'All his work from this point forward was affected by these lectures'[11] – a statement that certainly holds true for his theology of Scripture.

In this section, I argue that Bonhoeffer takes up the aporia of theology, which he had previously addressed as 'the problem of act and being', and resolves it within the structure of his Christology. The objectivity and non-objectivity of revelation find unity in Jesus Christ, who is wholly *present* and wholly *transcendent*. Whether or not this topic was in Bonhoeffer's mind as he prepared these lectures, the result is a way of dealing with the epistemological paradox of revelation with primary reference to Christology rather than a sociological interpretation of the church. Objectivity and non-objectivity in revelation are found in the promeity and transcendence of the person of Christ. While Bonhoeffer would still affirm the ecclesial form of Christ's presence, he bases this affirmation Christologically in the

---

9. DB-ER, 84.
10. DB-ER, 219.
11. Larry L. Rasmussen, 'Editor's Introduction to the English Edition', in DBWE 12, 37.

eternal promeity of Christ's *being*. And because his account of Christ's presence no longer rests on Jesus's social-ecclesial form, his theology of Scripture no longer hinges on the Bible's role in the church-community.

The transcendent Christ

For Bonhoeffer, revelation of God must be revelation of *God*. Therefore, theology has to do with the one who is wholly transcendent. This is a problem that Bonhoeffer addresses with his well-known how–who distinction. Christology, as the *logos* about Christ, is discourse about the God-human, who is the word of God in person. But how can such discourse get off the ground? Any attempt to fit this person into an existing system of thought – be it metaphysics, history, anthropology, religion, ethics, etc. – is bound to fail, because all such attempts take Jesus Christ as an idea rather than encountering him as a person. Christology cannot proceed by asking how Jesus could be both God and human, or how Jesus can be said to be present today. Christology must start at the encounter with this person and ask, 'Who are you?'

Christology founders whenever it occupies itself with questions about the relation of Christ's divinity to his humanity, whenever it asks 'how' rather than 'who'. Bonhoeffer regards the early church Christological controversies, which revolved around relating the divine and human natures in Christ, as hopelessly oriented around 'how' questions. Such questions always lead to a 'false Jesus Christ'.[12] 'The "how" question', Bonhoeffer concludes, 'subverts itself', because, as the christological controversies make clear, 'the "how" of relationship is impossible to think through'.[13] The only valid Christological question is, 'Who are you?' Even the form of this question implies that the questioner is already in the presence of the one being questioned, and that is precisely Bonhoeffer's point. Every how-Christology fails to contend seriously with the real, personal presence of Christ, because each operates within the structurally closed circle of human knowledge rather than from the actual encounter with the counter-Logos. In John Webster's apt description, Bonhoeffer understands that 'Jesus Christ is a question posed *to* the church, that the church is relentlessly interrogated by the fact that at the heart of its life is the presence of the incarnate one who cannot be assimilated into or clothed by a form of religious life'.[14]

Bonhoeffer's insistence on the 'who' question over the 'how' is one of the most striking and innovative features of his Christology, but it has clear precedents in his

---

12. DBWE 12, 351; DBW 12, 338.
13. DBWE 12, 353; DBW 12, 340.
14. John Webster, *Word and Church: Essays in Christian Dogmatics* (Edinburgh: T&T Clark, 2001), 120.

earlier works.[15] He had already argued at length in *Sanctorum Communio* and *Act and Being* that human beings are genuine persons only insofar as they encounter a genuine other as a boundary, at the limit of their own being. To transgress this boundary is to subsume the other into one's own will or mind, and thereby to negate their genuine otherness. In *Sanctorum Communio*, Bonhoeffer was concerned with the social-ethical boundary between human persons; in *Act and Being*, his concern was the limit of human knowledge in relation to revelation. In *Creation and Fall*, Bonhoeffer describes the *imago Dei* as humankind's reflection of God's freedom, which, as he had already established in *Act and Being*, is freedom *for* others rather than freedom *from* them. Throughout these works, Bonhoeffer is working out a theological anthropology as the inversion of the *cor curvum in se*. Rather than a heart turned in on itself, the genuinely human person is the one whose heart is turned outward for the other, for God and for other human beings. The *cor curvum in se* arises in human social-ethical relations (*Sanctorum Communio*), human knowledge (*Act and Being*) and in human freedom (*Creation and Fall*). For this reason, the otherness of the other must not be compromised, which is why Bonhoeffer emphasizes the *limit* posed by the other. Only in proper recognition of their limits can human beings be open to what lies beyond their limits. When it comes to Christology, if Jesus Christ is a person, then he is a genuine other and must be encountered as such. The 'who' question alone represents the heart turned outwards towards this other. This explains why Bonhoeffer asserts that 'the question of "who" expresses the otherness of the other', even while it 'interrogates the very existence of the one asking it'.[16] Thus, the 'who' question alone guarantees that the Christ of Christology remains legitimately beyond human grasp; if this were not the case, then Christology would no longer be about the transcendent word of God, the counter-Logos.

---

15. Alan Torrance suggests (without further explanation) that Bonhoeffer was 'under Barth's influence' in contrasting the 'how' and the 'who' questions (Alan J. Torrance, *Persons in Communion: Trinitarian Description and Human Participation* [Edinburgh: T&T Clark, 1996], 71; cf. 49 n. 99). Torrance later cites several quotations from CD I/1, 301, in which Barth prioritizes the doctrine of the Trinity as the answer to 'the concrete and decisive question: Who is God?' Bonhoeffer would have been familiar with CD I/1 by the time of his Christology lectures (note his letter of 24 December 1932 to Barth in DBWE 12, 82), but it cannot be said exactly how thoroughly he had read it or allowed it to govern his approach to Christology. He had, it must also be noted, attended some of Barth's lectures and met personally with him in July 1931. Bonhoeffer's letters from that time display his favourable reaction to Barth as a lecturer and person (DBWE 11, 32–40; DBW 17, 90–1; DBW 11, 15–22).
16. DBWE 12, 303; DBW 12, 283.

The present Christ

Revelation of God, Bonhoeffer insists, must not only be revelation of *God*, but also *revelation* of God. If the 'who' question secures the former, Bonhoeffer's account of the *presence* of Christ secures the latter. Christ is transcendent precisely as the one who is present. As one might expect from the preceding argument, the proper way to enquire about the presence of Christ is to ask, 'who is present, who is with us here and now?'[17] This question cannot be asked except by those who already recognize that they are in the presence of this person, that is, from the perspective of revelation. Christ's presence is Bonhoeffer's starting point, not his conclusion. The 'how' question about Christ's presence is flawed because it assumes a division between the Christ who is in himself and the Christ who is present. Where Christ's person and his presence are viewed separately, the result is the 'how' question seeking to unite them. Bonhoeffer, by contrast, wants to avoid making this separation in the first place.

Christology, he insists, begins with the question of the present person of Christ (hence the 'who' question). This means that the *works* of Christ are, on the level of theological epistemology, secondary to his person.[18] Works are always open to interpretation based on who performs them. Only in the revelation of who Christ is do the works of Christ take on their true meaning. Everything depends on who this person is. Putting the question 'in the abstract', Bonhoeffer says, 'the personal ontological structure … of the whole, historical Christ is the subject matter of Christology'.[19] The language of 'structure' recalls his discussion of the concept of person in *Sanctorum Communio* and simply refers to the make-up or constitution of a person. Because 'person' as a concept operates like a first principle for Bonhoeffer, he does not try to go behind the person to the 'stuff' that makes up a person. Rather, personal structure simply refers to a person's way of being. Thus it is fitting to ask the 'who' question of Christ's presence as Bonhoeffer does: 'By virtue of what personal ontological structure [Personstruktur] is Christ present to the church?'[20] This is not a 'how' question disguised as a 'who'; this is Bonhoeffer's genuine attempt to frame the question of Christ's presence in terms of his person (i.e. his being as the present one) rather than his works (i.e. his act in becoming present).

Bonhoeffer provides two answers to the *Personstruktur* question. The first, which he affirms with the caveat that it lacks specificity, is that Christ is present by virtue of his *Personstruktur* as 'God-humanity'.[21] The text of the Christology

---

17. DBWE 12, 313; DBW 12, 294.
18. Bonhoeffer is quick to say that there can be no separation in reality between Christ's person and works. 'The separation is only necessary for reasons of theological method' (DBWE 12, 310; DBW 12, 291).
19. DBWE 12, 310; DBW 12, 291.
20. DBWE 12, 314; DBW 12, 295.
21. DBWE 12, 314; DBW 12, 295.

lectures moves quickly past this point, but it bears some reflection. For Bonhoeffer, the real presence of Jesus cannot be asserted except in his being as the God-human. Only as God can he be present to all people simultaneously; only as human can he be present to anyone at any time. Yet it is not in uniting these two aspects that the picture of the God-human emerges; it is only the whole divine-human person who is present in this way. 'God in his timeless eternity is *not* God. Jesus Christ in his humanity, limited in time, is *not* Jesus Christ. Instead, in the human being Jesus Christ, God is God. Only in Jesus Christ is God present.'[22]

Bonhoeffer's second, and more specific, answer to the *Personstruktur* question is the '*pro-me*' structure.[23] With the *pro-me* structure, Bonhoeffer argues that Christ's presence is simply his way of being: 'His being-Christ is his being-for-me.'[24] Christ has no other way of being except as the one who is eternally and historically *pro-me*. There is no being of Christ behind or prior to his being *pro-me*; there is no access to an account of his aseity to ground an account of his promeity. 'It is not only useless to meditate on a Christ-in-himself but godless, precisely because Christ is not there in-himself, but rather is there for you.'[25] For Bonhoeffer, Christ is present not as an act incidental to his being, but by virtue of his being. However, this should be thought of in the categories of person and works, rather than being and act. Person, for Bonhoeffer, always means the unity of act and being.[26] By beginning with the *pro-me* structure of Christ, 'both the being and the [act] of Christ are maintained. Being-there-for-*you* comes together with being-*there*-for you.'[27] Anything less would, for Bonhoeffer, mean that Christ's presence is something extra to his being; but since Christ can only be known as the present one, it would imply that Christ cannot truly be known as he really is. Therefore, to say that the *Personstruktur* of Christ is *pro-me* is simply to identify the one who is present in the church as the whole Christ. The present

---

22. DBWE 12, 313; DBW 12, 294.
23. DBWE 12, 314; DBW 12, 295. In the latter portions of 'Christology', Bonhoeffer uses '*pro nobis*' language rather than '*pro me*'.
24. DBWE 12, 314; DBW 12, 295.
25. DBWE 12, 314; DBW 12, 296.
26. For example, DBWE 2, 122; DBW 2, 119. See also DeJonge, *Bonhoeffer's Theological Formation*, 71, summarizing Bonhoeffer's position: 'Person is the unity of act and being'.
27. DBWE 12, 315 (translation modified); DBW 12, 296. The English translators here render 'Akt' as 'works', which is peculiar, given that elsewhere Bonhoeffer uses the word 'Werke' in that capacity. Especially in the context of this statement, where *Akt* is parallel with *Sein*, it should be supposed that Bonhoeffer had the categories of act and being in mind. Nevertheless, close exegesis of the precise wording of these lectures is not always appropriate, given that it cannot be known which words are Bonhoeffer's and which represent the students' own interpretations or paraphrase.

Christ (*Christus praesens*) is the whole Christ (*totus Christus*).²⁸ There is no partial form of Christ's presence. Wherever Christ is, Christ is wholly there.²⁹

The whole Christ

The indivisibility of Christ does quite a bit of theological heavy lifting for Bonhoeffer. His Christology does not attempt to unite two separate 'natures' in one person, but rather proceeds from the whole Christ, the God-human. Therefore, it is not enough simply to identify Bonhoeffer's theology as Christocentric.³⁰ A theology centred around Christ might well begin with the deity of Christ in abstraction from the incarnation, that is, with the *logos asarkos*. The Christological task would then be to describe how this divine being or person took on flesh, became *logos ensarkos*. Not so for Bonhoeffer. In his view, the 'first premise' of theology is 'that God, out of mercy freely given, truly became a human being'.³¹ Theology has no point of departure apart from this particular human being who is God and this God who is a human being. It would therefore be inappropriate to classify Bonhoeffer's Christology as being 'from above' or 'from below'.³² His Christology proceeds from the whole Christ, in whom divinity does not exist without humanity, nor humanity without divinity. Thus, Bonhoeffer says that 'we should speak not of God becoming human [das Menschwerden] but of the God who became human [der Menschgewordene]'.³³ The only Christ with whom

---

28. Bernd Wannenwetsch makes this same connection in Bernd Wannenwetsch, 'The Whole Christ and the Whole Human Being: Dietrich Bonhoeffer's Inspiration for the "Christology and Ethics" Discourse', in *Christology and Ethics*, ed. F. LeRon Shults and Brent Waters (Grand Rapids: Eerdmans, 2010), 81.

29. Bonhoeffer is careful not to conflate the concept of revelation-as-presence with the divine attribute of omnipresence. He certainly affirms the latter: there is no place in the cosmos where God is not fully present. But if Christ is the presence of God, if he is *Emmanuel*, does the omnipresence of God's being not imply an omnipresence of God's revelation? And does this not warrant the search for revelation in other places besides Scripture, Sacrament and church-community? Here the key is simply to recognize that revelation-as-presence does not necessarily entail presence-as-revelation. Bonhoeffer later writes, 'Although God is indeed omnipresent, God does not intend that we perceive God just anywhere' (DBWE 14, 677; DBW 14, 679). In context, Bonhoeffer's meaning is clear: God is everywhere, but don't go looking for God in the Reich Church!

30. McCormack makes this same point with reference to Barth's theology. He rightly notes that 'the customary description of Barth's theology as "christocentric" has very little explanatory value unless one goes on to define concretely what "christocentrism" meant in his case' (McCormack, *Karl Barth's Critically Realistic Dialectical Theology*, 453–4). This is as true of Bonhoeffer's theology as it is of Barth's.

31. DBWE 12, 338; DBW 12, 322.

32. As per the schema in Wolfhart Pannenberg, *Jesus: God and Man* (Philadelphia: Westminster, 1968).

33. DBWE 12, 354; DBW 12, 341.

Christology has to do is the *whole* Christ, the person of the Mediator in his divine-human unity. Bonhoeffer regards any speech that divorces God from this human being or this human being from God as meaningless.

The indivisibility of the person of Christ is central for Bonhoeffer. He resists all talk of Christ's divinity in isolation from his humanity, and vice versa.[34] The Christological question can never be about how to reconcile divinity and humanity in Christ, about seeking the divine in the human or the human in the divine. The God-human is already given in revelation. As soon as Christology separates Jesus's divinity from his humanity, even for the sake of discussion, its object is no longer Jesus Christ. For Bonhoeffer, the stumbling block is not that God is hidden in the humanity of Christ but that the God-human is hidden in the humiliation of Christ. To identify the exalted God-human in the humble form of his contemporary presence as word, sacrament and church-community is the task of Christology.

This points to a key feature of Bonhoeffer's Christology, and indeed of his theology as a whole. 'One of the first statements in theology', says Bonhoeffer,

---

34. This might seem to put Bonhoeffer at odds with the Chalcedonian Definition, which carefully distinguishes between the two natures. David Congdon, rightly in my view, discerns that 'Bonhoeffer locates the theological truth of the Chalcedonian Definition precisely in its negativity' (David W. Congdon, *The God Who Saves: A Dogmatic Sketch* [Eugene, OR: Cascade, 2016], 105). For Bonhoeffer, the Chalcedonian statements about Christ's two natures are self-cancelling: without confusion, without change, without division, without separation. However, Congdon argues that Bonhoeffer has misunderstood the nature of the contradiction in Chalcedonian Christology, because, in Congdon's view, Bonhoeffer fails to see that 'Chalcedon ends up cancelling itself out *precisely because* it is the product of Hellenistic metaphysics' (ibid., 106). We must be cautious here, since the fragmentary notes that make up these lectures make it difficult to determine precisely what Bonhoeffer thought of Chalcedon and its relationship to Hellenistic metaphysics. Moreover, Bonhoeffer does not set out to defend Chalcedon as an anti-metaphysical project, but only to follow its basic logic (as he sees it). Nevertheless, Congdon is most likely correct in arguing that Bonhoeffer did not fully grasp the connection between the negative terms (unconfused, unchanged, undivided, unseparated) and the metaphysical concepts behind them (nature and person). In any case the conclusion stands: for Bonhoeffer, Chalcedon demonstrates the incoherence and self-defeating nature of the attempt to think through the relations of divinity and humanity in Christ. The Chalcedonian Definition resists 'how' Christologies by refusing to answer 'how' questions about the relationship of humanity and divinity in Christ. Rowan Williams has offered an insightful reading of the Chalcedonian logic of Bonhoeffer's Christology. He argues that Bonhoeffer deploys Chalcedon 'as a way of dismantling a false account of the finite/infinite distinction' (Rowan Williams, *Christ the Heart of Creation* [London: Bloomsbury Continuum, 2018], 195). The point that Bonhoeffer is trying to make, Williams writes, is this: '*In our apprehension of and response to* the presence of the God-human, we cannot isolate either a divine nature that is not bound up with the historical concreteness of Jesus or a human nature that is not suffused with divine agency' (ibid., 196).

is 'that wherever God is, God is wholly there'.[35] This is the most basic definition of divine simplicity: that God is not divisible. But for Bonhoeffer, this has a Christological corollary: wherever Christ is, it is the whole Christ who is there. The present Christ is always the whole Christ. Bonhoeffer's focus on the whole person of Christ results in his preference for 'states' over 'natures'. In his review of the early-church Christological controversies, he argues that each argument fails because it is based upon 'the attempt to unite two isolated existing realities'.[36] For Bonhoeffer, the serious question is not how divine and human natures relate to one another in Jesus Christ, but rather who this whole God-human person is in the states of humiliation and exaltation. He does not equate humility with humanity, nor exaltation with divinity. Instead, 'both in being humiliated and in being exalted, Jesus remains wholly human and wholly God'.[37] He frequently refers to the humiliated Christ as the 'stumbling block'. In his view, 'the doctrine of the stumbling block has its place not in the doctrine of God's taking human form but rather in the doctrine of the God-human's humiliation'.[38]

The subject of Christology is the Present One, Jesus Christ. This Christ is indivisible. There is no fitting speech about Jesus Christ that is not a speech about the whole God-human. This Christ is also transcendent. He can only be encountered as an absolute other and can never be incorporated into an existing body of knowledge. And this Christ is also present. There can be no question of Christ's presence except to acknowledge that being-for-me is simply Christ's way of being. Thus the aporia of theology, the basic paradox of God's objectivity and non-objectivity in revelation, finds unity in the person of Christ. He is present as the transcendent one; he is transcendent as the present one. And there is no competition between his presence and his transcendence. The counter-Logos is the present Logos is the whole Logos.

The presence of Christ means more (but not less) than 'Christ existing as community'. Despite a marked decline in usage, Bonhoeffer never expressly rejects this early formula. He continues to employ it here and later in his Finkenwalde lecture, 'The Visible Church in the New Testament'.[39] However, compared with his earlier writings, Bonhoeffer's middle- and late-period works do not make much of it. Indeed, a review of each occurrence of the expression, from its first appearance to its last, indicates that its dogmatic home was always in ecclesiology, specifically in Bonhoeffer's account of the presence of Christ in and as the church-community.[40] What does seem to have changed by 1933

---

35. DBWE 12, 349; DBW 12, 335.
36. DBWE 12, 354; DBW 12, 341.
37. DBWE 12, 355; DBW 12, 343.
38. DBWE 12, 314; DBW 12, 295.
39. DBWE 14, 449–55; DBW 14, 438–44.
40. Apart from *Sanctorum Communio* and *Act and Being*, see also DBWE 10, 407; DBW 10, 377, which is a summary of his argument in *Act and Being*; DBWE 11, 301; DBW 11, 271–2, which rehearses the ecclesiology of *Sanctorum Communio*; DBWE 12, 323; DBW 12, 305–6, which is the section on Christ's presence in the church-community; DBWE 14, 449–52; DBW 14, 438–40, again, in the section on the community as the presence of Christ.

is that the social-ecclesial framework was no longer Bonhoeffer's primary theological category. Specifically, in the 1933 Christology, Bonhoeffer's concern is to account for the presence of Christ in a way that includes but is not comprehended by his existence as church-community. Bonhoeffer begins with the whole divine-human person, crucified and risen, humiliated and exalted, transcendent and present. The person of Christ includes, by virtue of his promeity, his presence as church-community. But it also includes, by the same virtue, his presence as word and sacrament. Here Bonhoeffer affirms his own version of the 'threefold form' of revelation. Revelation as the present Christ takes the threefold form of word, sacrament and church-community.[41] Each of these shares the same ontological referent: Jesus Christ *pro-me*. Christ's personal structure of 'being-there-for-you' is the ground of Christ's presence in the threefold form of word, sacrament and church-community. The question of *how* Christ can be present as church-community is translated into the question of *who* the one present as church-community is. In order to flesh out the bibliology entailed by Bonhoeffer's 1933 Christology, I turn specifically to his theology of the word of God.

Bonhoeffer's theology of the word

In Frits de Lange's opinion, 'Bonhoeffer's theology of the Word does not appear to be all that massive'.[42] Against this, I argue that *word* does a lot of theological work for Bonhoeffer. To say that Christ is the word is to say very much indeed. The obvious starting point for Bonhoeffer's theology of the word is his Christology. But the word, as will soon become clear, is a far-reaching theme in Bonhoeffer's thought. It is, arguably, the conceptual link that grounds the systematic interdependence of Bonhoeffer's Christology, pneumatology, ecclesiology and bibliology. In this section, I will sketch the contours of Bonhoeffer's theology of the word, with particular attention to the relationship between intelligibility and embodiment. Although my emphasis is on the intelligible presence of Christ in revelation, in Bonhoeffer's thought the word seeking understanding cannot be separated from the word seeking flesh.[43]

---

41. DBWE 12, 314; DBW 12, 295. This does not appear to be a reference to Barth's 'threefold form'. Later in the Christology, Bonhoeffer notes the 'threefold being-there' of Christ (1) for humankind, (2) for history and (3) for nature (DBWE 12, 324; DBW 12, 307).

42. Lange, *Waiting for the Word*, 105.

43. An earlier version of this section appeared in Joel Banman, 'The Word of the Church to the World: Bonhoeffer's Concept of the Logos and the Bilingual Character of Public Theology', *The Bonhoeffer Legacy: An International Journal* 5 (2018): 47–62.

Intelligibility

I have already discussed Bonhoeffer's portrayal of Christ as the 'counter Word'[44] in connection with his emphasis on the transcendence of God in revelation. But there is more to be said about Bonhoeffer's understanding of Christ as Logos, specifically the relationship between the human logos and the Logos of God. God in Christ comes as the counter-Logos, which transcends every human logos and must either kill or be killed by the human logos. But what of the human logos that has been put to death by the Logos of God? What does it mean to speak of human understanding for those who have submitted their understanding to God's Word? Can there be any genuine human understanding of revelation? According to Bonhoeffer, Christology is 'the word about the Word of God. Christ is the Logos of God. Christology is logology. It is knowledge par excellence … Christology is the invisible, unrecognized, hidden center of scholarship'.[45] Bonhoeffer is well aware that this assertion could only ever be affirmed within the church. He is thinking squarely within the logic of revelation: the claim that Christ is the Word made flesh 'is the prerequisite, not the proof'.[46] Given this prerequisite, if Christ really *is* the word of God, then it follows that there is no alcove of human knowledge that lies outside of Jesus Christ. All human knowledge has its basis in God's word. And God's word is not a set of ideas or propositions; God's word is a person, namely, Jesus Christ. 'This human person is the transcendent.'[47] Knowledge is first and foremost a question of our existence, and human existence is determined in relation to the One who transcends human existence. All true knowledge exists only in relation to the Transcendent One, who confronts us as an unassailable boundary and who thereby 'interrogates' our very existence.[48] Christ is the ground of our being and the ground of our knowing. For Bonhoeffer, the presence of Christ is the beginning of knowledge.

For this reason, Christ's presence is inherently *intelligible*. This is not to say that the encounter with revelation involves an easy or automatic absorption of the content of God's word into the human intellect. The divine Logos and the human logos can never be collapsed into one another, nor can the human fully comprehend the divine. Christ is, after all, the *counter* Word, the *Gegenlogos*. But it is precisely as the counter-Logos that Christ encounters human beings in the sphere of the logos. Bonhoeffer's emphasis on Christ's *personal* presence does not exclude the encounter with Christ in the realm of the intellect. To speak of the intelligibility of Christ's presence is simply to affirm with Bonhoeffer, 'because the human being has a logos, therefore God encounters the human being in the Logos'.[49] Yet it would be a mistake to construe the word as idea rather than as 'the

---

44. DBWE 12, 302; DBW 12, 282.
45. DBWE 12, 301; DBW 12, 281.
46. DBWE 12, 301; DBW 12, 281.
47. DBWE 12, 301; DBW 12, 281.
48. DBWE 12, 303; DBW 12, 283.
49. DBWE 12, 316; DBW 12, 297.

living Word'.⁵⁰ The living word is *address*, spoken from one person to another, and as such is intrinsically relational and communal. Philip Ziegler has rightly noted that Bonhoeffer's 'ontological account of the promeity of Christ is a function of Bonhoeffer's theology of the Word of God'.⁵¹ Christ *pro-me* is not word in an abstract sense, but is God's word concretely addressed to human beings. Word as personal address occurs in personal community. Because Christ is the living word, his address to us always 'desires community' and 'seeks this community only by bringing the other person into the truth'.⁵² Where Christ is, he is there as the Logos.

To speak about the inherent intelligibility of Christ's presence is to raise the question of his perspicuity. According to Bonhoeffer, 'the truth of the human logos therefore originates in the Word, because the Word alone communicates clear and unambiguous meaning. Clarity and lack of ambiguity are the essence of the Word'.⁵³ I will have more to say about perspicuity when I draw out the bibliological implications of Bonhoeffer's theology of the word. Suffice it to say for now that Bonhoeffer regards perspicuity as an essential characteristic of the word. But this does not mean that human beings encounter the word in a way that overcomes all possible doubts or misunderstandings. The word that is clear and unambiguous is not identical with the biblical text or an interpretation thereof. It is, rather, Jesus Christ himself, the present word of truth. If Christ is present as word, then his presence is perspicuous to the eyes of faith, which is to say that the perspicuity of the word is the work of the Spirit of the word. The Spirit of truth leads the church into truth.

Embodiment

For Bonhoeffer, Christ's being the eternal word of God cannot be separated from his being the word made flesh. He is one and the same word. The one whose presence is inherently intelligible is the one whose presence is visible and takes up space. The presence of the word is an embodied presence. The word that seeks understanding is the word that seeks a body. The present word is always the incarnate one. Wherever the word is, there human beings in their sinful humanity are being borne by the one who became human. As embodied, the present word is visible. God's word is visible in the bodily form of sacrament and community.

Bonhoeffer says, 'The Word in the sacrament is the Word in bodily form.'⁵⁴ But he is careful not to lose sight of the sacrament's character as *word*: 'Christ is wholly Word, and the sacrament is wholly Word.'⁵⁵ The sacrament is not 'wordless' but

---

50. DBWE 12, 316; DBW 12, 298.
51. Philip G. Ziegler, 'Christ For Us Today: Promeity in the Christologies of Bonhoeffer and Kierkegaard', *International Journal of Systematic Theology* 15 (2013): 30.
52. DBWE 12, 316; DBW 12, 298.
53. DBWE 12, 316; DBW 12, 297.
54. DBWE 12, 318; DBW 12, 300.
55. DBWE 12, 318; DBW 12, 300.

rather 'is made holy and given its meaning by the Word'.[56] It proclaims the gospel, albeit in connection with the creaturely elements. The particular sacraments and their elements are also given their basis and validity solely by God's word. God's word, namely, Jesus Christ, is fully there *pro-me* in the sacraments. God's commitment to speak through these elements is so decisive that Bonhoeffer can even say that 'Jesus Christ is one who is bound by the sacrament'.[57] But, of course, this should not be understood as a strike against divine freedom. Christ's commitment to *these* sacraments is grounded in his free decision to be there for human beings in this way, as he himself instituted. The sacraments are Christ's presence as word. However, even though Christ's sacramental presence is intelligible, it is by no means reducible to raw intelligibility. The sacraments 'do not *mean* something – they *are* something'.[58] What they are is the present Jesus Christ, God's very word. What they say in being what they are is *gospel*. So Bonhoeffer: 'The promise of "forgiveness of sins" makes the sacrament what it is. Whoever believes in the Word in the sacrament has received the sacrament wholly.'[59] And yet this is not merely a matter of intellectual assent. The word of the sacrament is an embodied word: 'In the sacrament Christ is present to us in the sphere of our body's tangible nature.'[60] It is a fitting form for God's word, because God's word is the word made flesh.

The presence of the word made flesh must take up space in the world. And here Bonhoeffer's Finkenwalde ecclesiology is consistent with his earlier writings: 'The space of Christ in the world is occupied by the *church; it is the present Christ.*'[61] Where Christ is present, he is present *as* his body, and his body is the church. The church becomes the church as it hears and proclaims the witness of the prophets and apostles in the power of the Spirit. Purely intelligible words need only attentive learners; the incarnate word needs a community. This is why Bonhoeffer emphasizes the centrality of the sacraments. Baptism and the Lord's Supper both 'have their origin and goal in the body of Christ'.[62] Baptism is our once-for-all incorporation into Christ's body; the Lord's Supper is our ongoing participation in his body.[63] Christ's body is his visible presence.[64] In sum, 'the

---

56. DBWE 12, 318; DBW 12, 300.
57. DBWE 12, 319; DBW 12, 301.
58. DBWE 12, 319; DBW 12, 301.
59. DBWE 12, 318; DBW 12, 300.
60. DBWE 12, 322; DBW 12, 305.
61. DBWE 14, 446; DBW 14, 435.
62. DBWE 4, 216; DBW 4, 230.
63. In his essay, 'The Power of the Keys and Church Discipline', he describes the Lord's Supper as 'the repeated feeding of the confessing church-community of the baptized with the true body and blood of Christ. Believers are assured of their own bodily connection with the Lord and among each other and receive forgiveness for their sins through the body of Christ' (DBWE 14, 830; DBW 14, 835).
64. Bonhoeffer draws on Old Testament temple imagery in this connection (DBWE 14, 448–9; DBW 14, 436–8).

church-community of Christ is the present Christ in the Holy Spirit. It is Christ's visible body, and that body is always Christ'.[65]

Spirit

Bonhoeffer's theology of the word has a strong pneumatological character. Even in his Christology lectures, he alludes to the pneumatological implications of the Logos. The Holy Spirit, he says, is first and foremost 'Word and not power, action or feeling'; indeed, 'only as Word is the Spirit power and action'.[66] The Spirit is not the Logos; but because the Holy Spirit effects the presence of the Logos, the power of the Spirit is the power of the word, the activity of the Spirit the activity of the word. The Spirit *addresses* human beings with God's word, effecting the encounter with the risen and exalted Christ. In this sense, it would be appropriate to say that God's word is always the *inspired* word.

The word spoken by the Spirit is the word that seeks both understanding and flesh that drives towards both intelligibility and embodiment. And these cannot be disconnected. The church does not come into being wordlessly; it arises from and gathers around the proclamation of the word, and the proclaimed word seeks understanding. Bonhoeffer reads the story of Pentecost in Acts 2 as paradigmatic.[67] On the day of Pentecost, the Holy Spirit comes to an existing assembly, but this assembly is not yet the church. When the Spirit comes, it is a 'visible event'.[68] This event, namely, the 'language miracle', is not about giving secret, personal revelations. The Holy Spirit comes at Pentecost in the form of publicly intelligible words: 'The Spirit comes in the word itself, not in babbling and stammering, but precisely in words comprehensible to everyone.'[69] Peter's sermon that follows is, likewise, a coherent message – a message, moreover, whose coherence is grounded in the coherence of the Old Testament prophets.[70] It is precisely because people *understand* Peter's message that they are faced with the question, 'What should we do?' (Acts 2.37). In comprehending Peter's witness, the crowd begins to hear God's word of grace. But, as Bonhoeffer says, the presence of God's grace is judgement for those who do not know that this grace is really for

---

65. DBWE 14, 449; DBW 14, 438.
66. DBWE 12, 315; DBW 12, 297.
67. Bonhoeffer's exegesis of Acts 2 is found in his lectures on 'The Visible Church in the New Testament' (DBWE 14, 438–46; DBW 14, 425–34). Several sections from these lectures, or variations thereof, reappear in *Discipleship*, especially in the chapter, 'The Visible Church-Community' (DBWE 4, 225–52; DBW 4, 241–68).
68. DBWE 14, 439; DBW 14, 426.
69. DBWE 14, 439; DBW 14, 427.
70. Bonhoeffer draws a connection between the *filioque* and the unity of the Old and New Testaments. It is because the Spirit proceeds from Jesus Christ, the one who fulfils God's promises to Israel, that the church can never separate itself from Israel or Israel's Scripture: 'Wherever the "*filioque*" falls, so also does this tie to the people of Israel fall' (DBWE 14, 440; DBW 14, 428).

them. Those who repent, are baptized and receive the Holy Spirit become a new community, a new creation, in God's image. This, too, is an act of understanding, grounded in the intelligibility of the word they have heard. But in this act those who repent are also acted *upon* by the Holy Spirit. And it is not a one-off act, but an ongoing act of incorporation into a new community, which is God's new creation. Those who repent and believe become part of this new humanity. By the Spirit, they have heard and believed God's gracious presence in Christ through the intelligible word; and by the same Spirit, they become members of Christ's body, his embodied presence on earth.

But this does not mark the end of understanding. As it is recorded in Acts 2.42, the community 'remained constant in the apostles' teaching [*didache*]'.[71] The ongoing nature of the *didache* is decisive for Bonhoeffer. Unlike other kinds of instruction, the *didache* is not the sort of teaching that 'aims by definition at making itself superfluous'.[72] The church can never be done with the *didache*. This is because the apostolic preaching 'is truly God's Word in human words', and God's word 'has an inherent impulse toward community'.[73] As Bonhoeffer explains in his Homiletics lectures: '*Because the word by nature bears the new humanity, it is by nature always oriented toward the church-community.*'[74] God's word has become flesh in Jesus Christ, and this same word seeks flesh among us today, seeks to be embodied. The church is the community of God's word, and this community is always the work of the Holy Spirit. The apostolic teaching can never be isolated from this community, can never be separated from the Spirit-mediated bodily presence of Christ. So, although God's word is intelligible, it is not meant to remain in the intellect (lest it be made into an object to be put at human disposal). For Bonhoeffer, the apostolic teaching is not a human but a pneumatological event: 'In this *didache*, the Holy Spirit itself is speaking ... In this *didache*, the Holy Spirit exists.'[75] Apostolic teaching holds the promise of the Holy Spirit, who, as Bonhoeffer says elsewhere, 'is the present God and Christ'.[76] And Christ is not present as an idea or a teaching, but as a community. That is why Bonhoeffer connects the apostolic teaching and the church-community: 'This *didache* creates [*koinonia*].'[77] The proclamation of the word is both the origin and goal of the community: 'It is only through hearing the word that a fellowship comes into being, and once again all such brotherly life now stands in the service of the proclamation of that word.'[78] Word, Spirit and community are distinct, but inseparable.

---

71. Cited in DBWE 14, 443; DBW 14, 431; cf. DBWE 4, 226; DBW 4, 242.
72. DBWE 4, 227; DBW 4, 242; cf. DBWE 14, 443–4; DBW 14, 431–2.
73. DBWE 4, 227; DBW 4, 243.
74. DBWE 14, 511; DBW 14, 504.
75. DBWE 14, 444; DBW 14, 432.
76. DBWE 14, 417; DBW 14, 404.
77. DBWE 14, 445; DBW 14, 433.
78. DBWE 14, 445; DBW 14, 433.

In his Christology, his pneumatology and his ecclesiology, Bonhoeffer's concept of the Logos points to an account of revelation wherein God's word is by its very nature both intelligible and embodied. This is the key connection between his theology of revelation and the human encounter with revelation. For Bonhoeffer, revelation means *Christus praesens*. When this is viewed through the lens of his theology of the word, it becomes possible to speak of revelation as *verbum praesens*. In his thought, revelation as the presence of the word means that the Logos encounters me in my logos; it is the word seeking human understanding. Christ is there *pro-me* as the word *pro-me*. The word that is genuinely *for* human beings is there to be understood by human beings. But the being of the word is not intelligence or idea. There is no other word than the word made flesh. This means that the encounter with the incarnate word of God is never a matter of intelligence alone. The clarity of God's word is an embodied clarity; it is the word seeking human community. If the church is the body of Christ, then it is the body of the word.

Conclusion

Bonhoeffer's 1933 Christology represents a revision in his account of Christ's presence. *Christus praesens* still means 'Christ existing as community', but this is no longer its primary meaning. Bonhoeffer now situates his interpretation of Christ's presence within Christ's person, his existence *pro-me*. Thus he resolves the aporia of revelation within the structure of Christology rather than in his social interpretation of ecclesiology. His Christology extends to his theology of the word, which he interprets as inherently intelligible, embodied and, in the precise sense of being breathed out by the Holy Spirit, *inspired*.

It is on the basis of Bonhoeffer's theology of the word that it becomes possible to describe the connection between the word of God and the words of the Bible, between the present Christ himself and the semantic content of scriptural texts. In his earliest formulation he followed a very Barthian line and treated the Bible as a '*document that gives witness*'.[79] Under the category of 'witness', the Bible contains words through which God speaks and can be expected to speak. And this speaking is initiated by God and God alone. It occurs when and where God pleases. God speaks *through* the words of the Bible; only as such are these words God's own. The Bible points away from itself and towards God. One does not get hold revelation by employing the right sort of interpretation. Revelation is not what the text says or even what it means; it is the one to whom the text is pointing.

---

79. DBWE 9, 289; DBW 9, 311.

The term 'witness' suggests a basic distinction between the content of the text and the content of revelation, and undoubtedly this was its merit in Bonhoeffer's mind. It was always how Bonhoeffer, following Barth, framed the connection between the Bible and revelation, thus avoiding the error of objectifying revelation. But in light of the Christology I have outlined above, a *witness* to God's word cannot be so sharply distinguished from God's word itself. In fact, as I will show in the next chapter, Bonhoeffer's 1933 Christology becomes the basis for the claim that Scripture as the witness to God's word can rightly be identified and received as God's word itself.

5

THE WORD'S COMING TO WORD

I have been arguing that Bonhoeffer's early 'theology of sociality' resulted in an underdetermined ontology of Scripture, since he subordinated the Bible beneath proclamation (sociologically rendered) in his theology of revelation. With his account of revelation as 'Christ existing as church-community', Bonhoeffer portrayed Scripture's primary significance in its role in service of proclamation, which in turn he portrayed chiefly in its generative and sustaining role in and for the church-community. If, as I have argued in CHAPTER 4, Bonhoeffer's 1933 Christology signalled a revision in his account of Christ's presence, a revision that had ripple-effects in his theology of Scripture, do these revisions extend to his theology of preaching? Does proclamation still overshadow Scripture in his theology of revelation? How does his homiletic contribute to our understanding of his bibliology?

In this chapter, I show how Bonhoeffer's Christology undergirds a more fully realized affirmation of Scripture as God's word. I do this in conversation with his Finkenwalde lectures on homiletics and his 1935 essay, '*Vergegenwärtigung neutestamentlicher Texte*' (Making New Testament Texts Present). In both, I show how Bonhoeffer uses the category of *witness* to correlate the speaking of God's word with the presence of God's word. The preacher witnesses to Christ in the power of the Spirit of Christ on the basis of the scriptural witness to Christ. The strong connection between Christ's speaking and Christ's presence is how Bonhoeffer can identify the word of sermon with the incarnate Christ, as well as identifying the word of Scripture with the word of God. Scripture *is* God's word because it is the *witness* to God's word. The exegetical as well as the homiletical task is to attend to the Bible's character as witness. For Bonhoeffer, where the Word comes to word, the Word himself is present. Scriptural exegesis, I argue, involves asking the Christological 'who' question in constant dialogue with the biblical witness to Christ.

The present Christ as the word of proclamation

One of the developments I have traced in the preceding chapters is the gradual shift in Bonhoeffer's dogmatic centre of gravity from ecclesiology to Christology.

This process can be seen in the evolution of his Finkenwalde homiletics. In the first iteration of his lectures, he begins with a discussion of the preaching office and the pastoral office, offering an ecclesiological grounding for the sermon: '*I preach, because church exists, so that church may come into being.*'[1] This aligns comfortably with his earlier, academic theology. But from the summer of 1936, Bonhoeffer begins to ground his homiletic Christologically in the incarnation.[2] In an arresting series of expansions to the Finkenwalde homiletics, Bonhoeffer makes some of his most striking claims:

> *The sermon derives from the incarnation of Jesus Christ and is determined by the incarnation of Jesus Christ.* It does not derive from some universal truth or emotional experience. The word of the sermon is the incarnate Christ. The incarnate Christ is God. Hence the sermon is actually Christ. God *as* human being. Christ *as* the word. As the Word, Christ walks through the church-community.[3]

Here Bonhoeffer lays bare what he had already said in his Christology lectures that 'the Christ who is proclaimed is the real Christ'.[4] Without caveat or equivocation, Bonhoeffer says plainly, 'passing by the sermon means: passing by Christ'; the sermon is a '*sacramentum verbi*'.[5] Bonhoeffer's ontology of preaching, his account of what the sermon *is*, is thoroughly Christological, incarnational and sacramental. In the sermon, Christ is really present. The sermon is, in its very essence, *Christus praesens*.

This does not mean that the sermon ever ceases to be a thoroughly human word, full of error and sin, idolatry and heresy.[6] Bonhoeffer is all too aware of the tendency of preachers to use the pulpit as a soapbox. That is why he reminds the future preachers at Finkenwalde, 'A sermon is a witness to Christ and not a human endeavor.'[7] The preacher's task is to attend prayerfully to the witness of Scripture to Christ and to make this witness audible. 'Whenever *we* preach Christ', Bonhoeffer says, 'it can be done only by way of an outstretched finger' – but, he hastens to add, it is 'important that [Christ] is present'.[8] And Christ is present in the form of the proclaimed word. That is why Bonhoeffer can also say that a 'sermon is *not* a

---

1. DBWE 14, 491; DBW 14, 482.
2. See DB-ER, 443. Bethge correctly notes that this revision does not entail a rejection of his earlier ecclesiological claims.
3. DBWE 14, 509–10; DBW 14, 502–3.
4. DBWE 12, 313; DBW 12, 295.
5. DBWE 14, 514 ed. n. 108; DBW 14, 507 ed. n. 105.
6. In *Discipleship*, Bonhoeffer says, 'It is not always easy to recognize where a legitimate theological interpretation ends and heresy begins' (DBWE 4, 231; DBW 4, 247).
7. DBWE 14, 515; DBW 14, 508.
8. DBWE 14, 516; DBW 14, 509.

witness; is more'.[9] From the perspective of Bonhoeffer's ontology of preaching, 'the sermon is actually Christ'.[10] Christ's presence is assured wherever Christ himself speaks, and Christ has given authority to the church to speak his word on his behalf. Thus, in these lectures Bonhoeffer identifies the word as witness with the word as *Christus praesens*. The connection between the two is vital.

One of the clearest statements of this connection appears in a class discussion, following his expansions on the Christological foundation of preaching. Bonhoeffer cites the account in Luke 10.1–16, which tells of Jesus's commissioning of seventy disciples to go into the surrounding towns to speak on his behalf. At the end of this commissioning, Jesus concludes, 'Whoever listens to you listens to me, and whoever rejects you rejects me, and whoever rejects me rejects the one who sent me' (v. 16). Bonhoeffer refers to this passage in a way that clearly connects word as *witness* and word as *Christus praesens*: 'Where a disciple speaks, there Christ speaks; where Christ speaks, he *is present*. Luke 10[:16]. Wherever the word [is], there Christ [is] wholly.'[11]

Consider each claim separately. Firstly, where a disciple speaks, there Christ speaks. This does not mean that, in Bonhoeffer's mind, anything a follower of Jesus says automatically receives a divine endorsement. The speech in question is *proclamation*, which means testifying to Christ in the power of the Spirit. Christ is present in such proclamation as the Spirit ministers the word in the words. Secondly, where Christ speaks, he is really present. As I argued in CHAPTER 4, the presence of the word of God entails the real, personal presence of Christ. If Christ is speaking in the disciples' witness, then Christ himself is present. Finally, wherever the word is, Christ is fully there. This is simply a reassertion of the indivisibility of Christ, a point that Bonhoeffer had firmly established in his Christology lectures. If Christ is indivisible, then there is no question of Christ's being partially present, which includes his presence in proclamation. Where Christ is truly proclaimed in the power of the Spirit – even in the humble form of the sermon – the whole divine-human Christ is there.

It is on this basis that the word of the sermon *is* the incarnate Christ himself. But Bonhoeffer pushes this logic even further. Not only is it impermissible to make a division between divinity and humanity in Christ's person, it is likewise impermissible to make a division between Christ's person and his works. Accordingly, in Bonhoeffer's view, what Christ *does* in the form of proclamation is identical with what he does as the incarnate, crucified and risen one: he takes sinful humanity upon himself. Jesus of Nazareth, who lived in the first century, who was crucified, died and was buried, who descended into hell, rose from the dead on the third day, and ascended into heaven – it is this same Jesus who comes to the church in the form of preaching. Bonhoeffer does not distinguish the identity of the historical Christ, incarnate as the man Jesus of Nazareth, from the Christ

---

9. DBWE 14, 515, my emphasis; DBW 14, 509.
10. DBWE 14, 510; DBW 14, 503.
11. DBWE 14, 516; DBW 14, 509.

who is present in proclamation.¹² What God does in and through the sermon is precisely what God does in and through the incarnation, because it is the same Christ who is present and active in both. In the incarnation and in the sermon, God in Christ takes human nature upon himself and bears sinful human flesh. Whatever else might occur in a sermon – edification, instruction, conversion – Christ is there as the proclaimed word to take humanity upon himself: 'Christ as the sermon goes out to the congregation in order to embrace this congregation and to bear or sustain it.'¹³

Who, then, is the agent of proclamation? The primary agent of proclamation is not the preacher, but the Spirit of Christ. The proclaimed word has its own agency, grounded in the freedom of God who speaks his self-revelatory word by the Holy Spirit. Nevertheless, Bonhoeffer does warn about the possibility of hindering this autonomous word: 'The preacher should recognize this inherent movement of the word, should not impede it in any way or set his own movement into motion.'¹⁴ The preacher driven by the goal of speaking a word of exhortation, education or edification does not speak the word that has the capacity to bear sinful human flesh. The only word with this capacity is Jesus Christ.

Does the preacher, then, exercise any legitimate agency in the mediation of the word? More specifically, can the preacher make decisions, consciously or unconsciously, in preparation or delivery, that might render the incarnational presence of Christ more or less clearly – or even make that presence more or less likely to actually occur in the event of preaching? This problem is not unique to homiletics in Lutheran theology. The same question applies to the minister's agency in the administration of the Lord's Supper, and Bonhoeffer makes this connection explicit. In the question of Christ's sacramental presence, he says that the '*est*' (the 'is') of the sermon is the '*est*' of the sacrament.¹⁵ There is 'no gradation of reality' but 'the same measure of reality in both sermon and the Lord's Supper'.¹⁶ The question of Christ's incarnate presence as the word of the sermon is no more problematic than that of his presence in the bread and wine.

---

12. In this, Bonhoeffer is in line with Martin Kähler, *The So-Called Historical Jesus and the Historic Biblical Christ*, ed. and trans. Carl E. Braaten (Philadelphia: Fortress, 1964). Kähler's direct influence on Bonhoeffer is hard to measure, since much of it may have come by way of the dialectical movement. Carl Braaten notes the influence of Kähler on Barth, Brunner, Tillich and Bultmann in his introduction (ibid., 35–7). Bonhoeffer cites Kähler's work not only here in his homiletics lectures (DBWE 14, 510 n. 87; DBW 14, 503 ed. n. 84), but also in his Christology lectures (DBWE 12, 329; DBW 12, 312), and his lectures on twentieth-century Protestant theology (DBWE 11, 211–16; DBW 11, 177–83).
13. DBWE 14, 511; DBW 14, 504.
14. DBWE 14, 511; DBW 14, 504.
15. DBWE 14, 514–15; DBW 14, 508.
16. DBWE 14, 515; DBW 14, 508.

The question of human agency becomes somewhat less problematic when it is treated communally rather than individualistically, which is precisely what Bonhoeffer does. Following the Lutheran confessions, Bonhoeffer emphasizes the *office* of preaching over the individual preacher.[17] The fifth Augsburg Confession, 'Of the Ministry', states, 'To obtain such faith God instituted the office of preaching, giving the gospel and the sacraments. Through these, as through means, he gives the Holy Spirit who produces faith, where and when he wills, in those who hear the gospel.'[18] It is through the *office* of ministry, not the individual minister, that God has promised to be present by the Holy Spirit, and this promise cannot be revoked. Bonhoeffer exhorts his students to trust in this promise, and to uphold the trustworthiness of the sermon by their own obedience to the word.[19] Obedience is crucial, because the kind of church that corresponds to the truth of the sermon is the kind of church that obeys the commandments of Christ. Therefore, the preacher is to speak and enact the truth of the church's proclamation, thereby attesting to the trustworthiness of God's present word.

Bonhoeffer is not suggesting that the preacher somehow exercises control over Christ's presence in the event of proclamation. Christ is there in the form of preaching, yes, but never as an object at human disposal. The authority given to the church to speak Christ's word cannot be described as the power of a subject over an object. The relationship is that of call and promise, and Christ is the acting agent of both. So, consistent with his theology of revelation in *Act and Being*, Bonhoeffer's incarnational ontology of preaching maintains revelation's unidirectionality. There is no question of the preacher actively mediating Christ's presence via a sermon, even if the preacher adheres to particular exegetical standards. Christ's taking form as proclamation depends entirely on his word of promise to and for the church. That is why Bonhoeffer insists that 'only *the commission given by Christ* can support a sermon', hastening to add that 'the commission itself ... is given to the *church*'.[20] The commission to preach inheres in 'the *preaching office of preaching*'.[21] And whoever would serve in this office must bear its responsibility,

---

17. DBWE 14, 488–90; DBW 14, 479–82.
18. Robert Kolb and Timothy J. Wengert, eds, *The Book of Concord* (Minneapolis: Fortress, 2000), 40. It is quite likely that this article was under consideration in the discussion recorded in 'Questions That Reached Him' (DBWE 14, 514–16; DBW 14, 508–9), given that the phrase '*ubi et quando [visum est Deo]*' ('where and when it pleases God', translated above as 'where and when he wills') is explicitly discussed. The notes say that the *ubi et quando* refers not to the presence of the Holy Spirit but to the creation of faith: 'in any event, the presence is guaranteed' (DBWE 14, 515; DBW 14, 509).
19. DBWE 14, 491–2; 494; DBW 14, 482–3; 485–6.
20. DBWE 14, 490–1; DBW 14, 482.
21. DBWE 14, 489; DBW 14, 480. In his lectures on Church Constitution, Bonhoeffer states that the 'preaching office and pastoral office [are] different' (DBWE 14, 334; DBW 14, 315). The pastoral office is bound to a particular congregation, whereas in the preaching office the minister is 'ordained for service to the entire church' (DBWE 14, 334; DBW 14, 315).

empowered by the Spirit. In ordination, the preacher is given to participate in the promise of Christ that his word will be spoken through the preaching office. But it is Christ's commission to the *church* that grounds the promise of his presence in proclamation, and the preaching *office* that inherits this promise. In the 'preaching office of preaching', God makes himself '"haveable," graspable in the Word within the church'[22] – not as an object, but as the present person of Christ in the threefold form of word, sacrament and community.

Throughout the Finkenwalde homiletics, Bonhoeffer reminds his students that God is the speaker of God's word. It is on the basis of God's agency in proclamation that God can be said to be present in the word of proclamation.[23] The Holy Spirit speaks through the preacher's witness to Scripture's witness to Christ. Thus the proclaimed witness in the word of the sermon is inseparable from the written witness in the word of Scripture. Scripture, as God's witness to Christ, *is* God's word, and wherever this word comes to word, Christ is wholly there.

The present Christ as the word of Scripture

The bibliological implications of Bonhoeffer's Finkenwalde homiletics emerge in his essay, '*Vergegenwärtigung neutestamentlicher Texte*' (Making New Testament Texts Present).[24] This essay falls within the Finkenwalde period, and I consider it programmatic for his Finkenwalde exegesis. Bonhoeffer approaches the question of *Vergegenwärtigung* from two opposing angles: Is it the text that must be justified to the present, or the present to the text? In this essay, Bonhoeffer is building on his Christology to directly engage in the debate between the history-of-religions school and the dialecticians. The *pro-me* structure of Christ's person becomes the basis for reading Scripture as God's word for the present.

The question of making Scripture present revolves around two related questions: what does it mean to make something present, and what, really, is being made present? According to Bonhoeffer, there are two basic approaches to making Scripture present: 'Either one means that the biblical message must be justified before the present and therefore must prove itself presentable, or one means that the present must justify itself before the biblical message and therefore

---

22. DBWE 2, 91; DBW 2, 85.

23. Williams, in *Christ the Heart of Creation*, often construes God's presence in the world in terms of divine agency. For example, when discussing Bonhoeffer's doctrine of the mandates, he writes, 'where the interdependence of human life shows the radical quality of Christ's responsibility and representation, where familial, political or cultural action realizes a more and more unqualified degree of being-for-the-other, it becomes a manifestation of Christ's underlying and ongoing agency' (ibid., 204).

24. The titular term, *Vergegenwärtigung*, is fundamental to the coherence of Bonhoeffer's essay. It has been translated in DBWE 14 as 'contemporizing', but I have opted to leave it untranslated or to parse it as 'making present'.

the message must become present.'²⁵ Either the text is brought before the present and judged on the basis of contemporary values, mores, epistemologies, etc., or the present is laid before the text and judged on the basis of the biblical message. Bonhoeffer begins by accounting for the first kind of *Vergegenwärtigung*, which he regards as untheological. He traces a line from the 'age of rationalism' directly to the theology of the *Deutsche Christen*. This was not due to an alignment of their principles but rather to their shared presupposition of autonomous human reason. Everyone along this line had already determined their 'fixed, unquestionable point of departure'.²⁶ The attempt to ground theology in a universal point of departure recalls the history-of-religions search for a point of contact (*Anknüpfungspunkt*),²⁷ a supposed place of agreement between Christian theology and the contemporary zeitgeist. This, for Bonhoeffer, merely domesticates the biblical message. As the metaphor suggests, any part of the Bible that cannot be domesticated must be released back into the wilderness; only what is tame and serviceable can remain. This represents a kind of historical consciousness that absolutizes the present so that all other historical phenomena, including the Christian religion, must conform to it.

The key question of *Vergegenwärtigung* for this approach is how to find timeless ideas and principles embedded in the biblical text. For Bonhoeffer, this endeavour is rigged from the outset, because the only universal principles that can be found in Scripture are those principles that are already recognized and accepted *as* timeless and universal. Untheological *Vergegenwärtigung* cannot find anything in Scripture apart from what is already known. Interpreters must already 'have access a priori to the eternal standards they find in Scripture'.²⁸ The interpreter holds the keys to unlock Scripture. It becomes the interpreter's role to identify what in the Bible is eternal (and therefore applicable) and what is temporal (and therefore expendable). So they end up just the wrong way around: '*the norm of [Vergegenwärtigung] resides within us; the Bible is the material to which this norm is applied*'.²⁹ Bonhoeffer will argue for just the reverse.

For Bonhoeffer, it is not the present, but rather the biblical message that is the norm. More specifically, it is the *Sache* of the NT that must guide the question of

25. DBW 14, 400, my translation.

26. DBWE 14, 414; DBW 14, 401. Bonhoeffer identifies as examples eighteenth-century reason, nineteenth-century culture or twentieth-century *Volkstum*.

27. Bonhoeffer does perceive a difference between the liberal school and the *Deutsche Christen*, specifically in the latter's refusal even to raise the question of *Sache*. Liberal theologians like Troeltsch and Harnack had at least pursued the question of the essence of Christianity – and done so relentlessly – even if Bonhoeffer found their results wanting. But the *Deutsche Christen* had not even asked the question; they 'merely cried out for [*Vergegenwärtigung*]' (DBWE 14, 415; DBW 14, 402).

28. DBWE 14, 419–20; DBW 14, 406.

29. DBWE 14, 421; DBW 14, 408.

making it present.[30] So what is this *Sache*? Bonhoeffer's question of *Sache* echoes the question of essence (*Wesen*) posed by Troeltsch and Harnack. However, in Bonhoeffer's case the *Sache* of the Christian message is not an eternal truth or a universally valid ethic; the *Sache* of the NT 'is Christ and Christ's word', and *Vergegenwärtigung* occurs wherever this *Sache* 'genuinely comes to expression'.[31] This is the central claim of the essay and must be carefully unpacked.

Why is it that the expression of the *Sache* of the NT constitutes making these texts present? Is this not merely the first step towards making Scripture present? Liberal theology had sought to discover the essence of Christianity in order that it might speak to contemporary sensibilities, and because they regarded the essence of Christianity as a universal truth, it had to be expressed in universal terms. For them it was only by expunging Christianity of all historical contingencies that it could be brought into the present. Harnack's project in particular argued that there was a kernel of truth concealed within the scriptural husk, and that one could bring the text into the present only by uncovering the kernel (the essence) and discarding the husk (the original historical contingencies and subsequent developments).[32]

By contrast, Bonhoeffer views the *Sache* of the NT not as an ahistorical kernel of universal truth, but as the present Christ:

> True *Vergegenwärtigung* lies in the question of *Sache*. The *Sache* itself is trusted, that wherever it really comes to word, it is in itself the most present element; it needs then no additional special act of *Vergegenwärtigung*; *Vergegenwärtigung* occurs within the *Sache* itself. However, only because it is *this Sache* that the New Testament is concerned about, because the *Sache* here is Christ and his Word. Wherever Christ comes to word in the word of the New Testament, there is *Vergegenwärtigung*. Not where the present registers its claims before Christ, but rather where the present stands before the claims of Christ, *there is the present*.[33]

---

30. Like *Vergegenwärtigung*, *Sache* is a key term in Bonhoeffer's essay that I have opted to leave untranslated. In DBWE 14, *Sache* receives the idiosyncratic translation of 'substance'. To be sure, Bonhoeffer's meaning could be obscured if it were translated with the more common 'matter' or 'thing'. Bonhoeffer is following Barth's usage, specifically as it appears in the preface to the second edition of his Romans commentary. Barth says that 'a perception of the "inner dialectic of the *Sache*" in the actual words of the text is a necessary and prime requirement for their understanding and interpretation' (Barth, *The Epistle to the Romans*, 10). Bruce McCormack notes that Barth uses *Sache* to denote the real subject matter of Scripture, which is the 'Word in the words' (McCormack, *Karl Barth's Critically Realistic Dialectical Theology*, 270). Bonhoeffer is doing the same, directing attention to the 'What?' of the NT message, to its *Sache* (DBWE 14, 417; DBW 14, 403).

31. DBWE 14, 417; DBW 14, 403.

32. Harnack, *What Is Christianity?*, esp. 1–20.

33. DBW 14, 403–4, my translation; cf. DBWE 14, 417.

Bonhoeffer reorients the question of *Vergegenwärtigung* around the question of *Sache*, and then reinterprets the concept of the present around that *Sache*. In his view, when the *Sache* of the NT is correctly identified (i.e. Christ), it must at once be recognized as inherently contemporary (i.e. *Christus praesens*). His Christology lies beneath this assertion. If the *Sache* of the NT is 'Christ and Christ's word', then readers of Scripture already have to do with the *present* Christ. There is no other Christ than the Christ who is present by virtue of his *pro-me* structure. The being of Christ entails his presence.

In light of these close connections to his 1933 Christology, it is fitting to frame the question of *Vergegenwärtigung* as a 'who' question rather than a 'how' question. The key moment comes relatively early in the essay, when Bonhoeffer says that the false approach to *Vergegenwärtigung* asks about the 'what' of the present, whereas the true approach seeks the 'what' of the Christian message.[34] These two 'what' questions can actually be parsed according to the who–how dichotomy of his Christology. When *Vergegenwärtigung* is primarily concerned with the 'what' of the present, then it consists in answering *how* the NT message can be brought into the present, or perhaps *how* Jesus Christ can become present for us today. On the other hand, when *Vergegenwärtigung* is primarily concerned with the 'what' of the NT message, then it consists in enquiring about *who* is present here in God's word through Scripture. In short, the question of true *Vergegenwärtigung* is this: *Who* is present through the word of Scripture?[35]

Why is it that *Vergegenwärtigung* occurs in the genuine expression of *Sache* of the NT? For Bonhoeffer, genuine expression of the *Sache* does not depend on a particular methodology or any human capacity; it is solely as the Holy Spirit speaks the word of Christ through the word of Scripture that the *Sache* comes to expression. Therein lies the key. The Spirit-mediated presence of Christ by the speaking of Christ's word 'takes place not outside or alongside but only and exclusively *through the word* of Scripture itself'.[36] *Vergegenwärtigung* is not a matter of finding a way to make Scripture speak to contemporary sensibilities; it is a matter of being bound to Scripture in the church, through the proclamation of which the Holy Spirit comes to proclaim the present Christ, and thereby comes to *be* the present Christ. The idea that the text must be made concrete with a contemporary application is a hopeless abstraction, because it fails to recognize that nothing

---

34. DBWE 14, 416–17; DBW 14, 403. An editorial note for the first 'What?' indicates that Bonhoeffer originally framed it as a 'Who?' question, which suggests that he may have had the who–how dichotomy in mind at this point (DBWE 14, 417 ed. n. 27; DBW 14, 403 ed. n. 25).

35. To be sure, this 'who' question can only be asked within the church, where the revelation of Christ's identity and presence is already believed and proclaimed. But this is perfectly in line with Bonhoeffer's insistence that Christology is only possible within the context of revelation, that is, in the church.

36. DBWE 14, 417; DBW 14, 404.

could be more concrete or contemporary than the real Christ present in Spirit-led proclamation. At stake in preaching is nothing less than the mediation of the presence of Christ. Through scriptural proclamation, the Spirit of God mediates Christ's presence, where and where alone God posits the present. To be in the present, for Bonhoeffer, means to be in the presence of the present Christ.

The 'method' of *Vergegenwärtigung* is disarmingly simple: exegesis. Specifically, *Vergegenwärtigung* entails 'exegesis of the only word that has at its disposal the power of *Vergegenwärtigung*: scriptural exegesis'.[37] Scripture's unique suitability for this task entails and is entailed by Bonhoeffer's assertion that the *Sache* of the scriptural message is Christ and Christ's word. Scripture holds the promise of *Vergegenwärtigung* because its *Sache* is the present Christ. Note that this is a presupposition, not an argument. Only God can speak God's word; only the Spirit of Christ can make Christ present. Yet God has, precisely in the exercise of divine freedom, freely bound himself to Holy Scripture. Even though Bonhoeffer views the Bible as a thoroughly human book, he rejects outright the idea that human beings can decide where human words end and God's word begins. Scripture, by virtue of what God does through it, is 'as a whole *the witness* of God in Christ'.[38] It is not a depository of eternal truths, ethical norms or timeless myths; it is the witness to the word of God, which is the present Christ.

How should the preacher approach the word of Scripture in order to allow genuine *Vergegenwärtigung* to occur? Here the category of *witness* is crucial. Bonhoeffer says that everything depends on '*making the whole of Holy Scripture audible as a witness to the word of God*'.[39] All texts from the Bible have this character as witness, and the homiletical task is to make this character audible. The preacher cannot compel God to speak in the sermon, but the preacher can obscure the NT's character as witness. In fact, it is precisely in the misguided attempt to provide a concrete application that the human word can usurp God's word.[40] Preachers who aim to provide a 'concrete application' are generally concerned with the situation of the world inhabited by their congregation or the situation of the people within the congregation. In Bonhoeffer's view, the more concretely the preacher tries to render the situation of human beings, the more obscure their true situation becomes, namely, their situation before God.

How, then, does the preacher make Scripture audible as the witness to the word of God? Bonhoeffer has both an explicit, methodological answer, and an implicit, theological one. Explicitly, the method consists in treating each text as if its chief purpose was and is to proclaim the person and work of Christ – because for Bonhoeffer this is in fact the case. He intends this method for the whole of Scripture, both Testaments, each book, and all literary genres. He is well aware

37. DBW 14, 405, my translation; cf. DBWE 14, 418.
38. DBWE 14, 421; DBW 14, 408.
39. DBWE 14, 421; DBW 14, 409.
40. 'It is so easy for our words to cover up God's word', remarks Bonhoeffer in his lectures on twentieth-century theology (DBWE 11, 228; DBW 11, 196).

that critical scholarship would censure this approach; higher critical methods would study each biblical unit in light of its own original context so that it might be understood according to its original intent and meaning. Bonhoeffer does not reject the validity of the historical-critical approach, but he does relativize it. What historical criticism rightly understands is that the Bible is a human book, containing human words transmitted by human means. That is why historical criticism has its own validity. However, when preachers rely on this method in the pulpit, too often it is the preacher who decides which words in the Bible are human and which are divine, which bits are valid for contemporary listeners and which ones can be disregarded. For Bonhoeffer, 'the word of God and the word of human beings are bound together in the Holy Scriptures, but they are bound together such that God himself states where his word is and that he speaks that word *within the word of human beings*.'[41] The human character of the biblical word does not change in the event of proclamation, nor does the human character of proclamation itself. When God speaks God's word, it is through the human words of the Bible and preaching.

Bonhoeffer's approach also provides an implicit, theological answer to the method of *Vergegenwärtigung*. It emerges as soon as one asks *why* scriptural proclamation holds the promise of Christ's presence. If God is free to speak God's word, why is it through the Bible and the exegetical sermon, rather than, say through 'Russian Communism, a flute concerto, a blossoming shrub, or a dead dog?'[42] The assertion that God speaks through Scripture does not necessarily assert anything about the quality of the Bible itself. Bonhoeffer has emphasized how the biblical text becomes God's word as the Holy Spirit takes up the human event of proclamation; what about the text itself? The key is found in the distinction Bonhoeffer draws between God's freedom *from* human beings and God's freedom *for* human beings. God's absolute freedom from all that is not God stipulates that no created thing has any inherent claim to be an instrument of God's word. In the realm of pure possibility, God *could* speak through any created thing, and the Bible would have no priority over anything else in this regard. But Bonhoeffer does not deal in speculation or counterfactuals. Everything human beings can know about God is made known in God's actual exercise of divine freedom in revelation. And in revelation, 'God freely chose to be bound to historical human beings and to be placed at the disposal of human beings'.[43] So it is consistent with Bonhoeffer's earlier theology to say that God is bound to Scripture, not by any special quality of Scripture itself, but by God's free act of self-limitation, in which he binds himself to the witness of *this* book. The bond between Scripture and revelation is not inspiration but *election*. This is a vital aspect of Bonhoeffer's bibliology. The way he states it in his

---

41. DBWE 14, 421; DBW 14, 408.
42. CD I/1, 55.
43. DBWE 2, 90; DBW 2, 85.

Finkenwalde homiletics is that 'inspiration means that God commits himself to the word spoken by this human being despite all inadequacies'.[44] Thus, in making a claim about what God does through Scripture, Bonhoeffer implies something about what Scripture is.

In all this, Bonhoeffer wants to draw attention to the present-tense character of God's word in Scripture. In doing so, he challenges the idea that real exegetical work consists in bridging the historical gap that lies between the Bible and contemporary Christians. To focus exclusively on the question of how to make these ancient texts present (an accusation Bonhoeffer levels against the *Deutsche Christen*) is to lose sight of the *Sache* of Scripture altogether. The *Sache* does not need to be made present by a separate act of *Vergegenwärtigung*, because the word of Scripture is already a present word. Seen in this light, any attempt to make apparently outdated texts relevant for a modern audience has the paradoxical effect of increasing the distance between Scripture and hearer. Bonhoeffer was keenly aware of the ways in which Christians protected themselves from genuinely encountering God's word in Scripture. Given that he was delivering this lecture to pastors and vicars who had gone through formal theological education, and as one who himself had taught and been taught in that same environment, Bonhoeffer understood that higher biblical criticism had the potential to keep the educated reader of Scripture at a safe distance from the God who speaks therein. That is why he would later advise his Finkenwalde students, in his guide to scriptural meditation, 'Do not worry about incomprehensible passages, and do not flee to philology. This is not the place for the Greek New Testament but for our familiar Luther text.'[45] Using a familiar text like the Luther Bible helps foster the sense that the words of Scripture are not far off and remote, but are near us and for us.

Translation, then, is a key part of making biblical texts present. The textual or historical critic would argue that a translation of Scripture is already too far removed from the 'original' to serve its purpose (as, for that matter, would the defender of verbal inspiration).[46] But for Bonhoeffer, a translation, while one step further from the original text, is one step closer to *Vergegenwärtigung*. Indeed, '*translation* is the first, necessary, legitimate form of *Vergegenwärtigung*'.[47] It is for this reason that the Luther Bible plays a central role in presenting the *Sache* of

---

44. DBWE 14, 493 ed. n. 25; DBW 14, 485 ed. n. 24, recorded notes of a discussion that occurred around the same time as his essay on *Vergegenwärtigung*.

45. DBWE 14, 933; DBW 14, 948.

46. So Bonhoeffer, later in the essay: 'For any doctrine of verbal inspiration, a translation already represents a remove, since only the original text itself is inspired' (DBWE 14, 429; DBW 14, 417).

47. DBWE 14, 429; DBW 14, 417.

Scripture for the German church.[48] In Bonhoeffer's view, for Germany the human words of the Bible are distinctly *German* words: 'For those who are genuinely concerned with the substance [Sache], to wit, with the salvation of their soul, the German Luther Bible, *Luther's translation of the Holy Scriptures into German*, still best fulfills the demand for *Vergegenwärtigung* and *translating the gospel into German*. Here is present [vergegenwärtigtes] Christianity; here is German Christianity.'[49] This does not mean that the Luther Bible automatically works some kind of theological magic on German hearers, nor does it mean that German exegetes are prohibited from working with the original languages or deviating from Luther's translation.[50] Bonhoeffer's point is quite simple: the more we amplify the distance between the ancient world of Scripture and the contemporary world of the church, the more we mute the *Sache* of Scripture. The word is by its very nature a *present* word.

Scripture as witness and word

As I argued in CHAPTER 3, Bonhoeffer exhibited occasionalistic tendencies in his early academic theology, tendencies that were latent in his ecclesiocentric interpretation of revelation. But by the mid-1930s, his bibliology had developed beyond occasionalism. In CHAPTER 4, I showed how Bonhoeffer's 1933 Christology refines his account of revelation-as-*Christus-praesens*. Accordingly, Bonhoeffer's bibliology in the mid-1930s is characterized by a new kind of Christocentrism grounded in his theology of the word. The word, for Bonhoeffer, is the *Sache* of Holy Scripture, and Jesus Christ is both the speaking subject and the content of that word. The words that Christ speaks are nothing other than the words of Holy Scripture. God's word is God's address to human beings, and

---

48. Plant, in 'Uses of the Bible', 37–47, has shown some of the ways in which Bonhoeffer's dependence on the Luther Bible affected his interpretation of biblical texts. As Plant rightly points out, 'translation is not a theologically neutral activity', because it 'always involves theological decisions which interpret, often unconsciously, the meaning of a text' (ibid., 38). This is perhaps nowhere more obvious than Luther's interpretation of Pauline theology, especially his doctrine of salvation by faith alone. It pervades his translation of the New Testament, down to the ordering of the books themselves. It is quite right to say, as Plant does, that 'insofar ... that Bonhoeffer is reliant upon Luther's translation of the Bible, his own theology will certainly be affected by Luther's very particular interpretation of Paul's theology' (ibid., 42).

49. DBWE 14, 416 (translation modified); DBW 14, 403.

50. Bonhoeffer himself feels free to depart from Luther's translation, for example, in his exegesis of Psalm 119, where he occasionally follows Hermann Gunkel against Luther (DBWE 15, 506 ed. n. 36; DBW 15, 510 ed. n. 31). Bonhoeffer also had some facility with the biblical languages. See Plant, 'Uses of the Bible', 43–7.

when God speaks, these are the words he uses. Bonhoeffer's theology of the word, with its Christological, pneumatological and ecclesiological implications, provides the theological framework to account for this. Because Christ is the Logos, he addresses us as logos. The presence of Christ is an *intelligible* presence. It is thereby possible to assert that the witness of Scripture both *teaches* and *is* the present Christ. And yet it is equally important to emphasize that Christ's presence is his *embodied* presence. By the Holy Spirit, the teaching of Scripture grounds the community of the church. *Didache* creates *koinonia*.[51]

As for the relationship between text and revelation, we have already seen that Bonhoeffer's theology of revelation precludes any sense in which God's word could be identified with the biblical text *as such*. The Bible is not revelation. For Bonhoeffer, Scripture is revelation only insofar as the Holy Spirit speaks through it to testify to revelation in Christ. Bonhoeffer maintains this basic distinction between God's word of revelation and the words of canonical Holy Scripture throughout his theological development. But it becomes increasingly clear in his thought that as much as these need to be distinguished, they must never be divided. The Bible is not revelation, but God has bound his self-revealing word to the witness of the prophets and apostles. And, moreover, God has done so in a way that the Bible's semantic content must be taken with utmost seriousness. Christ is present where Christ himself speaks through the Holy Spirit. And, Bonhoeffer says, the speaking of the Spirit 'takes place not outside or alongside but only and exclusively *through the word* of Scripture itself'.[52]

The decisiveness of God's self-revelation in Christ extends to the decisiveness of his witness through the two Testaments of Christian Scripture. The prophets and the apostles testify to Christ, and the Spirit speaks through their testimony in witness to the same Christ. The bond between Scripture and revelation is not inspiration but election. It is grounded in God's free decision. But this does not mean that we should worry about whether or not God will indeed decide to speak through Scripture today. Bonhoeffer has moved beyond an occasional account of revelation in Scripture. Indeed, there could be no more decisive bond between revelation and Scripture than God's own decision. To say that Holy Scripture *is* God's word, then, means that Christ is present as the one who is speaking these words in testimony to himself. By his Spirit, he is present as the speaking subject and the content of these words. Bonhoeffer comes to the Bible in faith that Christ is speaking these words, and these words are speaking of Christ.

There is a close similarity as well as a discernible difference in Bonhoeffer's approach compared with his early theology. He still denies any identification between revelation and the biblical text, still regards the character of Scripture as witness to revelation, still emphasizes the church (word, sacrament and community) as the most essential form of God's coming to us in revelation. But in grounding his account of revelation in the person of Christ, he can express it more

---

51. DBWE 14, 445; DBW 14, 433.
52. DBWE 14, 417; DBW 14, 404.

simply: wherever Christ speaks, Christ is fully there. And if the Holy Spirit speaks through the witness of Scripture, then Christ is there as that very word.

This grounds a stronger ontology of Scripture than was possible with Bonhoeffer's earlier academic writings.[53] God's faithful commitment to Scripture means that these words are to be called God's word. Bonhoeffer avoids the language of Scripture as God's word for the early period of his writings, but it becomes more common after his 1933 Christology.[54] What is explicit in his catechetical outlines is implicit throughout his homiletics, namely, that because God has bound himself to Scripture as the witness to Christ, Scripture *is* God's word. Those who wish to find God should seek him in the pages of Holy Scripture. Scripture is God's word because God has committed himself to speak through it. So, in his practical advice on sermon preparation, Bonhoeffer recommends starting with a prayer for the Holy Spirit to speak through the text. This is to be followed by meditation on the text itself, which is not about exegesis but about meditation on 'the word that has just been spoken'.[55] The preacher can then consider how best to communicate this word to the church. Bonhoeffer believes that the Holy Spirit can and will speak through Holy Scripture even in private meditation.

Bonhoeffer's Finkenwalde writings also exhibit an increasing reverence for the Bible itself. In his catechetical outline, he makes the note, 'We should deal reverently with the Bible: Middle Ages.'[56] The reference to the Middle Ages probably intends to make the same point he makes in his homiletics: 'It is good to reflect occasionally on the time when Bibles were written and illustrated by hand, Bibles in which the name of Jesus was presented with particular devotion and beauty. It is perhaps precisely through its publication that the Bible has become such a despised book.'[57] Bonhoeffer's reverence for the Bible as a physical object reflects

---

53. This is the change perceived in Slot, 'The Freedom of Scripture', 101–22, although I am not convinced that 'canonicity' is the best framework for discussing this change.

54. It can be found in the 'Guide to Scriptural Mediation', which Bonhoeffer co-wrote with Bethge: '*Why do I meditate? Because I am a Christian* and because for that very reason every day is lost to me in which I have not deepened my knowledge of God's word in Holy Scripture' (DBWE 14, 931; DBW 14, 945–6). It also appears in his Finkenwalde catechetical work. In his notes for a 'Lecture Concept for Confirmation Instruction', he provides the following question and answer: '*What is Holy Scripture?* It is God's own word, in which, through the prophets and the apostles, he proclaims to me and to the church-community that Jesus Christ is God's Son and my sav[ior]' (DBWE 14, 785, brackets in original; DBW 14, 789). In his 'Catechetical Outline "Holy Scripture"', he says that Scripture 'is God's own word and will' (DBWE 14, 654; DBW 14, 653). These kinds of statements are nowhere to be found in his 1931 'Draft for a Catechism' which he co-authored with Franz Hildebrandt (DBWE 11, 258–67; DBW 11, 228–37). This catechism contains precious few mentions of the Bible, and aligns more comfortably with his earlier ecclesiocentric bibliology.

55. DBWE 14, 494; DBW 14, 486.

56. DBWE 14, 654; DBW 14, 653.

57. DBWE 14, 517; DBW 14, 510.

his growing sense that in its pages one can hope and expect to find God's witness to Christ. 'If the sermon is a witness only as a witness to the biblical witness, then one must revere the biblical word.'[58] So, not by virtue of its inherent qualities as a collection of human literature, but rather by virtue of God's commitment to this collection, Christians ought to treat the Bible with the same attitude as they would the elements of the sacrament – not because it is holy in and of itself, but because the Holy Spirit is active in and through it.

This is how Holy Scripture is God's word for Bonhoeffer. Not merely because God happens to speak through it from time to time, but because God has bound himself to testify to Christ through the words of this book. And although Bonhoeffer would never separate God's word from the church, he does come to speak of Scripture as God's word apart from its liturgical or homiletical context. God has committed himself to the witness of Scripture, to speak his word through it by the Holy Spirit. And where God's word is, Christ is fully there.

The exegetical 'who' question

In a 1936 letter to Rüdiger Schleicher, Bonhoeffer writes exuberantly about his love for Scripture and discusses his own approach to reading it. In this letter, he writes of his belief that 'God is speaking to us in the Bible'.[59] He continues, 'Thus do I read the Bible. I ask every passage: what is God saying to us here?'[60] He thereby identifies God as the speaker of the biblical words and describes his reading of Scripture as an enquiry into what God is saying in those words. I propose that Bonhoeffer's letter to Schleicher expresses two essential exegetical questions for the reading of Scripture: *Who* is speaking, and *what* is being said?

The primary exegetical question for Bonhoeffer is the 'who' question. *Who* is speaking the words of this text? And since we can only seek what we have already found, it turns out that the church knows the answer to the 'who' question in advance: God in Christ by the Spirit is speaking these words. But, just as certainly as this answer is known, it is likewise the kind of answer that can never be held in the act of knowing it. The 'who' question is the question of transcendence.[61] It 'interrogates the very existence of the one asking it'.[62] It does not enquire about an idea, and so it cannot be answered with an idea. The 'who' question involves the whole person and the whole Christ. It enquires about a person who is really present, whose otherness poses an absolute boundary to the questioner.

The secondary exegetical question is the question of content. *What* is this text saying? This question has two aspects. In the first place, the content of the biblical

---

58. DBWE 14, 535; DBW 14, 529.
59. DBWE 14, 167; DBW 14, 145.
60. DBWE 14, 168; DBW 14, 146.
61. DBWE 12, 305; DBW 12, 286.
62. DBWE 12, 303; DBW 12, 283.

text is identical with the speaker of that text: the crucified and risen Jesus Christ. This is the text's character as *witness*. In the second place, the content of the biblical text is identical with its semantic content: the Holy Spirit testifies to Jesus Christ precisely by speaking *these* words, and not others. Note the difference between asking what a text *says* versus what it *means*. The problem with looking for a meaning in the text goes back to the Barthian problem of God's non-objectivity in revelation. A text's meaning, as distinct from its content, is always an object immanent to human understanding. It is how interpreters take the text and turn it into an object of knowledge. It is on this basis that historical critics lay claim to the biblical text and turn it into purely human words. For Bonhoeffer, Scripture is the word of God's address, and this means that God does not convey meaning through Scripture but rather *speaks* it in Christ by the Spirit. Meaning, Bonhoeffer might say, is word-as-object. Speech, on the other hand, is word-as-encounter. To hear God speak is to encounter the living person of Jesus Christ. To read Scripture as God's witness to revelation is to attend to Jesus himself speaking these words by the Spirit. The goal is not a theological argument or an ethical application; the goal is to encounter the present Christ by hearing the voice of his Spirit.

Thus Bonhoeffer's bibliology suggests two basic exegetical questions: *who* is speaking, and *what* is being said? The first question ensures that God's word in Scripture is never confused with the words of the Bible, and the second ensures that they are never divided. And these questions are mutually interpretive. Bonhoeffer believes that it is only possible to hear what the text is really saying if we learn to hear it from the mouth of Jesus, and that we only learn who is speaking by hearing the words he is speaking to us about himself. The exegetical interplay is between these two questions. What is this text actually saying, given that it is Jesus Christ who is saying it? Who is this Jesus, given that he is speaking this text? Engagement in these questions is what carries Bonhoeffer more deeply into the Bible in the 1930s than he had gone before. It is only in hearing what the text says that we can truly face the question of who is saying this, and it is only in facing the one who speaks these words that we can actually hear the words that are being spoken. Although it is hardly breaking new ground to suggest that Bonhoeffer read the Bible 'christologically', what I aim to emphasize here is the character of his christological exegesis. In his thought, Christology is not what we pull out of the text, but rather what pulls us more deeply into it.

What looks like 'biblicism' on Bonhoeffer's part is actually an extension of his most fundamental theological conviction: revelation is the real presence of Christ, who is God's word. If Scripture is God's witness to revelation, then our task is to hear these words as the very words of Christ in our midst. Bonhoeffer resisted the idea that the proper use of a text was to find its proper meaning. He thought that you could face the text honestly and completely – including the many parts that elude understanding – by facing the crucified and risen Christ as the one who is speaking it. The task of the preacher is not first and foremost to edify or educate or exhort the congregation. The preacher's job is to preach the words of the Bible as the word of the living God. Where God speaks his word, Christ is fully there by the Spirit as the content and subject of God's address.

Within the framework of these two basic questions, Bonhoeffer's bibliology turns out to be quite accommodating to historical-critical methods of interpretation, despite his own misgivings about how these methods were practised. If Jesus is present in speaking the words of the biblical text, then it is perfectly appropriate to attend to the text as carefully as humanly possible. This means that the reader of Scripture may find it quite helpful to deploy the full range of critical tools, so long as these are aimed at a better understanding of the text, rather than at putting the text to some other use. But these tools will never be strictly necessary for faithful reading, and, in Bonhoeffer's opinion, they often get in the way. Hearing God speak through the human words of the Bible includes the demanding task of 'understanding' the human words of Scripture in their full humanity, which is the domain of historical criticism. The danger of these methods, from Bonhoeffer's perspective, is their tendency to treat Scripture as a dead letter. Bonhoeffer describes God's word as fully alive, since this word is 'the Resurrected One who has overcome death'.[63] Therefore, the 'meaning' of a text can be abstracted neither from the text itself nor from the one who speaks it. In this way, Holy Scripture is irreducibly God's word.

Because the 'who' question can only be asked in Christ's presence, it is important to locate the task of exegesis in the church. The community who reads the Bible as God's word is the church. Their communal identity is shaped by this reading, which is guided by the Spirit who ministers the words of Scripture as the word of God. Because the word is the word made flesh, the exegetical questions occur in and are directed towards the church. Bonhoeffer eschewed the 'application' question, but that doesn't mean he thought Scripture was impractical. The 'practical' question for Bonhoeffer was: how does this word that we have heard and understood take form among us as the church of Jesus Christ? In this way, Bonhoeffer's Finkenwalde exegesis involves an interplay between the word's intelligibility and its embodiment, between Scripture as *didache* and Scripture as *Christus praesens*. If this interplay were lost, then revelation would lose its character as revelation. Intelligibility without embodiment would turn Scripture into an object of human knowledge; embodiment without intelligibility would turn it into an object of human religiosity. Christ is present in and for the community grounded in the proclamation of Scripture as the witness to the present Christ. There is no hearing and believing of this witness apart from this community, no community apart from this hearing and believing.

What of truth and intelligibility? It is precisely Bonhoeffer's refusal to separate Christ's presence as word from the semantic content of the biblical text that legitimizes the task of exegesis. Exegesis, he says, 'means to recognize and understand God's word in Scripture as God's word'.[64] And we cannot hear the word as 'word' except in recognizing it in its intelligibility. To hear Jesus speak to us is to understand the words being spoken. It does not require that we *comprehend* the

---

63. DBWE 12, 305; DBW 12, 285.
64. DBWE 15, 517; DBW 15, 524.

full scope of what or who is addressing us. The task of exegesis is never complete. But speech is only speech if it is intelligible. For Bonhoeffer, Christ does not meet us in the form of a vague, indefinable *sensus divinitatis* or a wordless warming of the heart. Because Christ is the Logos, he meets us in our logos. The perspicuity of Scripture is grounded in the 'clarity and lack of ambiguity' that is the 'essence of the word'.[65] It is not because the words are so easy to understand, but because where the word is, he is fully there as the comprehensible and embodied word. This is the ministry of the 'Spirit of understanding'. And the word that the Spirit ministers to create and sustain the church as a community of shared understanding comes to us in the words of Holy Scripture.

Finally, because the exegetical 'who' question concerns a real encounter with Jesus Christ, the one who is in himself *pro-me*, it is not unfitting to frame it as a question of relation. In Bonhoeffer's Christology, 'the being of Christ's person is essentially relatedness to me'.[66] The exegetical extension of this would be to venture the 'who' question as follows: As the one who is speaking the words of this text, who is Christ for me today?[67] This question is not exhaustive, but it is a valid entry point, and it holds to Bonhoeffer's insistence that 'Christ can only be Christ *pro-me*'.[68] I will demonstrate in upcoming chapters that to ask the exegetical 'who' question of the biblical psalms, for example, is to ask about Jesus who is our *mediator*. And to ask the same question of biblical law is to ask about Christ who is our *Lord*. It is not that Jesus ceases to be our Lord when he acts as our mediator, or vice versa. But learning to hear the myriad words of the Bible as God's word spoken about and by Christ himself means learning to encounter Christ in the fullness of his being *pro-me*. Thus, a Bonhoefferian exegesis will explore the interplay between the 'who' question and the question of content. It is the present Christ who is here speaking these words, and these words are always speaking of Christ.

---

65. DBWE 12, 316; DBW 12, 297.
66. DBWE 12, 314; DBW 12, 295.
67. Here I am anticipating Bonhoeffer's question from prison: 'Who is Christ actually for us today?' (DBWE 8, 362; DBW 8, 402).
68. DBWE 12, 314; DBW 12, 296.

Part II

EXEGESIS

6

PRAYING THE PSALMS

The Psalter occupies a special place in Bonhoeffer's theological imagination. My goal in this chapter and the next is to draw out two significant connections between Bonhoeffer's bibliology and his exegesis of the Psalms. In the next chapter, I will discuss the relationship between *Christus praesens* and transformation in light of Bonhoeffer's 'Meditation on Psalm 119'. In this chapter, I examine Bonhoeffer's Finkenwalde writings, lectures and sermons on the Psalms in order to explore the connection between *Christus praesens* and prayer.[1] The Psalter is, as Bonhoeffer puts it, the 'prayerbook of the Bible',[2] and as such it is God's word in a unique way. In the Psalms, God's word to human beings takes the form of human words to God. Because of this distinctive characteristic, Bonhoeffer's use of the Psalms must be understood in light of his theology of prayer – and indeed it is in the context of his engagement with the Psalms that he most clearly expresses his theology of prayer. Learning to hear God's word in the form of human prayer begins with learning what it means for human beings to pray.

All prayer, in Bonhoeffer's view, is grounded in the mediation of Christ. Looking more specifically at the prayers of the Psalter, Bonhoeffer argues for another, more controversial, assertion: 'Because Christ was in David, Christ speaks in the Psalms.'[3] Although this statement attracted the criticisms of Bonhoeffer's contemporaries and his later interpreters, I will demonstrate that it is theologically consistent with his theology of revelation-as-*Christus-praesens*. I will then sketch the contours of Bonhoeffer's Christological exegesis of the Psalms, showing that his reading

---

1. For more comprehensive studies of Bonhoeffer's interpretation of the Psalms, see Brad Pribbenow, *Prayerbook of Christ: Dietrich Bonhoeffer's Christological Interpretation of the Psalms* (Lanham, MD: Lexington Books/Fortress Academic, 2018); Kuske, *The Old Testament as the Book of Christ*. For a shorter and theologically insightful introduction to Bonhoeffer's use of the Psalms, see Wolf Krötke, 'Dietrich Bonhoeffer's Exegesis of the Psalms', in *Karl Barth and Dietrich Bonhoeffer: Theologians for a Post-Christian World*, trans. John P. Burgess (Grand Rapids: Baker Academic, 2019), 177–89.

2. As per the title of his short book, *Prayerbook of the Bible* (DBWE 5, 141–218; DBW 5, 107–32).

3. DBWE 14, 393; DBW 14, 377.

of canonical psalms is directed towards hearing them as the prayers of Jesus and speaking them as the prayers of the church. This is grounded in his bibliological commitment to Christ's present word as the historical locus of revelation. Of the sermons that have been preserved from Bonhoeffer's Finkenwalde years, three are on the Psalms. Each demonstrates, in its own way, Bonhoeffer's ongoing attempt to hear God's speaking in the Psalter by learning to pray the psalms in and with the church, in and with Jesus Christ. As the 'prayerbook of the Bible' the Psalter is heard as a witness to Christ when and where the church recognizes and takes up these words in participation with Christ's own praying of them. Where Christ prays, there he is fully present.

Whose prayers are they anyway?

Bonhoeffer rejects the notion that prayer is 'simply pouring out one's heart'; it is, rather, 'finding the way to and speaking with God'.[4] This way is Jesus Christ, the Mediator. Christian prayer is therefore *mediated* prayer. Prayer does not come naturally to the human heart, nor does the human mind know what or how it ought to pray. For Bonhoeffer, any attempt to ignore or circumvent the mediation of Christ in prayer means that we have not understood our situation before God. We do not have immediate access to God: 'It is not simply a religious given that we can come to God in prayer but rather is made possible alone through Christ.'[5] We cannot come before the Father except as the Son brings us before him. For that reason, 'our prayer is bound prayer',[6] bound to Jesus Christ and to the witness of Scripture. Everything depends on the presupposition that 'God remains the one doing the speaking, the subject, that it is the Word of God, that is, the prayer of the high priest Jesus Christ'.[7] Bonhoeffer upholds Christ as the speaking subject of Christian prayer.

This becomes the theological basis for hearing the Psalms as God's word. If the speaking of God's word entails the personal presence of Jesus Christ as the content and speaker of that word, then the Psalms testify to God's word in a unique way. For Bonhoeffer, the Psalter's presence in the canon means 'that not only the word which God has to say to us belongs to the Word of God, but also the word which God wants to hear from us, because it is the word of God's dear Son'.[8] This casts new light on Bonhoeffer's theology of revelation. The previous chapters focused mainly on God's word as God's address to human beings, but in Bonhoeffer's reflections on the Psalms and Christian prayer, it becomes clear that God's word includes the address of human beings to God – provided this address is bound to the particular

---

4. DBWE 5, 155; DBW 5, 107.
5. DBWE 14, 388; DBW 14, 371.
6. DBWE 14, 388; DBW 14, 371.
7. DBWE 14, 388; DBW 14, 372.
8. DBWE 5, 157; DBW 5, 109.

human being called Jesus Christ. That is why Christians pray in the name of Jesus. Bonhoeffer certainly does not regard the invocation of Christ's name as a magical incantation, which somehow seizes control of divine activity in prayer. Prayer in Jesus's name 'is a reference not to a formula but to substance'.[9] Jesus Christ is the substance of prayer. As the Mediator, he is at the Father's right hand, interceding on our behalf. The church offers prayer 'in Jesus' name' precisely because it cannot offer prayer in its own name.

If Christian prayer is mediated by Christ, then the Psalter, as the prayerbook of the Bible, is first and foremost the book of Christ. But it is Christ's book in a special sense, because the Psalter is uniquely *Davidic*; it is David's book. Bonhoeffer does not ground this perspective in a commitment to Davidic authorship, but rather in recognition that Scripture itself connects King David and the Psalter. Not only is David directly or indirectly associated with the majority of the Psalms,[10] but, according to Bonhoeffer, 'no psalm from before the time of [David's] anointing has been handed down to us'.[11] Even psalms that have no apparent connection with David are, in that sense, *Davidic*. To hear the witness of Holy Scripture to Christ in the Psalter, then, requires careful attention to the biblical witness to David.

On this topic, Walter Harrelson offers a rather scathing evaluation: 'Bonhoeffer's ... biblical studies, illuminating though they are, also raise many problems. His study of David seems to be the worst of the lot.'[12] The study in question originated at Finkenwalde in October 1935, later published in *Junge Kirche* in 1936, but the same points can be found in his lecture on 'Christ in the Psalms' and in *Prayerbook of the Bible*. 'According to the witness of the Bible', Bonhoeffer says, 'David, as the anointed king of the chosen people of God, is a prototype of Jesus Christ'.[13] Christ is the descendant of David according to the *flesh* and according to the *promise*. 'According to the flesh' does not require a purely biological interpretation, since, as Bonhoeffer points out, biology breaks off at Joseph in the genealogy of Jesus. But the Davidic line 'according to the flesh' is the recipient of the promise, for which reason David's flesh and that of his offspring are never a trivial matter. The promise was made to David and his biological descendants. In a general sense, the incarnate Christ bears the flesh of David in bearing all human flesh, but Jesus specifically bears the

---

9. DBWE 14, 388; DBW 14, 371.
10. According to Bonhoeffer, 'of the 150 psalms, 73 are attributed to King David, 12 to the choir-master Asaph appointed by David, 12 to the levitical family of the children of Korah working under David, 2 to King Solomon, and one to each of the master musicians, Heman and Ethan, probably working under David and Solomon. So it is understandable that the name of David has been connected with the Psalter in special ways' (DBWE 5, 158; DBW 5, 110).
11. DBWE 5, 158; DBW 5, 110.
12. Harrelson, 'Bonhoeffer and the Bible', 125.
13. DBWE 5, 158; DBW 5, 110.

flesh of David by appearing in David's family tree ancestrally, if not genetically. 'According to the promise' describes the prophetic connection that Scripture draws between David and the Messiah, namely God's covenantal promise to David that his 'throne shall be established forever'.[14] David knows that he will beget the Messiah and even prophesies about the resurrection.[15] The Messiah fulfils the promise of David's everlasting rule and so inherits David's kingly office. The coming of the messianic king is the return of the Davidic king. 'Hence wherever the New Testament witness is taken seriously, any exposition of the stories of David must thus understand David in his person, his office, his words, and his stories as the one *in whom according to the witness of the New Testament Christ himself was present*, as a model and shadow of Christ.'[16] For Bonhoeffer, '*Christ was in reality in David according to the flesh and the promise – and David was his witness.*'[17]

Bonhoeffer's treatment of the Old Testament in Finkenwalde, and especially his work on the David–Christ connection, attracted criticism from all sides. Biblical scholars thought he was doing away with historical criticism and thereby disregarding the historicity of the biblical text. Theologians feared that he was reverting to a version of the 'orthodox thesis' of verbal inspiration, which Bonhoeffer himself had directly condemned not long before in his lecture, 'Christ in the Psalms'. The orthodox thesis, he says, '*postulates* that the I of the psalms is the voice of Christ in Christ's Old Testament community [Gemeinde]'.[18] This, perhaps surprisingly, makes the Psalter more fragile from a historical-critical perspective, because any suggestion that it was not actually David who penned the psalm is simultaneously an accusation against its divine inspiration. Martin Kuske worries that Bonhoeffer's study of King David, completed only a few months later, comes dangerously close to subverting his critique of the verbal inspiration. For Kuske, Bonhoeffer had 'abandoned the course' that he previously set in his lecture on the Psalms, 'and followed another which is not practicable for us, because it relativizes historical-critical research too much and speaks of a "personal presence" of Christ in the Old Testament'.[19] Kuske is not objecting to the idea of a Christological interpretation of the Old Testament, but rather to the idea of a 'personal presence' of Christ in the historical David. Martin Hohmann objected to this even more

---

14. 2 Sam. 7.16; cf. 7.4-17.
15. Bonhoeffer cites Acts 2.30-31 in this connection; see DBWE 5, 158–9; DBW 5, 110; DBWE 14, 872; DBW 14, 879.
16. DBWE 14, 874; DBW 14, 882.
17. DBWE 14, 872; DBW 14, 879.
18. DBWE 14, 390; DBW 14, 373.
19. Kuske, *The Old Testament as the Book of Christ*, 81.

strongly than Kuske.[20] If this personal presence is the basis for reading the Psalter as the prayer of Christ, then, it would seem, everything hinges on the Davidic authorship of any given psalm, on the genuine Davidic origin of all things by which David testifies to Christ.[21]

Is Bonhoeffer's account an intelligible position, or does it subvert some of his former insights? Does, for example, his insistence that Christ speaks in the Psalms because Christ was 'in' David not require a version of verbal inspiration? Does this not pin Christ's speaking in the Psalms to Christ's 'pre-incarnate' existence in the historical King David? These are questions not only of later interpreters like Kuske; Bonhoeffer's contemporaries raised similar concerns. For example, in 1936, Gerhard von Rad, citing Bonhoeffer's statement that David knew that he

---

20. Hohmann, *Die Korrelation von Altem und Neuem Bund*, 94–6. Hohmann objects to what he regards as pure 'eisegesis', of reading something (in this case, Christ) *into* the Old Testament that manifestly is not to be found there. In his view, Bonhoeffer inexplicably switched between a 'real presence' and a 'personal presence' of Christ in the Old Testament. The former can be acceptable – and indeed must be accounted for – but the latter is problematic to the point of being incomprehensible: '"Christ was in David" and its converse are statements that we cannot understand. Here the historical-critical exegesis against Bonhoeffer is correct' (ibid., 94). Hohmann cites Kuske at this point, who was likewise sceptical about 'personal presence' in a way that he wasn't about 'real presence'. The distinction between real and personal presence comes from Gerhard von Rad, *Fragen der Schriftauslegung im Alten Testament* (Leipzig: Deichertsche, 1938), 7ff. (cited in Kuske, *The Old Testament as the Book of Christ*, 67). Stephen Plant offers a helpful discussion of Bonhoeffer's correlation between the Old and New Testament in relation to the correlation between the ultimate and the penultimate his *Ethics*. See Plant, 'Uses of the Bible', 132–8. Plant observes that not only is there a double movement between the two testaments, 'but also a resolution in the personal presence of Christ within the penultimate' (ibid., 133).

21. It should be noted that Kuske's discussion does not take into account Bethge's concluding notes for the lecture, 'Christ in the Psalms', which show that Bonhoeffer was already thinking in terms of Christ's being 'in David'. Bethge's notes record the following discussion of Psalm 22, which Jesus quotes (Ps. 22.1) in his cry of dereliction from the cross (Matt. 27.46; Mark 15.34), and Hebrews 2.12 cites Psalm 22.22 as Jesus's own words: 'According to the Psalms, David speaking. According to the New Testament, Christ speaks; Heb. 2.12. *Because Christ was in David, Christ speaks in the Psalms*, hence Psalms of David' (DBWE 14, 393, my emphasis; DBW 14, 377). These notes are found in DBWE 14, 393; DBW 14, 377, but are not included in Dietrich Bonhoeffer, *Theologie-Gemeinde; Vorlesungen, Briefe, Gespräche, 1927 bis 1944*, vol. 3 (Munich: Kaiser, 1966), 294–302, which was the basis for Kuske's research. Bonhoeffer makes the same references in his study of David: 'Hence the New Testament quite naturally reads the words of the psalms of *David* as the *words of Christ*' (DBWE 14, 872, citing Heb. 2.12 [cf. Ps. 22]; DBW 14, 880). So the radical break that Kuske posits between the July lecture on the Psalms and the October study of King David is not supported by the textual evidence.

was bearing Christ in his loins and even knew about the resurrection, reacted like this: 'So there is – and apparently deliberately – something said by the texts that they do not want to say. Who can understand that?'[22] To von Rad, Bonhoeffer is reading directly against the grain of the Old Testament texts. And, to be sure, if reading with the grain means reading in a way that the original recipients of the text would have understood, then von Rad's criticism is well founded. But this is never Bonhoeffer's primary concern. For him, the grain of Scripture runs towards Christ, so reading with the grain always means reading Christologically.

As for the problem of relating Christ and David historically, it is important to remember that Bonhoeffer's interest in any biblical passage never lies in reconstructing history; his interest in Scripture concerns its witness to Christ in the present. This is not to say that Bonhoeffer posits Scripture against history or regards them in mutually exclusive terms. But in saying that Christ is present in the person and the office of David, Bonhoeffer prioritizes David's person and office as narratively rendered in the testimony of Scripture. His concern is always the capacity of the biblical account of David to bear contemporary witness to Jesus Christ. Christians rightly read David as the 'model and shadow' of Christ, not because Christ was historically pre-incarnate in David, but because Scripture testifies to David as the one to whom God has promised an everlasting, messianic kingdom. David's person and office, his psalms and stories have been passed down to the church through Scripture alone, which means that it is included in God's witness to the incarnate, crucified and risen Christ. So, 'David is important only insofar as he is a witness to Christ, not *in and for himself*, but for Christ and therefore for the church of Christ'.[23] It can hardly be supposed that Bonhoeffer has anything like a doctrine of verbal inspiration in mind here. Kuske's concern is that Bonhoeffer pins the Psalter's capacity to speak of Christ on something inherently true about the historical man David. This would certainly be out of character for Bonhoeffer, who consistently rejects any hint that revelation can inhere in a creaturely reality. But Kuske and Hohmann both overlook the connection Bonhoeffer draws between the speaking of Christ and the personal presence of Christ; thus, they miss the present-tense character of David's witness and invert Bonhoeffer's theological logic. Not: Christ was in David; therefore, David's words were actually Christ's words. But rather: Christ *speaks* in David; therefore, Christ *is* in David.

This is not to reduce the 'in' to a purely occasional interpretation. Bonhoeffer regards God's promise to David as having real, historical significance. Because God elected David to be the progenitor of the Messiah, a Christian reading of David must always include his being the 'model and shadow' of Christ. But this interpretation is necessarily retrospective. 'It is the incarnation that casts its

---

22. Gerhard von Rad, 'Sensus Scripturae Sacrae duplex? Ein Erwiderung', *Theologische Blätter* (1936), 32.

23. DBWE 14, 874; DBW 14, 882.

shadow on David',[24] not the other way around. We can seek only what we have already found, as Bonhoeffer often says. It must not be forgotten that Bonhoeffer's aim in his Bible study on King David is exegetical. On the cover sheet, he states, 'The following offers a guide for Christians, preachers, and teachers for correctly reading the books of Samuel … It is at the same time a practical exegetical contribution to the problem of Christ in the Old Testament.'[25] It is his attempt to show how the person and office, the words and stories of David in the Old Testament are to be read in the church as the witness to Christ. 'The God of the Old Testament', Bonhoeffer continues, 'is the father of Jesus Christ. The incarnate God in Jesus Christ is the God of the Old Testament. It is a triune God.'[26] For this reason, 'The Old Testament must be read from the perspective of the incarnation and cross, i.e., from the perspective of the revelation given to us', which means that 'the people and stories of the Old Testament are not moral models but rather witnesses to the election and promise of God'.[27] King David deserves special treatment because God elected to use him in a special way in the economy of salvation. From the retrospective position of the church, David in the Old Testament cannot be separated from Jesus in the New. If Jesus came in fulfilment of God's promise to David, as the messianic 'new David', then this reality ought to project backwards onto the church's interpretation of David in the days before fulfilment. Indeed, all Old Testament stories and figures are rightly interpreted only when they are rightly located in the history of God's election and promise fulfilled in Christ. Thus to the question of who prays the Psalter, Bonhoeffer responds: 'David … prays. Christ prays. We pray.'[28]

The psalms are heard as the witness to Christ as they are made recognizable as the prayers and the praying of Jesus. And where Christ speaks, including his prayers offered to his Father on our behalf, he is fully there. This perspective, however, is the beginning rather than the conclusion of Bonhoeffer's exegesis of the Psalter. His concern at Finkenwalde is not to promote this or that theological

---

24. DBWE 14, 873; DBW 14, 881.
25. DBWE 14, 871 ed. n. 2; DBW 14, 878 ed. n. 2.
26. DBWE 14, 871 ed. n. 2; DBW 14, 878 ed. n. 2.
27. DBWE 14, 871 ed. n. 2; DBW 14, 878 ed. n. 2.
28. DBWE 5, 160; DBW 5, 112. This distinctly Christian and Christological approach to Israel's Scripture undoubtedly raises objections over Bonhoeffer's potential to contribute to post-holocaust Jewish–Christian dialogue. It is worth noting here that Bonhoeffer's affirmation of the Old Testament as Christian Scripture was accompanied by his affirmation of the Jewish people. It is particularly telling that some of his harshest critics were just as offended – if not more so – by Bonhoeffer's supposedly anachronistic reading of the Old Testament as by his 'inclusion of Jewish thought and essence' into Christianity (Friedrich Baumgärtel, *Die Kirche ist Eine – die alttestamentlich-jüdische Kirche und die Kirche Jesu Christi? Eine Verwahrung gegen die Preisgabe des Alten Testaments* [Greifswald: Universitätsverlag Ratsbuchhandlung L. Bamberg, 1936], 16). I discuss this issue in CHAPTER 8. Krötke makes this point in 'Bonhoeffer's Exegesis of the Psalms'.

outlook, but to help his students learn to read Scripture as God's word for today and to show them how to proclaim and teach the same in their future congregations. So, while Bonhoeffer's Christocentric theology of Scripture might at first appear to be reductionistic, perhaps even deserving of the label 'Christomonism', a closer look at his exegetical work reveals otherwise. In actual practice, Bonhoeffer's Christological exegetical lens has an expansive rather than a reductive effect. Christology is not something he pulls out of the text, but rather something that pulls him more deeply into it.

Psalm 42 as the prayer of the church

As the following examples show, for Bonhoeffer it is precisely as Christ is perceived as the word and the *Sache* of Scripture – in this case as the speaking subject of the Psalms – that the text itself fully comes to expression. Hearing these prayers as the very words of Christ means hearing them more clearly and, in a way, more literally. It means confronting them head-on instead of sidestepping tricky passages. It also means learning to make the Psalms the prayers of the church. For Bonhoeffer, psalms can be heard as God's word precisely as the church learns to pray them. As his use of the Psalter during and after Finkenwalde demonstrates, Bonhoeffer's primary concern is that the church prays the Psalms in and with Jesus Christ. Rendered to God in Christ by the intercessory work of the Holy Spirit, these human words become God's very word to and for his church today.

It is not enough simply to teach the congregation to understand a psalm; the most fitting way to hear God's word in a psalm is for the church to pray it. That seems to have been Bonhoeffer's perspective when he preached on Psalm 42 in Zingst on 2 June 1935. This was shortly before his lecture, 'Christ in the Psalms' (31 July 1935), and indeed the sermon works as a practical application of what he would say there: 'There is no access to a psalm other than through prayer; that is to say, insofar as the church-community itself appropriates the words of a psalm by praying it.'[29] Both the content and the structure of Bonhoeffer's homily reflect his intention not merely to explain how the church could make Psalm 42 its own prayer, but actually to lead the congregation in praying it. For each verse in the psalm, Bonhoeffer follows the same pattern: (1) he reads the verse, (2) briefly expounds its meaning, especially its Christological significance, (3) offers a short prayer and (4) leads the congregation in song. This structure is unique among Bonhoeffer's extant sermons and is worth exploring in further detail.

(1) The basic verse-by-verse framework is certainly not unique. It is Bonhoeffer's preferred way to arrange a sermon. In his lectures on homiletics, he says that 'the text should provide the structure for a sermon', which is why the *homily* – that is, a sermon ordered in a verse-by-verse arrangement – 'is the most appropriate

---

29. DBWE 14, 387; DBW 14, 370.

form of textual interpretation'.[30] This comes through in his sermon on Psalm 42. He follows his own recommendation to 'begin with the beginning of the text and conclude with its conclusion'.[31] He does not pick out a theme and work out how the text supports or expresses it. He simply moves from one verse to the next, beginning at the first and ending at the last, exhibiting what he believes is 'unqualified confidence in the text'.[32]

(2) Each verse is followed by a short exposition. Here his Christological lens is on full display. He interprets the yearning for God in v. 1 as the longing for the God made known in Christ, citing his oft-repeated refrain: 'We can search for God properly only if God has already been revealed to us'.[33] The desire to see the face of God in v. 2 means learning to see God in the face of the crucified one. 'Where is your God?' asks v. 3, to which Bonhoeffer replies in his paraphrase of Luther, 'To this man [Jesus] you should point and say: that is God'.[34] The throng and the multitude in v. 4 are the church, the community of those who call on Christ. At v. 7, Bonhoeffer reminds his hearers that Jesus is the one who commands the wind and the sea. The wounds and mockery in v. 10 point to God's presence in the cross of Christ, so that 'God is closest to us precisely when we think God is farthest away'.[35] Throughout his exposition, Bonhoeffer does not concern himself with the psalm's original context, intended audience or *sitz im Leben*. There is no distance between the congregation and the psalmist. The words of one are the words of the other. And when he does this, the distinction between original author and contemporary hearer fades away.

(3) After each verse's explanation, Bonhoeffer prays. His prayers always resemble the verse that he is expounding, either as a paraphrase or as a variation on the theme. In most cases, the prayer builds on the preceding exposition, so that it makes sense in light of his interpretation. For example, in response to v. 4, he prays, 'God, Holy Spirit, send me Christian brothers with whom I can share faith and prayer, with whom I can bear everything laid upon me. Lead me back to your church, to your word, and to the Holy Lord's Supper. Amen'.[36] This prayer might not seem like a fitting response to v. 4, which recalls the joy of people keeping festival and processing to the house of God together. But Bonhoeffer has already reminded his hearers that fellowship with God cannot be disconnected from fellowship with Christ or the community of Christ. Bonhoeffer's prayer for fellowship, word and sacrament thereby expresses the same prayer as the psalmist: the prayer for fellowship with God in the fellowship of God's people. In other verses, the content of Bonhoeffer's prayer does not explicitly recall the exposition, but is nevertheless enriched by it. For example, in response to v. 2 Bonhoeffer prays, 'Lord, we long to

---

30. DBWE 14, 498; DBW 14, 490.
31. DBWE 14, 498; DBW 14, 490.
32. DBWE 14, 499; DBW 14, 491.
33. DBWE 14, 847; DBW 14, 852.
34. DBWE 14, 848; DBW 14, 854.
35. DBWE 14, 853; DBW 14, 859.
36. DBWE 14, 849; DBW 14, 855.

see you face to face.'³⁷ His Christological answer to the question about beholding God's face is not required to pray this, but if, as he argues, we truly see God in the face of the crucified Messiah, then the prayer takes on a new meaning. We do not ask that God show himself to us in a new way, but rather that we would learn to see God in the way he has already given to us, namely, the cross of Christ.

(4) The heading of Psalm 42 indicates that it is 'to be sung', and Bonhoeffer takes this literally. He concludes each section of his homily with a stanza from a hymn – related thematically to the verse at hand – which the congregation was to sing together. Bonhoeffer regarded the Psalter not only as the Bible's prayer book but also as its hymnal.[38] Christians sing psalms together because the Bible contains this book of songs. What's more, Christians sing psalms because 'in singing together it is possible for them to speak and pray the same Word at the same time.'[39] It is the best expression of the church's unity in prayer, prayer grounded in God's word and offered by the whole community. Music is a synchronous communal act. Words that are sung are sung together. The congregation follows the repetitions, rhythm and tempo of the hymn, speaking together as one voice, united in tune and time.[40] Music enforces its time on the congregation who prays in song: 'That which seems to be unnecessary repetition to us, who are accustomed to praying too hurriedly, is in fact true submersion in, and concentration on, the prayer.'[41] Singing a psalm, for Bonhoeffer, is the most appropriate form of communal prayer. Although Bonhoeffer does not lead the congregation in a verbatim antiphonal performance of Psalm 42, his use of thematically related hymns produces a very similar result.

As a whole, in both structure and content, Bonhoeffer's sermon aims to make Psalm 42 the prayer of the church – not only to raise the possibility but actually to bring it to reality as an integral part of the sermon structure. Bonhoeffer asks rhetorically, 'How are you to understand *what you have not yet prayed*?'[42] Although he does offer some exposition of Psalm 42, his goal is not that the congregation understands it but simply that they pray it. And not just that they leave the Sunday morning service with the exhortation to pray it, but that they actually pray it, then and there. But this was not the only way he sought to make the Psalms the church's prayer. He takes a different approach when he preaches on Psalm 90, and for good reason.

Praying Psalm 90 with the saints

The Bonhoeffer family gathered, as was their annual custom, to celebrate the New Year of 1936. Their New Year's Eve festivities always included a reading from

---

37. DBWE 14, 848; DBW 14, 853.
38. DBWE 5, 160–1; DBW 5, 113–14.
39. DBWE 5, 66; DBW 5, 50.
40. In DBWE 5, 66–8; DBW 5, 50–3, Bonhoeffer specifically advocates singing in unison.
41. DBWE 5, 161; DBW 5, 114. See also Harvey, *Taking Hold of the Real*, 242–5.
42. DBWE 14, 387; DBW 14, 370.

Psalm 90. They would not have known that only two weeks later Bonhoeffer would be preaching from this same psalm at the funeral service of his grandmother, Julie Bonhoeffer. She fell sick with pneumonia after Christmas that year and had succumbed to it quickly. Her death notice says that she 'died peacefully after a serious illness in her ninety-fourth year after a life lived up to the very end with spiritual vivacity'.[43] Describing her as spiritually vivacious was not hyperbole. One of the more memorable stories told of her is how, at the age of ninety-one, she openly defied the recent boycott of Jewish businesses, walking staunchly past a group of Nazi Storm Troopers to shop at the Jewish-owned department store, 'Kaufhaus des Westens'.[44] Bethge describes her as possessing 'revolutionary zeal', having 'inherited the alert critical sensibilities of her ancestors'.[45] She and Bonhoeffer corresponded regularly until the end of her life.[46]

As important as Psalm 90 was for his whole family, Bonhoeffer may have held it in an extra special connection with his grandmother. In a letter to her a few years earlier, he had quoted from Psalm 90.12: 'I've been thinking recently that by the time one is your age and has seen so many things come and go, one "may gain a wise heart," as the Bible says, and take a longer perspective.'[47] It was also a psalm that held special resonances for him on the topics of death and resurrection. In *Prayerbook of the Bible*, Bonhoeffer cites Psalm 90 in connection with both: 'Death is indeed the irreversible bitter end for body and soul. It is the wages of sin, and this must not be forgotten (Pss. 39, 90). But on the other side of death is the eternal God (Pss. 90, 102).'[48]

An examination of Bonhoeffer's sermon on Psalm 90 must therefore take into account its uniquely personal occasion and tone. It must also treat it in accordance with its more general occasion, being, as it is, a *funeral* sermon. Bonhoeffer instructed his Finkenwalde students on presiding over funeral services, which included special instructions about funeral sermons. He offers two guidelines that are relevant here. Firstly, for the burial of the Christian, the pastor must 'offer thanks for the person's life, recall the person's status as a Christian as well as the service the person rendered at home, at work, and in the church-community'.[49] Secondly, the pastor must offer 'the consolation of the gospel, not in a general sense but in reference to this particular deceased person in Christ'.[50] It is not clear from the student notes whether Bonhoeffer indicated how this is to be done in

---

43. DBWE 14, 127; DBW 14, 104.
44. This story is recounted in DB-ER, 11 and in Ferdinand Schlingensiepen, *Dietrich Bonhoeffer 1906–1945: Martyr, Thinker, Man of Resistance*, trans. Isabel Best (London: T&T Clark, 2010), 8.
45. DB-ER, 12.
46. Her last known letter to him is dated 24 October 1935; Bonhoeffer's reply is not extant.
47. DBWE 13, 59; DBW 13, 52 (letter dated 21 December 1933).
48. DBWE 5, 176; DBW 5, 131.
49. DBWE 14, 742; DBW 14, 746.
50. DBWE 14, 743; DBW 14, 746.

reference to a particular scriptural text, nor if he made any direct connection between the theology of preaching found in his homiletics lectures and the special case of preaching for a funeral service. In any case, a funeral is an occasion where preaching is rightly focused on a single individual in a way that would be inappropriate in the other preaching contexts. To be sure, it is still addressed *to* the congregation, but its content is driven by the particularities of the life that has departed. If the substance of the sermon is Christ's speaking through the witness of the biblical text, then the substance of the funeral sermon is Christ's speaking through the witness of the deceased.

Nevertheless, this does not mean that the funeral sermon is to be detached from Scripture. The example of Bonhoeffer's homily for his grandmother demonstrates this in a unique and remarkable way. In keeping with his pattern of preaching the Psalter as the church's 'prayerbook', he preaches Psalm 90 as the prayer of Julie Bonhoeffer, who prayed in Christ, and whose life invites all who knew her to pray this psalm in Christ with her. One of the features of this sermon is that Bonhoeffer really does preach through the psalm, quoting from seven of the seventeen verses, and doing so in sequence. At each point, he recalls different aspects of his grandmother's life, aiming to show how these words can be heard as her own prayers. Thus, it would seem, it is not only as we learn to hear Christ pray the psalms, but also as we learn to hear our fellow Christians pray them, that we can hear in them the very word of God. In this way, Bonhoeffer was able to preach Psalm 90 as a witness to his grandmother, as a witness to Christ and as the word of God to the congregation.

Bonhoeffer certainly follows his own advice to give thanks for the life of the deceased. He begins the sermon proper by saying that 'it is with enormous gratitude that we stand today at the grave of our dear deceased grandmother'.[51] His gratitude is focused almost entirely on her status as a Christian and God's presence throughout her life. Thus the opening verse of the psalm is a fitting prayer for her. Bonhoeffer puts this prayer in her mouth as he recalls that 'she had to learn repeatedly what she already had known as a child: "Lord, you have been our refuge in all generations"'.[52] This prayer was 'her support during her illness'.[53] Gratitude and remembrance mark Bonhoeffer's sermon at nearly every turn.

Verse 10 requires almost no additional comment: 'The days of our life are seventy years, or perhaps eighty, if we are strong; even then their span is only toil and trouble.' Julie Bonhoeffer outlived the psalmist's estimate, dying at the age of ninety-four. She had struggled her whole life for the sake of others. Her defiance of the Jewish boycott in 1933 was only one of many examples of her toiling for the rights of the oppressed. Bonhoeffer recalls that 'her final years were clouded by the great suffering she endured because of the fate of the Jews among our people, which she bore and suffered in sympathy with them'.[54] The 'toil and trouble' of

---

51. DBWE 14, 909; DBW 14, 922.
52. DBWE 14, 909–10; DBW 14, 923.
53. DBWE 14, 910; DBW 14, 923; cf. Ps. 90.1.
54. DBWE 14, 910–11; DBW 14, 924.

Psalm 90, when heard through her voice, are understood as the struggle against evil and suffering, the struggle to which all Christians have been called. Yet this is a fight that cannot be won in this life. Thus Bonhoeffer cites v. 12, which he had quoted in a letter to her in December 1933: 'But her death as well as her life can teach us a lesson. "So teach us to count our days that we may gain a wise heart".'[55] The good that she had worked for all her life was bounded by the limitation of her days. God alone can bring the work to completion. And for this reason, Psalm 90 must also be directed to Christ.

A life such as Julie Bonhoeffer's, marked by the striving for justice that could not be fully realized in her lifetime, serves as a reminder to take refuge in the Lord alone. Thus Bonhoeffer, once again following his own advice about funeral sermons, offers 'the consolation of the gospel, not in a general sense but in reference to this particular deceased person in Christ'.[56] Her toil was not in vain, because she called on the Lord as her refuge. And so, Bonhoeffer asks, 'What else can we say about this sort of full, rich life? We call on the God who is our refuge, to whom we can flee in any distress and any sadness, Jesus Christ, in whom is all truth, all righteousness, all freedom, and all love.'[57] Her defiance of the boycott in 1933 did not reverse the direction of Nazi oppression, and she did not live to see the end of Hitler's Germany. At the time of her death, the future of her country was still shrouded in uncertainty and ambiguity. Bonhoeffer's prayer, with the psalmist, is that she 'might view in eternity what is yet cloaked and hidden here under sin and death, that she might view in peace and clarity the eternal countenance of God in Jesus Christ'.[58]

In all this, Bonhoeffer is not so much interpreting Psalm 90 as he is showing how Julie Bonhoeffer's life interprets it. From this vantage point, he summons his hearers, those who knew and loved her, to make Psalm 90 their own prayer. He urges them not to be sad, but to return to their work, as she would have wanted. He exhorts them to 'go away from her grave strengthened. Strengthened by her image, by her life and death, but strengthened even more by faith in the God who is both her and our own refuge forever'.[59] And he concludes by praying the words of v. 17: '"Let the favor of the Lord our God be upon us, and prosper for us the work of our hands – O prosper the work of our hands!" Amen.'[60] This was her prayer; Bonhoeffer invites his hearers to make it theirs.

Admittedly, neither Psalm 42 nor Psalm 90 presents overwhelming exegetical hurdles, even for the modern German churchgoer wondering if the ancient prayers of the Psalter have anything to do with their own. There are other psalms that are not so easily incorporated into the prayers of 'civilized' Christians, and Psalm 58 is a key example.

---

55. DBWE 14, 911; DBW 14, 924; cf. Ps. 90.12.
56. DBWE 14, 743; DBW 14, 746.
57. DBWE 14, 911; DBW 14, 924–5.
58. DBWE 14, 911; DBW 14, 925.
59. DBWE 14, 911; DBW 14, 925.
60. DBWE 14, 912; DBW 14, 925.

Psalm 58 as the prayer of Christ

Bonhoeffer preached on Psalm 58 at Finkenwalde on 11 July 1937. Psalm 58, according to *Prayerbook of the Bible*, falls squarely under the category of the psalms of *vengeance*. It asks for God's violent retribution against the wicked, rejoices in revenge and describes the righteous as bathing their feet in the blood of the wicked. Bonhoeffer reflects, 'All attempts to pray these psalms seem doomed to failure. They really seem to lay before us the so-called preliminary religious stage [religiöse Vorstufe] in relation to the New Testament.'[61] Such a view was common in the historical-critical guild at the time. Whatever such psalms might tell us about the history of Israelite religion, they offer nothing constructive to the church's liturgical and prayer practices. But for Bonhoeffer biblical psalms are not there primarily as a model for Christian prayer. Grounded in a reconstructed 'original' context, the text loses its theological intelligibility. A human being, even such a man as King David, cannot pray Psalm 58 and remain innocent. And so we cannot hear the prayer of Psalm 58 both as the words of King David and as the word of God. But, Bonhoeffer thinks, if we learn to hear the words of David as the words of Christ, we can begin to hear them as the word of God and, thereby, learn to pray them in Jesus's name. He therefore employs a particular kind of Christological exegesis in his reading of this difficult text.

Bonhoeffer opens his sermon by asking, 'Is this terrible psalm of vengeance really our prayer?'[62] The answer at once is no, although for Bonhoeffer this is not because the psalm offends modern moral sensibilities, but rather because it is directed against the very same evil of which all people are culpable. 'Only people who are themselves completely without guilt can pray thus.'[63] This presents a problem, since, as Bonhoeffer notes, 'David himself is not innocent.'[64] But David's innocence is not the primary referent, since, as Bonhoeffer reads the Psalter, 'Christ, and thus the church of God, is in David'.[65] It is Christ 'in David' who prays this, which is why the church is permitted to pray it too.

Recall that later interpreters of Bonhoeffer (e.g. Kuske) see in these kinds of words a version of the orthodox thesis, as if Bonhoeffer is trying to justify David's prayer for vengeance based on his being somehow infallible as a pre-incarnate Christ. My proposal, by contrast, is that the statement, 'Christ ... is in David', must be interpreted from the perspective of the biblical testimony of David as a witness to Christ, namely, on the basis of God's election of David to be the one through whom the Messiah will come and establish an everlasting kingdom. Christ is 'in' David in the same way he is 'in' the Bible, that is, not on the basis of a quality inherent in or endowed upon the creaturely reality (since this would be to objectify revelation), but because God has freely bound himself to David in his gracious

---

61. DBWE 5, 174; DBW 5, 129.
62. DBWE 14, 964; DBW 14, 981.
63. DBWE 14, 964; DBW 14, 981.
64. DBWE 14, 965; DBW 14, 981.
65. DBWE 14, 965; DBW 14, 981.

election of him to bear the Messiah. We have no direct access to the 'historical' David; we have only Scripture's witness to David. And Scripture, Bonhoeffer believes, renders David narratively and prophetically as the 'model and shadow' of Jesus Christ. In order for God's promise to David to be fulfilled, David must not be allowed to perish at the hands of evildoers, not because he himself is innocent, but because God has promised to bring forth 'innocence itself' from his lineage. Contra the 'orthodox thesis' of verbal inspiration, Bonhoeffer's interpretation does not stand or fall with the authenticity of Davidic authorship. It stands or falls with the biblical witness of David to Christ, which inheres in God's gracious election of David to be the ancestor of the promised Messiah. Put another way, Psalm 58 can be heard as God's word not because the historical man David was innocent enough to pray these words piously, but because Scripture itself presents David as the 'model and shadow' of Christ the innocent one.

This is an important point, because it is only by hearing this psalm as the prayer of a truly innocent person that it can truly be heard. If we close our ears to the violence of this text, we fail to hear it at all. Bonhoeffer says, 'Anyone who shrinks back in horror from such joy in God's vengeance and from the blood of the wicked does not yet understand what happened on the cross of Christ.'[66] For Bonhoeffer, the answer to David's prayer comes at Golgotha. Shunning the violence of God's judgement means shunning the cross of Christ. It is as we learn to recognize Jesus Christ as the praying subject of Psalm 58 that we can also learn to recognize him as the recipient of the very judgement and violence that he prays for. 'When we look at him, the Crucified, we recognize God's true, living wrath on us, the wicked, and in that very same moment we also recognize our liberation from this wrath, and we hear: Father, forgive them; for they do not know what they are doing.'[67] This psalm leads those who pray it in Jesus's name to the cross of the crucified. The church prays it not as the innocent ones who have the right to call upon God for divine judgement, but as the guilty ones on whom God's judgement rightly falls. To hear ourselves pray this violent psalm is to hear how much it cost Christ to utter his word of forgiveness from his cross. This psalm is not permission for the church to ask for God's violent judgement upon others, far less to execute this judgement themselves. On the contrary, 'those who commend vengeance to God renounce the possibility of taking such vengeance into their own hands.'[68] God has taken vengeance into his own hands, and he has allowed this vengeance to fall upon himself.

Bonhoeffer regards this as God's word for the *present*, a message with ongoing significance in the context of the 1937 German church: 'Satan will continue to rouse up enemies against Christ and his community through injustice, violence, and falsehood.'[69] Yet Bonhoeffer proclaims the hope that Christ in fact prays this

---

66. DBWE 14, 968–9; DBW 14, 986.
67. DBWE 14, 969; DBW 14, 987.
68. DBWE 14, 967; DBW 14, 984. He quotes Deut. 32.35 (cf. Rom. 12.19) in this connection: 'Vengeance is mine, I will repay, says the Lord'.
69. DBWE 14, 970; DBW 14, 988.

psalm vicariously: 'He accuses the wicked, summoning God's vengeance and righteousness down upon them, and offering himself on the cross for the sake of the wicked with his own innocent suffering.'[70] When the church prays this in participation with Christ, Psalm 58 expresses our 'humble gratitude for the cross of Christ having saved us from wrath', our 'ardent petition that God bring all our enemies to the cross of Christ and grant them mercy' and our 'fierce yearning that the day might soon come when Christ visibly triumphs over all his enemies and establishes his kingdom'.[71]

Bonhoeffer's goal is clear: to preach Psalm 58 as God's word for today. And because it is God's word to us in the form of a human prayer to God, it can be heard as the witness to Christ as the church learns to pray it in participation with Christ. If Bonhoeffer had tried to offer a historical explanation for the original context and reception of this psalm, he would not have been able to draw these conclusions. If he had tried to take Psalm 58 as a model for Christian prayer, he would not have been able to affirm, 'Thus have we learned to pray this psalm.'[72] But in attending to Christ's own speaking of this psalm, Bonhoeffer was able to help his hearers learn to pray it along with Christ. It testifies to Christ because it is Christ's own prayer. Because and only because it is Christ's prayer, the church can and does pray it with him in his name.

Coming before God with words such as these, when they are offered in participation with Christ's mediation of our prayers, can only be done with a posture of humility and thanksgiving. In the context of the church struggle in Germany, Psalm 58 becomes for Bonhoeffer a prayer of hope that the wicked might find judgement and forgiveness in the cross of Christ and that Christ would thereby overcome evil and bring about his promised kingdom. It may not have been what was in the mind of the original author, but for Bonhoeffer the only thing that matters is what God is saying through Scripture today. In allowing Scripture to say nothing except the singular word of God in Christ, Bonhoeffer does not think that he has imposed arbitrary limits on what the text can mean. On the contrary, the more fully the Christological substance of the text comes to expression, the more fully the text itself comes to expression too. Bonhoeffer's exegesis entails a mutual deepening in knowledge of both the text that testifies to Christ and the Christ to whom the text testifies.

Conclusion

For Bonhoeffer, the Psalter is God's word in a unique way. Biblical psalms come to us as human words not only in form but also in content. We can hear these prayers as God's word only when we hear them as the prayer of the incarnate Christ, in whose mouth they become God's own word to us and in whose name they

70. DBWE 14, 970; DBW 14, 988.
71. DBWE 14, 970; DBW 14, 988.
72. DBWE 14, 970; DBW 14, 988.

become our words to God. Because our prayers can only come before the Father on the basis of Christ's mediation, the first exegetical task is to hear these words as Jesus's own prayer. The question is not only how the church can pray this, but how *Christ* can. These questions should not be isolated from one another. As the above examples show, Bonhoeffer does not draw a hard and fast line between God's word to us and our words to God in any given psalm. It is always as the church prays a psalm that the church learns to hear it as God's word. And it is always as the church learns to hear the same psalm as God's word that they can learn to pray it.

To be clear, Bonhoeffer's interpretation of the Psalms as Christ's prayers does not constitute his 'method' of exegesis. Indeed, the search for a consistent method, even among the small sample of sermons I have examined in this chapter, yields inconclusive results. Bonhoeffer's methodological inconsistency becomes even more apparent when his Finkenwalde sermons are compared with his later work on the Psalms, for example, his exegesis of Psalm 119.[73] What remains consistent, however, is his conviction that Christ is really present when and where God speaks. If revelation is God's personal presence in Christ, then it is by its very nature a *relational* event. It is an interpersonal encounter with the living Jesus. Bonhoeffer's treatment of the Psalms is therefore consistent with his bibliology, grounded in his theology of revelation-as-*Christus-praesens*. Because of this, we do not read a psalm from a detached, objective position, evaluating it by this or that external standard, judging for ourselves whether it might be or contain a revelatory word. Revelation as the present Christ always claims the whole person. In the case of the Psalms, revelation means that by the Holy Spirit we encounter Christ in his mediatorial work at the right hand of his Father. The Mediator is present *pro-me* in and through the church's prayer. The prayers of the church, bound to Scripture and prayed in Jesus's name, have the promise of Christ's presence, the promise of God's self-revealing word. Revelation, for Bonhoeffer, entails a human response – not as a prerequisite, since God's act of self-disclosure is always grounded in his free and gracious act for us, but as an integral part of the event itself, since this event is a personal encounter with the present Jesus. We are encountered in revelation not by information about God but by God himself in person. There is no place external to this encounter from which it might be evaluated. Bonhoeffer continues in his dialectical roots (as defined in CHAPTER 2), allowing revelation to function as the *petitio principii* of his theology. Only the one who already stands within revelation can hear God's word as revelation. The Psalms can be heard as God's word only for those who pray them in Jesus's name, and they are prayed rightly only by those who have learned to hear them as God's word.

---

73. Brad Pribbenow argues this point in *Prayerbook of Christ*, for example, 113–31; 180–1. I examine Bonhoeffer's exegesis of Psalm 119 in more detail in the next chapter.

7

MEDITATING ON THE WORD

As Bonhoeffer continued to spend time in the Psalter, and especially as he found himself more cut off from the Christian community and set out on a dangerous, isolated path of conspiracy, his emphasis shifts from the communal aspects of prayer to the personal.[1] If the previous chapter explored the Psalter in the context of 'the day together', this chapter's interest is 'the day alone'. And this shift in emphasis brings out another important aspect of Christ's presence in the psalms. As I stated in the beginning of this study, one of the key questions of bibliology is what God *does* with Scripture. Thus far, I have demonstrated that Bonhoeffer's bibliology turns on his conviction that where God speaks his word, Christ is fully there *pro-me*. What God does with Scripture, then, is minister his life-giving and salvific presence in the word, personally present in Jesus Christ. In 'Meditation on Psalm 119', Bonhoeffer discloses another aspect of revelation-as-*Christus-praesens*: formation. Where Christ is there for human beings, there human beings are being formed into his image. The right reading of Scripture, then, not only depends on our having hearts that seek Christ, but also results in the renewal of our hearts so that we become formed into Christ's image. The fruit of scriptural meditation is that we come not only to understand God's word, but to love it.

I have already demonstrated that Bonhoeffer's exegesis of the Psalter was driven by his attempt to pray the psalms in the name of Jesus. He endeavoured to show how any given psalm should first be heard as Christ's own prayer before it can become the church's prayer. When the church prays a psalm as the prayer of Christ, the words can be recognized as human words to God and God's words to humanity at the same time. The best way to preach a Psalm, in other words, is to teach the congregation how to pray it. Bonhoeffer's 'Meditation on Psalm 119' is likewise meant to lead to prayer, but his approach differs compared with the sermons I reviewed in CHAPTER 6. The difference between 'Meditation on Psalm 119' and the Finkenwalde sermons can be traced along the line that divides meditation and exegesis. But before I can demonstrate this, I must first show how Bonhoeffer sought to make Psalm 119 his own prayer and the prayer of the church.

---

1. On this, see Krötke, 'Bonhoeffer's Exegesis of the Psalms', 179–80.

Praying Psalm 119

The 'way' of God's word

One of the most germane images in Psalm 119 for Bonhoeffer is that of God's word as a *way*.[2] He takes up this image immediately in his comments on v. 1. Walking along an established way means walking from a beginning to an end. It is a trajectory along which moving forward means genuine progress towards a goal. To walk in the way of the Lord means to go between God's beginning and God's end. As Bonhoeffer says, 'The way between this beginning and this end is the walk in the law of God.'[3] This theme was not a new one for Bonhoeffer. At a significant moment in the funeral sermon for his grandmother, he had quoted Fritz Reuter's tombstone inscription:

> Beginning and end, O Lord, are yours,
> the span between, life, was mine;
> and though I might have wandered around in the dark, not finding my way –
> with you, Lord, there is clarity, and light is your house.[4]

He had an astute sense that life was nothing but aimless wandering unless it was firmly situated along the way of the Lord, between God's beginning and God's end.

For this reason, he regards the law not as restriction but as *freedom*, 'the freedom from the murderous law of never-ending beginnings'.[5] Bonhoeffer was critical of Christian movements that emphasized personal conversion.[6] The one who walks in the law of the Lord need not worry about ever-new conversions and reconversions. This one is free to make progress, to advance in God's ways. This one is free *for the gospel* rather than being a slave to the law. Bonhoeffer comments, 'To wait for a new beginning, day after day, thinking that one has found it countless times only to declare it lost in the evening: this is the complete

---

2. For more on this theme in relation to Bonhoeffer's ethics, see Brian Brock, 'Bonhoeffer and the Bible in Christian Ethics: Psalm 119, the Mandates, and Ethics as a "Way"', *Studies in Christian Ethics* 18 (2005): 7–29.

3. DBW 15, 500, my translation. The DBWE 15 edition typically translates Wandel as 'change' or, as in this case, 'turn', which results here in an odd rendering: 'The path between this beginning and this end is the turn [Wandel] within God's law' (DBWE 15, 497). In my translation, I have taken my cue from David Gracie, who correctly translates Wandel with its more archaic meaning of 'walk' (Dietrich Bonhoeffer, *Meditating on the Word*, 1st Rowman & Littlefield ed., ed. and trans. David McI. Gracie [Lanham, MD: [Cowley], Rowman & Littlefield, 2008], 96).

4. DBWE 14, 911; DBW 14, 925.

5. DBWE 15, 497; DBW 15, 500.

6. According to Bethge, 'He had always been repulsed by the pietists' deliberately told stories of their conversions' (DB-ER, 206).

destruction of faith in that God who set the beginning once through his forgiving and renewing word in Jesus Christ.[7] Although Ps. 119.1 could be read as a continual call to conversion, to renew one's commitment to being blameless in God's law, Bonhoeffer's interpretation argues for exactly the reverse. Walking in God's ways is not a question of what we might do (or redo) for God, but rather of what God has already done for us. On the basis of God's irrefutable beginning for us, we are already walking along God's path. Bonhoeffer thereby calls us 'to understand ourselves as people who have been placed on the path and now cannot do otherwise than walk the path as well'.[8]

The connection between God's word as *way* and God's word as *law* emerges here. Bonhoeffer quotes Deut. 6.20–25 and concludes, 'No one understands the law of God who does not know of the redemption that has already occurred and the future promise.'[9] The meaning of the law of God is found in God's redemptive act, which is his beginning with us, and in his future promise, which is his end with us. The law, then, does not throw us back on our own moral agency but upon the path that God has established between the beginning and the end. Those who walk in the law of the Lord are 'happy', because 'they are freed from the agony of their own beginnings'.[10] They walk in the clarity of God's word, which, the psalmist says, is 'a lamp to my feet and a light to my path' (Ps. 119.105). The happiness of those who walk in the law of the Lord has nothing to do with the self-satisfaction of living up to the standards of an ethical system. Envisaged as a 'way', the law is more than just a way of life; it is the definite path from God's accomplished beginning to God's promised end. And although Bonhoeffer takes the psalmist's imagery as his point of departure, he does not hesitate to interpret the 'way' Christologically. Jesus, according to John 14.6, *is* the Way: 'The way of God is God's way to human beings, and only in this way is it the way of human beings to God. Its name is Jesus Christ.'[11] For Bonhoeffer, it is only possible to walk blamelessly in the way of God's law because in Christ we are already on the way.

Learning to love God's law

Commenting on the length and repetitiveness of Psalm 119, Bonhoeffer says: 'We recognize, then, that the apparent repetitions are in fact always new variations on one theme, the love of God's word. As this love can have no end, so also the words that confess it have no end.'[12] Although the love of God's word does not appear to be an especially challenging theme to embrace, especially for a Lutheran like Bonhoeffer, Psalm 119 specifically equates God's word with the *law*, the Torah.

---

7. DBWE 15, 497; DBW 15, 500.
8. DBWE 15, 498; DBW 15, 501.
9. DBWE 15, 498; DBW 15, 502.
10. DBWE 15, 500; DBW 15, 503.
11. DBWE 15, 505; DBW 15, 509.
12. DBWE 5, 165; DBW 5, 119.

Theologians in the tradition of Luther are bound to have difficulty with this. Is not the primary use of the law to show human sinfulness and guilt? Psalm 119 seems to praise the law in and for itself. Can the Lutheran interpreter really pray this?[13]

Luther himself exhibited a certain degree of ambivalence towards the praise of the law in Psalm 119. He treated the psalm as a 'comparison between the old and the new law'.[14] It is *prophecy*. The key to its interpretation, he thought, was in sharing the prophet's vision. And the prophetic vision is this: 'The prophet looks with spiritual eyes at the law of Moses and sees hidden and enclosed in it the law of faith, the Gospel of grace, and the invisible things promised, like the kernel under the shell or the treasure under the ground.'[15] For Luther, beneath the problematic surface of this psalm (and it *is* problematic from the standpoint of his law–gospel dichotomy) lay the treasures of the gospel. But these treasures did not sit open and available on the surface; they had to be found and excavated. Luther and Bonhoeffer both say that we are on the way of God's law, but for Luther, the goal is to get off of this path: 'The whole psalm is nothing but a petition that the spiritual law be revealed and the letter be removed, that the spirit be brought forth and the veil taken away and the face appear, that Christ come and Moses pass away.'[16] The only laudable law, as far as Luther was concerned, is the law of the Spirit. The grand error would be to mistake the law of Moses for the law of faith. In fact, Luther said openly that the 'law of the Lord' identified in Ps. 119.1 is *not* the Torah; the blessed one is the one who walks in the law of the Lord *as opposed to* 'the law of Moses or of man'.[17] For Luther, those who delight in the Mosaic law are cursed rather than blessed, because they are seeking salvation by works rather than by grace through faith.

Luther is demonstrating a certain kind of Christological exegesis, although a very different sort than Bonhoeffer. Luther's reading of Psalm 119 as a prayer for the law of grace would make little sense from a historical-critical perspective (and it would be anachronistic to expect Luther to adhere to this in any case), but it does make sense in light of his affirmation of *sola fide*. If Psalm 119 praises the law, then it must be praising the only law that is worthy of praise, namely, the law of faith. Luther would consider his interpretation of Psalm 119 as an example of reading Scripture from its centre, that is, allowing Scripture to impose its meaning on him. He condemned those who 'impose their meaning on Scripture and do not permit its sense to be imposed on them'.[18] And because, in his view, Scripture 'imposes' *sola fide* as the true meaning of the law, the law of faith must lie at the heart of Psalm 119.

---

13. In the present context, my concern is not Bonhoeffer's evaluation of the law overall, but his exegesis of Psalm 119, especially in comparison to Luther's.
14. LW 11, 415.
15. LW 11, 414.
16. LW 11, 422.
17. LW 11, 415.
18. LW 11, 432.

Bonhoeffer takes a different tack than Luther here. Even if we set aside questions about the law and Luther's emphasis on *sola fide*, there is a broader distinction between their approaches to Psalm 119. Luther regarded this psalm as *prophecy* and thought that the way to read it correctly was to read it through the prophet's eyes. The prophet's vision, according to Luther, was the law of faith hidden inside the law of Moses. Those who walk in the law are blessed, so long as we understand that 'the law' in Psalm 119 is the spiritual law made known in the gospel. For Bonhoeffer, Psalm 119 is *prayer*, the prayer of Christ and of Christ's church. The first thing to be done is to pray it. To extract a Christological truth from Psalm 119 might be a perfectly valid way to hear it as God's revelatory Word, but, Bonhoeffer thinks, this cannot be done until the church in the Spirit offers these words in Jesus's name to the Father in prayer. The fundamental difference between Luther's and Bonhoeffer's treatment of Psalm 119 is the way each envisages God's speaking through the text. For Luther, God has spoken through the prophet in testimony to Jesus Christ. For Bonhoeffer, God's word is present in Christ as the church prays in his name in these words that testify to him and which he brings to his Father on the church's behalf.

One of the most prominent themes in 'Meditation on Psalm 119' is the joy and blessedness of God's word, even in the form of law. Bonhoeffer refers time and again to the gratitude and joy that arise along the way of God's law. Joy in the law flows from the heart that has learned to love God's law. Commenting on v. 2, Bonhoeffer rejects the idea that 'a purely external fulfillment of the commandments' could lead to true happiness. On the contrary, 'the entire undivided heart must be involved'.[19] For Bonhoeffer, the heart that can truly love God's law is the heart that never ceases to seek God.[20] And a heart that seeks God in God's word is a heart that can really progress along God's way.

Praying with the psalmist

In CHAPTER 6, I argued at length that Bonhoeffer's exegesis of the Psalter rests on his conviction that the only way to hear them as the word of God is to learn to hear them as the prayers of Christ, and to pray them in his name. It is striking, then, that 'Meditation on Psalm 119' does not make any explicit references to this mode of interpretation. Bonhoeffer does not directly name Jesus as the speaking subject of Psalm 119, but rather refers throughout to 'the psalmist' and 'the person who prays the psalm'.[21] He identifies himself with the 'I' of the Psalm.[22]

19. DBWE 15, 503; DBW 15, 507.
20. Unsurprisingly, Bonhoeffer immediately points out that God can be sought only because God has already made himself known (DBWE 15, 503–4; DBW 15, 507).
21. 'Thus, we are being addressed as those who are on the same path as the psalmist' (DBWE 15, 497; DBW 15, 501). 'The person who is praying says …' (DBWE 15, 513; DBW 15, 519). 'But is the person who prays our psalm … is he blind?' (DBWE 15, 520; DBW 15, 528). The English translation occasionally inserts 'the psalmist' where the German uses only the masculine pronoun (e.g. DBWE 15, 496; DBW 15, 499).
22. This is also noted in Krötke, 'Bonhoeffer's Exegesis of the Psalms', 179.

Given what we know about Bonhoeffer's exegesis of the Psalter, why does he not emphasize Christ as the praying subject of this psalm? This cannot be explained as a development in his thought, since his writings both before and after his work on 'Meditation on Psalm 119' support the centrality of Christ as the praying subject of the Psalter.[23] There is nothing to suggest that his thinking had changed, so why the difference?

In *Prayerbook*, he categorizes Psalm 119 under the heading, 'The Law', offering some general guidelines for reading these psalms.[24] He states that God's commands are not burdensome (quoting 1 John 5.3), that they make our way certain, bringing freedom, not subjugation. The law is therefore grace in Christ, and is to be obeyed and loved. For Bonhoeffer, this means that it is possible to rejoice in and love the law, just as the psalmist does, but only on the basis of faith in Christ. Because Jesus was the only one to fully obey God's law, he alone can fully rejoice in it. For the sinful heart, God's word is judgement and imprisonment, but in Christ, it is grace and freedom. If Christ alone can truly love God's law, Christ alone can truly pray the words of Psalm 119, and therefore we can only pray this prayer truly in Christ's name.

Because God's law is God's word to those on God's way, the contemporary reader of Psalm 119 is in the same situation as the psalmist: 'We are being addressed as those who are on the same path as the psalmist.'[25] Bonhoeffer's exegetical decisions are geared towards showing how the prayer of the psalmist is a fitting prayer for anyone on that path, for anyone walking in God's way. Psalm 119 expresses our situation before God; we are on the way that has its beginning in God's act of redemption and its end in God's promise. God in Christ has already walked this way. Christ by the Holy Spirit is with us along the way. His word concerning this way – which is not a separate word from the Word whose name is Jesus Christ – encounters us as both demand and gift, and we must learn to hear it and to love it as both. The prayer of Psalm 119 is God's word, not only as God's way of standing before us in Christ, but also as our way of standing before God in Christ. The Psalter as revelation, Bonhoeffer believes, is God's word to human beings in the form of human words to God, words that can and are offered to God only on the basis of God's own speaking of them in the incarnate and ascended Christ. This is why he says in *Prayerbook* that Christ gives thanks 'in us' for the law, and we 'pray it in the name of Jesus Christ'.[26] Thus Bonhoeffer has not abandoned the course he set out in his 1935 lectures on the Psalms, but reaffirms it. We pray Psalm 119 only because Christ prays it in us, and we pray it only in his name. Christ who fulfilled the law and thereby rejoiced in it likewise 'grants us joy in its

---

23. He outlines this approach in his 1935 lecture, 'Christ in the Psalms', puts it into practice throughout his Finkenwalde sermons and reiterates the same principle in his 1940 book, *Prayerbook of the Bible*, which was published after he had ceased his work on 'Meditation on Psalm 119'.
24. DBWE 5, 164; DBW 5, 118–19.
25. DBWE 15, 497; DBW 15, 501.
26. DBWE 5, 164; DBW 5, 118–19.

fulfillment'.[27] We are on the same way as the psalmist because we are in Christ, who is the beginning and the end, the origin and the fulfilment of the law. It is in Christ alone that we can fulfil the law, in Christ alone that we can love it.

Meditation vs exegesis

Bonhoeffer reads Psalm 119 as the prayer of those who are in Christ, because those who are in Christ are on the same *way* as the psalmist. And the one who has learned to pray this psalm has learned to love God's law and to be drawn into the rich depths of his Word. This is where the theme of scriptural meditation must come to the fore. Bonhoeffer believed that a life in God's way was a life of meditation on God's word. What does this mean?

It will be useful to begin by clarifying the difference between exegesis and meditation in Bonhoeffer's thought. His comments on Psalm 119.15 make a good starting point. Meditation is 'a matter not only for those especially called to this but rather for everyone who wants to walk in God's ways'.[28] This practice is to be upheld alongside exegesis, and 'a theologian who does not practice both denies his office'.[29] Bonhoeffer identifies the difference this way: 'Meditation means to take God's word prayerfully into my heart; exegesis means to recognize and understand God's word in Scripture as God's word.'[30] The distinction is subtle but important.

At first glance, it may appear that Bonhoeffer is alluding to a distinction between head and heart. But not only is such language perilously imprecise, the distinction it indicates runs directly against the grain of Bonhoeffer's theological anthropology.[31] The human person, for Bonhoeffer, is an *integrated whole*, and cannot be pulled apart into mind and body, body and soul, or head and heart. He writes, 'The "heart" in the biblical sense is not the inner life but rather the whole person before God.'[32] He makes a similar point with respect to the body–soul dichotomy in *Creation and Fall*: 'A human being does not "have" a body or "have" a soul; instead a human being "is" body and soul.'[33] As irreducible wholes, human beings cannot set one part of themselves against another without rejecting their entire existence.[34] The idea that a person could actively engage one part of the self in meditation, and a completely separate part in exegesis, is based on a concept of the human person that Bonhoeffer actively rejects.

---

27. DBWE 5, 164; DBW 5, 119.
28. DBWE 15, 517; DBW 15, 524.
29. DBWE 15, 517; DBW 15, 524.
30. DBWE 15, 517; DBW 15, 524.
31. See Joseph McGarry, 'Con-formed to Christ: Dietrich Bonhoeffer and Christian Formation', *Journal of Spiritual Formation & Soul Care* 5 (2012): 228.
32. DBWE 8, 457; DBW 8, 511.
33. DBWE 3, 77; DBW 3, 71.
34. Bonhoeffer makes this point about human embodiedness: 'People who reject their bodies reject their existence before God the Creator' (DBWE 3, 77; DBW 3, 71–2).

There is also a Christological reason why the line between exegesis and meditation cannot be drawn between the head and the heart. As I have argued in CHAPTER 4, Bonhoeffer locates intellectual reflection on revelation within his theology of the word. Christ's presence as the Logos supersedes but nevertheless involves the human logos. Exegesis, understood as recognizing and understanding God's word in Scripture, demands intellectual attention to that which counters and surpasses the intellect. It cannot be located in the intellect, because the word of God in Scripture is the *counter*-Word.[35] It is a matter of God's real presence in Christ by the Spirit, and Christ's presence cannot be divided into head and heart. Christ is an indivisible whole. The present Christ is the whole Christ, and the whole Christ encounters the whole human person.

Therefore, owing to the nature of the human being who encounters God's word in Scripture as well as the nature of the word there encountered, exegesis and meditation cannot simply be differentiated along the lines of head and heart. Both ways of engaging with Scripture are concerned with the *whole person*, head and heart together. Nevertheless, there are genuine differences between the two practices. As Bonhoeffer understands them, meditation and exegesis correspond to the following set of contrasting pairs: silence and speech, solitude and community, and stillness and action. All three are hinted at in his comments on Psalm 119.15, and can be further elucidated with reference to his other writings on scriptural meditation.

Silence and speech

Meditation and exegesis have the same object, God's word as the present Christ. What distinguishes them, in Bonhoeffer's conception, is our posture and intention in each practice. The first distinction is between *speech* and *silence*. Exegesis wants to bring God's word to word;[36] meditation wants to be silent under God's word. Silence is the mark of meditation, speech of exegesis. But silence is not the same as 'wordlessness'. For Bonhoeffer, both speech *and* silence are essentially related to the word. Meditation is 'the simple act of the individual who falls silent under the Word of God'.[37] Exegesis is oriented towards *proclamation*, towards turning God's word to human speech, whereas meditation is oriented towards *formation*, towards receiving God's word *pro-me* today.

One of the fruits of meditation is the growing wisdom to speak rightly. As Bonhoeffer says, 'Silence before the Word leads to proper hearing and thus also

---

35. Moreover, Bonhoeffer's critique of theologies that 'objectify' revelation, which he discusses in *Act and Being* as theologies of 'being', necessarily includes any that would reduce revelation to something that exists purely in the structures of the mind.

36. Here I follow Bonhoeffer's language in '*Vergegenwärtigung neutestamentlicher Texte*': 'Wo Christus im Wort des Neuen Testaments *zu Wort kommt*, dort ist Vergegenwärtigung' (DBW 14, 404, my emphasis).

37. DBWE 5, 84; DBW 5, 67.

to proper speaking of God's Word at the right time.'[38] The silence that Bonhoeffer endorses does not reflect 'a mystical desire to get beyond the Word',[39] but the simple desire to live under the word. It is a 'listening silence'.[40] Bonhoeffer quotes Thomas à Kempis at this point: 'No one speaks more confidently than the one who gladly remains silent.'[41] True spiritual silence means receptivity to God's word: 'We remain silent solely for the sake of the Word, not thereby to dishonor the Word but rather to honor and receive it properly.'[42] Thus, the heart of meditative silence is not the absence of words, but the presence of God's word alone.

But this should not obscure the genuine distinction that Bonhoeffer perceives. Despite its fruitfulness in engendering right speech, meditation seeks silence, not words. In this way, it is markedly different from exegesis. In his Finkenwalde guide to scriptural meditation, Bonhoeffer advises, 'Do not look for new ideas and connections in the text as for a sermon! Do not ask: How can I pass these words along? But rather: What are they saying to me!'[43] Meditation is not the time for pulpit preparation; in fact, Bonhoeffer specifically recommends that pastors not meditate on the passage for an upcoming sermon.[44] The goal is to receive God's word openly, without worrying how this word might be delivered to others. Meditation has no agenda save one: 'What we want is to encounter Christ in his own word.'[45]

Silence and speech are connected: 'Genuine speech comes out of silence, and genuine silence comes out of speech.'[46] Exegesis and meditation work together to acknowledge this assertion with respect to Holy Scripture; neither practice on its own can fully discern the word within the words of the Bible. As Bonhoeffer notes, quoting from Ecclesiastes 3.7, 'There is a time … to keep silence and a time to speak.'[47] Exegesis acknowledges that God's word must be understood and proclaimed in speech. Meditation acknowledges that God's word must be received and accepted in silence.

Solitude and community

The next distinction falls between *solitude* and *community*. In contrasting meditation and exegesis along these lines, I do not mean that Bonhoeffer

38. DBWE 5, 85; DBW 5, 68.
39. DBWE 5, 84; DBW 5, 67.
40. DBWE 5, 85; DBW 5, 68.
41. DBWE 5, 85; DBW 5, 68; cf. Thomas à Kempis, *The Imitation of Christ*, ed. Harold C. Gardiner, trans. Richard Whitford (New York: Doubleday, 2009), 27.
42. DBWE 5, 85; DBW 5, 68.
43. DBWE 14, 933; DBW 14, 947.
44. Evidently, this was an issue with the Finkenwalde students. Bethge reports that many of them had difficulty with the mandatory time set aside for scriptural meditation. Unsure what to do with themselves, many slept, read or worked on sermon preparation (DB-ER, 463).
45. DBWE 14, 932; DBW 14, 946–7.
46. DBWE 5, 83; DBW 5, 67.
47. DBWE 5, 84; DBW 5, 67.

recommends practising meditation alone and exegesis with others. Both are generally to be practised alone. Solitude and community are not the respective conditions under which meditation and exegesis are to be undertaken, but rather their respective intentions. With its intention towards proclamation and speech, exegesis aims at the community of faith, whereas meditation's intention towards formation and silence sets it towards the individual before God. Bonhoeffer's description of meditation as '[taking] God's word prayerfully into my heart'[48] not only suggests a solitary activity, but also describes an encounter between God's word and the individual. Meditation is solitary in practice and intent. Exegesis, on the other hand, may be solitary in practice, but, in its pursuit of bringing God's word to word, necessarily intends the community.

Bonhoeffer draws out these connections most directly in *Life Together*. In his chapter on 'The Day Alone', he says, 'The mark of solitude [Einsamkeit] is silence, just as speech is the mark of community. Silence and speech have the same inner connection and distinction as do being alone [Alleinsein] and community.'[49] What, then, is this 'inner connection and distinction' that Bonhoeffer references here? Why is silence the mark of solitude, and speech the mark of community? Once we understand these relationships, the place of meditation and exegesis in this schema becomes clearer.

The relationships between these concepts derive from how each relates to God's word. Bonhoeffer had always affirmed, with his Lutheran tradition, that the church is wherever 'the word of God is rightly taught and the sacraments are rightly administered'.[50] That is, the church is a community gathered around the *proclamation* of God's word, both in the pulpit and at the altar. In *Life Together*, Bonhoeffer's description of the community's 'life together under the Word'[51] revolves around the ways in which the word is *spoken*. 'The profound silence of morning is first broken by the prayer and song of the community of faith.'[52] The community gathers, and the people are no longer silent. Even singing together is to be regarded as the spoken word: 'Our song on earth is speech. It is the sung Word.'[53] As I noted in CHAPTER 6, Bonhoeffer advocates specifically for the community to sing psalms together, that they may 'speak and pray the same Word at the same time ... for the sake of uniting in the Word'.[54] Their uniting in the word is uniting in the spoken word, spoken in Scripture readings, in songs and in prayers.[55] Speaking the word goes hand in hand with fellowship in the word. The mark of community is speech.

---

48. DBWE 15, 517; DBW 15, 524.
49. DBWE 5, 83; DBW 5, 66–7.
50. DBWE 14, 690; DBW 14, 692.
51. DBWE 5, 51; DBW 5, 37.
52. DBWE 5, 51; DBW 5, 37.
53. DBWE 5, 66; DBW 5, 50.
54. DBWE 5, 66; DBW 5, 50.
55. Bonhoeffer insists that unity under the word cannot be established on the basis of mutual agreement or goodwill; it is always a 'bestowed unity' (DBWE 14, 663; DBW 14, 663).

It stands to reason, then, that solitude goes hand in hand with silence. But the meaning of both must be drawn from their relation to God's word. Just as there is a difference between genuine silence and the inability to speak, so there is a difference between genuine solitude and isolation. Bonhoeffer warns his readers, 'Whoever cannot be alone should beware of community. Whoever cannot stand being in community should beware of being alone.'[56] The one who cannot be alone cannot heed Christ's call to discipleship, because Christ's call makes everyone into an individual before God.[57] He minces no words about it: 'If you do not want to be alone, you are rejecting Christ's call to you, and you can have no part in the community of those who are called.'[58] Thus, he envisages both solitude and community as originating in Jesus's call to discipleship.

Just as God addresses his people individually and corporately, Christians must stand before the word in solitude and in community. For Bonhoeffer, 'meditation does not allow us to sink into the void and bottomless pit of aloneness [Alleinsein], rather it allows us to be alone [allein] with the Word'.[59] Thus, the heart of meditative solitude is not the absence of companions, but the company of God's word alone. To be sure, Bonhoeffer is not positing a division in the one word of God. He does not think that God has one kind of word to say in meditation and another in exegesis. There is only one word: Jesus Christ, who is personally and fully present wherever God speaks his word. Both meditation and exegesis are meant to receive this word openly, but the difference is in what kind of receptivity is intended. Exegesis stands before God's word in the community. Meditation stands before God's word alone.

Stillness and action

Finally, meditation and exegesis differ along the lines of *stillness* and *action*. Meditation takes a posture of stillness. This comes through in Bonhoeffer's comments about *time* in Psalm 119.15:

> I need time for God's word and often have to ponder the words for a long time in order to understand the precepts of God correctly ... True, God often demands fast and immediate action, yet he also demands silence and contemplation. Thus I may and must often stay for hours and days with one and the same word before

---

56. DBWE 5, 83; DBW 5, 66.

57. His best-known writing on this topic is in *Discipleship* (DBWE 4, 92–9; DBW 4, 87–95), but he echoes the same points in *Life Together*: 'Alone you stood before God when God called you. Alone you had to obey God's voice. Alone you had to take up your cross, struggle, and pray and alone you will die and give an account to God' (DBWE 5, 82; DBW 5, 65).

58. DBWE 5, 82; DBW 5, 65.

59. DBWE 5, 86–7; DBW 5, 70.

I am enlightened with the correct realization ... God's word claims my time ...
To be a Christian is not the matter of a moment but takes time.[60]

Meditation means *waiting* on God's word. Bonhoeffer has long been admired as a man of decisive action, but by this period of his life he had learned to acknowledge the time and patience required to hear God's word rightly.

Waiting on the word of God in Scripture is a fundamental mark of meditation, which distinguishes it from exegesis. The exegete must not be impatient with Scripture, but nevertheless often works under specific time constraints: the preacher must preach on Sunday morning; the teacher must teach when the class begins. The one meditating, by contrast, has no deadlines, no specific agenda. In his Finkenwalde guide to meditation, Bonhoeffer recommends selecting a text of ten to fifteen verses, and to keep to this text for the whole week.[61] And in *Life Together*, he suggests that even a single word or phrase will be enough: 'Are not the words "father", "love", "mercy", "cross", "sanctification", or "resurrection" often enough to fill amply the brief time set aside for our meditation?'[62] The unhurried pace and lack of agenda attest to meditation's meaning, which is simply 'waiting for God's Word to us'.[63] And waiting for God's word means hearing God's word in God's time.

The basic intention of meditation is patient receptivity, which is fitting given what we know about Bonhoeffer's bibliology. Only God can speak God's word in Scripture. Human beings cannot force God's hand, but can only wait on God to speak. And waiting on God means expecting God to do something really *new*. To borrow an analogy from Bonhoeffer's prison letters, the patient expectancy of scriptural meditation resembles the season of Advent: 'One waits, hopes, does this or that – ultimately negligible things – the door is locked and can only be opened *from the outside.*'[64] Meditation waits upon the word, because the text cannot be unlocked by an exegetical key that is already at hand. It can only be opened *from the outside*, by the God whose coming is hoped for and anticipated each day in the Scriptures. The heart of meditative stillness, then, is not the absence of activity, but the action of God's word alone.

The result of waiting on God in Scripture is encountering God's word in its continual newness. This is why Bonhoeffer says that 'there is no standing still. Each gift, each realization that I receive, only drives me more deeply into the word of God'.[65] One is never done with Scripture. One must return to it again and again, waiting on God's word. In Bonhoeffer's words, 'God's word is not the sum of a few general sentences that could be in my mind at any time; rather it is God's daily new

---

60. DBWE 15, 517; DBW 15, 523–4.
61. DBWE 14, 934; DBW 14, 949.
62. DBWE 5, 87–8; DBW 5, 71.
63. DBWE 5, 87; DBW 5, 70.
64. DBWE 8, 188; DBW 8, 197.
65. DBWE 15, 517; DBW 15, 523.

word addressed to me, expounded in its never-ending wealth of interpretation'.[66] Stillness before God's word, then, can be viewed as a certain kind of movement; it means moving more deeply into God's scriptural word.

But none of this is meant to negate the importance of attending to the breadth of Holy Scripture. For Bonhoeffer, personal meditation is the time to deepen our understanding, whereas communal contexts (chiefly, preaching and public reading) provide the place to broaden our understanding. It is fitting that, by his recommendation, communal readings of Scripture are to be lengthy, whereas personal meditation should focus on short passages. In the former case 'we are led more into the whole length and breadth of the Holy Scriptures', and in the latter 'we are guided into the unfathomable depths of a particular sentence and word'.[67] Both are necessary for the theologian and indeed for all Christians. Bonhoeffer calls for the church to become fully acquainted with the whole of Scripture. How else, he asks, 'are we ever to gain certainty and confidence in our personal deeds and church activity if we do not stand on solid biblical ground?'[68] This is the work of communal reading, of proclamation, of exegesis. This is the work that leads to 'personal deeds and church activity'. Exegesis therefore acknowledges that God's word must be acted upon. Meditation acknowledges that God's word must be waited upon.

The transforming presence of Christ

To summarize the basic difference between exegesis and meditation, exegesis involves speech, community and action; meditation involves silence, solitude and stillness. This schema is meant to emphasize the distinction between exegesis and meditation in Bonhoeffer's thought, but in reality the categories are not so cut and dry. Bonhoeffer never suggests that meditation and exegesis are mutually exclusive practices. He emphasizes the importance of each in his effort to describe the encounter with God's word in its fullness. But, unlike Barth,[69] he is comfortable making some distinctions. The reader of Scripture does not control her encounter with God's word in Scripture, but she can direct her intention one way or another.

Bonhoeffer alludes to the necessity of meditation in the reading of Psalm 119. In *Prayerbook of the Bible*, he writes that 'Psalm 119 becomes especially difficult for us perhaps because of its length and uniformity. Here a rather slow, quiet, patient movement from word to word, from sentence to sentence is helpful'.[70] This is a better description of meditation than of exegesis. He even suggests that exegesis is

---

66. DBWE 15, 517; DBW 15, 524.
67. DBWE 5, 87; DBW 5, 70. Bonhoeffer here quotes Eph. 3.18 in this connection: 'that you may have the power to comprehend, with all the saints, what is the breadth and length and height and depth'.
68. DBWE 5, 63; DBW 5, 47.
69. DBWE 14, 268; DBW 14, 252.
70. DBWE 5, 164–5; DBW 5, 119.

not the most fitting way to engage with Psalm 119. In *Life Together*, he notes that the repetition in Psalm 119 is so pronounced that 'it seems it does not want to end and becomes so simple that it is virtually impervious to our exegetical analysis'.[71] In this regard, prayerful persistence becomes more important than exegetical technique, which is why Bonhoeffer asks rhetorically, 'Is there not the suggestion that every word of prayer must penetrate to a depth of the heart which can be reached only by unceasing repetition?'[72] Thus for Bonhoeffer the proper use of Psalm 119 is embedded in its form. It is not primarily to become the object of exegetical analysis, nor is it making an argument with which we can choose to agree or disagree. It is to be *prayed* – prayed repeatedly until the words of the psalm become our own, until the psalmist's prayer and our prayer are one and the same. Bonhoeffer embraces the repetition of this psalm, drawing his readers into the same, so that his exegesis is not only born of meditation but leads to it too.

If the *form* of Psalm 119 suggests a posture of patience and receptivity towards God's word, its *content* makes this point unavoidable. As I have shown, Bonhoeffer's 'Meditation on Psalm 119' discloses the themes he found to be most prominent in the psalm, especially the 'way' of God's word, the blessedness and joy of those who love God's law, and the need for continual meditation on God's word. All of these, in their own ways, illuminate his thinking about scriptural meditation. Moreover, his interpretation of Psalm 119 reveals striking connections between meditation and *formation*. Bonhoeffer expects the patient, silent receptivity of scriptural meditation not only to lead to new realizations, but to a renewed heart. As Christians take up the regular discipline of scriptural meditation, they open themselves up to God's word, that it may dwell in and transform their hearts. Meditating on the word aims to bring God's word to expression, not as human speech, but in our very selves. Its fruit is the Word's becoming flesh in the hearts and lives of God's people. Thus, we pray with the psalmist not because we have hearts that can already pray these words, but because we hope that through our continued prayers these words will come to dwell in our hearts, thereby turning us into people who *can* pray these words. Meditative prayer begins not with the representation of the heart, but with its transformation.

This is the point that can offer a substantive contribution to our understanding of Bonhoeffer's bibliology. Christ who is present in the word of Scripture transforms us by that very word into his very form. The presence of Christ in Scripture is a *transforming* presence. In the Finkenwalde guide to scriptural meditation, Bonhoeffer makes two parallel assertions. Under the question, 'What is my goal with meditation?', he says, 'In any event, we always want to come away from meditation differently than we go to it. What we want is to encounter Christ in his own word.'[73] The first statement asserts that meditation has a *formative* effect, the second that meditation entails Christ's *presence* in the word. The connection

---

71. DBWE 5, 57; DBW 5, 42.
72. DBWE 5, 57; DBW 5, 42.
73. DBWE 14, 932; DBW 14, 946–7.

between these two statements can be traced through his growing emphasis on God's word as a *way*, a concept that is not entirely absent from his earlier works, but comes into especially sharp focus in 'Meditation on Psalm 119'.

In his effort to expound the text of Psalm 119, Bonhoeffer speaks of formation in the psalmist's language of walking in God's ways, seeking God with one's whole heart and meditating on God's word. He draws attention to the psalmist's language about the heart and its desires. The heart is not a particular part of a person but indicates the person as an undivided whole, and the heart that prays Psalm 119 is a heart that has been made new in God's word. Bonhoeffer does not envisage life in the way of the law as 'a purely external fulfillment of the commandments'.[74] Bonhoeffer renders v. 5 as 'O, that my way would be directed toward keeping your statutes'.[75] He writes that this prayer expresses *desire*, the desire to keep God's commandments. But he also recognizes that 'the O! of our wishes and the O! of our prayers are two different things'.[76] In the former, we simply *express* our existing desires to God; in the latter, we ask God to *transform* our desires, so that our hearts will seek God's word and God's will. After all, Bonhoeffer says, 'We cannot bring forth even the right "O!" from our own heart. God has to teach us through the Holy Spirit how to call it out.'[77] In other words, we do not pray Psalm 119 *out of* a desire for God's law, but, with the Spirit's help, *into* such a desire.

In keeping with the imagery of the way, Bonhoeffer envisages formation as a process.[78] This means that there can be genuine progress – as well as regress – and this is true only because there is a definite goal. The goal is the form of Jesus Christ, who is the end, the *telos*, of the way God has established for us. The *telos* of God's way is the reconciled and renewed human being, fully revealed and realized in Jesus Christ. This process is not a gradual ontological change from one kind of human being to another. The change has already occurred.[79] Nor does Bonhoeffer imagine that formation occurs in a piecemeal fashion, as if human thoughts could become more Christ-like while human actions are unaffected. Because a human being is an indivisible whole, formation involves the whole person: 'When God's word has struck us, we may say: I seek you *with my whole heart*. For we would seek an idol halfheartedly, but never God himself. God needs the whole heart.'[80] The whole human person must encounter the whole Christ, and this encounter is transformative.

---

74. DBWE 15, 503; DBW 15, 507.
75. DBWE 15, 506; DBW 15, 510.
76. DBWE 15, 506; DBW 15, 510.
77. DBWE 15, 506; DBW 15, 510.
78. See DBWE 4, 286; DBW 4, 302; DBWE 15, 504; DBW 15, 508; DBWE 6, 134; DBW 6, 125.
79. See McGarry, 'Con-formed to Christ', 231.
80. DBWE 15, 513; DBW 15, 519.

Conclusion

Bibliology asks not only what Scripture is but also what God does with it. Bonhoeffer's incomplete 'Meditation on Psalm 119', along with related, contemporary works, indicates that his bibliology includes Christian formation within the real encounter with Christ in the word of Scripture. In scriptural meditation, Christians place themselves before God's word in Scripture so as to receive it by the Holy Spirit, that they may be transformed into the form of Christ who encounters them in the word of Scripture today. We do not transform ourselves by sheer force of effort or discipline, but the one who is on God's way meditates on God's word, and meditation invites an encounter with Christ in the word that is uniquely transformative. Our hope for transformation must be directed to God, since 'it is God, the Holy Spirit himself, who makes for me the reality of what was true for Jesus Christ alone: my will is your word'.[81] Psalm 119 is for Bonhoeffer the endlessly repeated prayer that must accompany all people on God's way: May my ways be your ways, my will your word.

---

81. DBWE 15, 510; DBW 15, 515.

8

READING IN THE PRESENT TENSE

At a retreat for his Finkenwalde seminarians in the summer of 1936, Bonhoeffer presented two essays that would cause him more trouble than he could have anticipated. His essay, 'On the Question of Church Communion', quickly gained notoriety due to Bonhoeffer's application of the *extra ecclesiam* principle: 'Whoever knowingly separates himself from the Confessing Church in Germany has separated himself from salvation.'[1] It was published in the June 1936 edition of *Evangelische Theologie* to resounding critical disdain.[2] His other essay, a theological interpretation of Ezra-Nehemiah, received less attention, but was likewise contentious. The piece ran in *Junge Kirche* under the title, 'The Reconstruction of Jerusalem According to Ezra and Nehemiah' (hereafter, 'Reconstruction').[3] The arch-critic of 'Reconstruction' was Friedrich Baumgärtel, who declared that Bonhoeffer's exegetical decisions were indefensible, his deployment of texts arbitrary and his conclusions baseless. According to Eberhard Bethge, it 'destroyed Bonhoeffer's reputation as an interpreter of the Old Testament'.[4]

In this chapter, I reconsider the critical objections to 'Reconstruction' in light of Bonhoeffer's bibliology. I begin by reviewing Bonhoeffer's exegesis of Ezra-Nehemiah and Baumgärtel's criticisms against it. Then, building on the bibliology I have outlined in the preceding chapters, I articulate the present-tense character of divine and human speech in Bonhoeffer's thought. His bibliology is built upon a *present-tense* concept of revelation, which is grounded in his Christology, and his exegesis of Ezra-Nehemiah is consistent with this concept. Much of this chapter proceeds as a critical dialogue with Baumgärtel, who released a scathing response to 'Reconstruction' shortly after its publication. I show that Baumgärtel operates with a fundamentally different concept of revelation and its relationship to history and Scripture, and that this concept is at the root of much critical reaction

---

1. DBWE 14, 675; DBW 14, 676.
2. Bethge reports that this statement quickly morphed into a simplistic refrain, so that Bonhoeffer's detractors would sarcastically exclaim, 'Anyone without a Red Card won't go to heaven!' (DB-ER, 520). Bethge notes that, in most provinces, the membership commitments to the Confessing Church were signed on a red card.
3. DBWE 14, 917–31; DBW 14, 930–45.
4. DB-ER, 526.

against Bonhoeffer's study. For Bonhoeffer, exegesis is not the task of establishing the one true meaning of the text, nor does it aim at producing an authoritative, standalone 'interpretation'. Exegesis means prayerfully discerning the 'right word' for the present and aims at a present-tense act of 'telling the truth' about Scripture. When reconsidered in this light, both the contributions and the limitations of 'Reconstruction' to our understanding of Bonhoeffer's scriptural exegesis become clearer.

The reconstruction of Jerusalem

On 12 January 1936, Bonhoeffer read from the pulpit a proclamation from the Council of Brethren, formally rejecting the governance of the provincial church committee, which had been established on 27 December 1935. In open disobedience to state authority, Bonhoeffer read to the congregation: 'Complying with the Minister's request and handing over the leadership of the church to the state's church committees is not an option .... [W]e have to make it quite clear to ourselves that we shall not arbitrarily abandon the claims of the Confessing church, even if this should lead us along a fresh path of suffering.'[5] After reading this proclamation, Bonhoeffer preached a sermon from Ezra-Nehemiah about the reconstruction of the wall. Although the text of this sermon has been lost, Bethge takes it for granted that the published version of 'Reconstruction' represents an elaboration of the January sermon.[6]

'Reconstruction' is structured thematically rather than chronologically, although his arrangement broadly corresponds to the history narrated in Ezra-Nehemiah. He offers no rationale for his choice of texts or his organizational scheme, but it seems plausible that he is attempting to work through the historical narrative while drawing attention to parts with special resonance with the situation of the Confessing Church. The essay has four sections: 'The Awakening' (Ezra 1–2); 'The Reconstruction' (Ezra 3); 'The Enemies' (Ezra 4; Neh. 4); and 'Purification of the Community' (Ezra 10; Neh. 7.73b–8.12). Thematically, each section discusses the call, the promise, the external conflict and the internal conflict, respectively. The word of call and promise ground and sustain the community, while the external and internal conflicts threaten to break it apart. Bonhoeffer had been addressing these issues already in his involvement with the Ecumenical Movement and the Confessing Church, and these are the issues he perceives in the text of Ezra-Nehemiah.

Central to Bonhoeffer's exegesis is his presentation of Israel as the community of God's *word*. He does so in different ways in the different sections of 'Reconstruction'. In the time of *awakening*, God's word takes the form of God's call, which awakens

---

5. Joachim Beckmann, ed., *Kirchliches Jahrbuch für die Evangelische Kirche in Deutschland 1933–1944* (Gütersloh: Bertelsmann, 1948), 107–8; quoted in DB-ER, 501–2.

6. Indeed, Bethge quotes from the April Bible study in such a way that readers might think he is quoting directly from the January sermon. See DB-ER, 501.

and gathers the community. During *reconstruction*, the community clings to God's word in the form of God's promise to David to build an everlasting kingdom from his offspring. This dependence on God's promise entails their rejection of the empty promises of political powers, which reveal themselves to be Israel's *enemies*. The community, called by God and trusting in God's promise alone, builds itself upon God's word in Scripture. The *purification of the community* follows from their serious desire to be a community under God's word, that is, under the law. In each case, the word of God is essential to who and what God's people are, whether this word comes in the form of call, promise or law.

Although Bonhoeffer speaks of the word in these different forms, its content remains unequivocal. As call, law or promise, there is only one word: Jesus Christ. Before the time of Christ, God's word has a promissory character. In Bonhoeffer's reading, the community in the time of reconstruction has no possession except the promise. When Ezra reads the law (Neh. 7.73b–8.12), he addresses a people who have already been constituted on the basis of the promise. The community of the word is the community of the promise. Bonhoeffer thereby regards Israel and its history from the perspective of its end in Christ. And if God's word is eternally the word revealed in Christ, then the community of the word is always the community of Christ. Therefore, Bonhoeffer refers to the community in Ezra-Nehemiah as the *church*, using the terms 'community of God', 'people of God', 'Israel' and 'church' interchangeably.[7] The oneness of the community of God's word inheres in the oneness of God's word. Thus, Bonhoeffer assumes throughout his Bible study, and states explicitly in the closing paragraph, that 'the church of God is One both then and today'.[8] Accordingly, his portrayal of the community in Ezra-Nehemiah often strikes distinctly ecclesiological notes.

Bonhoeffer's first two sections on 'the awakening' and 'the reconstruction' largely centre on God's word as call and promise. The restoration and reawakening of the church can only come about through the will of God and his call, and any attempt to rebuild the community of God apart from God's call is tantamount to rebellion against God. God's people must wait for God to awaken them with his word and must accept and pass through God's judgement. The book of Ezra begins after God's people have suffered through God's judgement in the exile and introduces God's call to rebuild the temple in Jerusalem. Bonhoeffer argues that although God's call comes externally through the pagan ruler, Cyrus (Ezra 1.1–4), it comes internally through the Spirit to the exiled community, according to Ezra 1.5. That the call comes through a political power does not indebt the church to the state. The political rulers give space to God's community, but the community is founded on God's word alone.

---

7. Bonhoeffer refers to post-exilic Israel both as a 'Gemeinde' and as a 'Kirche'. The translators of DBWE 14 normally render 'Gemeinde' as 'church-community', following the precedent set in DBWE 1, 14–19. However, in this case they have opted for the more literal translation: 'community'. See their explanation in DBWE 14, 918 ed. n. 5.
8. DBWE 14, 930; DBW 14, 944.

In Bonhoeffer's reading, the rebuilding that takes place is a genuine renewal of faith, among those 'whose spirit God had stirred' (Ezra 1.5). The action is not coerced; the obedience of the people is completely voluntary. God's call commands free obedience, and the community is united in their obedience, acting as one person. At great risk to themselves, they return. As the community called by God's word, they are truly the *ecclesia*. God's call is certain because God's promises are sure. The rebuilding of the temple proceeds on the basis of God's promise and the community's faith in that promise. Being roused by God's call does not result in a frenzy of enthusiasm but in disciplined, diligent obedience. The community, led by their king and high priest, begins worship of God at an altar that they built before any work on the temple had begun. They were an 'emergency church'[9] under the promise, patiently waiting on God's time in the reconstruction. When rebuilding finally begins, the people respond with a mixture of despair and hope: despair from the older generation who lamented the loss of Israel's former glory and hope from the younger in God's promise and steadfast love.

In David's son, Zerubbabel, God's promise was being fulfilled. Zerubbabel builds the second temple 'in the power of the Christ to whom the promise applies in David'.[10] The name of the high priest, Jeshua, regularly stands next to Zerubbabel's in the text of Ezra,[11] and the kingly and priestly figures together evoke the figure of Jesus Christ. Bonhoeffer was experimenting with allegorical interpretation of the Old Testament at this time, most prominently in his Bible Study on King David and his work with the Psalter.[12] Just as Christ is 'prefigured' in David,[13] so is he prefigured in those who inherit the Davidic promise. The God who has called the community has called them according to the word of promise that was given to David, passed to Zerubbabel and is fulfilled in Christ. Ezra-Nehemiah therefore testifies to God's election of Israel and his promise to establish a kingdom through David's line. The return of Israel and the rebuilding of Jerusalem after the Babylonian captivity by a Davidic king witness to God's ongoing faithfulness to his promise.

Bonhoeffer's third section on 'the enemies' concerns the external threats to the community. The church's early success is a visible event, and the restored community has an unavoidable impact in the wider political sphere. The political powers first try to exploit the church for its own ends, which comes as an offer of assistance, to work together in reconstruction (Ezra 4.1–2). Bonhoeffer, following Zerubbabel's response in Ezra 4.3, insists that the church must reject such an offer. Only God builds God's church, and his word alone is the church's foundation.

---

9. DBWE 14, 922; DBW 14, 935.

10. DBWE 14, 922; DBW 14, 935.

11. Bonhoeffer cites Ezra 2.2; 3.2, 8; 4.3; 5.2 (DBWE 14, 922; DBW 14, 935).

12. See 'King David' in DBWE 14, 870–93; DBW 14, 878–904, and 'Christ in the Psalms' in DBWE 14, 386–93; DBW 14, 369–77.

13. 'The office and reign of Christ are prefigured [vorgebildet] in David' (DBWE 14, 872; DBW 14, 880).

After being refused, the political powers try to stop the church's reconstruction by force. Bonhoeffer jumps to Nehemiah 4 to show that political violence, while it may succeed for a time, is weaker than God's word. Bonhoeffer emphasizes that the success of the reconstruction of Jerusalem is owed to God alone, despite the state's active opposition. Accordingly, he draws attention to passages of Ezra-Nehemiah – such as Ezra 4.3 and 8.22, and Nehemiah 6.16 – that depict Israel's rejection of political power and state assistance.

Having rebuilt the temple and the city walls, the community itself must also be rebuilt. This is the framework of Bonhoeffer's fourth and final section on the 'purification of the community'. Anticipating the language of *Discipleship*, he says that the rebuilding of the community must be done in 'simple obedience to the word of God'.[14] The reading of the Torah in Nehemiah 8 is significant in this context. Not according to political power, calculation or influence but only on the ground of Scripture can the church stand before God. Gone were the days when belonging to Israel included political or economic advantages. The people sought God and God's word alone, as their response to the reading of the law indicates. The people weep when they hear Ezra read the law, they repent and are assured that God is with them. 'God's law is his grace', Bonhoeffer says.[15] The people freely commit themselves to God's law in the power of God's grace and word. Thus, the word of Scripture is the basis of the newly awakened and rebuilt community, who obeys the word wholeheartedly and voluntarily, a pure community of the word. However, purity cannot come without discipline. Disobedience to God's word poses a perennial threat to the community, so a complete and shocking separation occurs between true believers and unbelievers. For Bonhoeffer, outrageous as this action may seem, this kind of extreme 'church discipline' signifies that God's word is being taken with utmost seriousness.

Bonhoeffer's conclusion is as close as he comes to addressing the contemporary situation of the Confessing Church. He concludes with a statement on the continuity of God's word, God's church and God's ways:

> The church of God is One both then and today. The paths along which God leads the church are always the same; through judgment and punishment and destruction, the community hears God's call and promise anew. But wherever God's promise is perceived and is taken seriously, the church emerges; wherever a community is prepared to possess nothing other than the word, it stands before [God] as the community of justified sinners. And ultimately it comes about: 'And when all our enemies heard of it, all the nations around us were afraid and fell greatly in their own esteem, for they perceived that this work had been accomplished with the help of our God.'[16]

---

14. DBWE 14, 928; DBW 14, 941.
15. DBWE 14, 929; DBW 14, 943.
16. DBWE 14, 930–1; DBW 14, 944–5. This is the second time he quotes from Neh. 6.16 (the first occurs, with slightly modified wording, in DBWE 14, 927; DBW 14, 940).

Baumgärtel's critique

Friedrich Baumgärtel was the professor of Old Testament in Greifswald when 'Reconstruction' was published in *Junge Kirche*, and it was not long before he responded with a rebuke.[17] The Greifswald Superintendent Karl von Scheven had been appointed as the leader of the provincial church committee, which the Council of Brethren had formally rejected in the statement that Bonhoeffer read on 12 January 1936.[18] Needless to say, tensions were already high between Finkenwalde and Greifswald, but Baumgärtel states his wish to put issues of church politics aside in order to address the exegetical and theological issues at stake.[19] For him, the problem with 'Reconstruction' ran deeper than Bonhoeffer's idiosyncratic exegetical decisions. He was more concerned with the principles of Old Testament interpretation that undergirded Bonhoeffer's study. 'If Bonhoeffer's way of interpreting the Old Testament succeeds in the church', Baumgärtel declared, 'the Old Testament will be surrendered and lost to the church'.[20]

Baumgärtel's main point of contention was Bonhoeffer's assertion that the 'church then' can be identified with the 'church today', that the post-exilic Israelite community described in Ezra-Nehemiah is 'one' with the Protestant Church in 1930s Germany. In Baumgärtel's judgement, this conclusion is indefensible, not only on the grounds of historical research, but even from a plain reading of the biblical texts. His attack against Bonhoeffer is twofold. Firstly, he uses passages from Ezra-Nehemiah to counter Bonhoeffer's conclusions directly. His purpose in this section, as he notes, is to follow Bonhoeffer's example and deploy only the texts, ignoring what historical science might have to add. Secondly, he broadens his scope to address the implications of 'Reconstruction' for the interpretation of the Old Testament as a whole. He concludes that Bonhoeffer's selection of passages from Ezra-Nehemiah is arbitrary, that Bonhoeffer ignores historical research at his peril and that the parallels drawn between the 'church then' and the 'church today' are invalid. For Baumgärtel, Bonhoeffer wilfully misrepresents the meaning of Old Testament texts, and if the church were to follow suit, it would lose the Old Testament as Holy Scripture.

It will help to unpack Baumgärtel's objections at greater length. In his first section, he raises basic exegetical objections against Bonhoeffer. Whereas Bonhoeffer had portrayed the community's return as a risky venture and an act of sheer dependence on God, and therefore of complete *independence* from the state, Baumgärtel contends that the texts offer a different portrait altogether. The community receives plenty of financial assistance from the

---

17. Baumgärtel, *Die Kirche ist Eine*. All translations from this booklet are my own.
18. For more on this history, see DB-ER, 495–506.
19. Baumgärtel, *Die Kirche ist Eine*, 3.
20. Baumgärtel, *Die Kirche ist Eine*, 17.

royal treasury (Ezra 6.3-10). Ezra enjoys the support of the Persian King Artaxerxes (Ezra 7.6), who offers to outfit the temple with everything required (Ezra 7.15-24). Historical research, Baumgärtel cannot resist adding, suggests that Persian welfare was very generous towards subjugated religions, and so it would hardly have been a great risk to venture out in response to Cyrus's command.[21] As for the church's refusal of worldly political power, which Bonhoeffer sees in Zerubbabel's rejection of state assistance and Nehemiah's resistance of violent opposition, Baumgärtel simply finds this implausible, given the extent to which the religious and political leaders of Israel were involved and entangled with the political powers. The 'church then' was, in fact, quite comfortable establishing its foundation *'in league with state authority'*.[22] The state, then, was not the primary opponent of the rebuilding of the temple and of Jerusalem. Baumgärtel argues that the main obstacle was the community itself. Specifically, the community's apathy and selfishness threatened to halt God's work at every turn. It took the prophets Haggai and Zechariah to rouse the people back into action, and they do so by proclaiming a messianic ideal that is incompatible with Christ's. The hope that awakened the 'church then' was the promise of worldly power and glory, which Jesus explicitly rejected. Therefore, for Baumgärtel, 'the "church then" pursued the messianic ideal that was broken by the one on whom the church today is founded'.[23]

Additionally, Baumgärtel disagrees with Bonhoeffer's portrait of the post-exilic community as a 'community of the word'. It seems to Baumgärtel that Bonhoeffer's equating the 'church then' with the 'church today' follows from the premise that both are, in the most genuine sense possible, communities of God's word. But Baumgärtel thinks this premise is simply false. The Israelite community was not an ethnically and culturally diverse group united by a common faith in God's word. By the post-exilic period, Baumgärtel contends, Israel had become *'an ethnic-legal-cultic [völkisch-rechtlich-kultische] community* in a certain delimited geographical district and endowed with the rights of local self-government'.[24] He asserts that, from the perspective of the Old Testament, *'the community of God is identical with the "nation"* [*"Volk"*]'.[25] These direct parallels between the Old Testament people of God and the 'Volk' would have posed a particular challenge to Bonhoeffer as a Confessing Church interpreter of the Old Testament. After all, if the church is the same today as then, does it follow that there is an *ethnic* dimension to what it means to be the people of God? This challenge reaches its pinnacle when Baumgärtel turns to the purification of the community in Ezra 9-10. What Bonhoeffer views as 'church discipline', Baumgärtel views as something more extreme: 'The separation is certainly the separation of the unbelievers from the "church," but at the same

---

21. Baumgärtel, *Die Kirche ist Eine*, 7.
22. Baumgärtel, *Die Kirche ist Eine*, 8.
23. Baumgärtel, *Die Kirche ist Eine*, 9.
24. Baumgärtel, *Die Kirche ist Eine*, 10.
25. Baumgärtel, *Die Kirche ist Eine*, 11.

time it is the separation of the ethnic foreigners from the ethnic community. This separation is not merely "church" discipline, it is at the same time the intense process of ethnic purification [völkische Reinigungsprozeß] carried out by the "church then.""[26] What could Bonhoeffer say to this? Did he really want to model the Confessing Church after a nationalistic community that would expunge all ethnic diversity from its ranks?

Baumgärtel, by appealing to the same books of the Old Testament that Bonhoeffer did, argued for a completely different conclusion. The 'church then' was not a church at all. It was an ethnic community that took full advantage of political powers and influence, that enforced religious laws with governmental force, that excluded foreigners for the sake of the purity of the people. The 'church' that was built up at that time was not the 'church today'. It was the church of bondage, not of freedom. It was the church of the Pharisees, the church that crucified Jesus. 'The church is one, both then and today?', Baumgärtel asks in his incredulous refrain. No, he concludes, quite the opposite. The Second-Temple Judaism that was founded in the days of Ezra and Nehemiah is the very 'church' that Jesus came to overturn.

Baumgärtel does not limit his critique to the text of Ezra-Nehemiah. He perceives a larger problem with Bonhoeffer's seeming disregard for historical research. Exasperated, he says that theologians tend to forget a basic fact about theological exegesis: 'The Old Testament is a testimony of the leading of the people of God in history, so it has to do with the theological interpretation of history, and it has to strive for the historical facts to the best of its knowledge and conscience. Failure to do so will eliminate the historical moment from God's revelation.'[27] The theological interpretation of Scripture, in other words, goes hand in hand with responsible historical science. Note, however, that Baumgärtel's reason for saying this is not because history better illuminates the *text*. Rather, it is because both the text *and* historical research illuminate 'the historical moment' of revelation. Scripture, for Baumgärtel, testifies to God's *history* with his people, and that is where revelation is to be found. If revelation simply is this history, then theological exegesis is a historical enterprise. This marks a clear distinction between Baumgärtel and Bonhoeffer, which I will discuss in more detail below.

For Baumgärtel, the most dangerous outcome of Bonhoeffer's approach is the collapse of the two Testaments of the Christian Bible. The Old Testament must remain the *Old* if the New is to have any significance. The meaning of the New Testament can only be understood in relation to what it supersedes. That is why Bonhoeffer's reading of Ezra-Nehemiah is so disastrous. Jesus, Baumgärtel avers, came to undo the errors of the Jewish religion that began in the days of Ezra and Nehemiah; the last thing Christians should be doing

---

26. Baumgärtel, *Die Kirche ist Eine*, 13.
27. Baumgärtel, *Die Kirche ist Eine*, 14.

with Israel's Scripture is following its example. To say that the church is already there in the Old Testament, and that the church today only needs to transform itself to look like the church then, is to make a categorical theological error. The 'church' did not exist before Christ: 'The Old Testament that is no longer the *Old* Testament because "the church" is already in it, and yet which knows nothing of the cross and the empty tomb, is for us Christians a dead book; it is meaningless for the Christian, because we cannot separate the church from the death and resurrection of the Lord.'[28] It was for the sake of the very essence of the church and Scripture's place within it that Baumgärtel could not allow Bonhoeffer's Bible study to go unchallenged. He sought to correct Bonhoeffer not only on the particulars of his exegetical decisions, but also on broader theological issues. Interpretation of the Old Testament is the theological interpretation of *history*, and Christian interpreters must take care to maintain the Old Testament's character as the *Old* and not the New. Baumgärtel thus challenged Bonhoeffer on both exegetical and historical-critical grounds. With the former, he showed how even the text taken on its own terms disagrees with Bonhoeffer's presentation, and with the latter, he accused Bonhoeffer of ignoring the historical character of revelation.

The present-tense character of revelation

According to Bethge, Baumgärtel's critique was widely accepted,[29] not least by Bethge himself. Bethge agrees that Bonhoeffer 'had ignored the context of the verses he had selected' and 'had been too hasty in compiling the material'. He suspects that Bonhoeffer may have 'sensed the weakness of his exegetical method, for not long afterward he thought of drafting an article on "hermeneutics"'.[30] Martin Kuske, another sympathetic reader of Bonhoeffer, agrees with Baumgärtel that Bonhoeffer was being 'one-sided' and concedes that 'Bonhoeffer arbitrarily interpreted the Old Testament and therefore surrendered it when it concerned the exegetical-dogmatical question regarding the identity of the church at that time and today'.[31] Ernst Georg Wendel accepts Baumgärtel's position that Bonhoeffer's exegesis is untenable,[32] and Ferdinand Schlingensiepen notes Bonhoeffer's neglect

---

28. Baumgärtel, *Die Kirche ist Eine*, 18.
29. Bethge quotes a reply from the Westphalian church paper: 'Baumgärtel's demand for clarification is patently necessary. Bonhoeffer's "Bible study" cannot remain uncontested' (*Das Evangelische Westfalen* [September 1936], 142; quoted in DB-ER, 528).
30. DB-ER, 528.
31. Kuske, *Old Testament as the Book of Christ*, 83.
32. Wendel, *Studien zur Homiletik Dietrich Bonhoeffers*, 100–2.

of serious Old Testament scholarship during his education, reporting that Gerhard von Rad took Bonhoeffer to task for his approach to the subject.[33]

Nevertheless, these reviews are not entirely negative. Bethge concludes that the Bible study 'does not stand up to an examination of its biblical-historical context, but its message remains valid'.[34] Kuske likewise argues that Bonhoeffer was less concerned with standing up to historical-critical scrutiny than with conveying God's message for the present situation. Proclamation thus proceeds 'not with the goal of assisting the hearer to reach an opinion about past events, but to move him toward the simple action of the Word heard in the present'.[35] Bethge and Kuske both reject the method of Bonhoeffer's interpretation but affirm his broader message. In their evaluation, 'Reconstruction' is best read as a compelling sermon based on faulty exegesis. But if this is the case, then what are theological exegetes to make of 'Reconstruction'? What about Bonhoeffer's questionable exegetical moves throughout? Is his exegesis something to be emulated, or is it nothing more than a cautionary tale, a failed exegetical experiment?

I propose that 'Reconstruction' offers something far more constructive for the discipline of theological interpretation, but that its potential contribution is obscured by the kinds of criticisms that have long been levelled against it. In light of the bibliology I outlined in the preceding chapters, I argue that giving due attention to the present-tense character of revelation in Bonhoeffer's thought helps to explain his approach to Ezra-Nehemiah in 1936. Bonhoeffer's reading of Scripture is informed by his account of what Scripture is and does, which in turn follows from his Christological account of divine revelation. For Bonhoeffer, revelation is *Christus praesens*, and therefore God's word is to be found not somewhere in history, but rather in the present. This frees him to discern a present word for his present situation in the text of Ezra-Nehemiah, and to pursue this word in ways that the historical-critical guild would not allow.

Revelation-as-*Christus-praesens*, I have argued thus far, is a central theme in Bonhoeffer's thought. It has important implications not only for his understanding of revelation and bibliology, but also for his understanding of the relationship between history and Scripture. For Bonhoeffer, it is impermissible to talk of Jesus

---

33. Schlingensiepen, *Bonhoeffer 1906–1945*, 191: 'The Old Testament was the one theological discipline that Bonhoeffer had neglected somewhat during his own studies. Thus it was no wonder that his Bible study was rejected even by Old Testament scholars in the Confessing Church. His friend Gerhard von Rad, with whom he had often played music when they were schoolboys, wrote in his diary that he ought to "take Bonhoeffer by the collar" here. Rad had shown, as no one else had done, that there was no need to bend Old Testament texts out of shape in order to interpret them in the spirit of the Confessing Church. So during a visit of Bonhoeffer's to the University of Jena, the two theologians, friends since their youth, had a lively but friendly dispute over the interpretation of the Old Testament for the present time.'

34. DB-ER, 528–9.

35. Kuske, *Old Testament as the Book of Christ*, 84.

Christ in a way that divorces his person from his presence. 'It is not only useless to meditate on a Christ-in-himself but godless, precisely because Christ is not there in-himself but rather is there for you.'[36] Reading Scripture as the book of Christ, therefore, means reading it as the book of the *present* Christ. As I demonstrated in CHAPTER 5, this development had important implications for Bonhoeffer's bibliology. 'Reconstruction' represents one of Bonhoeffer's exegetical applications of his bibliology.

Bonhoeffer does not wish to negate the historical character of revelation. On the contrary, the present-tense character of revelation is how he maintains its historicity. God's word is by nature a present word. The present, however, is not a static reality. It is forever becoming the past, becoming *history*. History includes the many present moments in which God spoke to and acted for human beings, and these are what have been recorded in Scripture and passed down to the church. Revelation is 'historical' because it occurs in history, but historical revelation does not exist frozen in the past, nor can it be uncovered by unearthing the history. God's word can only be heard as a present word. Historical research can help to bring out the full, historical character of revelation,[37] but exegesis is always for the sake of hearing God speak today. The church is the community that believes God has spoken and will continue to speak today in the words of historical revelation recorded in Holy Scripture. As a word that occurs in the present, revelation is intrinsically historical, but it cannot be reduced to the history in which it occurred. Even if we could perfectly reconstruct the events that prompted the biblical written record, we would not thereby have obtained revelation. For revelation 'exists' only in the present. Its being is in its being spoken today.

It is not only the present-tense character of God's speech in revelation that must be considered, but also the present-tense character of human speech. Exegesis discerns the present word in order to proclaim a word in and for the present. 'Reconstruction' is not Bonhoeffer's once-for-all statement about the 'meaning' of Ezra-Nehemiah; it is meant to serve proclamation. For Bonhoeffer, the final goal of exegesis is not a standalone document called an 'interpretation', but rather the event of proclamation as a present-tense act of 'telling the truth' about Scripture.

Bonhoeffer's incomplete essay, 'What Does It Mean to Tell the Truth?', is instructive here. For Bonhoeffer, telling the truth consists in the claim that '*what is real is to be expressed in words*'.[38] All truth is grounded in reality, which means the reality of God. Lying, in Bonhoeffer's understanding, 'is first of all the denial of God as God has been revealed to the world'.[39] It is not a contradiction between one's thoughts and one's words, but 'a contradiction of the word of God as it was spoken in Christ and in which creation rests'.[40] Human speech is not merely to

---

36. DBWE 12, 314; DBW 12, 296.
37. DBWE 14, 390; DBW 14, 374.
38. DBWE 16, 603; DBW 16, 622.
39. DBWE 16, 607; DBW 16, 627. Bonhoeffer quotes 1 John 2.22 in this connection.
40. DBWE 16, 607; DBW 16, 627.

correspond to discrete facts, but to reality. 'Cynics', Bonhoeffer says, 'want to make their word true by always expressing the particular thing they think they understand without regard for reality as a whole. Precisely in this way they utterly destroy the real, and their word becomes untrue, even if it maintains the superficial appearance of correctness'.[41] Truthful speech cannot be attained by baldly stating the facts, because speech is a relational event that happens between persons. Speech is *address*, not idea, a point that Bonhoeffer had already made in his 1933 Christology: 'The word as idea remains essentially within itself, but the word in the form of address is only possible as word between two persons, as speaking and response, responsibility'.[42] Speech is word addressed to a concrete other. And here Bonhoeffer's distinctive way of relating history and the present once again shows itself. Word as address 'is not timeless but rather takes place within history. Thus, it is not generally accessible to anyone at any time but rather happens there where it is spoken to someone by another'.[43] That speech is a present act means that it is historical, but it also means that speech occurs only in the *present* historical moment.

Although Bonhoeffer's essay on truth-telling was occasioned by quite different circumstances than the question of scriptural interpretation,[44] his reflections offer a promising way to reframe his exegesis in 'Reconstruction'. Proclamation can be regarded as a present-tense act of 'telling the truth' about Scripture, insofar as it addresses the congregation with the scriptural text as the witness to the ultimate reality in which all reality is embedded. In proclamation, ultimate reality is expressed in words. It speaks the 'right word' for the concrete situation, the word that concretely discloses the word of God in the words of Scripture. If, as Bonhoeffer says elsewhere, 'exegesis means to recognize and understand God's word in Scripture as God's word',[45] then the task of exegesis is analogous to the process of determining the 'right word': 'To discover this is a matter of long, earnest, and continual effort that is based in experience and the perception of reality. In order to say how something is real – i.e., to speak truthfully – one's gaze and thought must be oriented toward how the real is in God, and through God, and toward God.'[46] Exegesis that drives towards truthful proclamation is therefore concerned primarily with how God is speaking in the words of the text to reveal himself in Christ today. If historical-criticism is employed, it is solely for the purpose of discerning this present word in order to proclaim it concretely in the present.

Theological exegesis, following Bonhoeffer, requires that we stand fully in the present, in our various concrete situations and contexts, while recognizing that the true meaning of the present consists in encountering the present Christ in

---

41. DBWE 16, 608; DBW 16, 628.
42. DBWE 12, 316; DBW 12, 298.
43. DBWE 12, 316; DBW 12, 298.
44. See DBWE 16, 601 ed. n. 1; DBW 16, 619 ed. n. 1 for more details.
45. DBWE 15, 517; DBW 15, 524.
46. DBWE 16, 603; DBW 16, 622.

the word of Scripture. 'The concept of the present', Bonhoeffer claims, 'is not a temporal determination; instead it is [determined] through the word of Christ as the word of God'.[47] Therefore, even the concept of the present requires a Christological interpretation. Revelation and word exist only in the present, and the present is constituted by the present Christ. Human words that testify to revelation are always contingent and provisional. This is partly why Bethge and others have been able to affirm that Bonhoeffer spoke the 'right word' for his time while simultaneously disavowing his exegetical moves. The problem with this perspective is that, for Bonhoeffer, the 'right word' is not something that can stand apart from textual exposition. The word of proclamation is not a standalone word that arises from or is based upon the biblical text. God speaks 'only and exclusively *through the word* of Scripture itself'.[48] Therefore, 'the sermon is a witness only as a witness to the biblical witness'.[49] 'Telling the truth' about Scripture requires continual discernment and humility to hear what the Spirit is saying to the church through the biblical words today. Bonhoeffer's posture of naive receptivity towards the text of Ezra-Nehemiah follows from his commitment to hearing Christ speak today in the words of Scripture.

In sum, Bonhoeffer's affirmation of the historicity of revelation derives from his more fundamental affirmation of its irreducible present-tense character. The 'being' of revelation is *Christus praesens*, and Holy Scripture is God's chosen witness to this self-revelatory word; theological exegesis is the spiritual and prayerful discernment of this present word in Scripture, in the service of proclaiming the present word of God in the words of the biblical text today. God is present in history precisely in being present today.[50] The present-tense nature of revelation demands both a full appreciation of revelation as a historical event and a refusal to reduce revelation to any such event. God's word occurs as God's speaking in the present, that is, into the historical moment. But the historical event of God's speech cannot simply be exported into the present, as if this would bring yesterday's revelation into today. Revelation occurs for us if and only if God himself speaks today.

Reading out of context

Recall Baumgärtel's statement about the need for historical research: 'The Old Testament is a testimony of the leading of the people of God in history, so it has to do with the theological interpretation of history, and it has to strive for the historical facts to the best of its knowledge and conscience. Failure to do so will

---

47. DBWE 14, 417; DBW 14, 404.
48. DBWE 14, 417; DBW 14, 404.
49. DBWE 14, 535; DBW 14, 529.
50. In Bonhoeffer's somewhat awkward phrasing, 'God is for us "always" *God* precisely "*today*"'. DBWE 11, 360; DBW 11, 332.

eliminate the historical moment from God's revelation.'[51] Accordingly, Baumgärtel's interest lies in uncovering the historical events behind the biblical text. It is in the *history*, not the text, that God's revelatory activity has occurred. The text merely gives evidence about this history. The historical record, therefore, can and should be read alongside the biblical account. Bonhoeffer himself could approve of this practice in principle. The historical element of the scriptural witness is, after all, inextricably bound up with the scriptural words in which God speaks. But Bonhoeffer and Baumgärtel construe the historicity of revelation differently. Revelation, for Baumgärtel, is a divinely orchestrated event in history. For Bonhoeffer, however, revelation is the presence of Christ as God's contemporary word. To put it another way, for Baumgärtel, *history* is the point of contact between revelation and our present situation, whereas for Bonhoeffer, the *present* is the point of contact between revelation and history. For Bonhoeffer, making Scripture present means one of two things: 'Either one understands it to mean that the biblical message must justify itself to the present … or that the present must justify itself to the biblical message.'[52] In his view, exegesis begins and ends with God's present word. All revelation extends from God's word in Christ, and this word is *Christus praesens*.

What, then, does Bonhoeffer make of the historical events that lie behind the biblical testimony? Apart from a passing reference to the 'entirely uncertain'[53] chronology, Bonhoeffer shows little interest in the question, and this aligns with his insistence on the present-tense character of revelation. God speaks only in the present; revelation necessarily occurs historically but is not reducible to the history itself. The language of Barth's later interpreters is apt: revelation is *in* history but not *of* history.[54] Bonhoeffer reads Ezra-Nehemiah as history but seems unconcerned to ask whether it can be verified as such. After all, if God is speaking through this text, this word is spoken only in the present. In the eyes of his historical-critical interlocutors, Bonhoeffer was frustratingly naive, but his naivety was intentional. Consider his letter to Rüdiger Schleicher, dated 8 April 1936 – only a few weeks before he presented 'Reconstruction' to his students on 21 April 1936. He tells Schleicher that, because only God can speak God's word, the reader should be willing to surrender his or her own understanding to be open to what God might be saying in the biblical words. He remarks, 'What a joyous thing it is when one finds one's way back to these primitive things after losing one's way along the false

---

51. Baumgärtel, *Die Kirche ist Eine*, 14.
52. DBWE 14, 413; DBW 14, 400.
53. DBWE 14, 927; DBW 14, 941.
54. Although this exact phrase does not occur in *Church Dogmatics*, it has become a common way to express the basic problem of revelation and history as Barth saw it. See, for example, McCormack, *Barth's Dialectical Theology*, 209; Trevor Hart, 'Revelation', in *The Cambridge Companion to Karl Barth*, ed. John Webster (Cambridge: Cambridge University Press, 2000), 45.

paths of so many theologies.'⁵⁵ Gesturing to patience and humility as exegetical virtues, he says, 'I am willing to grant that this or that passage of Scripture cannot yet be understood, though with the certainty that one day this passage will indeed be revealed as God's own word.'⁵⁶ The perspicuity of God's word depends on God's initiative in revealing himself through his word rather than the sophistication of our critical methods. The task of exegesis is a process of listening and discernment, which demands patience, silence and an attitude of receptivity. Exegesis means waiting on the Holy Spirit to disclose God's word in Scripture as God's word in Christ.

Nowhere is the difference between Bonhoeffer and Baumgärtel more pronounced than in their treatments of the post-exilic Israelite community vis-à-vis the twentieth-century Protestant church. Bonhoeffer refers to the Israelite community as the 'church' without further explanation. As I summarized above, a good portion of Baumgärtel's booklet is occupied with showing how the community described in Ezra-Nehemiah is *not* in fact the same community as the Protestant church. There are simply too many differences between the community of Israel in the time of reconstruction and the church today, and so any attempt to remodel the church after the portrait given in Ezra-Nehemiah is doomed. What Ezra-Nehemiah offers, in Baumgärtel's view, is a portrait of God's people in bondage to the law, a spiritually dead community. It shows the process whereby Israel 'began to shed the stream of living knowledge of God that was given to the people of Israel in Moses and the prophets'.⁵⁷ If it serves as a model for the church today, it does so only negatively.

This is an instance where Baumgärtel's concept of revelation blinds him to Bonhoeffer's logic. Kuske rightly notes, 'The statement that the church then and now is one, against which the attack of Baumgärtel arose, was not the goal, but *only* the presupposition of his Bible study.'⁵⁸ Bonhoeffer does not interpret *towards* the unity of the 'church then' and the 'church today' but *from* it. A community that is truly a community of the word cannot be essentially different from another community of that same word, because each has the present Christ as its origin, substance and goal. To deny this, in Bonhoeffer's view, is to deny the scriptural testimony of Ezra-Nehemiah, which presents the community as 'a community of the word'.⁵⁹ Baumgärtel views Ezra-Nehemiah as a *source* for the history of Israel building itself into a community of law and bondage. Bonhoeffer reads Ezra-Nehemiah a *witness* to Christ and thereby as God's address to the church today.

A striking example of this difference is found in Bonhoeffer's and Baumgärtel's respective treatments of Ezra 9–10. Bonhoeffer interprets this passage as 'church discipline', whereas Baumgärtel reads it as 'ethnic purification'. It might seem that Baumgärtel is acknowledging the true difficulties of the text and that Bonhoeffer,

55. DBWE 14, 169; DBW 14, 147–8.
56. DBWE 14, 169; DBW 14, 147.
57. Baumgärtel, *Die Kirche ist Eine*, 13.
58. Kuske, *Old Testament as the Book of Christ*, 83.
59. DBWE 14, 928; DBW 14, 942.

by comparison, is simply glossing over what should be recognized as a disturbing moment in the narrative. But this is precisely where attention to the present-tense character of Bonhoeffer's theology of revelation is useful, specifically as it pertains to the place of the *interpreter* in relation to exegesis. If God's word is a contemporary word, then exegesis means hearing God's word today, which can only happen in the event of genuine encounter with God's word. The 'difficulty' of Scripture is not primarily that it sounds objectionable, but that it addresses us with God's commanding word. Therefore, facing the difficulties of the text does not mean simply turning up the volume so everyone can hear how offensive the Bible sounds to modern ears. It means allowing oneself and one's community to be implicated by these texts. Baumgärtel's exegesis tends to run in the opposite direction. He draws attention to the ways in which the post-exilic community depended on state assistance and revelled in political power. He points out the disturbing ethnic basis of the purification of the community and the legal enforcement of religious adherence. In all this, he is careful to highlight the *distance* between the 'church then' and the church today. In an emphatically supersessionist move, Baumgärtel opposes 'the inclusion of Jewish thought and essence into our faith',[60] asserting that 'the old covenant must remain the old'.[61] With this attitude, Baumgärtel refuses to allow the problematic events in Ezra 9–10 to sully his hands.

To be sure, Bonhoeffer has not evaded the charge of supersessionism. His conflation of the community in Ezra-Nehemiah and the Confessing Church in Germany is one of many instances where his Christological reading of Old Testament texts raises serious questions about his potential to contribute to post-Holocaust Jewish–Christian dialogue.[62] What should not be missed, however,

---

60. Baumgärtel, *Die Kirche ist Eine*, 16.
61. Baumgärtel, *Die Kirche ist Eine*, 18.
62. Victoria Barnett concludes that he exhibits a persistent 'theological anti-Judaism' that complicates his legacy in post-Holocaust Jewish–Christian dialogue, in Victoria J. Barnett, 'Dietrich Bonhoeffer's Relevance for Post-Holocaust Christian Theology', *Studies in Jewish–Christian Relations* 2 (2007): 53–67. Some scholars have noted that Bonhoeffer's only explicit treatment of the subject – his 1933 essay, 'The Church and the Jewish Question' (DBWE 12, 361–70; DBW 12, 349–58) – is inconclusive, because discrepancies between Bonhoeffer's draft and the published version call into question the origin of the essay's most offensive claims. See Harvey, *Taking Hold of the Real*, 185–6; cf. DBWE 12, 361 ed. n. 1; DBW 12, 349 ed. n. 1. For a helpful review of various perspectives on Bonhoeffer's contribution to post-Holocaust theology, see Stephen R. Haynes, 'Bonhoeffer, the Jewish People and Post-Holocaust Theology: Eight Perspectives; Eight Theses', *Studies in Jewish–Christian Relations* 2 (2007): 36–52. Haynes concludes that, despite Bonhoeffer's many admirable actions and words on behalf of the Jews, ultimately he 'is not a sufficient or even a reliable guide for Christian post-Holocaust theological reflection' (Haynes, 'Bonhoeffer, the Jewish People and Post-Holocaust Theology', 52). Timothy Stanley, 'Bonhoeffer's Anti-Judaism', *Political Theology* 17 (2016): 297–305, argues that theological anti-Judaism has often been conflated with racial anti-Semitism and that Bonhoeffer's success in rejecting the latter has obscured his failure in the former.

is that Bonhoeffer's reading of Ezra 9–10 constitutes an unequivocal rejection of anything resembling 'ethnic purification'. For Bonhoeffer, the 'purification' of Ezra 9–10 speaks directly to the Confessing Church's need to 'purify' itself of the Reich Church government. The proximity of 'Reconstruction' to Bonhoeffer's essay, 'On the Question of Church Communion', is instructive. In 'Reconstruction', he states, 'one of the most severe aspects of God's word, once it has been perceived, is that it causes people to separate from one another for the sake of that word'.[63] Bonhoeffer believed that the Confessing Church had perceived the word of God. So, in 'Church Communion', he says plainly, 'the Reich Church government has separated itself from the Christian church. The Confessing Church is the true church of Jesus Christ in Germany'.[64] The word of God both unites the community and draws distinct boundaries around it. Bonhoeffer discerned in Ezra 9–10 the address of God to the Confessing Church in and for the present moment, a word that demanded obedience. Obedience, in this instance, certainly did not entail drawing an ethnic line in the sand and dividing the church accordingly. Indeed, as corroborated in 'Church Communion', the element that needed to be purged from the Confessing Church was the influence of the Reich Church!

My purpose here is not to justify Bonhoeffer's exegetical approach by its results. I only aim to show how his attention to the present-tense address of God in Scripture enables him to discern the 'right word' for his situation in ways that would have been strictly prohibited by the standards of historical criticism. His goal is to 'tell the truth' about Scripture by attending to its present witness to God's word, and this is consistent with his account of revelation as *Christus praesens*.

Does this justify interpreting verses out of context, as Bonhoeffer seems to have done in 'Reconstruction'? This is the element of Baumgärtel's charge that Bonhoeffer's later interpreters have generally conceded. It appears that Bonhoeffer was selective in the verses he included and, more importantly, those he excluded. Not only did he ignore the extra-biblical historical material, he ignored the biblical record too! So, the argument goes, Bonhoeffer used select verses from Ezra-Nehemiah to make a different point than the text of Ezra-Nehemiah, taken as a literary whole, actually makes. The biggest target of this critique, as summarized above, is Bonhoeffer's portrayal of Israel as acting in voluntary obedience to God's word independently of and in opposition to the state.

An understanding of Bonhoeffer's bibliology is vital here, because this exegetical critique, like the historical one described above, assumes a past-tense concept of revelation. Its emphasis on the text rather than the history behind the text does, to be sure, have greater affinity with Bonhoeffer's bibliology, but the problem is that it relies on an external, objective standard by which to judge exegesis. For Bonhoeffer, the final measure of exegesis cannot be its fidelity to the immediate literary context any more than it can be its fidelity to the historical events behind the text. Both

---

63. DBWE 14, 930; DBW 14, 944.
64. DBWE 14, 668; DBW 14, 668.

represent attempts to reconstruct the original conditions of revelation in order to gain access to it. It portrays revelation as an event in the past that needs to be brought into the present.

The charge of arbitrariness and selectivity levelled against Bonhoeffer seeks an objectively discernible unity within the biblical text itself, and so contradictions pose an unavoidable exegetical roadblock. But Bonhoeffer was not bothered by the presence of contradictions in the Bible. 'Scripture is harmonious and clear', he says, 'not because it does not contain contradictions but because it is the same God. The harmony of Scripture is not a fact but is instead the presupposition with which one reads it'![65] A contradiction between passages within a biblical book is not substantively more problematic than a contradiction between passages from different books, or even different Testaments. Bonhoeffer reads through a Christological lens rather than a historical- or textual-critical one, because he believes that the unity of Scripture inheres in its witness to God's word in Christ. Pointing out contradictions does not overturn what Bonhoeffer was trying to accomplish. Indeed, from the perspective of Bonhoeffer's bibliology, Baumgärtel's decision to limit his exegetical critique to the text of Ezra-Nehemiah was itself arbitrary and selective!

Bonhoeffer intentionally brings theological presuppositions to Ezra-Nehemiah that are not to be found within the text itself. This includes the presupposition about the unity of the 'church then' and the 'church today'. It also includes presuppositions based on the church's doctrines, creeds and confessional statements. Once again, Bonhoeffer's essay on church communion helps establish the context of his exegetical decisions. In his present situation, there was no question of colluding with the Reich Church government, because that decision had already been made in Barmen. He believed that God had really spoken in Confessing Church's synods. He puts it in rather stark terms in 'Church Communion': 'Either the Barmen Declaration is a true confession to the Lord Jesus effected by the Holy Spirit, in which case its character can be constructive or schismatic for the church; or it is a nonbinding expression of the opinion of several different theologians, and the Confessing Church itself has since then been traveling down a fateful, false path.'[66] Obedience to Ezra-Nehemiah cannot require disobedience to God's revealed word, and therefore the command of God in these texts, as far as Bonhoeffer is concerned, cannot negate the word that the church had discerned and outlined in the Barmen Declaration.

Bonhoeffer sought to read Ezra-Nehemiah as the testimony to God's present word. In his situation, this meant reading it in harmony with the Barmen Declaration along with the church's other creeds and confessional statements. The objective criterion of Bonhoeffer's exegesis is constituted by what God is saying today, not what the biblical text is thought to have meant in its own time. Bonhoeffer's refusal to stand at a historical distance from the text gives his Finkenwalde-era exegesis

---

65. DBWE 14, 492; DBW 14, 484.
66. DBWE 14, 694; DBW 14, 696.

a distinctive vitality and immediacy. He does not hold himself to the external measures of interpretive 'correctness' espoused by the historical-critical guild. He does not think that God's voice in Scripture is found in reconstructing the history behind the text or working out what the supposed original meaning might have been. For him, the interpretive context of Scripture is not an objectively available historical background, but the living Lord Jesus Christ. He wants to hear the Spirit of Christ speak the scriptural words in testimony to Christ. He does not aim to provide the once-for-all interpretation of Ezra-Nehemiah, but to hear and heed the voice of the present Christ.

Conclusion

Bethge's conclusion about 'Reconstruction' has set the pace for subsequent reception of this piece: 'It does not stand up to an examination of its biblical-historical context, but its message remains valid.'[67] This statement is not incorrect, but his concession to Baumgärtel's criticisms obscures the potential contribution of 'Reconstruction' in contemporary conversations about theological interpretation. It is not that the message should be affirmed and the method discarded. If Bonhoeffer has a 'method', it is not a rigid set of rules that purport to unlock all of Scripture as God's word all at once. Exegesis is a spiritual, prayerful activity and can only occur under the guidance of the Holy Spirit. God's word in Scripture cannot be unleashed by an exegetical method, no matter how sophisticated. The only way to hear God speak is to attend to the presence of his word in Christ. The exegetical task, then, is discerning how the scriptural witness discloses this very word today.

Bonhoeffer's approach does not lend itself to the production of various 'interpretations'. It is far more congenial to what John Webster describes as 'faithful reading'. 'Reading', Webster notes, 'is a more practical, low-level term, less overlain with the complexities of hermeneutical theory, less patent of exposition through a theory of the human subject, and less likely to be overwhelmed by psychological or philosophical abstraction'.[68] My preference for 'reading' over 'interpretation' to characterize Bonhoeffer's exegesis is not meant to deny the inevitable and often unconscious involvement of the reader in the act of reading, but simply to emphasize his posture of receptivity to the speaking God and his openness to encountering God in the scriptural word. When 'Reconstruction' is regarded as an instance of 'reading' Scripture with the aim of 'telling the truth' about it, Baumgärtel's criticisms lose their edge and Bonhoeffer's study of Ezra-Nehemiah can be more clearly evaluated for its contributions to our understanding of his scriptural exegesis. I propose two.

---

67. DB-ER, 529.
68. Webster, *Holy Scripture*, 86.

Firstly, 'Reconstruction' exemplifies Bonhoeffer's approach to allegorical interpretation. Bonhoeffer allows that allegorical exegesis, when practised responsibly, can be a faithful way of praising the fullness of Scripture's witness to Christ. The key parameters for responsible allegorical interpretation are: (1) that only the *scriptural* word can be allegorized and (2) that the results of allegorical exegesis must yield the same *content* as 'literal' exegesis, namely, Jesus Christ.[69] Within these limitations, allegory belongs to the realm of freedom in the church, so that the strict semantic meaning of the text does not limit what the Spirit might speak in testimony to Christ in the words of Scripture. Some of Bonhoeffer's contemporaries viewed 'Reconstruction' in this light.[70] But it would be an overstatement to describe 'Reconstruction' as the conscious application of a clearly defined allegorical 'method' of interpretation. He is not comprehensively decoding the various layers of symbolism in the text, after the manner of Bede's early commentary on Ezra-Nehemiah.[71] His bibliology overtly resists the notion that objectively identifiable layers of meaning might inhere within the text itself. On the other hand, it embraces the possibility that the figural connections between Israel and the church, between Zerubbabel and Christ, might be included in how God is addressing the church in the words of Ezra-Nehemiah today. Allegorical interpretation, following Bonhoeffer, does not try to assert something about what the text 'really' means beneath the superficial layer of its apparent meaning. Biblical criticism has its place. 'It merely is not the use that genuinely discloses the essence of the Bible; it discloses merely its surface.'[72] Bonhoeffer's bibliology lends itself to this kind of 'pre-critical' exegesis without negating the validity of modern biblical criticism.[73]

Secondly, Bonhoeffer's bibliology allowed him to give more weight to his present situation in his exegesis than Baumgärtel would permit. However – and this point is crucial – for Bonhoeffer, the 'present situation' is determined by the present Christ. The present is not a moment in time into which Christ may or may not speak; the present 'is [determined] through the word of Christ as the word of God'.[74] As Webster puts it, 'The historical location of Scripture is the present which is constituted by Jesus Christ's presence and work.'[75] It is not, then, the present understood as the current cultural moment or a contemporary milieu, but only

---

69. DBWE 14, 428–9; DBW 14, 416–17.

70. Karl Ludwig Schmidt, who at the time was the editor of *Theologische Blätter*, said as much in a letter dated 23 September 1936. From Schmidt's perspective, Bonhoeffer's Bible study had, 'in a methodically rather insightful way, supported the necessity of allegorical scriptural interpretation' (DBWE 14, 259; DBW 14, 242).

71. Bede, *On Ezra and Nehemiah*, ed. and trans. S. DeGregorio, Translated Texts for Historians 47 (Liverpool: Liverpool University Press, 2006).

72. Bonhoeffer, DBWE 14, 167.

73. My use of the term 'pre-critical' follows David C. Steinmetz, 'The Superiority of Pre-Critical Exegesis', *Theology Today* 37 (1980), 27–38.

74. DBWE 14, 417; DBW 14, 404.

75. Webster, *Domain of the Word*, 41.

the present understood as God's present address to the church that can direct the theological reading of Scripture. Thus, 'Reconstruction' demonstrates the way in which the church might read scriptural history in the present tense, to hear God's present word in the words. Moreover, it shows how the church's present situation of being addressed by God's word might direct its reading of Scripture. This process is circular, to be sure, but its circularity reminds us that hearing God's word is an ongoing task of the church. To say that God's word never changes is not to say that it can be calcified into static formulas; God's word is a living person. The risen Christ encounters us in the present moment of his address.

'Reconstruction' confronts us with an almost embarrassing degree of historical naivety, but this follows naturally from Bonhoeffer's bibliology. That is not to say that the particular exegetical moves Bonhoeffer takes in 'Reconstruction' are the only way to 'make present' the text of Ezra-Nehemiah. In fact, if we take Bonhoeffer's emphasis on the present-tense character of revelation and proclamation seriously, we are obliged to consign his exegesis to *history*. This, to be sure, does not mean disregarding it, but it does suggest a different set of questions than have often been asked of it. The primary concern should not be whether Bonhoeffer's exegesis is historically defensible, or whether he has unearthed the one true meaning of Ezra-Nehemiah, or whether we can freely ignore the verses he seems to ignore. The question is whether Bonhoeffer's reading of Ezra-Nehemiah facilitates the church's contemporary hearing of God's living address in this text. Those who seek revelation in Scripture should seek it where it is to be found, namely, in the *present* and in the *presence* of Christ.

9

THE CALL OF THE PRESENT LORD

Bonhoeffer's *Discipleship* has become something of a spiritual classic. It is filled with memorable phrases, undoubtedly coloured by our retrospective knowledge of the course his life took. 'Cheap grace is the mortal enemy of our church', he says. 'Our struggle today is for costly grace.'[1] Empty faith will not do; obedience is required: 'Only the believer obeys, and only the obedient believes.'[2] And this obedience may cost us our lives: 'Whenever Christ calls us, his call leads us to death.'[3] Unfortunately, a point that is sometimes lost is that the bulk of *Discipleship* is basically an extended theological interpretation of Scripture, centrally the Sermon on the Mount. Bonhoeffer says in the preface, 'In times of church renewal holy scripture naturally becomes richer in content for us. Behind the daily catchwords and battle cries needed in the Church Struggle, a more intense, questioning search arises for the one who is our sole concern, for Jesus himself.'[4] This intense questioning, this necessary search for Jesus is what drives the church back to Holy Scripture, precisely because Scripture's content is Jesus Christ. The point of those breath-taking opening chapters is not, as is sometimes assumed, to swing the faith-works pendulum a bit closer to the centre. Bonhoeffer is not trying to find a place for works-righteousness in the Lutheran church. He is trying to remind the church that at the centre of its life together is the person of Jesus Christ, and that Christian life means hearing and heeding Christ's call to follow him.

In this chapter, I demonstrate how Bonhoeffer's exegesis of the Sermon on the Mount in *Discipleship* is consistent with his bibliology.[5] *Discipleship* is governed by Bonhoeffer's theology of revelation-as-*Christus-praesens*, and his exegesis of the Sermon on the Mount is driven by the interrelated exegetical questions: *who is*

---

1. DBWE 4, 43; DBW 4, 29.
2. DBWE 4, 63; DBW 4, 52.
3. DBWE 4, 87; DBW 4, 81.
4. DBWE 4, 37; DBW 4, 21. This point is also made in Ziegler, 'A Theologian of the Word of God', 32–3.
5. An abridged and modified version of this chapter appeared in Joel Banman, 'Discipleship as a "Who" Question: Bonhoeffer on Reading Scripture as the Call of the Present Christ', *Stimulus: The New Zealand Journal of Christian Thought and Practice* 26 (2019): 18–23.

speaking this text, and *what* does this text say? Bonhoeffer's concern is to unfold the commandments of Jesus as the scriptural witness to the present Christ who is the *Lord*. The Lord who commands is the incarnate, crucified and risen one, and he alone is the giver and fulfilment of the law. As such, Bonhoeffer prioritizes hearing over interpretation, and pays special attention to the cruciform shape of discipleship. Moreover, Bonhoeffer finds in the concept of discipleship a way to speak about the life of the church in the presence of Christ today. The Jesus who is present in the word and sacrament is the same Jesus who called his disciples in first-century Palestine.

Discipleship and revelation

The story of Bonhoeffer's 'discovery' of the Sermon on the Mount has been told many times, and I have nothing to add to this biographical narrative.[6] But as far as his theological development is concerned, arguably it was Bonhoeffer's ongoing commitment to his theology of revelation-as-*Christus-praesens* that made the concept of discipleship so germane to his thought in the 1930s. In treating the Christian life as the life of discipleship, Bonhoeffer was able to relate everything to the *present* Christ: incarnate, crucified and risen. The image of *following after* (*Nachfolge*) a living person proved to be endlessly compelling for the young pastor and theological educator. It was a vision of Christianity that, unlike the purely ethical interpretations of the liberal Protestants, simply could not do without the risen Christ. Christianity as discipleship means life in the presence of the living Jesus. 'Christianity without the living Jesus Christ remains necessarily a Christianity without discipleship; and a Christianity without discipleship is always a Christianity without Jesus Christ.'[7] Ethical and practical questions about what it means to be a Christian thus give way to Christological and biblical questions about who we are following and what he is saying in calling us to follow him.

In the opening chapters of *Discipleship*, Bonhoeffer sets the question of discipleship in the terms of his theology of revelation. In 'Costly Grace', he critiques revelation as object or system and advocates for an understanding of grace as God's living word. He demonstrates the intrinsic link between faith and obedience grounded in Christ's personal presence in 'The Call to Discipleship'. In 'Simple Obedience', he takes 'interpretation' to task for the way it turns God's word into an easily digestible human word. 'Discipleship and the Cross' is where he reiterates his Christological conviction that God's word in Christ is always the 'counter-logos', which never simply corresponds to human ways of knowing, but is rather the way of the cross. And in 'Discipleship and the Individual', Bonhoeffer stresses that Christ's call must be heard as the call of the mediator, before whom

---

6. See, for example, DB-ER, 202–6; Schlingensiepen, *Dietrich Bonhoeffer*, 93–5.
7. DBWE 4, 59; DBW 4, 47.

alone we stand, and therefore in whose presence alone we encounter the call to discipleship. Throughout these opening chapters, Bonhoeffer is setting the stage for an account of the Christian life that is grounded from beginning to end in the presence of Christ.

It is worthwhile to expand on some ways in which he does this. In the first chapter, 'Costly Grace', he presents a version of his critique of theologies that turn revelation into an object at the disposal of human beings. In his judgement, too many in his contemporary church paid no mind to actively following the living Christ, content to reassure themselves of their good standing before God with the doctrine of *sola gratis*. Bonhoeffer did not wish to deny this doctrine, but he perceived that it was being misunderstood and misused as an excuse not to obey the commands of Jesus, specifically the Sermon on the Mount. This is what he describes as cheap grace. 'Cheap grace', he says in the chapter's memorable opening words, 'is the mortal enemy of the church. Our struggle today is for costly grace'.[8] In juxtaposing the two types of grace, Bonhoeffer is not pitting works-righteousness against *sola gratis*. As he continues, it becomes clear that the real difference between cheap and costly grace is the difference between revelation-as-object and revelation-as-*Christus-praesens*. Recalling his critique of 'being-theologies' in *Act and Being*, several statements in this first chapter become especially striking in this regard: 'Cheap grace means grace as doctrine, as principle, as system. It means forgiveness of sins as a general truth; it means God's love as merely a Christian idea of God.'[9] Cheap grace means putting God's word at human disposal, turning revelation into an object. It is the mistake of saying, 'If only our church is in possession of a doctrine of justification, then it is surely a justified church.'[10] Cheap grace always means reducing God's word into a word that is merely human; it is a 'denial of God's living word, denial of the incarnation of the word of God.'[11] 'Costly grace', on the other hand, 'is grace as living word, word of God, which God speaks as God pleases'.[12] And this living word is none other than the crucified and risen Lord Jesus.

When Bonhoeffer speaks in the third chapter about simple obedience, his aims are the same. He wants to show how certain kinds of biblical interpretation turn God's living word into something that is simply at human disposal. Here he makes an interesting distinction, which is programmatic throughout his exegesis of the Sermon on the Mount: he distinguishes between sophisticated *interpretation* and simple *hearing and obeying*. Bonhoeffer perceives in the former 'a principle of scripture foreign to the Gospel [ein unevangelisches Schriftprinzip]'.[13] Such a principle means that

8. DBWE 4, 43; DBW 4, 29.
9. DBWE 4, 43; DBW 4, 29.
10. DBWE 4, 53; DBW 4, 40.
11. DBWE 4, 43; DBW 4, 29.
12. DBWE 4, 45; DBW 4, 31.
13. DBWE 4, 82; DBW 4, 74.

in order to understand scripture, one first must have a key to interpreting it. But that key would not be the living Christ himself in judgment and grace, and using the key would not be according to the will of the living Holy Spirit alone. Rather, the key to scripture would be a general doctrine of grace, and we ourselves would decide its use.[14]

God must be the one to speak God's word. As soon as it is delivered into the hands of the interpreter, it is not God's word. The mediator between God and human beings is not a method of biblical interpretation, but the person of Christ. Revelation as the call to discipleship means that God's word can never be merely an object for human consideration; God and human beings are fully implicated in revelation, in as much as revelation is the word of the mediator, the incarnate God-human. As Bonhoeffer says, 'Discipleship is bound to the mediator, and wherever discipleship is rightly spoken of, there the mediator, Jesus Christ, the Son of God, is intended.'[15] That is why simple obedience is a more fitting response than interpretation in the encounter with Christ's call. If the content of his call were a new law or set of principles to apply, then interpretation would indeed be an appropriate task. But Christ himself is the content of his call, and so, Bonhoeffer thinks, the only response can be to follow him.

The true word of grace, then, is the call to discipleship. And the reason for this, according to Bonhoeffer, is that Jesus is himself both the speaking subject and the content of this call. In his second chapter, on the call to discipleship, Bonhoeffer makes this point clear. In his view, 'there is only one good reason for the proximity of call and deed: *Jesus Christ himself.* It is he who calls'.[16] And yet what Christ calls his disciples to is not a new law but simply himself: 'No further content is possible because Jesus is the only content.'[17] If, as Bonhoeffer believes, Christ is the content of the call as well as the one calling, then it should not be surprising to find Christology at the heart of his account of discipleship. The call to discipleship entails the Christological 'who' question: Who is calling? For Bonhoeffer, everything hinges on this question. 'Jesus calls to discipleship, not as a teacher and a role model, but as the Christ, the Son of God.'[18] As the incarnate Son of God, Jesus is the Lord. When dealing with the Sermon on the Mount, Bonhoeffer believes that we have to do with a Lord who is present before we have to do with a command that is uttered. Nevertheless, it is in the form of the command that the present Christ is revealed to be the Lord. That is why faith and obedience cannot be separated in Bonhoeffer's thought. Faith and obedience have their unity as the singular response appropriate to a genuine encounter with the living Lord.

14. DBWE 4, 82; DBW 4, 74.
15. DBWE 4, 59; DBW 4, 47.
16. DBWE 4, 57; DBW 4, 45.
17. DBWE 4, 59; DBW 4, 47.
18. DBWE 4, 57; DBW 4, 45.

For Bonhoeffer, Jesus encounters us as the one who calls, as the Lord who is *pro-me*. Because Christ is the Lord, his presence entails a decision. Law and gospel, obedience and faith find their unity in the presence of the risen Lord Jesus. When Bonhoeffer approaches any scriptural text, including the Sermon on the Mount, he is asking a 'who' question. The commandment is truly God's word, and therefore it cannot be heard in isolation from the presence of the one who *is* God's word. Correspondingly, the word cannot be encountered in isolation from the particular form of God's word as commandment. It is in the form of commandment that God is revealed to be the *Lord*. The presence of Christ as the Lord entails the presence of his lordship. That is, he is not just the Lord in some general sense. He is the Lord precisely because he is *my* Lord. In the form of law, God's word posits God's lordship as the relationship between Creator and creature, and the creature's response can only be to accept this relation or to reject it. To deny God's lordship is to deny one's own creatureliness. But the key for Bonhoeffer is that one's acceptance or denial of God's lordship cannot be abstracted from one's response to God's command. There is no external arbiter that can validate God's command before it is to be obeyed. That would already be to deny God's eternal lordship. The only way to hear and believe God's command is to hear and obey it. The genuine encounter, the real 'who' question, involves the questioner as much as – if not more than – the one questioned. This enquiry involves that which is genuinely outside of ourselves; it interrogates *us*.

Discerning our encounter with Jesus as Lord begins by recognizing that 'Lord' is not merely a title but a relation. A confession of Christ's lordship without obedience to him as our Lord would really be a denial of his lordship. To encounter Jesus as Lord is to find ourselves in a particular kind of relationship to him, a relationship where his words have an ultimate claim on us. That is why, in Bonhoeffer's famous expression, '*only the believers obey*, and *only the obedient believe*'.[19] The truth of this axiom depends on the indivisibility of the identity and the presence of Christ. Where Christ is present, he is present as the Lord. In the Sermon on the Mount, his lordship takes the form of command, and our belief in him as the Lord takes the form of obedience to that command. Faith and obedience cannot be separated from each other. One is not a result of or a prerequisite for the other. Faith and obedience constitute the singular human response to the concrete encounter with the living Lord. The commandment cannot be understood apart from the Lord, nor the Lord apart from his commandments. A fragment from his essay, '*Vergegenwärtigung neutestamentlicher Texte*', perfectly encapsulates his approach in *Discipleship*. He argues that scriptural commandments are, like all parts of Scripture, the *witness* to Christ. They are not to be taken 'as eternal norms and laws but as commandments of a Lord, in which the commandment is only understood correctly where the Lord is recognized'. The lordship of the one who commands

---

19. DBWE 4, 63; DBW 4, 52.

and the commands issued by the Lord are inseparable. Therefore, he continues, 'Only those who hear and heed the commandment perceive in it the witness of Christ. Hence the commandments of the New Testament are not the principles of a Christian ethics but rather the unique witness of the present and commanding Christ, and it is as such that they are to be interpreted.'[20]

Thus, for Bonhoeffer, the law is revelation, because the incarnate, crucified and risen Word of God is himself the Lord and giver of the law. In the commanding form of the law, Christ is himself present as our Lord. Bonhoeffer's answer to the exegetical 'who' question in this case is simply: *Jesus is Lord*. But words alone can never constitute a full answer to any 'who' question. The real answer comes about in response to the encounter with the Lord who gives the law. The presence of Christ entails a decision, because to encounter Christ as the Lord is to encounter his lordship over us. In sum, the law is revelation because it is the word of the present Christ.

The Sermon on the Mount

Bonhoeffer's approach to the Sermon on the Mount in *Discipleship* is all the more striking for its distance from his earlier writings on the topic. In his 1929 lecture to his congregation in Barcelona, 'Basic Questions of a Christian Ethic', he takes a rather different approach. His Barcelona lecture anticipates several key moves that he will take in his mature *Ethics*, specifically his rejection of ethical systems built on universal moral laws. The problem is, if there can be no Christian ethic along the lines of principles, what is to be done with all the ethical teachings throughout the Gospels and Epistles? Pointedly, Bonhoeffer asks, 'what is the Sermon on the Mount doing in the New Testament?'[21] In his Barcelona lecture, he argues that history-of-religions research has debunked the idea that Christianity had introduced a fundamentally new ethic. What was new was not its moral teachings, but its construal of the human situation before God. So, Bonhoeffer says, the significance of the Sermon on the Mount is not to bring new moral instruction, but to say, 'You stand before the face of God, God's grace rules over you.'[22] All human actions are taken before God, and therefore the will of God for today must guide all Christian behaviour. God's will for the present moment is the only thing that can determine Christian ethical acts.

This means that the significance of the Sermon on the Mount is decidedly *not* what it actually says. The commandments of Christ have, at most, a general significance, a meaning that does not necessarily bear an intelligible connection to the content of those commandments. As Bonhoeffer puts it, 'There is no law with a specific content, but only the law of freedom, that is, bearing responsibility alone

---

20. DBWE 14, 427; DBW 14, 415.
21. DBWE 10, 363; DBW 10, 327.
22. DBWE 10, 365; DBW 10, 329.

before God and oneself.'[23] For this reason, 'it is the most serious misunderstanding to turn the commandments of the Sermon on the Mount once again into a law by applying them literally to the present.'[24] He singles out pacifism in particular, rejecting it as a principle along with all ethical principles. Bonhoeffer goes so far as to argue in favour of war, not only as an act of defence, but even as an offensive act of expansion. This kind of war, he says, accords with God's call within every nation 'to create its history, to enter into the struggle that is the life of nations'.[25]

Some years later, in a 1936 letter to Elisabeth Zinn, he writes about how much he had changed since then. He reflects, 'Christian pacifism, which for a brief time before ... I had still passionately disputed, suddenly came into focus as something utterly self-evident.'[26] And what was it that shifted his perspective so suddenly? By his own account, it was 'the Bible, especially the Sermon on the Mount'.[27] Evidently, his shift in perspective meant, among other things, that he was no longer willing to distinguish between the general significance of the Sermon on the Mount and the particular content of its teachings. He had come to believe that 'God is speaking to us in the Bible',[28] and so, when reading Scripture, he would ask of every text, 'What is God saying to us here?'[29] He could no longer hold that what God was saying through the Sermon on the Mount was a general statement about how human beings stand before the divine. On the contrary, the words of Jesus in the Gospels are the very words with which the Spirit of God speaks in testimony to Christ. Therefore, the words themselves could not be ignored.

Notably, this implies a certain way of reading scriptural texts, a way that does not ignore literary questions. Genre, authorship, implied audience and other features of the biblical literature are not irrelevant to Bonhoeffer's Christological exegesis. The Sermon on the Mount cannot be properly understood in abstraction from how the Gospel of Matthew frames it. So, when Bonhoeffer begins his exegesis of Matthew 5, he does not skip ahead to the third verse. He opens with a discussion of the crowds and the disciples. It is important for Bonhoeffer that the Sermon on the Mount is understood to be Jesus's address 'to those who are already under the power of his call'.[30] It is Jesus's message to his disciples. The verses that follow the Sermon on the Mount disclose the identity of the one who preached it. Commenting on the crowds' astonishment in Matthew 7.28-29, Bonhoeffer writes,

---

23. DBWE 10, 367; DBW 10, 332. This statement anticipates his *Ethics*, where he discusses freedom and responsibility at greater length. In his *Ethics* manuscript, 'History and Good [2]', for example, he argues that 'the structure of responsible action involves both *willingness to become guilty* ... and *freedom*' (DBWE 6, 275; DBW 6, 275). 'Responsibility and freedom', he says, 'are mutually corresponding concepts' (DBWE 6, 283; DBW 6, 283).
24. DBWE 10, 367; DBW 10, 332.
25. DBWE 10, 373; DBW 10, 339.
26. DBWE 14, 134; DBW 14, 113.
27. DBWE 14, 134; DBW 14, 113.
28. DBWE 14, 167; DBW 14, 145.
29. DBWE 14, 168; DBW 14, 146.
30. DBWE 4, 101; DBW 4, 100.

'What had happened? The Son of God had spoken.'[31] Everything that Jesus has said in the Sermon on the Mount must be heard as the words of the Son of God.

Is it then to be taken 'literally' as his message to the church today? This is the wrong question. The question is *who* is issuing these commands, and *what* these commands say. If it is Jesus Christ, the crucified and risen Lord, who issues the commands, and if these commands are heard as his call to discipleship, then the content of the Sermon on the Mount takes on a specific import. It is no accident that Bonhoeffer prefers the language of hearing and obeying to that of interpreting and applying. 'From the human point of view', he says, 'there are countless possibilities of understanding and interpreting the Sermon on the Mount. Jesus knows only one possibility: simply go and obey. Do not interpret or apply, but do it and obey. That is the only way Jesus' word is really heard'.[32] Doing and obeying is the only way to hear Jesus's words because Jesus is not just another rabbi. If he were, interpretation and application would be appropriate responses. The teachings of the Sermon on the Mount mean something quite different if they are understood, as the Gospel of Matthew presents them, to be the address of God's Son to his followers. And these questions involve the whole scriptural witness.

Throughout, Bonhoeffer is advocating for a 'Gospel-oriented [evangelischen] hermeneutic'.[33] This means an exegesis that reads the *whole* of Scripture as the proclamation of Christ. There is no hierarchy of 'inspiration' in the Bible, as if the words attributed to Jesus were closer to God's word than words attributed to his disciples. Bonhoeffer is not interested in a red-letter edition of the Bible, which would read the words of Jesus as God's word and the words of the disciples as a model for how to respond to God's word. Nor are contemporary readers to identify themselves straightforwardly as contemporaries of the disciples. It is both the call and the response that together constitute the scriptural witness to Christ. If Scripture contains commandments to obey, it is only because they are presented as the very word of God in Christ by the Spirit.

Bonhoeffer, who had worried in 1929 that the Sermon on the Mount might be turned into a new law, now advocates for simple obedience to the call of discipleship. But this does not represent a fundamental change to the core of his theology of revelation. What had changed is Bonhoeffer's understanding of Scripture's role in disclosing the present Christ. Simple obedience is not a form of legalism, but of response to the genuine encounter with Christ the risen Lord. And this perspective is grounded in Bonhoeffer's exegesis of the text, wherein the questions of *who* is speaking and *what* is being said are mutually interpretive and enriching. It is because the living Lord, the crucified and risen Son of God is speaking that the commandments of the Sermon on the Mount can be heard only as they are obeyed. And, because the one speaking is the Lord, it is only as these commandments are obeyed that they can really be heard. It is only in obedience to

---

31. DBWE 4, 182; DBW 4, 192.
32. DBWE 4, 181; DBW 4, 191.
33. DBWE 4, 82; DBW 4, 74.

the commandment that the present Christ is encountered as the Lord. As a series of ethical principles, the Sermon on the Mount cannot be applied literally to the present. But as the call to follow the crucified and risen Lord, it can and must be obeyed. Anything else represents the denial of God's self-revelation in Christ.

The cruciform shape of discipleship

The exegetical 'who' and 'what' questions interact even more clearly in Bonhoeffer's portrayal of discipleship as the way of the *cross*. The cross is central to Bonhoeffer's theology of revelation in the 1930s. If revelation means God's self-revealing word in Christ, over against any words human beings could say about God, then God must be allowed to reveal himself where he pleases. But the place God has revealed himself is the cross. 'And those who want to find God there must live beneath that cross just as the Sermon on the Mount demands.'[34] Bonhoeffer's exegesis of Matthew 5–7 unfolds the cruciform shape of discipleship by showing how Jesus's call is a call to follow him to his cross. The call to follow Christ means the call to follow the Crucified One. Because Christ is present as the *crucified* Lord, his lordly call to discipleship is always a call to follow him to the cross.

Bonhoeffer seems to have found in the *theologia crucis*, a notable Lutheran distinctive, a way to reinforce the divine initiative in revelation; it is not any human being, but God alone, who says where God's word is. God's word includes the cross, is found at the cross and is not heard apart from the cross. The word of the cross contradicts human nature and understanding. Revelation encounters human beings as a genuine limit, as a confrontation, as transcendence. This insight connects to what Bonhoeffer had said in his Christology lectures: 'There are only two possibilities when a human being confronts Jesus: the human being must either die or kill Jesus.'[35] For Bonhoeffer, there is no other option, because Jesus, as the very revelation of God, cannot 'fit into the classification system that I already have at hand'.[36] The cross ensures that human beings do not simply find a God who corresponds to themselves.

The centrality of the cross in *Discipleship* was there from its inception. According to Bethge, the composition of the book was a lengthy process of development and refinement, but 'the chapter "Discipleship and the Cross" was a cornerstone of the work from the beginning'.[37] The cross, it should be noted, does not denote generic human suffering or trials. 'The cross is neither misfortune nor harsh fate. Instead, it is that suffering which comes from our allegiance to Jesus Christ alone.'[38] Here,

---

34. DBWE 14, 168; DBW 14, 146.
35. DBWE 12, 307; DBW 12, 288.
36. DBWE 12, 301; DBW 12, 281.
37. DB-ER, 450.
38. DBWE 4, 86; DBW 4, 79.

Bonhoeffer is drawing a sharp divide between Christianity as respectable, civil religion and Christianity as discipleship. Certainly his emphasis on this point was warranted in his context, as the Lutheran church in Germany struggled to find its proper place in relation to the state. 'Being shunned, despised, and deserted by people', he says, 'is an essential feature of the suffering of the cross, which cannot be comprehended by a Christianity that is unable to differentiate between a citizen's ordinary existence and a Christian existence'.[39] The cross is not a general idea or concept. The cross is the cross of Christ. And Christ's cross is Bonhoeffer's key to the Sermon on the Mount. The shape of discipleship is cruciform.

Take Matthew 5.3, for example, which reads, 'Blessed are the poor in spirit, for theirs is the kingdom of heaven.' Bonhoeffer identifies two misguided interpretations of this passage. The first is a purely ethical interpretation. In this view, poverty is an ultimate good in its own right. Blessing is inherent in the practice of voluntary poverty, and so the only important thing is that we make ourselves poor. Bonhoeffer's problem with this view is that it has no necessary connection with Jesus. The blessing comes from our own works, rather than from Christ. The other misinterpretation that Bonhoeffer identifies is the way of 'cheap grace'. In this view, Jesus is not setting up a new law in the Sermon on the Mount, but rather is calling human beings to faith. It follows that, since faith can be had irrespective of personal wealth, the important thing is not to let possessions interfere with genuine faith. The application of this view, as Bonhoeffer frames it, is that 'you are free to keep your possessions, but have them as if you did not have them'.[40] Thus, Jesus's command is not to be taken literally, but to be followed in spirit. For Bonhoeffer, this is the kind of 'cheap grace' that comes of interpreting and applying Jesus's command, rather than simply hearing and obeying it. This approach, for all its apparent interpretive sophistication, leads to nothing but inaction: 'When the storm comes, I will lose the word quickly and I will learn that ... I did not have the word of Christ. Instead, I had a word I wrested away from him and made my own by reflecting on it, but not doing it.'[41] The content of discipleship, Bonhoeffer insists, is not an interpretation and application of Christ's call, but rather Christ himself who calls us to faith and obedience.

For Bonhoeffer, the blessings of the Beatitudes come neither from the inherent good of the ethical principle nor from our doctrinally correct interpretation of the commandment. The blessing comes from Christ. To be poor for poverty's sake is of no value. To be poor for the sake of Christ is to receive the kingdom of heaven. What poverty means in this context is simply to be 'needy in every way'.[42] Wealth, security, spiritual riches and power – all this is lost. 'When [the disciples] followed [Jesus], they lost themselves and everything else which could have made

---

39. DBWE 4, 87; DBW 4, 80.
40. DBWE 4, 78; DBW 4, 70.
41. DBWE 4, 182; DBW 4, 191–2.
42. DBWE 4, 102; DBW 4, 101.

them rich.'⁴³ The Beatitudes are not, then, ethical principles. They describe the cruciform shape of the life of discipleship and promise blessing for the sake of Christ who calls us to discipleship. There is no distinction in Bonhoeffer's mind between different kinds of Beatitudes, nor between Matthew's 'spiritualized' or Luke's 'politicized' versions. Such dichotomies, he thinks, arise from the attempt to ground the blessedness of the Beatitudes in something other than Christ's call and promise.⁴⁴

In Bonhoeffer's hands, the Beatitudes mean this: Jesus looks to his followers, who for the sake of following him have become poor, who mourn, who are meek, who hunger and thirst for righteousness, who are merciful, pure in heart, peacemakers and persecuted. He recognizes their humble state now that they have heeded the call to follow him, and he promises them his blessing. All they now lack because of Christ they will receive back from Christ. It is for this reason that he interprets each Beatitude in terms of *renunciation*. The poor have renounced dependence on everything that would offer security. Those who mourn have renounced happiness, the meek their rights, those who hunger and thirst their righteousness, the merciful their honour, the pure in heart their moral purity, the peacemakers violence and strife. Bonhoeffer reads this passage as descriptive rather than prescriptive. *What* it describes is the lives of those who have obeyed the call to discipleship, and *how* it does so is by outlining all that must be left behind for the sake of following Jesus. They are not, in and of themselves, commandments of Christ, but they work to expand on the singular commandment: Follow me! And the blessings that come are not intrinsic to the renunciation. They do not arise from the cause-and-effect of inherent moral goods or a merit-based system of sacrifice and reward. Renunciation and blessing are based in the call and promise of the Lord Jesus.

How, then, is Bonhoeffer making this text audible as a witness to Christ? The Beatitudes, in his view, are addressed to 'those who are already under the power of his call'.⁴⁵ And Christ's call to discipleship leads inexorably to the cross. Those who would follow Christ to his cross cannot lay claim to human ways of security and self-sufficiency. Following Christ makes us poor in every way; yet, the one who calls us there also promises us blessing, the blessing of the kingdom of heaven. The validity of this promise rests purely in the authority of the one who makes it. If Jesus were giving us an ethical teaching, then the blessedness of poverty would rest in the validity of the ethical principle behind it. But if the one who calls and promises is the Lord, then he alone is the basis for the promised blessing.

What must not be overlooked is that the immediacy of Christ's call is entailed by the presence of the one who calls. Bonhoeffer emphasizes the presence of Christ's call because he believes that Christ is really present as the Lord who calls.

---

43. DBWE 4, 103; DBW 4, 102.
44. See his footnote in DBWE 4, 102 n. 2; DBW 4, 100 n. 2.
45. DBWE 4, 101; DBW 4, 100.

Christ is the content of the call to discipleship, and he is there in person when and where this call is spoken. Because Christ is present as the crucified Lord, his call leads us where we would not and could not go on our own. He calls us to find him at the place of his cross. He calls us to 'live beneath that cross just as the Sermon on the Mount demands'.[46] The Christological question must guide our approach. Not: *How* can we live according to the Sermon on the Mount today? But rather: *Who* is this one calling me today? And if the Holy Spirit leads us to say, 'Jesus is Lord', then we will find ourselves interrogated by this 'who' question. For Bonhoeffer, the one we meet in the Sermon on the Mount is the Lord Jesus who encounters us as the Word in the form of his call to discipleship, which is the call to his cross.

Bonhoeffer draws attention to the cruciform shape of each beatitude and points to the blessing that comes only from the crucified and risen Christ.[47] The poor are poor because their real treasure, the kingdom of heaven, is hidden in the total poverty of the cross. Those who mourn bear the suffering of those around them as Christ bears all human suffering on the cross, and their comfort is communion with Christ the crucified. The meek have surrendered their rights to worldly justice as Christ did when he was unjustly put to death, and their inheritance is the new creation that begins at the cross. Those who hunger and thirst for righteousness have given up their claim to be righteous, recognizing that the true righteousness with which they will be filled can only be found in God who forgives us on the cross. The merciful live without any claim to their own dignity, sharing in the humility and guilt of others as Christ did to the point of death, the Christ who is now exalted and will mercifully exalt the lowly and grant them true honour. The pure in heart live without the justification of their own conscience; their purity comes not from knowing about good and evil but from knowing Christ alone, and in seeing Christ they see God.[48] Peacemakers have renounced the power of violence and willingly endure suffering inflicted upon them, because they understand the true peace comes only through the death of the Son of God, for whose sake they are called God's children. The disciples are persecuted for the sake of their alien righteousness, which the world despises; they are thus made poor and fittingly receive the same promise as the poor.

For Bonhoeffer, it is important to recognize that the word of blessing is always uttered from the cross. There is nothing inherently blessed about what the disciples have become in following Christ. Their blessing is Christ alone. And the cross is where this blessing is to be found, because the cross is where Christ is to be found. That is why Bonhoeffer directs the exegetical 'who' question about the Beatitudes to the cross. There is no genuine enquiry into the 'who' question that does not go by way of the cross. The one calling is the Lord. The Lord calling is the Crucified.

---

46. DBWE 14, 168; DBW 14, 146.

47. The following is found in DBWE 4, 102–10; DBW 4, 101–10.

48. Note that Bonhoeffer's interpretation of this beatitude is unique among the others in that it does not include any direct mention of the cross.

The church and discipleship

Discipleship is all about hearing and heeding the call of the present Lord Jesus. Arguably, Bonhoeffer's account of Christ's presence requires little explanation throughout the first half of *Discipleship*. After all, Bonhoeffer is working with passages that speak of Jesus literally walking and talking in first-century Palestine. But one might rightly point out that Jesus is no longer present in this way. What, then, does the call to discipleship imply for the contemporary church? In Bonhoeffer's view, the New Testament testifies to this call in different ways. The Synoptic Gospels and the Pauline Epistles employ different concepts, but the same reality is intended. Discipleship is life in the presence of Christ, and, for Bonhoeffer, life in the presence of Christ is life in the church-community.

In a short but pivotal chapter, Bonhoeffer poses 'Preliminary Questions' about the relationship between the present-day church and the call to discipleship during Jesus's earthly ministry. 'To his first disciples', Bonhoeffer notes, 'Jesus was bodily present, speaking his word directly to them. But this Jesus died and is risen. How, then, does his call to discipleship [Ruf in die Nachfolge] reach us today?'[49] The problem with this enquiry, however, is that it circumvents the 'who' question. The issue is not about asking *how* Jesus's call to discipleship applies today, but rather *who* this one is who calls to discipleship. The one who calls is the risen Lord Jesus, who 'is not dead but alive and still speaking to us today through the testimony of scripture'.[50] To hear his call to discipleship, 'we need to hear it where Christ himself is present. It is within the church that Jesus Christ calls through his word and sacrament'.[51] There is no difference between the identity of the one present in word and sacrament and of the one present in first-century Palestine. It is the same Jesus Christ in both cases. 'Here he is', Bonhoeffer says, *'the whole Christ'*.[52]

As I argued in CHAPTER 4, the present Christ is always the whole Christ for Bonhoeffer. This means that wherever Christ meets us through the testimony of Scripture, it is the whole Christ whom we meet. This encounter is as decisive for us today as it was for those who encountered him in first-century Palestine. Bonhoeffer argues that the New Testament writers testify to this same encounter using different terminology. 'What the Synoptics describe as hearing and following the call to discipleship', Bonhoeffer says, 'Paul expresses in the concept of baptism'.[53] The connection between these concepts is perhaps not immediately obvious. But remember that, for Bonhoeffer as for Barth, the *content* of God's word is always the same, even if it comes in different forms. God's word is from beginning to end Jesus Christ. This means that one cannot distinguish between different kinds of encounters with Jesus, as if one kind of encounter might have more or less

---

49. DBWE 4, 201; DBW 4, 215.
50. DBWE 4, 201; DBW 4, 215.
51. DBWE 4, 202; DBW 4, 215.
52. DBWE 4, 202, my emphasis; DBW 4, 216.
53. DBWE 4, 207; DBW 4, 221.

significance than another. Being baptized is not an encounter of a lesser order than being called; Paul is not talking about a different Jesus than the Synoptics. Human beings do not take more or less initiative in baptism than in being called by Jesus. Baptism does not require less of us than the call required of the disciples. Baptism is not less decisive. Even in the practice of infant baptism, there is no less of a decision to be made, no less responsibility. The call to discipleship and baptism both denote the decisive encounter with the living Jesus, who meets us as our Lord and Saviour and brings us to the point of death. Although the mode of Christ's presence is different in each case, his identity is the same, as is the totality of the claim he makes on those he encounters. 'Whenever Christ calls us, his call leads us to death.'[54] This well-known statement is equally apt, in Bonhoeffer's thought, to describe the call to discipleship as to describe baptism.

Throughout *Discipleship*, Bonhoeffer affirms 'that Jesus Christ and his call are the same, then and now'.[55] And this is where the question of Scripture comes into sharpest focus. 'Scripture does not present us with a collection of Christian types to be imitated according to our own choice. Rather in every passage it proclaims to us the one Jesus Christ. It is him alone whom I ought to hear.'[56] The unity of the Jesus attested in Scripture and the Jesus who is present in the church is the basis for Bonhoeffer's exegesis of the Sermon on the Mount, the Pauline epistles, and indeed all of Holy Scripture. Thus, Bonhoeffer says,

> If it is indeed scripture alone that assures us of Christ's presence, then it must be scripture as a whole, the scripture which also testifies to the ongoing presence of the synoptic Jesus Christ. The synoptic Christ is neither more nor less distant from us than the Christ of Paul. The Christ who is present with us is the Christ to whom the whole of scripture testifies. He is the incarnate, crucified, risen, and glorified Christ; and he encounters us in his word.[57]

Scripture discloses that our situation before God is the same as that of the first disciples. The barrier between them and us, between the Synoptics and Paul, Bonhoeffer thinks, is artificial. In his view, the situation was not clearer for the disciples than for us, because in both cases 'it is the *hidden* Christ who calls'.[58] In his Christology lectures, Bonhoeffer had argued that the hidden Christ does not mean a divine person hiding inside a human being. Rather, it means the whole God-human hidden in his humiliated state. In Bonhoeffer's sacramental theology, this is exactly how to describe the real presence of Christ in baptism. Christ humbles himself in order to encounter us, but he does not thereby tip the balance of his personal constitution towards the 'human' side of the scale. Jesus is God and

---

54. DBWE 4, 87; DBW 4, 81.
55. DBWE 4, 203; DBW 4, 217.
56. DBWE 4, 204; DBW 4, 218.
57. DBWE 4, 206; DBW 4, 220.
58. DBWE 4, 202, my emphasis; DBW 4, 216.

human being united in one person, and it is this whole, divine-human person who comes to us in the humble form of word and sacrament.

It is on this basis that Bonhoeffer interprets Pauline baptismal language in unity with the Synoptic concept of baptism. Like the call to discipleship, baptism is, paradoxically, a passive action. 'Baptism is not something we offer to God. It is, rather, something *Jesus Christ offers to us.*'[59] Like discipleship, baptism means the total break from the world and total allegiance to Jesus Christ. Being baptized is a once-for-all visible act of obedience, through which we participate in Christ's death, are justified from sin and enjoy ongoing community with Christ by the gift of the Holy Spirit. Specifically, this Spirit-given community with Christ means being made into members of Christ's body. Christ's presence is no less embodied today than during Jesus's earthly ministry. Those in the church 'are in the community of the first disciples and followers of Jesus'.[60] Bonhoeffer thereby points to an interpretation of discipleship that extends beyond the Synoptic narrative. In the church, the community of the baptized that is therefore the community of disciples, Christ encounters human beings as their crucified and risen Lord today.

Conclusion

Throughout *Discipleship*, Bonhoeffer expounds the Sermon on the Mount according to two basic, mutually informative exegetical questions: *Who* is addressing us in this text, and *what* does this text say? The seemingly simplistic exegesis in *Discipleship*, then, is a direct result of Bonhoeffer's ongoing struggle to come to terms with the challenge of Barth's theology as well as his own Lutheran tradition. The categories of law and gospel do surprisingly little work in Bonhoeffer's exegesis, which leans far more heavily on the categories of obedience and faith – categories that, crucially, arise from his exegesis of the scriptural text. Specifically, they follow from his exegetical 'who' question, by which he seeks to encounter the Sermon on the Mount as the present word of the present Lord Jesus, present as the incarnate, crucified and risen Lord, the same Lord present in word and sacrament in the church today. It is faith in Jesus as the present *Lord* that grounds the immediacy of call and obedience: to believe that Jesus is the Lord is to obey his commandments. And his commandments in the Sermon on the Mount outline the call to discipleship that bids his disciples to follow him to the cross.

Discipleship has an undeniably ethical bent, but it is a work of exegesis before it is a work of ethics. When Bonhoeffer takes up the topic of Christian ethics directly, he takes a somewhat different approach. The relationship between scriptural exegesis and Christian ethics is important to grapple with, which is why I now turn to his ethical writings of the early 1940s.

59. DBWE 4, 207; DBW 4, 221.
60. DBWE 4, 222; DBW 4, 237.

10

DOING THE TRUTH

It is perhaps surprising that I now turn to Bonhoeffer's *Ethics*, because it would seem to offer little to our understanding of his bibliology and exegesis. Bonhoeffer's *Ethics*, after all, contains relatively little scriptural exposition. This, however, does not mean that *Ethics* evinces a waning interest in Scripture in Bonhoeffer's post-Finkenwalde years. On the contrary, as I will argue in this chapter, the way in which Bonhoeffer correlates revelation and ethics helps illuminate the place of Scriptural exegesis in his ethical thought. This is important, because the way Bonhoeffer uses Scripture in *Ethics* is not obvious. Only one of the manuscripts contains extensive exegetical material, and Bonhoeffer consistently allows his argument to turn on doctrinal-theological, rather than scriptural-exegetical, grounds.

This chapter will not be a comprehensive study of how Bonhoeffer uses Scripture in *Ethics*.[1] Instead, it is an enquiry into the exegetical logic of Bonhoeffer's ethical thought. I argue that, for Bonhoeffer, the exegetical route to praxis runs through doctrinal theology. By the Spirit, God teaches the truth in Scripture, and doctrinal theology is concerned with expressing this truth. Ethics means 'doing the truth', which, owing to the historical nature of human life, cannot be known in advance

---

1. For such a study, see Plant, 'Uses of the Bible'. Plant notes at least six different features of Bonhoeffer's uses of Scripture in the *Ethics* manuscripts: (1) Scripture testifies to the 'Gestalt' of Christ; (2) the Old Testament correlates to the New as the penultimate to the ultimate; (3) the ultimate word of Scripture is a word of grace; (4) Scripture demarcates the space in which ethical action in obedience to God's will occurs; (5) Scripture, especially the account of the Fall, critiques all ethical systems based on static ideas of 'good' and 'evil'; (6) the Bible narrates instances of divine command and human obedience (or disobedience) – not as ethical examples to be superimposed on contemporary situations, but as witnesses to God's ongoing involvement in human history by his commanding word (ibid., 279–82). Even in summary, it is clear (as Plant rightly argues) that Bonhoeffer's various uses of Scripture in *Ethics* do not coalesce into a unified exegetical 'method'. Plant follows David H. Kelsey, *The Uses of Scripture in Recent Theology* (London: SCM, 1975), by keying in on Bonhoeffer's *uses* of Scripture, and identifies two major motifs that drive his exegetical decisions: ethics as *formation* and ethics as *command*. Under the motif of formation, Bonhoeffer reads Scripture as a witness to the 'Gestalt' of Christ, and therefore it is the *narrative* of the Bible that is authoritative, since it presents the form of the one to whom Christians are conformed

as a list of 'thou shalts' and 'thou shalt nots'; rather, the Spirit teaches us the truth of our historical situation through Scripture's witness to the Real One. The good, as 'accordance with reality', entails the freedom to be responsible for others in the context of the Christ-reality, a reality that we learn in Scripture as the witness to Christ by the Spirit of Christ.

Revelation, reality and good

In this first section, I argue that Bonhoeffer's distinctive theology of revelation is the red thread that runs through his *Ethics*, and, moreover, that it can be found at the foundation of the architectonic shape of his ethical vision. His critique of ethics as static principles had always been based in his (Barthian) conviction that God's word can never be made into an object at human disposal. A new focus throughout *Ethics* is the concept of *reality*, which at once sharpened his critique of 'principle' ethics and offered a firm foundation for a constructive ethical proposal. It is his Christological interpretation of reality that places revelation-as-*Christus-praesens* at the centre of Christian ethics. And that is precisely where bibliology can be mapped onto his theological ethics.

Reality is the key to Bonhoeffer's *Ethics*. He found this key, however, not in the writings of Luther or Kierkegaard or Barth, but in the work of the German Catholic philosopher and Thomist, Josef Pieper.[2] Bonhoeffer had underlined the following sentences from the beginning of Pieper's book, *Reality and the Good*,[3] and there is perhaps no better summary of his own approach to ethics: 'Reality is the foundation of ethics. The good is that which is in accord with reality.'[4]

(Plant, 'Uses of the Bible', 272; cf. 79–117). Under the motif of command, Bonhoeffer locates the authority of Scripture in its presentation of God's direct address to his people. To be clear, Scripture does not contain commands that must be arbitrarily followed, irrespective of ever-changing historical contexts; rather the commands of God in Scripture 'have the logical force of reports of the way God's commands are spoken, and potential sites of encounter with God's commands in ever new places, situations and times, between God and the Christian' (ibid., 273). For Plant, these two major 'metaphorical construals' (i.e. formation and command) coexist in Bonhoeffer's *Ethics*, and the tension and interplay between them suggest a plurality in Bonhoeffer's doctrine and use of Scripture (ibid., 278).

2. For a contemporary Thomistic appropriation of Pieper's ethics, see Reinhard Hütter, *Bound for Beatitude: A Thomistic Study in Eschatology and Ethics* (Washington, DC: The Catholic University of America Press, 2019), 151–74.

3. Josef Pieper, *Die Wirklichkeit und das Gute* (Leipzig: Jakob Hegner, 1935). The underlining in Bonhoeffer's copy is noted in DBWE 6, 50 ed. n. 14; DBW 6, 34 ed. n. 13. In what follows, I quote from Stella Lange's English translation of *Reality and Good*, which is found in Josef Pieper, *Living the Truth*, trans. Lothar Krauth and Stella Lange (San Francisco: Ignatius, 1989), 107–83.

4. Pieper, *Living the Truth*, 111.

Nevertheless, as sympathetic as Bonhoeffer was to this foundation, he does not adopt Pieper uncritically, nor does he discuss the contents of *Reality and the Good* explicitly. Typical of the way he engages with other theologians, his use of Pieper has the character of 'an ongoing, silent dispute'.[5] Nevertheless, reality emerges as the most clear mark of Pieper's influence on Bonhoeffer's approach to ethics.[6] Pieper's grounding of ethics in *reality* (*Wirklichkeit*) and his understanding of 'the good' in terms of *what is in accord with reality* (*das Wirklichkeitsgemäße*) framed the problem of Christian ethics in a new way for Bonhoeffer. It is worth looking at some of the details of Pieper's argument in *Reality and the Good* in order to identify (1) what elements Bonhoeffer adopted, (2) why he found the concept of reality to be so germane for his own project and (3) how and why he diverged from Pieper in his unfolding of key ideas. The answers to these questions, I propose, provide important clues about the underlying theological structure of Bonhoeffer's argument, in the context of which I will identify the systematic place and function of bibliology in his incomplete magnum opus.

Pieper says that reality has two meanings, corresponding with the Latin words *realis* and *actualis*. Reality as *actualis* refers to that which is *actual*, what is realized as opposed to what is merely (unrealized) potential. What is in accord with *actualis* is what is directed towards the realization – the *becoming real* – of a thing's potential. For all created things, direction towards realization means direction towards its creator. Pieper's main interest, however, is the other sense of reality. Reality as *realis* means everything that exists objectively, the reality of objects. *Realis* is what is presented to the senses and the intellect from the outside; its existence is independent of our knowledge of it. The good, as that which is in accord with *realis*, is what is faithful to objective being. Therefore, Pieper says, 'the man who wishes to realize the good does not look upon his own act but upon the truth of real objects'.[7] He quotes Goethe to the same effect: 'In our doing and acting everything depends on this, that we comprehend objects clearly and treat them according to their nature.'[8] Action that is in accord with reality is grounded in true knowledge of the reality itself.

---

5. This is how Bonhoeffer described his engagement with Barth during the composition of *Discipleship* (DBWE 14, 252–3; DBW 14, 235).

6. Evidence of Pieper's influence on Bonhoeffer's thought can be pursued by identifying Pieperian ideas and expressions that appear in Bonhoeffer's work and then cross-referencing them with passages that Bonhoeffer had marked in his own copies of Pieper's books. Fortunately, the editors of *Ethics* have noted several such occurrences. See DBWE 6, 50 ed. n. 14; 66 ed. n. 69; 175 ed. n. 16; 202 ed. n. 108; 217 ed. n. 160; 222 ed. n. 18; 270 ed. n. 91; DBW 6, 34 ed. n. 13; 53 ed. n. 65; 116 ed. n. 94; 167 ed. n. 16; 103 ed. n. 103; 216 ed. n. 149; 221 ed. n. 15; 270 ed. n. 77.

7. Pieper, *Living the Truth*, 113.

8. Ibid., 108, quoting from Goethe's 'Maximen und Reflexionen'. The English translation can be found in Johann Wolfgang von Goethe, *Maxims and Reflections*, trans. Thomas Bailey Saunders (New York: Macmillan, 1906), 84.

But where does this knowledge of reality come from? How does it arise in human cognition? For Pieper, it begins in the voice of primordial conscience. This voice is 'a natural, innate "attitude" (*habitus*) of the human mind by which it is destined to have a primary and infallible judgment about the good as the end and meaning of human action'.[9] Its content is the natural law. But this law is not something additional to reality; it derives from reality itself. If the good is defined as 'that towards which everything strives', then the imperative of the primordial conscience states that 'we must love the good'.[10] The voice of primordial conscience is born of the disunity between essence and existence in all created beings. Only in God are essence and existence identical. By contrast, existence and essence are not identical in created things; the 'that' of any creature is separate from its 'what'. The good, as the essential 'what' towards which all things strive, is the realization of a creature's essence. This is the good that the voice of primordial conscience cries out for.

The voice of primordial conscience is natural and infallible, but this does not mean that human beings necessarily obey its demands. Prudence is the virtue by which human beings discern and will the concrete good in any given situation. According to Thomas Aquinas, Pieper observes, prudence is 'partly cognitive (*cognoscitiva*) and partly commanding (*praeceptiva*)'.[11] It is a 'directing knowledge'.[12] As such, it is the final bridge between one's truthful perception of objective reality and one's concrete willing of the good in history. Pieper thus commends 'objectivity as an ethical attitude'.[13] Objectivity means allowing one's will and action, one's practical reason, to be determined entirely by objective reality. In adopting the ethical attitude of objectivity, the human subject becomes self-effacing. One never regards one's own actions, but only the reality, and thereby the good, of the object. True knowledge of reality entails willing the good. Ethics, in other words, means 'doing the truth'.[14] Reality provides the ultimate ground of morality, insofar as the good is what is in accord with reality, and moral action must will the good for all things. Thus, the ethical will expresses the inherent movement of all things from their existence into their essence. In short: 'Become what you are'.[15]

The *Ethics* owes its unique approach and content to a wide variety of intellectual sources and influences, to say nothing of Bonhoeffer's own situation and experiences. Nevertheless, Pieper was decisive in determining how Bonhoeffer approached the topic of Christian ethics, what kinds of questions he raised and

---

9. Pieper, *Living the Truth*, 153.
10. Ibid., 154.
11. Ibid., 163.
12. Ibid., 165.
13. Ibid., 171.
14. Ibid.
15. Ibid., 162.

the kinds of answers he found satisfactory.[16] *Reality* is a central – arguably *the* central – theme.[17] Two manuscripts in particular, 'Christ, Reality, and Good' and 'History and Good', turn on the concept of reality and bear the marks of Pieper's influence. I would go so far as to say that these two manuscripts together constitute Bonhoeffer's Christological exposition of Pieper's opening sentences: 'Reality is the foundation of ethics. The good is that which is in accord with reality.'[18] Bonhoeffer unpacks these fundamental propositions Christologically: the *Christ*-reality is the foundation of ethics, and the good is what is in accord with 'reality as it has been taken on by God in Christ'.[19]

The concept of reality proved to be the key in Bonhoeffer's account of Christian ethics. The idea of the good is not governed by some other idea, but is grounded in reality itself. It is for this reason that ethical principles can never be the measure of the good. The good, Bonhoeffer agrees with Pieper, is what is in accord with reality, *das Wirklichkeitsgemäße*. Having its basis in reality, ethical action is measured by reality itself. And this gives him something to say with respect to the *content* of

---

16. In addition to the evidence adduced below, I would also point to the letter of 9 October 1940 that Bonhoeffer wrote to Bethge, in which he says that his work on *Ethics* was progressing and that he anticipated spending the rest of the week outlining the whole project (DBWE 16, 78; DBW 16, 66). Significantly, he notes in this same letter that Protestant ethics lacks 'selfless self-love', which is a direct citation from Josef Pieper, *The Four Cardinal Virtues: Prudence, Justice, Fortitude, Temperance*, trans. Daniel F. Coogan et al. (New York: Harcourt, Brace, & World, 1965), 149. He cites the same in DBWE 8, 375; DBW 8, 417.

17. Bonhoeffer had been deploying the language of *reality* (*die Wirklichkeit*) in service of the ethical prior to his reading of Pieper. Perhaps most significantly (and enigmatically), he speaks of reality as 'the sacrament of the commandment' in his 1932 lecture in Ciernohorské Kúpele, 'On the Theological Foundation of the Work of the World Alliance' (DBWE 11, 361; DBW 11, 334). Plant, in *Taking Stock of Bonhoeffer*, 97–113, has shown that this aspect of Bonhoeffer's thinking about reality has its roots in Lutheran sacramentology (rather than in Catholic moral philosophy), and moreover that he consistently held this view until at least his 1941 piece, 'On the Possibility of the Church's Message to the World' (DBWE 6, 352–62; DBW 6, 354–64). The way Bonhoeffer speaks of reality in these contexts, however, differs from the use Pieper makes of it (and, as I will argue, from Bonhoeffer's adoption of Pieper's formulation). Prior to his reading of Pieper, Bonhoeffer tended to use the word *reality* to speak of the *historically concrete* and, specifically in the 1932 lecture, of the 'concrete visibility of the church's word' (Banman, 'The Word of the Church to the World', 59). To be sure, this sense of *reality* certainly persists throughout the *Ethics* manuscripts – not least in the aforementioned 1941 essay (whether or not it was intended to be included in the *Ethics*). Nevertheless, his discussion of the good in connection with 'ultimate reality' represents a genuine development in his thinking about how ethics relates to reality, an insight that is clearly articulated in Pieper's writing.

18. Pieper, *Living the Truth*, 111.

19. DBWE 6, 224; DBW 6, 223.

God's will: 'The will of God is nothing other than the realization of the Christ-reality among us and in our world.'²⁰ God's will is not reducible to this or that particular commandment in this or that concrete situation; God wills the whole of reality, and his will is accomplished in the person of the Son.

This does not mean that Bonhoeffer accepts Pieper's argument as is. For one thing, Pieper supposes that human reason has the innate capacity, via the voice of primordial conscience, to recognize the true essence of an existing thing, whereas Bonhoeffer is less optimistic. Bonhoeffer discusses this in his manuscript, 'Natural Life'. By locating the category of the 'natural' in the sphere of the 'penultimate', Bonhoeffer gives natural life a distinctly Christological interpretation. 'The natural', he says, 'is that form of life preserved by God for the fallen world that is directed toward justification, salvation, and renewal through Christ.'²¹ The natural is *penultimate* reality, because it precedes and prepares the way for the ultimate, namely, the justification and redemption of human beings. It can be recognized only in revelation, by looking to Jesus Christ. But because Jesus Christ is the reconciliation of God and the world, one cannot look to Christ without looking to the natural life that he has taken upon himself. 'Only by Christ's becoming human does natural life become the penultimate that is directed toward the ultimate.'²²

As far as reason is concerned, he says that reason is included in the natural, and as such it is included in the fall. Bonhoeffer uses the word *Vernunft* (perception) for 'reason' in this context, which follows Pieper's usage.²³ But, unlike Pieper, he does not regard reason as a direct connection with reality itself, but only as 'the organ for recognizing the natural'.²⁴ He contrasts his view with 'Catholic theory' – without naming Pieper but undoubtedly relying on him as an exemplar – in which 'reason has retained an essential integrity'²⁵ even after the fall. For Bonhoeffer, knowledge of reality must be grounded in God's *revelation*. The natural, as the penultimate, can only be perceived in light of Christ, who takes natural life unto himself. Bonhoeffer is consistent on this point. 'Only insofar as the ultimate reality is revelation, that is, the self-witness of the living God, is its claim to ultimacy fulfilled.'²⁶ This means, moreover, that 'the decision about the whole of life depends on our relation to God's revelation'.²⁷

This basic point of divergence also reveals another key difference between Bonhoeffer and Pieper. Although Bonhoeffer follows Pieper in discussing the good as what is in accord with reality, the fact that Bonhoeffer understands reality

---

20. DBWE 6, 74; DBW 6, 60–1.
21. DBWE 6, 174; DBW 6, 166.
22. DBWE 6, 174; DBW 6, 166.
23. Pieper, *Living the Truth*, 116.
24. DBWE 6, 174; DBW 6, 167; cf. DBWE 16, 590; DBW 16, 607: 'The organ through which the lex naturae comes into play is the ratio.'
25. DBWE 6, 175 n. 1; DBW 6, 167 n. 1.
26. DBWE 6, 48; DBW 6, 32–3.
27. DBWE 6, 49; DBW 6, 33.

in terms of revelation means that the measure of human action cannot originate within the human person. This measure must come 'from the outside'. Thus, where Pieper speaks of *prudence* as the measure of the good, Bonhoeffer prefers to speak of *responsibility*. The question of the good, for Bonhoeffer, 'has to do with the claim of the one who, in his own person, fulfilled the essence of history – the claim of Jesus Christ, the one in whom God became human, upon history, whose ultimate reality is none other than himself'.[28] And the claim of Jesus Christ 'is a claim that encounters us *from outside*, which we either believe or contradict'.[29] The assertion that human existence is historical existence means that 'a human being necessarily lives in encounter with other human beings and that this encounter entails being charged … with responsibility [Verantwortung] for the other human being'.[30] This claim goes all the way back to the theological anthropology that Bonhoeffer developed in *Sanctorum Communio*, where he describes human personhood as arising in *response* to the concrete claim of the human 'other'.[31] Responsibility means responding to the address of another, which means it is always determined by a reality outside of the self. Because Christ is the ultimate 'other', responsibility is life 'lived in answer to the life of Jesus Christ'.[32] This includes our encounter with other human beings, because Christ has taken all of humanity upon himself. Moreover, this encounter also includes the encounter with Christ in God's word. After all, for Bonhoeffer we do not meet Christ only in the human other; Christ is present in the threefold form of word, sacrament and community.[33]

To return to the broader sweep of Bonhoeffer's ethical vision, he enthusiastically endorses Pieper's claims that reality is the foundation of ethics and that the good is what is in accord with reality. There are, however, many aspects of Pieper's account that Bonhoeffer does not follow: Bonhoeffer interprets reality with reference to Christology rather than Thomistic metaphysics; he asserts that knowledge of reality begins with revelation rather than reason; and he unpacks 'accordance with reality' through a discussion of responsibility rather than prudence. In his Christological picture of reality, ethics is found in 'the relation between reality and becoming real, between past and present, between history and event (faith) or, to replace the many concepts with the simple name of the thing itself, the relation between Jesus Christ and the Holy Spirit'.[34] This point is crucial, but often overlooked. In the theological logic of *Ethics*, the relation between Jesus Christ and the Holy Spirit describes and encompasses all the other concepts under discussion, and it has profound implications for the bibliological question. Dogmatically speaking, a theological account of how reality relates to its becoming real is an exposition

---

28. DBWE 6, 235; DBW 6, 234.
29. DBWE 6, 250, my emphasis; DBW 6, 249.
30. DBWE 6, 220; DBW 6, 219.
31. DBWE 1, 48; DBW 1, 28.
32. DBWE 6, 254; DBW 6, 254.
33. DBWE 12, 315; DBW 12, 297.
34. DBWE 6, 50; DBW 6, 34.

of the relationship between Christology and pneumatology.[35] Christian ethics, then, is theologically 'derivative' of these more fundamental doctrines. And, as I have demonstrated at length in CHAPTER 4, the link between Christology and pneumatology for Bonhoeffer is his theology of the word. The ministry of the Spirit is to 'present' Christ as God's word, and Holy Scripture is God's chosen instrument for this ministry. Given the dogmatic locus of revelation in the architectonics of the *Ethics*, I now turn to the question of how Scripture functions in his ethical thought.

The path according to Scripture

Coordinating bibliology and ethics in Bonhoeffer's mature thought begins with locating the theology of revelation in his *Ethics*, and this, as I have shown, is found in the central concept of *reality*. Bonhoeffer makes a telling comment early in 'Christ, Reality, and Good': 'The *subject matter of a Christian ethic is God's reality revealed in Christ becoming real [Wirklichwerden] among God's creatures*, just as the subject matter of doctrinal theology is the truth of God's reality revealed in Christ.'[36] Here Bonhoeffer draws an important distinction between Christian ethics and doctrinal theology, a distinction that I will follow for the remainder of this chapter. Doctrinal theology is concerned with the articulation of reality as revealed by God, and Christian ethics is concerned with this reality's becoming real. The relationship, as Bonhoeffer puts it plainly, is the relationship between Jesus Christ and the Holy Spirit. In his bibliology, Christ and the Spirit are related as Word and Speech. The Holy Spirit speaks the words of Scripture as the word of God, and where God's word is spoken, God's word is *present*. Because God is present as his word, his presence is intelligible, and doctrinal theology testifies to this intelligibility. It is concerned, in other words, with the *knowledge* of revelation, which is really knowledge of reality itself. Yet knowledge of the word is not the sort of 'existing thing' that can be had in abstraction from the presence of the word. It is not knowledge as a once-for-all acquisition, but an ongoing process of learning and transformation. The Holy Spirit instructs the church about the reality of God and world through Scripture's witness to Christ, the Real One in whom the reality of God and the reality of the world are reconciled.

---

35. Mawson, *Christ Existing as Community*, 129, notes that, as early as *Sanctorum Communio*, Bonhoeffer was careful not to make the work of the Spirit merely an extension of the work of Christ. Contrasting Bonhoeffer with Hegel, Mawson shows that Bonhoeffer's pneumatology involves the actualization of a *reality* completed in Christ, rather than of a *potentiality* made possible by Christ. Quoting from DBWE 1, 144; DBW 1, 89: 'The counterpart of actualization [*Aktualisierung*] by the Holy Spirit is not potentiality [*Potentialität*] in Christ, but the reality [*Realität*] of revelation in Christ.'

36. DBWE 6, 49; DBW 6, 34.

Grounding ethics in the ultimate reality of God's reconciliation of the world in Christ does not negate the difficulties and uncertainties of the penultimate reality in which all ethical decisions and actions are carried out. The course of history is ethically ambiguous to us, and it is impossible to know whether our motives are truly good or whether our actions will yield genuinely good outcomes.[37] In their real, historical existence, human beings act without the benefit of 'an absolute criterion by which to choose continually and exclusively between a clearly recognized good and a clearly recognized evil'.[38] The ethical problem arises in the concrete encounter with the concrete other. Therefore, 'accordance with reality' is not a principle that can be universally applied, but a call that must be answered ever and again. Because we do not encounter reality as a unified whole, but only in fragments, 'accordance with reality' names the call to responsibility that arises in the present moment of being addressed.

What this means is that Bonhoeffer's ethic is continually aimed at 'taking the next necessary step'.[39] Responsible action 'has to proceed step-by-step, ask what is possible, and entrust the ultimate step, and thus the ultimate responsibility, to another hand'.[40] This is how Bonhoeffer seeks to renounce self-justification in the sphere of the penultimate. The word of justification is, after all, *God's* ultimate word for human beings; human attempts at self-justification represent the rejection of this ultimate word. Thus, Bonhoeffer envisages life in the sphere of the penultimate as the *way* between God's beginning and God's end. The penultimate is about 'preparing the way for the word'.[41] When Bonhoeffer speaks about Christ as the 'origin, essence, and goal' of life, of responsible action, of history, he is situating us 'in the middle'.[42] Therefore, Brian Brock is right to argue that Bonhoeffer conceives of ethics as a 'way'.[43] And this has important implications for how Bonhoeffer thinks Scripture should and should not be used in service of ethical discernment.

Bonhoeffer's lecture, 'Our Path According to the Testimony of Scripture', is especially illuminating in this context. He delivered this lecture at a meeting of

---

37. Early in 'Christ, Reality, and Good', Bonhoeffer rejects both an ethic of motive and an ethic of consequence. Both systems, as he sees them, depend on aligning judgements (either about the intention behind an action or its results) with abstract moral principles. And even if one did have access to such principles, it is impossible to know all the factors that might motivate one's decisions, and no one can predict all the effects that any given action might have. Therefore, no final judgement on the goodness of motive or consequence can be rendered. Our judgements about motive and consequence are severely limited by our knowledge of history as a whole. For Bonhoeffer, any attempt to remove ethical ambiguity by correlating moral principles to either motive or consequence represents the negation of the historicity of human beings as ethical agents. See DBWE 6, 52–3; DBW 6, 37–8.
38. DBWE 6, 219; DBW 6, 218.
39. DBWE 6, 225; DBW 6, 224.
40. DBWE 6, 225; DBW 6, 224.
41. DBWE 6, 161; DBW 6, 153.
42. Brock, 'Bonhoeffer and the Bible in Christian Ethics', 23.
43. Ibid., 7–29.

the Confessing Church Council of Brethren in Pomerania on 26 October 1938, in which he was to address the question, 'Has the synod of Barmen and especially of Dahlem taught according to Scripture?'[44] He begins by noting the potentially mixed motives that might be driving such a question. Are the Confessing Church pastors, he wonders, doubting the path they have been on? Are they questioning whether Barmen and Dahlem were indeed reliable expositions of Scripture? Are they, perhaps, even wondering if Scripture can offer the needed guidance in times such as theirs? In any case, Bonhoeffer clarifies up front that 'the kinds of questions we bring to Scripture also determine the kind of answer we receive'.[45] Therefore, what Scripture has to say about the doctrinal correctness of Barmen and Dahlem is not the same as what it has to say about the path they have since taken.

One of the main questions concerns the nature of 'scriptural evidence'. Bonhoeffer makes an important distinction: 'Scriptural evidence applies only to the truth of a doctrine, but never to the correctness of a path'.[46] With this statement, Bonhoeffer takes aim at a particular kind of objectification of revelation that can creep into 'biblical' ethics, the sort where I seek an 'insurance policy' in Scripture for my actions, putting scriptural proofs 'in my pocket as the guarantee for my path'.[47] Scriptural evidence, in this case, becomes nothing more than self-justification. An ethic grounded in revelation cannot have scriptural evidence at its disposal in this way, and so the sphere of ethics is not the place for adducing scriptural proofs. Such proofs belong in the sphere of doctrinal theology, the question of truth. Accordingly, when addressing the Confessing Church's question about Dahlem, Bonhoeffer says that 'it is not our Dahlem path but the truth that was pronounced and witnessed to in Dahlem that is justified by Scripture'.[48] Nevertheless, this does not mean that doctrinal truth – and by extension Scripture – stands in isolation from our various paths. 'Our path follows self-evidently, plainly, and necessarily from the truth that is witnessed to.'[49] In the language of John's Gospel, our path is 'the doing of the truth'.[50] Bonhoeffer assures his audience, 'If we abide in truth and in truth alone, our path will be the right one.'[51] It may seem as though Bonhoeffer has simply transferred the objectivity of revelation from ethics to doctrine, but it is important to keep in mind that he does not regard the truth of doctrinal theology in static terms. Doctrine testifies to the intelligibility of God's word, and Bonhoeffer's commitment to theological truth stems from his commitment to testify to Christ who *is* the Truth. Christ's presence as the Word is an intelligible presence, and doctrinal theology is the servant of the Word as Truth.

---

44. DBWE 15, 416–17; DBW 15, 407.
45. DBWE 15, 418; DBW 15, 409.
46. DBWE 15, 419; DBW 15, 410.
47. DBWE 15, 420; DBW 15, 412.
48. DBWE 15, 419; DBW 15, 411.
49. DBWE 15, 419; DBW 15, 411.
50. DBWE 15, 420; DBW 15, 411, citing John 3.21. Pieper also uses this language in Pieper, *Living the Truth*, 171.
51. DBWE 15, 420; DBW 15, 411.

In making this argument, Bonhoeffer is not trying to sneak ethical certitude in by the back door of doctrine. His whole point is to resist the various ways human beings use Scripture to justify themselves, and to direct our attention away from the rightness of our own actions and towards the God we encounter in Christ. To be 'in accordance with Scripture' means something different for doctrine than for discernment. Scripture teaches and testifies to the truth, and at the same time it 'calls us to faith and obedience in the truth that we know in Jesus Christ'.[52] Knowledge of the truth and walking on the way cannot be separated, because Christ who is the Truth is also the Way. This is why Scripture, for Bonhoeffer,

> does not spare us from faith but actually leads into the venture of faith and obedience to God's word, and it strengthens us in this. According to Scripture we do not first know and comprehend the way and then decide to follow it; it is rather the one who is on the journey who knows that he is on the right way. Knowledge comes only in action and decision. Only he who is in truth will recognize the truth. Jesus says: 'Anyone who resolves to do the will of God will know whether the teaching is from God' (John 7.17). For this reason, scriptural evidence can be provided only *along the way*, that is, for the one who believes.[53]

One does not read the Bible in order to be assured of his or her own goodness. To adapt the language of Bernd Wannenwetsch, Scripture 'is not the *foundation of* our moral knowledge, but the *interlocutor to* our moral discourse'.[54] As interlocutor, the word of Scripture confronts us with the call to faith and obedience in the present, freeing us *from* rigid ethical systems and freeing us *for* responsible action for others.

This is the dynamic, I suggest, at work in *Ethics*, although it largely operates behind the scenes. Two of Bonhoeffer's 1942 essays, written during the same period he worked on his *Ethics* manuscripts, exhibit this same dynamic: '"Personal" and "Objective" Ethics' and 'The Question of Baptism'. Both essays follow the same argumentative structure: exegesis of Scripture, consultation with Lutheran confessional writings and systematic doctrinal reflections. Consistent with his view that Scriptural evidence can be deployed to test the truth of our doctrines but not the rightness of our paths, Bonhoeffer's biblical exegesis in these essays serves his doctrinal conclusions. Neither essay concludes with an ethical 'application' or a required praxis; instead, his doctrinal conclusions become the framework for praxis, determining the possibilities of free responsibility without stipulating

---

52. DBWE 15, 420; DBW 15, 412.
53. DBWE 15, 421, my emphasis; DBW 15, 412.
54. Wannenwetsch, 'The Whole Christ and the Whole Human Being', 96. Wannenwetsch is parsing the relationship of Bonhoeffer's Christology and ethics in this context, and is not discussing Scripture exclusively. However, owing to Bonhoeffer's conviction that the word of Scripture is the present Christ, it is appropriate to speak of Scripture as 'interlocutor' in this way.

particular actions or proposing certain ethical principles. Bonhoeffer's exegetical route to praxis moves from scriptural testimony to doctrinal theology, which in turn identifies the ethical sphere wherein free, responsible action can be discerned and undertaken. He does not look to 'scriptural evidence' to justify one action or another, but rather to establish a doctrinal framework in which the church must venture a concrete decision. Scripture does not justify our ways; Scripture sets us on our way.

The place of Scripture in Ethics

My question in this chapter concerns the nature of Bonhoeffer's use of Scripture throughout the *Ethics* manuscripts, which cannot be answered with reference to the sheer number of biblical citations alone. Given Bonhoeffer's conviction that 'scriptural evidence applies only to the truth of a doctrine, but never to the correctness of a path',[55] it is fitting that he would appeal to scriptural evidence more frequently in a doctrinal argument than in an ethical one.[56] Here it is important not to misunderstand the terms. I am following Bonhoeffer's distinction between the subject matter of doctrinal theology and that of Christian ethics, respectively, as the *truth* and the *becoming-real* of God's reality revealed in Christ. It is certainly possible to take up the topic of Christian ethics doctrinally, as Bonhoeffer himself does throughout the *Ethics*, by discussing it in its systematic relationship to other areas of Christian doctrine and with reference to scriptural evidence, but this would still be an essentially doctrinal argument. Bonhoeffer's distinctive *doctrine* of Christian ethics, grounded as it is in revelation-as-*Christus-praesens*, carefully limits the extent to which concrete issues can be answered in advance, which thereby limits the amount of ethical 'application' in the *Ethics* manuscripts.[57]

Nevertheless, in ethics no less than in proclamation, he believes that the present Christ is always the most concrete element of all, and he therefore rejects pure formalism as strongly as uncontrolled casuistry. These twin errors arise from the conviction that the good and the real are ultimately irreconcilable. At their extremes, formalism conceptualizes the good to the exclusion of the concretely real, while casuistry delineates the concrete good in every conceivable situation

---

55. DBWE 15, 419; DBW 15, 410.
56. Plant draws a similar conclusion in 'Uses of the Bible', 195.
57. There is, as Philip Ziegler has noted, 'remarkably little ethics in Bonhoeffer's *Ethics*'. It is, as Ziegler argues, 'thoroughly metaethical in character, being pre-eminently concerned with the fundamental presuppositions, commitments and dispositions of moral discourse, reflection and action, rather than with the content of particular moral judgments or the form of discrete moral acts' (Philip G. Ziegler, '"Completely within God's Doing": Soteriology as Meta-ethics in the Theology of Dietrich Bonhoeffer', in *Christ, Church and World: New Studies in Bonhoeffer's Theology and Ethics*, ed. Michael Mawson and Philip G. Ziegler [London: Bloomsbury T&T Clark, 2016], 101).

until the concept of the good disappears. In Christ, Bonhoeffer insists, the good and the real are reconciled, and therefore a concrete Christian ethic 'can proceed from the reconciliation of the world with God in the human Jesus Christ, in God's acceptance of real human beings'.[58] When Bonhoeffer says that the subject matter of Christian ethics is the becoming-real of the reality of revelation, he means Christ's taking form in the world. 'Ethics as Formation', he writes, 'is the venture of speaking about the form of Christ taking form in our world neither abstractly nor casuistically, neither programatically nor purely reflectively. Here we must risk making concrete judgments and decisions. Here decision and deed can no longer be shifted onto the individual's personal conscience. Here concrete commandments and guidance are given, for which obedience will be demanded'.[59] In this final section, I examine how Bonhoeffer uses and does not use Scripture when he ventures concrete judgements and decisions throughout the *Ethics*. In order to focus the discussion, I have selected two manuscripts that help demarcate the exegetical and ethical scope of Bonhoeffer's project, as he seeks to offer a concrete Christian ethic that does not slip into pure formalism or casuistry. As I will show, his use of Scripture in each manuscript is determined by the kind of argument he is making.

'God's Love and the Disintegration of the World'

One of the most compelling manuscripts in Bonhoeffer's incomplete *Ethics* is called 'God's Love and the Disintegration of the World'. He wrote it relatively late in the composition process, but most likely he intended it to be his introductory chapter.[60] It contains by far the most biblical exegesis of any *Ethics* manuscript. Nearly the whole of the argument proceeds in close dialogue with Scripture, and many sections are presented plainly as biblical commentary. For present purposes, what is interesting about this section of the *Ethics* is not only the extent of the exegetical material, but the conclusion it presses towards: I propose that the exegetical argument we find here is essentially doctrinal in character and that its doctrinal conclusion places important limits on the ways in which exegesis can function in the ethical arguments that follow.

Bonhoeffer's opening sentences set up and encapsulate the argument as a whole: 'The knowledge of good and evil appears to be the goal of all ethical reflection. The first task of Christian ethics is to supersede that knowledge.'[61] What follows is a sweeping account of the fall and its effects on the human capacity for ethical action. He begins with an exegesis of Genesis 3, which was familiar territory. In

---

58. DBWE 6, 100; DBW 6, 87.
59. DBWE 6, 102; DBW 6, 89.
60. For a discussion concerning Bonhoeffer's intended order of *Ethics* manuscripts, see DBWE 6, 440-9; DBW 6, 447-56; concerning the composition history, see DBWE 6, 467-76; DBW 6, 12-22.
61. DBWE 6, 299; DBW 6, 301.

keeping with his prior work in *Creation and Fall*, he interprets the knowledge of good and evil as *ethical* knowledge. The original temptation, in his reading, was to deny God as the origin and source of all good and to take up moral judgement as a human capacity.[62] Adam and Eve in their origin saw only God, and in God saw and did nothing but the good. Having eaten from the tree, they have become 'like God' (*sicut deus*), gods against God.[63] The ethical consequence of the fall is not that human beings have chosen evil over good, but that they have chosen their own good and evil over God. Therefore, one of the results of the fall is the *conscience*. As he puts it in *Creation and Fall*, 'Conscience is not the voice of God within sinful human beings; instead it is precisely their defense against this voice.'[64] Ethical reflection is therefore *self* reflection, whereby the human being becomes the final judge and arbiter of what is good and evil.

By framing the knowledge of good and evil in Genesis 3 in ethical terms, Bonhoeffer presents the doctrine of the fall as the beginning of (what we call) ethics. *Christian* ethics, if it is to be grounded in God rather than in human sin, must supersede the knowledge of good and evil. Although Bonhoeffer is flirting with the Nietzschean language of 'beyond good and evil', he does not wish to dispense with good and evil as ethical categories.[65] The good, he wants to say, does not exist as an independent entity; the good finds its meaning only in God. For Bonhoeffer, 'the knowledge of good and evil is thus disunion with God. Human beings can know about good and evil only in opposition to God'.[66] This is how Bonhoeffer affirms the reality of the good – not by regarding it as an ideal or a moral principle, but rather by affirming that the good is reality itself and that good acts are in accord with reality. Bonhoeffer's exegesis of Genesis 3 prepares the way for this argument by shattering the idols of our own knowledge of good and evil.

---

62. He cites Gen. 3.22 in this connection: 'The human being [Mensch] has become like one of us, and knows what good and evil are' (DBWE 6, 301; DBW 6, 302).

63. This is how the English translation renders the German *Gegengott*, 'god-against-God' (DBWE 6, 302; DBW 6, 304).

64. DBWE 3, 128.

65. In his 1929 Barcelona lecture, 'Basic Questions of a Christian Ethic', he signals his (very limited) agreement with Nietzsche: 'One particularly profound feature of the old story of the fall is that it was caused by eating from the tree of the knowledge of good and evil. The primal – let us say, childlike – community between human beings and God stands beyond this knowledge of good and evil; it knows only one thing: God's limitless love for human beings. Hence the discovery of the world beyond good and evil is by no means to be attributed to the enemy of Christianity Friedrich Nietzsche … It belongs rather to the original, albeit concealed material of the Christian message' (DBWE 10, 363; DBW 10, 327). For a more thorough analysis of Nietzsche's influence on Bonhoeffer, see Peter Frick, 'Friedrich Nietzsche's Aphorisms and Dietrich Bonhoeffer's Theology', in *Bonhoeffer's Intellectual Formation*, ed. Peter Frick (Tübingen: Mohr Siebeck, 2008), 175-99.

66. DBWE 6, 300; DBW 6, 302.

In order to discover what is really good, we must learn to look 'beyond good and evil', that is, to look beyond ourselves and to look instead to God alone.

He develops this theme further with reference to the figure of the Pharisee in the Synoptic Gospels. In his reading, the Pharisee represents 'the epitome of the human being in the state of disunion'.[67] Looking to the various conundrums that the Pharisees and teachers of the law present to Jesus, Bonhoeffer concludes that Jesus overcomes these 'temptations' by refusing to get caught up in the ethical conflict.[68] Jesus does not answer their questions, but supersedes them. Bonhoeffer thus juxtaposes the narrative of the fall in Genesis 3 with these stories from the Gospels, wherein Jesus shows himself to be beyond the situation of ethical conflict.[69] His exegesis of these Gospel narratives thereby provides 'scriptural evidence' against legalistic systems of morality.

Bonhoeffer also makes substantial use of the Epistle of James. He draws on James's contrast between 'hearers' and 'doers' of the law (Jas. 1.22-25), arguing that, by the logic of the Epistle, this is in fact a false distinction. One cannot 'possess' the law by knowing it and not doing it, nor is doing the law something separate from hearing it. Our eyes are to be on the word alone, not on ourselves or on others in judgement. Hearing without doing leads to judging, and judging, he argues 'stands in absolute opposition to doing'.[70] He points to the story of Mary and Martha (Luke 10.38-42) as a converse example. Although the story seems to favour hearing (Mary) over doing (Martha), here as in James the problem is separating the two. James condemns those who are 'merely hearers', which leads to judging; Jesus rebukes Martha for doing without hearing, which leads to mere busyness.

---

67. DBWE 6, 310; DBW 6, 311. In this context, 'the Pharisee' is undoubtedly a caricature, best understood as a kind of moral 'type' or 'characterization'. This would be in line with his earlier manuscript, 'Ethics as Formation' (DBWE 6, 78-80; DBW 6, 64-6), where he contrasts various moral characters with the *Gestalt* (figure or form) of Jesus Christ. Plant makes this connection in 'Uses of the Bible', 187. Plant is especially helpful in drawing attention to the narrative – even literary – dimensions of the German word, *Gestalt*, and to the specifically *narrative* exegesis that 'Ethics as Formation' entails. See Plant, 'Uses of the Bible', 79-117, esp. 95-8.

68. DBWE 6, 311; DBW 6, 312-13; Bonhoeffer cites Matt. 12.1-14; 22.15-22, 23-33, 34-40; Luke 10.25-37.

69. One might point to the temptation narrative as a counter-example (Luke 4.9-12), in which the Slanderer quotes Ps. 91.11-12, and Jesus rebuts by quoting Deut. 6.16. Bonhoeffer, in his lecture on temptation, describes this encounter as follows: 'Jesus's answer sets God's word against God's word, not in such a way that results in unholy uncertainty, but in a way such that here truth stands against lie' (DBWE 15, 393; DBW 15, 380). The 'lie' is that God can be tested and controlled like other realities, as if God can be 'put to the question' like the rest of nature. Jesus's reply expresses, in the form of a biblical commandment, a truth about God that leads directly to his action in accordance with that truth.

70. DBWE 6, 327; DBW 6, 330; cf. James 4.11.

Bonhoeffer envisages human beings who have been 'freed from the disunion of their own knowledge of good and evil to be in unity with Jesus'.[71]

Having recast the doctrine of the fall in terms of ethical knowledge, Bonhoeffer dismantles the foundations for many ethical systems. (One thinks particularly of Kant's categorical imperative.) The world is in this state of disunion; how can it be set right? For Bonhoeffer, *love* 'is the decisive word that distinguishes the human being in disunion from the human being in the state of origin'.[72] But this decisive word cannot be identified with a particular human behaviour or attitude. As the First Epistle of John says, 'God is love' (1 John 4.16). This oft-quoted biblical text, Bonhoeffer insists, must be understood as a definition of love before it can be understood as a definition of God. To say that God is love is not to identify God with a concept that we already understand, but to identify love with the mystery of God revealed in Christ: 'Thus nobody knows what love is except through God's self-revelation. Love is therefore God's revelation. God's revelation, however, is Jesus Christ'.[73] The New Testament unfolds the concept of love in its witness to Christ, through the richness of the events and teachings connected to the name of Jesus. In Scripture, love consists in 'the reconciliation of human beings with God in Christ'.[74] Picking up on the language of 1 John 4.19, Bonhoeffer argues that any human activity rightly called love springs from being loved and chosen by God in Christ, since 'we love him because he first loved us'. In short, God's love overcomes the disintegration of the world. It is on this basis that a Christian ethic must proceed.

Compared with other *Ethics* manuscripts, this one contains much more exegetical material, and much less that is directly ethical. Even Bonhoeffer's condemnations of judging should be read less as ethical exhortations, and more as a doctrinal discussion about the significance of the fall. To be a fallen human being is to be the judge of good and evil; no moral exhortation can subvert this state of affairs. This manuscript functions as Bonhoeffer's exegetical introduction to his *Ethics*, and it is a doctrinal argument through and through. It deploys scriptural evidence in the service of the doctrine of the fall, which disassembles countless ethical false-starts and establishes a new ethical foundation in the reality of Christ. Bonhoeffer thereby uses scriptural evidence to make a doctrinal argument that severely limits the extent to which scriptural evidence can be used in ethical discourse. When biblical texts are used to justify our ways, they are being used in accordance with the fallenness of human beings, rather than in accordance with the reality of revelation in Christ.

---

71. DBWE 6, 330; DBW 6, 333.
72. DBWE 6, 332; DBW 6, 335.
73. DBWE 6, 334; DBW 6, 337.
74. DBWE 6, 335; DBW 6, 339.

'Natural Life'

Bonhoeffer's manuscript on 'Natural Life' is noteworthy as the first theological ethic of human rights by a twentieth-century German Protestant. Although incomplete, Bonhoeffer's draft includes a lengthy section on 'the freedom of bodily life', in which he discusses various ethical topics, including euthanasia, suicide, marriage rights, birth control, abortion, forced sterilization and torture. Writing to Bethge during his work on this manuscript, he admitted that traditional Protestant ethics had failed to provide adequate theological resources to address these questions, and that he had found Catholic moral theology invaluable.[75] He declares up front in 'Natural Life' that the Catholic concept of the natural must be recovered in Protestant thought. Without it, Protestant ethics will lack the orientation it needs to respond to the countless new situations that press in from all sides.

Given the specificity and concreteness of the issues he raises in this manuscript, it is perhaps surprising how rarely he directly cites Scripture in the course of argument. In this, the second longest of all the *Ethics* manuscripts (only the second draft of 'History and Good' is longer), he cites or quotes Scripture only eight separate times.[76] Moreover, his use of scriptural texts does not follow any obvious pattern, ranging from direct quotations to general statements about biblical teaching. What is consistent and particularly noteworthy, however, is that Bonhoeffer never uses scriptural citations as the argumentative fulcrum in any

---

75. DBWE 16, 126; DBW 16, 114.

76. (1) Bonhoeffer refers to 'the destruction of the natural' as a sign of the end as prophesied in Luke 21.16 (DBWE 6, 177; DBW 6, 170). (2) He contrasts the idealism of Kant, who placed duty over rights, with the view of Holy Scripture, which speaks 'first of what is given to life, and only then of what is demanded of it' (DBWE 6, 180; DBW 6, 173). (3) He accompanies his discussion on the right to bodily joy and pleasure with a string of quotations from Ecclesiastes (DBWE 6, 187; DBW 6, 181; citing Eccles. 2.24-25; 3.12; 9.7-9; 11.9). (4) He references the story of the rich man and Lazarus (Luke 16.19-31) to exemplify the value God places on lives that have seemingly no social utility. (5) He concludes his discussion of euthanasia by quoting Exod. 23.7, 'Do not kill the innocent' (DBWE 6, 193, 196; DBW 6, 188, 191). (6) When considering the question of suicide, he argues that Scripture neither forbids it nor approves of it, but that suicide appears in the Bible 'only as the consequence of the deepest sin', and that 'instead of prohibiting it the Bible wants to call the despairing to repentance and grace' (DBWE 6, 199-200; DBW 6, 195-6). In this context, he cites the examples of Ahithophel (2 Sam. 17.23) and Judas (Matt. 27.5), but he alludes to some possible exceptions without naming specific references (the editors suggest 1 Sam. 31.4 and Ps. 37.15 as possibilities). (7) When discussing the rights of reproduction, he argues that 'the biblical view of marriage' affirms sexual union that is 'distinct but never separated from the right to reproduction' (DBWE 6, 210; DBW 6, 208). Here he quotes from Gen. 1.28; 2.18; 2.23-24, citing 1 Cor. 7 and Exod. 21.10. He also references Gen. 38. (8) Finally, he quotes Matt. 5.29 as the 'boundary' concerning the natural right to dispose of certain parts of one's own body (DBWE 6, 213-14; DBW 6, 212).

of the topics he discusses. Scripture, at most, *accompanies* his ethical discourse, the shape of which is determined by Bonhoeffer's theology of the natural life. Why is this?

One explanation is that the apparent lack of biblical material in *Ethics* is due to the more 'universal' (i.e. less particularly Christian) scope required of a work on ethics. For example, the editors of the German edition of *Ethics* assume that 'the terminology of a book on ethics cannot adhere as closely to the language of the Bible and of proclamation as is the case in *Discipleship*'.[77] However, this is unconvincing, given that Bonhoeffer's ethical point of departure, as the editors themselves acknowledge, is 'the theological question of how the reality of God revealed in Jesus Christ can take form in human life in the world'.[78] Precisely how Bonhoeffer might pursue this question without adhering to the language of the Bible and of proclamation is anybody's guess. God's revelation in Christ *is* the subject matter of the Bible and of proclamation. A Christological ethic, in his view, could not be anything but a scriptural ethic, and vice versa. Even 'Natural Life', arguably the most 'universal' of the manuscripts, is unavoidably Christological in orientation. It is hard to imagine a more thoroughly Christological definition of the natural than Bonhoeffer provides: 'The natural is that which, after the fall, is directed toward the coming of Jesus Christ.'[79] And one could hardly offer a more Christocentric call to the natural life than Bonhoeffer's: 'Only through Christ's becoming human do we have the right to call people to natural life and to live it ourselves.'[80]

What *does* account for the seemingly marginal role of scriptural quotations in 'Natural Life' is what I described above, namely, Bonhoeffer's warning against relying on 'scriptural evidence' to justify ethical decisions 'along the way'. Bonhoeffer's ethics of the natural life envisages what 'doing the truth' might mean in light of the truth that God has reconciled fallen humankind to himself in Christ. Far from following a pragmatic impulse to accept the reality of things as they are, Bonhoeffer is building on the doctrine of the incarnation, which grounds his simple, Christological insight that 'Christ has entered into natural life'.[81] The 'way' of the natural follows from this incarnational truth of natural life. The reason Bonhoeffer does not adduce 'scriptural evidence' is because the doctrine of the incarnation was not his point of contention, but his point of departure. The concept of the natural, lost as he saw it to Protestant thought, offered a profoundly scriptural way to address ethical questions related to the penultimate reality of being human. Thus, the place of Scripture in 'Natural Life' goes much deeper than the number of biblical quotations. The doctrine of the incarnation is in Bonhoeffer's view indisputably 'in accordance with Scripture', and this doctrine is at the heart of his exposition of the natural.

77. DBW 6, 418; DBWE 6, 414.
78. DBW 6, 413; DBWE 6, 409.
79. DBWE 6, 173; DBW 6, 165.
80. DBWE 6, 174; DBW 6, 166.
81. DBWE 6, 174; DBW 6, 166.

In 'Natural Life', therefore, Bonhoeffer does not deploy scriptural evidence in the service of 'moral proof-texting', which would be tantamount to justification by works. To be sure, his references to specific biblical passages, few as they may be, indicate his ongoing dialogue with Scripture in thinking through these concrete ethical problems. But deeper than this, Scripture is at the very centre of the Christology that grounds his exposition of the natural. The marginal place of scriptural evidence in 'Natural Life' is consistent with Bonhoeffer's assertion that 'Scriptural evidence applies only to the truth of a doctrine, but never to the correctness of a path'.[82] The 'path' of ethics, the concrete venture of judgements and decisions in history, is to be made in accordance with reality, and this reality is revealed in Scripture and articulated by doctrinal theology. Implicitly in 'Natural Life' and explicitly in 'God's Love', Scripture is the basis for the doctrinal framework in which Christian ethical discourse can occur. Scripture does not and cannot tell us what the right thing to do is in any given situation. Scripture testifies to God's word in Christ, in whose truth our given situations can be seen for what they truly are. Doctrine situates ethics, but it never frees people from the risk and responsibility of concrete action.

Conclusion

Christian ethics concerns the becoming-real of the reality of revelation, and doctrinal theology concerns the truth of this reality. For Bonhoeffer, scriptural evidence grounds the latter in a way that it cannot ground the former. This dynamic is at work explicitly and (more often) implicitly throughout *Ethics*. My study of *Ethics* in this chapter offers the following bibliological nuance to my larger project: What God does with Scripture in speaking his word by the Spirit is to *teach reality*.

To be sure, calling the church to more doctrine may not seem to evoke the picture of Christ-like love and the call to free responsibility that Bonhoeffer endorses in his *Ethics*. The key, however, is not to confuse doctrinal theology with theological authoritarianism. Doctrinal theology, as a witness to the intelligible truth of God's present word in Christ, is an endlessly creative and lively enterprise. One can never be done with it. It is not a system that, once finalized, can sit on the shelf undisturbed. Neither does it represent disengagement from the world; it is not a retreat into the private sphere of the intellect. It is the fruit of the church's ongoing participation in the reality of God reconciled to the world in Christ, a reality disclosed in Scripture. It is when one's concrete situation is understood as embedded in the reality of Christ that the command of God can be rightly heard.

In pursuit of responsible action, Bonhoeffer believes there are more and less responsible ways of appealing to scriptural proofs. Scripture is the basis for the doctrinal framework in which Christian ethical discourse can occur. Scripture

---

82. DBWE 15, 419; DBW 15, 410.

does not and cannot tell us what the right thing to do is in any given situation. Scripture testifies to God's word in Christ, in whose truth our given situations can be seen for what they truly are. Doctrine situates ethics, but it never frees people from the risk and responsibility of concrete action. This is why Bonhoeffer's *Ethics* is best regarded 'as thoroughly *metaethical* in character.'[83] His primary concern is not in determining the moral value of particular human actions, but in establishing the doctrinal framework in which human beings can venture concrete ethical decisions. Thus, the main feature of Bonhoeffer's *Ethics* is also its most stubborn bug: we who live by God's grace alone can never justify our own actions as moral or immoral. There is nothing, not even scriptural evidence, that can justify our moral decisions apart from God's grace. Anything else is tantamount to justification by works. Therefore, if we want to follow Bonhoeffer's lead, we must first surrender the security of knowing when we are acting ethically.

I do not regard this conclusion as especially controversial. All Bonhoeffer is proposing is that we read Scripture as if it is about *God* before it is about us. As we go to Scripture to learn revelation, to discover ever and again who God is, what God has done and what God is doing, the way we live and act will be transformed by our deepening perception of the reality we find ourselves in. Scripture, by the Spirit of truth, leads us into truth, and by the same Spirit, the church's life becomes the doing of the truth. When the church ventures concrete actions in history, it should not look to scriptural proofs to justify its decisions. It should look to Scripture in order to hear and discern its witness to reality. Exegesis serves ethics first and foremost by furnishing a theological account of reality: God and world reconciled in the person of Christ.[84] It is in the context of this reality that the venture of free, responsible action occurs, actions whose goodness cannot be guaranteed in advance nor assured after the fact, but actions that stand – with all things – under the judgement and grace of God.

And this is where Bonhoeffer's way of using – and not using – Scripture for Christian ethics connects with his fundamental insight about revelation-as-*Christus-praesens*. The reality that Scripture teaches is that Christ is present in and for the world as the incarnate, crucified and risen reconciler. Bonhoeffer's writings from the 1940s evince his growing interest in locating the worldly presence of Christ. This is one of his primary concerns as he writes to Eberhard Bethge from prison, and is the topic of the next chapter.

---

83. Ziegler, 'Completely within God's Doing', 101.
84. This proposal is fleshed out in Christopher R. J. Holmes, *Ethics in the Presence of Christ* (London: T&T Clark, 2012), 137–53.

11

THE WORD FOR OTHERS

Bonhoeffer's writings from prison continue to be one of the most widely read parts of his corpus – and justly so. The letters he wrote from his cell at Tegel contain many moving passages, depicting a young man struggling to face his uncertain and fearful circumstances with honesty and faithfulness. These letters also contain some of Bonhoeffer's most intriguing theological proposals. It seems fitting to conclude this study by considering Bonhoeffer's prison theology in light of the preceding conclusions. Specifically, this chapter addresses the relationship between Bonhoeffer's bibliology and his developing interest in the nonreligious interpretation of biblical concepts.

Nonreligious interpretation of biblical concepts is not identical to what I will later discuss under the heading of nonreligious exegesis, but the latter cannot be discussed without first reviewing the former. In what follows, I begin by demonstrating that Bonhoeffer's critique of religion and of Barth's 'positivism of revelation' was grounded in his theology of revelation-as-*Christus-praesens*. Next, I show how Bonhoeffer's interpretation of Scripture during his final years remained Christological to its core, in a way that represents both continuity with and development beyond his earlier exegetical writings. I conclude with some remarks about what nonreligious exegesis might entail. I argue that Bonhoeffer's prison Christology has exegetical implications and that nonreligious exegesis is fundamentally about learning to read Scripture as God's word-for-others.

Revelation in a religionless age

Before I can address the relationship between Bonhoeffer's bibliology and nonreligious interpretation, it is worth considering whether his bibliology, specifically his interpretation of revelation as *Christus praesens*, is consistent with his prison theology. In this section, I argue that it is not only consistent, but that *Christus praesens* remains central to his thought.

In a letter to Bethge dated 30 April 1944, Bonhoeffer begins his exciting new theological enquiries with a pair of questions: 'what is Christianity or who is Christ actually for us today?'[1] The juxtaposition of these two questions is telling.

---

1. DBWE 8, 362; DBW 8, 402.

He assumes that what Christianity is cannot be separated from who Christ is for us. Christianity, to begin, 'is' not a religion, but it has always been 'clothed' in religion. And if it is the case that Christianity is not reducible to any particular religious garb, Bonhoeffer wonders if it is possible to remove this garb altogether, to speak of an entirely religionless Christianity. If so, it would mean that being or becoming religious is not a prerequisite for being or becoming a Christian. If Christ is for the religionless person *as* religionless, then Christianity can be for the religionless age – and not in order to change the nonreligious into the religious, but in order for Christ to 'become Lord of the religionless as well'.[2]

---

2. DBWE 8, 363; DBW 8, 404. For the purposes of this chapter, I must leave aside the question of how accurate Bonhoeffer was in his assessment of the 'world come of age'. His proposal seems in line with certain kinds of secularization theory, which either argue or assume that modernization brings with it secularity. Charles Taylor, in his magisterial *A Secular Age* (Cambridge, MA: Harvard University Press, 2007), helpfully distinguishes between three types of secularity. The first type refers to the divide between the sacred and the secular, between that which is oriented towards the eternal and spiritual, and that which is oriented towards the temporal and earthly. The second type refers to a kind public space that is, or endeavours to be, religiously 'neutral'. It is not necessarily anti-religious, but religion and/or belief in God is regarded as a private matter, and will hold no essential place in the political and economic makeup of the society. The third type of secularity, and the kind Taylor is most interested in, refers to the conditions of belief. A secular person in this third sense may or may not believe in God and may or may not be religious, but what makes this person secular is the *contestability* of their beliefs. Accordingly, Taylor's sprawling narrative traces 'a move from a society where belief in God is unchallenged and indeed, unproblematic, to one in which it is understood to be one option among others, and frequently not the easiest to embrace' (ibid., 3). One of his arguments is that secularization does not occur by subtraction: secular society is not simply what remains after old superstitions and archaic beliefs have been removed. Secularism is an *achievement*, and one that depends on the invention of an exclusive humanism that offers human beings a sense of meaning and fullness within a completely 'immanent frame' (ibid., 25–89). Obviously, we cannot fault Bonhoeffer's account for failing to match the scope and nuance of Taylor's, and it would be too simplistic to equate Bonhoeffer's discussion of religionlessness in a world come of age with Taylor's account in *A Secular Age*. For example, Bonhoeffer suggests that 'people as they are simply cannot be religious anymore' (DBWE 8, 362; DBW 8, 403), whereas Taylor is more concerned with the contestability of belief – whether or not someone identifies as religious. But Taylor's account aligns with Bonhoeffer's insofar as both recognize that religious affiliations and beliefs can no longer be held as the default position, certainly not in Europe and North America. Ralf K. Wüstenberg has identified several other resonances between Bonhoeffer's account of religionlessness and Taylor's account of secularity in his essay, 'Religion and Secularity', in *The Oxford Handbook of Dietrich Bonhoeffer*, ed. Michael Mawson and Philip G. Ziegler (Oxford: Oxford University Press, 2019), 321–30.

This is where Bonhoeffer levels the first of several criticisms of Karl Barth's 'positivism of revelation' (which I will return to shortly), but he also has an unnamed target in his sights. He writes that

> our entire nineteen hundred years of Christian preaching and theology are built on the 'religious a priori' in human beings. 'Christianity' has always been a form (perhaps the true form) of 'religion'. Yet if it becomes obvious one day that this 'a priori' doesn't exist, that it has been a historically conditioned and transitory form of human expression, then people really will become radically religionless – and I believe that this is already more or less the case.[3]

His argument turns on this questioning of the religious *a priori*, which was a key tenet of Troeltsch and the history-of-religions school. Bonhoeffer had already critiqued the *a priori* in *Act and Being*, where he argued that human beings do not have an inherent ability to receive revelation, nor are they naturally drawn towards faith; the human being has a heart turned in on itself (*cor curvum in se*), not towards God.[4] But note that Bonhoeffer is not here objecting to the existence of the *a priori*; he simply thinks that it cannot become the ground of theological discourse. In this 1944 prison letter, by contrast, Bonhoeffer is no longer convinced that any such natural drive towards religion even exists. Perhaps, he speculates, it will turn out that all human religiosity was merely a form of human expression, and not something hardwired in the human mind. In *Act and Being*, Bonhoeffer objected to the *a priori* because he thought it made for bad theology; now he objects because he thinks it makes for bad anthropology!

Bonhoeffer is not far from his early academic years in Berlin, heeding Barth's call to abandon Troeltsch's brand of theological liberalism. Yet it is in this same letter from prison that Bonhoeffer begins to signal some newfound misgivings about Barth's proposals. Considering the possibility of religionless Christianity, Bonhoeffer credits Barth (specifically the Barth of the second edition of the Romans commentary) as 'the only one to have begun thinking along these lines'.[5] But he immediately chastises him for failing to follow his insights to their logical conclusion. This is where Bonhoeffer's infamous charge of 'positivism of revelation' first appears.[6] What does he mean by this? He is by no means rejecting revelation as the ground of theological discourse. In his view the problem is that Barth did not carry his critique of religion via revelation

---

3. DBWE 8, 362–3; DBW 8, 403.
4. DBWE 2, 58; DBW 2, 52.
5. DBWE 8, 363–4; DBW 8, 404; cf. DBWE 8, 428–9; DBW 8, 480–1.
6. DBWE 8, 364; DBW 8, 404. See also DBWE 8, 373, 429; DBW 8, 415, 481. This topic has been studied frequently in Bonhoeffer scholarship. See, for example, Pangritz, *Karl Barth in the Theology of Dietrich Bonhoeffer*, 76–87; Ralf K. Wüstenberg, *A Theology of Life: Dietrich Bonhoeffer's Religionless Christianity*, trans. Douglas W. Stott (Grand Rapids: Eerdmans, 1998), 60–5; Slot, *Negativism of Revelation*, 208–26.

far enough and that what he ended up with was another kind of fundamentally religious discourse: a take-it-or-leave-it set of doctrines that offers little to the person who is genuinely outside (and wishes to remain outside) the sphere of religion. Bonhoeffer regards this type of religiosity as an insurmountable and unnecessary obstacle between religionless people and God. Is it not enough to genuinely encounter God? Must one also formulate the right kinds of thoughts about that encounter. Edward van't Slot puts it well when he concludes that doctrinal theology 'displays a *"positivism of revelation"* if it *overemphasizes theological reflection on revelation, and neglects the simple, faithful ministry to a world that is not interested in theology*'.[7] The situation of real people in their real situations, as Bonhoeffer sees it, involves a steep waning of the religious trappings that, until then, could largely have been taken for granted. Can we really demand of this world, if it has truly 'come of age' in this way, that it revert to the way things used to be? For Bonhoeffer, if Christ is to be 'for us' in this new situation, then Christ must be the 'Lord of the religionless'.

Bonhoeffer is not thereby rejecting theological discourse altogether. He simply wants to ensure that it occupies its proper place in the world. Here it is helpful to see the 'arcane discipline' as a counterpoint to 'positivism of revelation'. Bonhoeffer does not want the classical Christian doctrines to fade into oblivion, but he wonders if perhaps the best place to preserve these mysteries is in the arcane discipline of the church. He had written about this already in his 1932 ecclesiology lectures. In that context, he was distinguishing between confession and confessional*ism*, and the latter is not far from positivism of revelation: 'Confessionalism uses confession as a means of propaganda against the godless. Confession of faith belongs in the Christian assembly of the faithful ... Confession belongs as *arcanum* within the worship service.'[8] When the church's confessions are treated as weapons to be deployed against the world, or as a set of truth claims to be lorded over the world, or even as a barrier that divides the church from the world, there we have positivism of revelation. Bonhoeffer envisions the mysteries of faith in the context of the arcane discipline being used to sustain the community that is called to be radically *for* the world.

In *Discipleship*, Bonhoeffer expresses his concern that grace not be distributed willy-nilly as if it were cheap, but that its costliness be protected: 'Costly grace is grace as God's holy treasure which must be protected from the world and which must not be thrown to the dogs'.[9] As he outlines in his Finkenwalde lectures on catechesis, the ancient church withheld the sacraments from those who had not received proper preparation, instruction and baptism. The arcane discipline meant that the most sacred parts of the liturgy were shrouded in secrecy – largely a necessity

---

7. Slot, *Negativism of Revelation*, 226. Slot proposes 'positivism of faith' as an alternate term for Bonhoeffer's critique of Barth (ibid.).
8. DBWE 11, 314–15; DBW 11, 285.
9. DBWE 4, 45; DBW 4, 31.

that arose out of state persecution – which ensured that the holiest things of the church were not exposed to mockery.[10] The deepest mysteries of the faith ought to be treated with due reverence, rather than paraded before every passer-by. To put it simply: Christianity doesn't work as the presentation and enforcement of doctrinal beliefs – certainly not in the 'world come of age' that Bonhoeffer perceived. He wanted to know how to speak about God with people who lacked familiarity with and interest in religion. But it does not mean giving up the core doctrines of the Christian faith; it would mean, rather, keeping them in their rightful place, in the deepest recesses of prayer, worship and sacrament. In this way, church dogma is not to be understood as the unwieldy key that unlocks the door to the sanctuary, but rather as the treasure hidden in its innermost chambers.

In all this, Bonhoeffer is exploring how to be a theologian of revelation (which he never ceased to be!) in the context of a world come of age. His opening question guides his enquiry, and the echoes of his 1933 Christology are clear: 'Who is Christ actually for us today?'[11] Rather than asking *how* Christians can reach a religionless world, he is asking *who* Jesus is for this religionless world. Moreover, his Christological question assumes the promeity of Christ: who is Jesus Christ *for us*, here and now, in the real world? Bonhoeffer thought that if one faced facts honestly, one would have to admit that the world no longer needs 'God' the way it once did. The 'God' that the world has outgrown is, in the last analysis, nothing but a human fabrication, an idol. Bonhoeffer notes with disdain how 'religious people speak of God at a point where human knowledge is at an end (or sometimes when they're too lazy to think further), or when human strength fails'.[12] But this is nothing but a *deus ex machina*. Religious people invoke 'God' when nothing else can solve the problem or answer the question before them. God becomes a 'gap-filler' in human knowledge.[13] The outcome is, as Bonhoeffer points out, 'inevitable': 'when the boundaries of knowledge are pushed ever further, God too is pushed further away and thus is ever on the retreat'.[14] Bonhoeffer has no interest in the 'God of the gaps' whose domain is shrinking every day. He wants to find God in the centre of human life, not at its outermost margins. In his memorable phrase, 'God is the beyond in the midst of our lives'.[15]

It is Bonhoeffer's ongoing concern to find God at the centre that indicates the consistency of his core theological convictions. Discussing his topic further, he clarifies: 'The ground for this lies in the revelation of God in Jesus Christ. God is the center of life, and doesn't just "turn up" when we have unsolved problems to be

---

10. See DBWE 14, 554; DBW 14, 549 and DBWE 14, 532; DBW 14, 526. Similarly, in *Discipleship*: 'What happened to the insights of the ancient church, which in the baptismal teaching watched so carefully over the boundary between the church and the world, over costly grace?' (DBWE 4, 54; DBW 4, 40).
11. DBWE 8, 362; DBW 8, 402.
12. DBWE 8, 366; DBW 8, 407.
13. Or 'stopgap' (*Lükenbüßer*). See DBWE 8, 405; DBW 8, 454.
14. DBWE 8, 406; DBW 8, 454.
15. DBWE 8, 367; DBW 8, 408.

solved.'[16] If God's revelation in Christ is the basis of our knowledge of God, then we must recognize God in the midst of life, not at the edges. He never loses sight of the God who, in Christ, is really present for us today. But what does God's presence look like in a world that has no need of God? 'Before God, and with God, we live without God',[17] he writes. Godlessness characterizes the world come of age, but, as Bonhoeffer reminds us, Godlessness is not a foreign theme to Christianity; it is there at its very heart: 'God consents to be pushed out of the world and onto the cross; God is weak and powerless in the world and in precisely this way, and only so, is at our side and helps us.'[18] Thus it is as the crucified Christ that God is present in the world, 'present as an absent one', as Wolf Krötke puts it.[19] Given the way in which Bonhoeffer's reflections on religionless Christianity and nonreligious interpretation of biblical concepts grow out of his concern to find Christ at the centre of human life, it is clear that *Christus praesens* remains a central theme in his thought, even in his prison writings. As Gerhard Ebeling puts it, 'The problem of non-religious interpretation arises for Bonhoeffer not from any doubt of Jesus Christ, but precisely from faith in Jesus Christ ... The question of non-religious interpretation derives directly from the foundation and heart of his theology, from his Christology.'[20] Specifically, his concern remains the same to speak of Jesus Christ as really present in and for this world.

In keeping with his 1933 Christology, he does not ask *how* Jesus could possibly be present in such a godless age, but rather *who* Jesus is as the present one today. In his Christology lectures, Bonhoeffer had answered the 'who' question of Christ's presence with the *pro-me* structure: Christ is present by virtue of his being for me and for us.[21] In his 'Outline for a Book', enclosed in his letter to Bethge of 3 August 1944, he switches from Christ's being-for-me to Christ's being-for-others. Christ's being 'there for others' means that he is present as the suffering and powerless one. It was on this principle that Bonhoeffer wanted to base his (non-religious) interpretation of biblical concepts.[22]

Bonhoeffer and the Bible in prison

As the day of Eberhard and Renate Bethge's son's baptism approached, Bonhoeffer began suggesting biblical texts that Bethge might use for the service. Among his

16. DBWE 8, 406–7; DBW 8, 455.
17. DBWE 8, 479; DBW 8, 534.
18. DBWE 8, 479; DBW 8, 534.
19. Wolf Krötke, 'The Meaning of God's Mystery for Dietrich Bonhoeffer's Understanding of the Religions and "Religionlessness"', in *Karl Barth and Dietrich Bonhoeffer*, 146.
20. Gerhard Ebeling, *Word and Faith*, trans. James W. Leitch (Philadelphia: Fortress, 1960), 107.
21. DBWE 12, 314; DBW 12, 295–6. Bonhoeffer uses *pro nobis* (for us) later in his lectures (DBWE 12, 359; DBW 12, 347).
22. DBWE 8, 501–2; DBW 8, 558–9.

suggestions were 2 Timothy 2.1, Proverbs 4.18, 23.26, Psalm 90.14 and Isaiah 8.18.[23] Although for obvious reasons Bonhoeffer could not preside over the baptism, he sent a letter to Eberhard and Renate containing a meditation for the event. His letter contains many references to Scripture, mostly Old Testament texts. Throughout, he reflects on the kind of world that his godson will inherit – which he believes will be quite different from the one he experienced in his childhood – and what it might take to navigate through the uncertain times ahead. There is nothing overtly Christological or groundbreaking about the way he deploys biblical texts in this meditation. In nearly every paragraph, he is simply quoting Scripture that relates to the topic at hand. Perhaps his prognostications and advice arose from his repeated reading of Scripture in prison; perhaps the biblical passages he cites occurred to him as he wrote. Rhetorically, the latter seems more likely, if only because his paragraphs tend to conclude, not begin, with relevant Scripture quotations – but this hardly matters in any case. The point is that Bonhoeffer had so internalized the Scriptures that he could – and, when the context was appropriate, would – quote the Bible liberally. The final paragraph is where Bonhoeffer's meditation reveals that he was still thinking about the world come of age and religionless Christianity. He states the church has failed by fighting for nothing but its own survival, and has thereby surrendered the power of its word to the world. It must therefore be renewed until it can once again speak in a new language, 'perhaps quite nonreligious language',[24] and that, until then, Christianity will continue quietly and inconspicuously. Bonhoeffer's final words quote from Proverbs 4.18 (as it happens, the only one of the passages he had suggested to Bethge that he ends up using in the meditation), a verse that had captivated him in the days leading up to the baptism: 'The path of the righteous is like the light of dawn, which shines brighter and brighter until full day.'[25]

This is just one of many examples of Bonhoeffer's ongoing engagement with Scripture throughout his prison writings. Indeed, one of the striking features of Bonhoeffer's 'new theology' is just how biblical he is trying to be.[26] Whatever else might be said about religionless Christianity, it is patently clear that Bonhoeffer never intends it to mean *scriptureless* Christianity. Not only does Bonhoeffer develop his ideas in conversation with the Bible, he presents them as ideas that have arisen directly from his reading of the Bible. This is the case with some of his most famous statements from prison. For example, on the 'suffering God', he writes, 'Human religiosity directs people in need to the power of God in the world, God as deus ex machina. The bible directs people toward the powerlessness and the suffering of God; only the suffering God can help.'[27] Human religiosity, he

---

23. DBWE 8, 379; DBW 8, 422; DBWE 8, 381; DBW 8, 425.
24. DBWE 8, 390; DBW 8, 436.
25. DBWE 8, 390; DBW 8, 436; cf. DBWE 8, 379; DBW 8, 423.
26. Moreover, he had not lost interest in questions of how scriptural interpretation ought to proceed; see the first of his July 1944 notes in DBWE 8, 452; DBW 8, 506.
27. DBWE 8, 479; DBW 8, 574.

believes, constructs a very different God from the God of the Bible. Again, in the midst of one of his critiques of Barth's 'positivism of revelation', he characterizes Barth's theology as a 'like it or lump it' proposition. And what is Bonhoeffer's complaint? 'That's not biblical.'[28] As he grasps after his own alternative, Bonhoeffer writes, 'At the moment I am thinking about how the concepts of repentance, faith, justification, rebirth, and sanctification should be reinterpreted in a "worldly" way – in the Old Testament sense and in the sense of John 1:14.'[29] If this is what he envisaged as non-religious interpretation, it is clear that he is still interested in biblical interpretation. Thus, his interest in worldly, nonreligious interpretation of biblical concepts remains as ever an interest in exegesis.

It is well known that Bonhoeffer's appreciation for the Old Testament grew during his time in prison. A passage from his letter of 5 December 1943 is worth quoting:

> By the way, I notice more and more how much I am thinking and perceiving things in line with the Old Testament; thus in recent months I have been reading much more in the Old than the New Testament. Only when one knows that the name of God may not be uttered may one sometimes speak the name of Jesus Christ. Only when one loves life and the earth so much that with it everything seems to be lost and at its end may one believe in the resurrection of the dead and a new world. Only when one accepts the law of God as binding for oneself may one perhaps sometimes speak of grace. And only when the wrath and vengeance of God against God's enemies are allowed to stand can something of forgiveness and the love of enemies touch our hearts. Whoever wishes to be and perceive things too quickly and too directly in New Testament ways is to my mind no Christian.[30]

Now, this attitude towards the Old Testament might be seen as simply another way of marginalizing its importance, since, taking this quotation on its own terms, it still treats Israel's Scriptures as nothing but a prologue to the *real* good news of the New Testament. I will address this concern at the conclusion of this chapter. What matters at this point is the simple fact that Bonhoeffer was learning to perceive things in new ways, in 'Old Testament ways'. Significantly, Bonhoeffer found in the Old Testament a profound affirmation of the world, a view that stands in stark contrast to what he saw as the religious impulse to be whisked out of the world.

The Old Testament, as Bonhoeffer reads it, is a profoundly this-worldly book.[31] Ernst Feil suggests that there is a 'significant difference' between Bonhoeffer's

---

28. DBWE 8, 373; DBW 8, 415.
29. DBWE 8, 373; DBW 8, 416.
30. DBWE 8, 213; DBW 8, 226.
31. For an excellent study of Bonhoeffer's view of this-worldliness in creative conversation with contemporary issues, see Harvey, *Taking Hold of the Real*. Harvey's chapter on Bonhoeffer's reading of the Old Testament is particularly valuable (ibid., 209–33).

former reading of the Old Testament as 'the book of Christ' and his reading of the Old Testament in prison: 'He no longer looked primarily at Christ in the Old Testament but, with Christ, at the world, at thisworldliness.'[32] An example of the biblical pattern of this-worldliness, Bonhoeffer observes, appears in the nature of Old Testament redemption. Unlike other redemption myths, the story of Israel is 'redemption *within history*, that is, *this side* of the bounds of death ... Israel is redeemed out of Egypt so that it may live before God, as God's people on earth'.[33] The fundamentally religious question of saving one's soul is, Bonhoeffer believes, foreign to the Old Testament, which is far more interested in God's action in and justice for this world.[34] And he believes that this same pattern continues in the New Testament: 'The Christian hope of resurrection is different from the mythological in that it refers people to their life on earth in a wholly new way, and more sharply than the OT.'[35] How does the New Testament refer Christians to their earthly life? Bonhoeffer continues, 'Like Christ ... they have to drink the cup of earthly life to the last drop, and only when they do this is the Crucified and Risen One with them, and they are crucified and resurrected with Christ.'[36] Thus the this-worldliness of the Old Testament dovetails perfectly into the New Testament Christological narrative of incarnation, crucifixion and resurrection.

It is crucial not to forget that this world-affirming narrative always goes by way of Christ's suffering and pain. Twice Bonhoeffer makes reference to Jesus's final hours in Gethsemane (Matt. 26.36-46), stating that genuine, Christological worldliness means staying awake with Jesus, remaining with God through God's suffering.[37] In his poem, 'Christians and Heathens', he makes the same point. Through the three stanzas of this poem, the only difference between 'Christians' and 'heathens' is that 'Christians stand by God in God's own pain'.[38] This is the kind of worldly Christianity that Bonhoeffer envisages. One of the problems with religious Christianity, apart from its tendency towards individualism and an over-dependence on metaphysics,[39] is that it covers up the godlessness of the world with a mask of religion. One cannot follow Jesus to the cross while remaining under the illusion that the world would never actually send him there.

The path of Christianity follows the messianic suffering of Jesus, which Bonhoeffer refers to Isaiah 53.[40] He traces this pattern in the Gospels: Jesus's call to discipleship, his eating with sinners, his healing of the sick at as fulfilment of Isaiah 53.4-5 (as in Matt. 8.14-17). And those who respond to Jesus in faith do so

---

32. Feil, *The Theology of Dietrich Bonhoeffer*, 94.
33. DBWE 8, 447; DBW 8, 500.
34. Bonhoeffer asks, 'Does the question of saving one's soul even come up in the Old Testament?' (DBWE 8, 372–3; DBW 8, 415).
35. DBWE 8, 447; DBW 8, 500.
36. DBWE 8, 448; DBW 8, 500–1.
37. DBWE 8, 480; DBW 8, 535; DBWE 8, 486; DBW 8, 542.
38. DBWE 8, 461; DBW 8, 515.
39. DBWE 8, 372; DBW 8, 414.
40. DBWE 8, 480; DBW 8, 536.

in various ways, and rarely in the way 'religious' people are expected to respond: Zacchaeus gives away half of his possessions (Luke 19.1-10); the 'sinful woman' anoints Jesus with oil and tears (Luke 7.36-50); the centurion at Capernaum does not confess his sins, but his faith is commended (Matt. 8.5-13; Luke 7.1-10); the shepherds and wise men alike come to see the infant Jesus, not in order to gain something from him, but because they are guided there.[41] Bonhoeffer provides several other examples and offers this conclusion: 'The one thing they all have in common is their sharing in the suffering of God in Christ. That is their "faith." There is nothing about a religious method; the "religious act" is always something partial, whereas "faith" is something whole and involves one's whole life. Jesus calls not to a new religion but to life.'[42]

The call to fullness of life is a reminder that Bonhoeffer's vision of non-religious Christianity is not all about pain and suffering. He is also very concerned with the presence of God in and among human strength and vitality. This is, in fact, where his reflections began in the inaugural letter of 30 April 1944. He took umbrage with the religious strategy of creating an artificial 'need' for God by first convincing someone of the disaster of sin or mortality and then offering God as the solution to this newfound problem. This kind of religious predation is most effective on people when they are at their most vulnerable, and Bonhoeffer describes it as 'religious rape'.[43] But where is God for those who are not overcome by anxiety over their sin or death? After all, Bonhoeffer argues, in the world come of age, people simply are not bothered by these questions. He wants to 'speak of God not at the boundaries but in the center, not in weakness but in strength, thus not in death and guilt but in human life and human goodness'.[44] The best response to unanswerable questions, he concludes, is not 'working hypothesis: God' but reverent silence. When Bethge questions whether Scripture actually says anything about health, happiness and strength, Bonhoeffer responds that the Old Testament at least addresses these themes constantly via the concept of *blessing*. 'This blessing is the addressing and claiming of earthly life for God, and it contains all [God's] promises.'[45] And Bonhoeffer disputes the notion that the cross of the New Testament negates the blessing of the Old. He suggests that 'the difference between the OT and NT may consist solely in the fact that in the OT the blessing also includes the cross and in the NT the cross also includes the blessing'.[46]

His growing appreciation for the worldliness of the Old Testament was leading him to read the New Testament in light of the Old, but in a way that kept the centrality of Christ in view. To be sure, he had already been reading the Old Testament 'Christologically', as I have shown in previous chapters.[47] But his

---

41. DBWE 8, 481; DBW 8, 536-7.
42. DBWE 8, 482; DBW 8, 537.
43. DBWE 8, 363; DBW 8, 404.
44. DBWE 8, 366-7; DBW 8, 407.
45. DBWE 8, 492; DBW 8, 548.
46. DBWE 8, 493; DBW 8, 549.
47. See also Kuske, *The Old Testament as the Book of Christ*.

intensified emphasis on the this-worldliness of Christianity, along with his critique of human religiosity, enabled him to discern the presence of Christ in Scripture in ways that did not blunt (what might be called) the *profanity* of Scripture. Why, Bonhoeffer asks Bethge, do we encounter so much immorality in the Old Testament?[48] Sometimes, to be sure, the characters are condemned in the narrative for their actions, but not all the time. The answer provided by the history-of-religions school was simple: the Old Testament represents a preliminary stage of human religion; the New Testament marks a development towards better, more civilized expressions of human religiosity. Bonhoeffer had always rejected this. After all, 'it is one and the same God'.[49]

Bonhoeffer's interpretation of Scripture in prison is no less Christological than it had been, no less focused on the real presence of Christ in scriptural revelation, but it does gain a new emphasis. The more he learns to find Christ on every page of Scripture – especially the parts that exhibit profound this-worldliness – the more he learns to find Christ in the world, and vice versa. Gerhard Ebeling's assessment in 1960 was correct: 'Non-religious interpretation is for Bonhoeffer nothing other than Christological interpretation.'[50] Granted, this is not precise enough to define a particular approach to Scripture, given that there are seemingly countless ways an exegete can claim to be 'Christological' – a point that Ebeling himself notes. However, in light of my present study, I would clarify as follows. Non-religious interpretation means learning to hear and encounter Christ in Scripture as the one who is radically in and for *this* world, as the one who only 'is there for others'.[51] Christology, as I have said earlier in this study, is not what Bonhoeffer pulls out of Scripture, but rather what pulls him more deeply into it. In his prison letters, Bonhoeffer makes it clear that a Christological reading of Scripture entails a worldly reading, because Christ has reconciled God and the world in his very person.[52]

The worldly, nonreligious reading of Scripture intensifies the Christological in another way, namely, by shattering the illusion that God is somehow welcome in this world. This is an important point to clarify. The alignment of the worldly and the Christological is not due to some false equivalence between Christ's call and the world's. (Some of the early enthusiasm over Bonhoeffer's ideas about religionless Christianity no doubt stemmed from the eagerness to simply go on with life without too much interference, without 'costly grace'.) Genuine worldliness, for Bonhoeffer, always means an affirmation of the world as reconciled to God in Christ. The question he was grappling with in prison was how to speak of this in the context of

---

48. DBWE 8, 214; DBW 8, 227.
49. DBWE 8, 214; DBW 8, 227. As I argued in CHAPTER 8, the continuity of the two testaments is for Bonhoeffer a presupposition, not a conclusion.
50. Ebeling, *Word and Faith*, 107.
51. DBWE 8, 501; DBW 8, 558.
52. He had made this point quite clear already in his *Ethics* manuscript, 'Christ, Reality, and Good' (DBWE 6, 47–75; DBW 6, 31–61).

a religionless age, an age in which God was no longer a necessary piece of anyone's intellectual furniture. Rather than be dismayed at this situation, Bonhoeffer saw it as an opportunity to interpret Scripture and the Christian faith with even greater fidelity. 'Religion' had created a world that was, frankly, imaginary. It was certainly a far cry from the world Bonhoeffer saw all around him. In a world of our own making, we will always find a God of our own making. The real presence of Christ occurs in the real world that he has made and reconciled. If we dare to face the religionlessness of the world come of age, we will find that we are facing in the right direction to see Christ there. If, as I have argued in the preceding chapters, Bonhoeffer reads Scripture as the witness to the present Christ, in prison he learns to read Scripture as the witness to the Christ who is present only as the suffering and powerless one in the world.

Polyphonic exegesis

Thus far, I have expounded two features of Bonhoeffer's prison theology that are relevant for the larger scope of my study. Firstly, I demonstrated that his critique of religion (and Barth's 'positivism of revelation') was grounded in his theology of revelation-as-*Christus-praesens*. Secondly, I showed how his this-worldly interpretation of Scripture, especially the Old Testament, was Christological to its core, in a way that is both consistent with and developed beyond his earlier exegetical writings. In this final section, I turn to his tantalizingly incomplete project of nonreligious interpretation of biblical concepts. Indeed, to call it an incomplete project suggests more progress than he had actually made. He admitted to Bethge, 'I am more able to see what needs to be done than how I can actually do it.'[53] As usual, it is easier to identify the problem than to articulate its solution.

The problem is straightforward enough, and Barth had laid it out forcefully in his second Romans commentary.[54] 'Religion' is humanity's way to God, but what is needed is for God to come to human beings. The Bible discloses God's revelation in Christ by the Holy Spirit, and as such its subject matter is revelation, not religion. To be sure, there is plenty of religion in the Bible – divine law, cult and ritual, prayers and prophecy – and in a religious world the Bible is naturally read as offering the 'true' or 'absolute' version of what everyone is already seeking. But if the world turns out to be radically religionless, what is to be done with Scripture? Must people first be made, in some general sense, 'religious' so that they can then be made to accept the biblical religion? Bonhoeffer doesn't think so. His enquiries continue to revolve around the question he had raised in his 30 April 1944 letter: who is Christ actually for us today? How can Christ become the Lord of the religionless? Given Bonhoeffer's disillusionment with so-called religious people, one might wonder why he never raises the converse question: How can

---

53. DBWE 8, 475; DBW 8, 529.
54. Barth, *The Epistle to the Romans*, 229–70.

Christ become Lord of the *religious*? But his concern was not whether religious people were more open to the gospel than nonreligious, but whether nonreligious people were required to become religious in order to become followers of Christ.[55] And if not, what kind of interpretation of core biblical concepts (creation, fall, reconciliation, repentance, faith, new life, eschatology) would be suitable for this new kind of nonreligious Christian?[56]

This would not have been the first time he offered something of a *dogmatica minora* through an idiosyncratic lens. He did something similar in *Sanctorum Communio*, where he presented the basic Christian concepts of person, primal state, sin and revelation through the lens of sociality. What might a similar project have looked like through the lens of religionlessness? What kind of exegesis might this have entailed? The kinds of constructive moves that might be made in 'nonreligious' or 'worldly'[57] interpretation cannot be determined simply by these adjectives. Fortunately, Bonhoeffer has not left us without guidance. Religious Christianity, he thinks, has all too often understood God as the absolute power who rushes in only where humanity is too weak to solve its own problems or too ignorant to answer its own questions. But the world's coming of age has exposed the emptiness of this approach. God as *deus ex machina* is not the God of the Bible. Thus, Bonhoeffer writes that the world come of age 'frees us to see the God of the Bible, who gains ground and power in the world by being powerless. This will probably be the starting point for our "worldly interpretation".[58] Similarly, in his 'Outline for a Book', he writes that 'our relationship to God is no "religious" relationship to some highest, most powerful, and best being imaginable – that is no genuine transcendence. Instead, our relationship to God is a new life in "being there for others," through participation in the being of Jesus'.[59] It is Christ, the crucified 'being for others', who reveals the transcendence of God. In this way, the deepest mystery is not the God who remains far off, but the God who has come nearest to us.[60] Immediately following this, Bonhoeffer outlines the next section of

---

55. He connects this question directly to Paul's question of circumcision. As far as Bonhoeffer is concerned, Paul's statements about circumcision (e.g. Gal. 6.15) mean that in Christ human beings are freed from religion (DBWE 8, 366, 430; DBW 8, 406, 482).

56. Bonhoeffer lists these concepts in his 'Outline for a Book' (DBWE 8, 502; DBW 8, 559).

57. He uses the two terms synonymously when describing the interpretation of biblical concepts. See DBWE 8, 457, 480; DBW 8, 512, 535.

58. DBWE 8, 479–80; DBW 8, 534–5.

59. DBWE 8, 501; DBW 8, 558.

60. Noting mystery as an important theme in the letters, Krötke, 'The Meaning of God's Mystery', 135–49, draws a connection to Bonhoeffer's 1934 sermon on 1 Cor. 2.7-10 (DBWE 13, 360-3; DBW 13, 359-63). In that sermon, Bonhoeffer meditates on the mystery of revelation, stating emphatically that '*mystery does not mean simply not knowing something. The greatest mystery is not the most distant star; to the contrary, the closer something is to us, the better we know it, the more mysterious it becomes to us*' (DBWE 13, 361; DBW 13, 360).

his book, which is to be 'the interpretation of biblical concepts on this principle'.[61] The interpretive principle in question is just this, that God's omnipotence and transcendence are expressed precisely in his powerlessness and nearness.

If this is the hermeneutical key to nonreligious interpretation, then it would mean rethinking biblical concepts in terms of their relationship to the God who 'is there for us' as the suffering and godforsaken one, and whose presence and power take this form and no other. In this way, nonreligious interpretation stands in striking continuity with the exegetical trajectory I have been tracing throughout this study. Put simply, Bonhoeffer is reading Scripture as God's witness to the present Christ, with the recognition that Christ is present in and for *this* world as the crucified one.

The exegetical question, then, is still basically the Christological 'who' question, and the basis for speaking of Christ's presence is still Christ's person, his 'being for others'. The change from *pro me* and *pro nobis* language is subtle but important. It emphasizes the fact that Christ is not only there for me and for us, but also and primarily for *others*, for those that have no religion whatsoever. Bonhoeffer was appalled at how the Confessing Church had fought harder for its own self-preservation than for others who were in need.[62] The church, as he puts it in his 'Outline', 'is church only when it is there for others'.[63] Analogously, we might say that Scripture is God's word only when it is God's word for others. And, moreover, the only divine word that is truly 'there for others' is Jesus Christ. Christ is the word-for-others, and the key to nonreligious exegesis is to discern this word in every page of Scripture.

This approach, it must be said, might not seem to square with Bonhoeffer's 'this-worldly' reading of the Old Testament in prison. His conviction that Christians should not rush too quickly into New Testament ways of thinking would seem to require that the Christological reading of the Old Testament not overtake other ways of reading. And here I think Bonhoeffer offers a helpful image for how we might envisage the exegetical task: polyphony.[64] Polyphony in music is when

---

61. DBWE 8, 502; DBW 8, 559.

62. Although he doesn't use the phrase 'positivism of revelation' in his 'Outline', he does level a related complaint against Barth and the Confessing Church, who, according to him, 'have encouraged people to entrench themselves again and again behind the notion of the "faith of the Church" rather than asking and stating honestly what they really believe' (DBWE 8, 502; DBW 8, 559). The dialectical alternative is equally dishonest, which claims that 'I do not have my faith at my disposal and therefore cannot simply state what I believe' (DBWE 8, 503; DBW 8, 560). In both cases we have avoided the simple question of what we believe – not, to be clear, what we think Christians *must* believe, but what we actually believe 'in such a way that our lives depend on it' (DBWE 8, 502; DBW 8, 559). How many people recite the Apostles' Creed with that kind of seriousness?

63. DBWE 8, 503; DBW 8, 560.

64. For more on Bonhoeffer and the polyphony of life, see Andreas Pangritz, *Polyphonie des Lebens: Zu Dietrich Bonhoeffers 'Theologie der Musik'* (Berlin: Alektor, 1994); Harvey, *Taking Hold of the Real*, 234–68.

multiple, independent melodies are played simultaneously.⁶⁵ He uses this imagery only three times in the extant letters, and all within the span of three letters less than two weeks apart.⁶⁶ Bethge had written to him expressing some of the tension he had felt between his love for his wife and his duties to the church and his country. Bonhoeffer replies that Bethge should feel no obligation to dampen his earthly loves for the sake of heavenly ones. He calls Bethge to embrace the 'polyphony of life'. He explains: 'What I mean is that God, the Eternal, wants to be loved with our whole heart, not to the detriment of earthly love or to diminish it, but as a sort of cantus firmus to which the other voices of life resound in counterpoint.'⁶⁷ Earthly love is a contrapuntal theme to be played alongside and in harmonious relationship with the cantus firmus. When rightly ordered to the cantus firmus, love of God and earthly loves can be 'undivided and yet distinct'.⁶⁸

With the image of a polyphonic composition, Bonhoeffer is setting up a way of understanding what might otherwise be viewed as mutually exclusive loves in a non-competitive way. I propose that this image can also be deployed in relation to scriptural exegesis. Bonhoeffer had already acknowledged that the fullness of Scripture is not exhausted by a single interpretation, or even a single kind of interpretation. This was why he allowed for the possibility of allegorical exegesis. His main stipulation was that allegorical interpretation must never disclose something other than Christ as the content of Scripture. But within this guideline, he thought that allegorical interpretation was permissible 'as praise for the fullness of the scriptural witness to Christ'.⁶⁹ A 'polyphonic exegesis' of Scripture would not need to regard the literal, the Christological, the 'worldly' or any other kind of interpretation as necessarily excluding all others. Each could be pursued and developed, so long as each is rightly ordered to Christ as the exegetical cantus firmus.

The trajectory set in Bonhoeffer's prison letters suggests that nonreligious interpretation would have Jesus Christ, the suffering and powerless 'being for others', as the exegetical cantus firmus. But with this firmly established, one would be free to explore other aspects of the biblical text, such as the affirmation of this world, the critique of religion, the place of God in human strength and vitality, and countless others. It was this kind of exegetical logic (although he may not have expressed it as such) that allowed him to tell Bethge that reading Song of Songs as an earthly love poem was 'probably the best "christological" interpretation'.⁷⁰ It was why the time he spent learning to think in 'Old Testament ways' was fruitful not only for his appreciation of Israel's Scriptures, but also for his new theological

---

65. An accomplished musician himself, Bonhoeffer was particularly fond of Bach's fugues. See DBWE 8, 306; DBW 8, 336.
66. DBWE 8, 393, 397, 405; DBW 8, 440, 445, 454.
67. DBWE 8, 393–4; DBW 8, 440–1.
68. DBWE 8, 394; DBW 8, 441. Bonhoeffer is intentionally echoing the Chalcedonian definition here.
69. DBWE 14, 429; DBW 14, 417.
70. DBWE 8, 410; DBW 8, 460.

reflections on Christ and the world come of age. Exegetical polyphony is, of course, only a metaphor, not a method, but it is useful for illuminating this important point about Bonhoeffer's use of the Bible.

With Christ as God's word-for-others as the interpretive cantus firmus, nonreligious exegesis can and must mean more than emphasizing the biblical critique of religion (although Bonhoeffer would certainly want to include this). The polyphonic exegete will explore the full richness of Scripture by discerning the presence of the 'being for others' in the scriptural words. But this will not necessarily require an allegorical reading of Old Testament texts. Old Testament passages can be read as independent, this-worldly melodies that are sung in time and tune with Christ. After all, it is *this* world, and not another, that Christ has reconciled to God. This is why it may be that a worldly interpretation of a biblical text is also the best Christological interpretation. For Bonhoeffer, the more God's word-for-others is discerned on every page of Scripture, the more we will learn to find this word in and for the world. But the order cannot be reversed. If 'worldliness' in some general sense were to become the exegetical cantus firmus, we would lose not only the Christological but even the worldly resonances of Scripture. In Bonhoeffer's logic, in looking to Christ, we see both God and the world reconciled in one person, but if we look to the world apart from Christ, we see neither God nor the world as it is in reality.

Nonreligious exegesis, then, is thoroughly Christological exegesis. And if this sounds limiting, it is only because the scope of Bonhoeffer's Christology has not been fully appreciated. As it says in Col. 1.17, in Christ 'all things hold together', and this means that learning to see Christ in Scripture means learning to see everything in Scripture, even if what we find there doesn't seem particularly Christological. It may, in fact, appear quite worldly and profane. What polyphonic exegesis facilitates is a way of appreciating the worldliness of Scripture *as worldliness* rather than as preparatory work for appreciating an otherworldly sequel. This recalls a question I raised earlier in this chapter: does reading the Old Testament as a prologue to the New not simply relativize it? On the contrary, a polyphonic reading of the Old Testament is precisely how the Christian can appreciate it both in anticipation of the central theme to follow and as an independent melody that has its own place and dignity. It is not about enduring a cacophonous prelude that helps one better appreciate the beauty of the main theme. Polyphonic exegesis is about deepening one's knowledge and love of the cantus firmus by exploring the full depths of all its contrapuntal themes.

12

CONCLUSION

Reading in the presence of Christ

I quoted Walter Harrelson at the beginning of this study: 'Bonhoeffer's greatest contributions to Christian theology do not lie in the area of biblical exegesis.'[1] If we look at the history of Bonhoeffer's reception, Harrelson's assessment has proven largely correct. Interpreters of Bonhoeffer generally have not emphasized his scriptural exegesis or his bibliology. My operating assumption, however, has been that attending to Bonhoeffer's bibliology offers a fruitful framework for appreciating and evaluating his exegesis. And, to discover what Bonhoeffer is up to with the biblical text, we must first understand what he thinks God is up to with it.

Accordingly, I have found that the uniting factor of Bonhoeffer's middle-period exegetical works is not found in methodology but in bibliology. Although he does not systematically outline an ontology of Scripture or a theological account of the Bible's place in the divine economy, his theology of revelation is at work throughout his exegesis. It has been my aim to trace the development of Bonhoeffer's theology of revelation, to draw out its implications for his (often implicit) bibliology and to explore how his bibliology informs his exegetical decisions. As I demonstrated in CHAPTER 2, Bonhoeffer committed himself enthusiastically to the theological *petitio principii* of revelation. From the earliest phase of his theological development, he was a theologian of God's word. In CHAPTER 3, I identified *Christus praesens* as the central theological concept by which Bonhoeffer resolves the aporia of revelation, a concept that gains traction in his 1933 Christology lectures. These lectures, as I showed in CHAPTER 4, indicate that the dogmatic locus of *Christus praesens* had shifted from ecclesiology to Christology in his thought. In my attention to the development of Bonhoeffer's theology of revelation, I have identified *Christus praesens* as the leitmotif in his bibliology.

---

1. Harrelson, 'Bonhoeffer and the Bible', 139.

A common trait in studies of Bonhoeffer's interpretation of Scripture is the search for a Bonhoefferian 'method'.[2] Indeed, this was my intention when I first began this study. As I examined the range of Bonhoeffer's biblical writings, I had to reconfigure my approach. Bonhoeffer neither describes nor follows any particular exegetical method, and to extract a methodology from his exegesis would be to go against the grain of some of his most deeply held theological concerns. Bonhoeffer's theological project is built upon the foundation of God's non-objectifiability, the 'infinite qualitative distinction' between Creator and creature. God is the content of the word of Scripture, and no exegetical method can deliver this content into human hands. An exegetical method, after all, is a particular set of instructions for how to extract a particular kind of meaning from a text.[3] But God cannot be placed under methodological conditions, and it would be impossible to extract God out of the text of Scripture by any human method.

A helpful analogy is found in Bonhoeffer's discussion of Barth's dialectics.[4] It is not that Barth endorses dialectics as the proper technique for rendering divine revelation into human speech. On the contrary, dialectics emphasizes Barth's contention that all human words fall short of God's word. Dialectics as a method is not the master but the servant of theology, and it serves in this capacity by acknowledging the incomprehensibility of God. The way of theology follows from the nature of theology's subject matter. Likewise, the way of Scriptural exegesis follows from the nature of Scripture. To recall John Webster, 'bibliology is prior to hermeneutics'.[5] That is why I have sought to establish Bonhoeffer's bibliology before exploring his exegetical works.

At the outset of this study, I identified two key bibliological questions: (1) What is Holy Scripture? (2) What does God do with Scripture? In more technical terms, bibliology accounts for Scripture's ontology and its place in the divine economy. The answers given to these two questions will have implications for a third: (3) What are we do to with Scripture?

---

2. The lack of consistency in Bonhoeffer's interpretation of the Psalms is one of the critiques in Pribbenow, *Prayerbook of Christ*.

3. Here I am drawing on how Robert Jenson describes a *critical theory*, or in the older parlance, a *hermeneutical principle*. Robert W. Jenson, *Canon and Creed*, Interpretation (Louisville, KY: Westminster John Knox, 2010), 80. More on this below.

4. DBWE 11, 233–4; DBW 11, 202. See also DBWE 2, 86 n. 11; DBW 2, 80 n. 11, where Bonhoeffer quotes from Barth, 'Fate and Idea', 59: 'A real theology of God's Word is ... not the sort of thing one can take or leave ... Real theology of God's Word is the sort of thing by which one can only be taken or left ... If I am called to do this theology, then so I am. Not because I found a way to God, but because God found a way to me. Not because I bind myself to God, but because God binds me to himself. Not because my dialectics are so great, but because God condescends to make use of me and this my doubtful tool.'

5. John Webster, *The Domain of the Word: Scripture and Theological Reason* (London: T&T Clark, 2012), 4.

What is Scripture?

Biblical ontology is an account of what Scripture *is*. One model, which Bonhoeffer always rejected, is verbal inspiration.[6] This model makes revelation identical with the Bible's semantic content. Revelation is the event of divine inspiration in which the biblical authors wrote the words that have been transmitted in the canonical Christian Bible. Revelation is essentially an event that happened in the past, was written down and accurately transmitted. Because these words are identical with God's word, they are eternally true and valid, even though they have the trappings of historical contingency. Interpretation of the verbally inspired Bible hinges on finding the eternally true propositions in the historically contingent text.

Another model is historicism. In its strongest form, historicism would not have any place for revelation at all. But it is possible to conceive of a theologically adjacent historicism. This is what the theological faculty in Berlin espoused during Bonhoeffer's education. This kind of historicism posits a historical link, however tentatively, between revelation and the Bible's semantic content. Revelation is understood as God's activity throughout history, and the Bible is thought to contain the writings of those who have experienced or witnessed this divine activity. It is a record of religious history portrayed from the distinct perspectives of those who recorded it. Interpretation hinges on treating the text in its own original context by reconstructing the author's history, his point of view, his theological motives, the textual history, the situation of the original audience, etc.

A third model is what I identified in CHAPTER 3 as occasionalism. At its most extreme, occasionalism makes a total break between revelation and the semantic content of the biblical text. Revelation 'occurs' today when the biblical text is read, in the event that is classically understood as illumination. But the *content* of revelation bears no essential relation to the 'meaning' of the biblical text. The Bible is the occasion of God's address, but is not in any meaningful sense the content of that address. This model would fall under what Bonhoeffer critiqued as 'act-theology' in *Act and Being*. The contingency of revelation is described in terms of God's inscrutable freedom and will. Interpretation hinges on discerning what God is saying today 'through' these words, which may or may not resemble what the words themselves (seem to) intend.

For Bonhoeffer, Scripture is the word of God, not by virtue of a quality inherent in the texts themselves, but by virtue of God's gracious decision *for* these texts, the decision to speak in and by these words. Two errors must be avoided here. Firstly, to say that God chooses these texts is not to posit a kind of bibliological adoptionism. God does not choose to use writings that happen to suit the divine purpose but which arose quite apart from those purposes. Rather, God's decision for the canonical biblical texts includes and encompasses the history that gave rise

---

6. A clear contemporary description of this view is what Christian Smith calls 'biblicism' in *The Bible Made Impossible: Why Biblicism Is Not a Truly Evangelical Reading of Scripture* (Grand Rapids: Brazos, 2012).

to their composition, preservation and transmission. Thus, the history 'behind' the texts cannot be separated from the texts themselves; but neither can this history exercise normative force over the text's range of valid uses and interpretations. Secondly, although the text of Scripture is not identical with revelation, it would be inadequate to say that Scripture 'becomes' revelation in the moment of divine speech. Bonhoeffer's bibliology, in its most developed form, is not occasionalist. It is more fitting to speak of Scripture as the *instrument* of divine revelation. To avoid misunderstanding: instrumentality is not occasionalism by another name. What is done by means of this instrument maintains an indissoluble connection to the nature of the instrument itself. (The same melody can be played on both piano and violin, but it will not be the same music!) God not only uses Scripture as the instrument of divine speech; God crafted this particular instrument for this very purpose.

Bonhoeffer's ontology of Scripture rests on his (largely implicit) pneumatology, which emphasizes the Spirit's ministry of the *word*. The freedom of God to speak in Scripture is the freedom of the Spirit, but this does not primarily mean the freedom to *withhold* his revelatory speech. Revelation means the free and gracious outpouring of the divine self. The Spirit ministers God's word when and where Scripture is received in faith. And where does this faith come from? It comes from the Spirit, whom the Father has sent in Jesus's name, who teaches and reminds the church of everything Jesus taught and commanded. The Spirit of truth, who is present and active, testifies concerning the Son. For this reason, Scripture as the instrument of revelation does not sit idle until God (apparently arbitrarily) decides to do something with it. Scripture is living and active as the Spirit is living and active.

Scripture is God's word by virtue of election, God's free and decisive act that includes the whole history of these texts and the communities that have been shaped by them. God's decision for Scripture is a decision for his word, for Jesus Christ, the Logos made flesh. This is why it is necessary to discuss Bonhoeffer's bibliology as a function of his Christology. Biblical ontology runs downstream from Christological ontology. Thus I indicated *Christus praesens* as the master theme in Bonhoeffer's bibliology, because it is the master theme in his Christology.

What does God do with Scripture?

This leads naturally into the second bibliological question. What God does with Scripture is make his word present to human beings who receive Scripture in faith. According to Bonhoeffer's theology of the word the presence of the Logos of God – who *is* God – is both an intelligible and an embodied presence. We can and should go to Scripture to 'learn' revelation, which is the theologian's task and vocation. God makes himself known as the Present One, the Word made flesh, the crucified and risen Christ. But this knowledge cannot be separated from the embodied presence of God in Christ, in sacrament and community. The embodiedness of revelation draws special attention to Bonhoeffer's conviction that God's Word does not and cannot be made to fit inside a human mind. It is not an idea that can be incorporated into existing categories and ways of knowing. God's word is the *person* of Christ. Although our intellects can (and hopefully sometimes do!) testify to this truth, our words about God are never the whole truth. Only Christ is the truth.

Why this Christological emphasis? If revelation is divine *self*-revelation, would it not be more prudent to ground bibliology in the doctrine of God rather than in Christology? If the content of revelation is God himself, should we not begin, as Barth did, with the doctrine of the Trinity? Does Bonhoeffer not short-change himself by focusing so intently on the Second Person of the Trinity? As I discussed in CHAPTER 3, the doctrine of the Trinity does not do much theological work for Bonhoeffer. Whereas Barth connects the doctrine of revelation explicitly to the Trinity with his discussion of God as Revealer, Revelation and Revealedness,[7] Bonhoeffer does not base other doctrinal arguments upon prior statements about the inner-life of God. Nevertheless, it is important to recognize that Bonhoeffer's bibliology is fundamentally Trinitarian in shape: God is present in the person of the Logos by the Spirit's ministry of the word. The whole structure would collapse without the foundation in the Triune God. The doctrine of the Trinity, for Bonhoeffer, rarely becomes the object of theological enquiry, but it does enable and support the theological enterprise.[8] In the case of bibliology, the doctrine of the Trinity allows Bonhoeffer to speak of the presence of the Logos as the undivided presence of God by the Spirit. Such a claim is only coherent because it is about the *Triune* God. It is nevertheless fitting and appropriate to speak of revelation in terms of the *Second* Person, because this Person is the Logos of God, the revelation of whom surpasses and fulfils all prior revelation, and who is himself the Son, the radiance of God's glory and the perfect representation of God's being. Jesus Christ, as the Word incarnate, crucified and risen, is the proper subject matter of bibliology.[9]

What should we do with Scripture?

Thus the final question: What are we to do with Scripture? Bonhoeffer's answer, as I have traced it, is that we are to hear God speaking in the Bible, and thereby to

---

7. CD I/1, 295–347.

8. This perspective echoes Charles Marsh's argument about Bonhoeffer's emphasis on the 'secondary objectivity' of God in revelation. See Marsh, *Reclaiming Dietrich Bonhoeffer*, 29–33.

9. Christopher Holmes has argued that Bonhoeffer's Christology can be enriched with a more overt and robust Trinitarian foundation. See Christopher R. J. Holmes, 'Bonhoeffer and Reformed Christology: Towards a Trinitarian Supplement', *Theology Today* 71 (2014): 28–42; Christopher R. J. Holmes, 'Beyond Bonhoeffer in Loyalty to Bonhoeffer: Reconsidering Bonhoeffer's Christological Aversion to Theological Metaphysics', in *Christ, Church and World: New Studies in Bonhoeffer's Theology and Ethics*, ed. Michael Mawson and Philip G. Ziegler (London: Bloomsbury T&T Clark, 2016), 29–43.

encounter God himself present as his spoken word. Recall the following sequence, which describes the essential connection between the written witness of Scripture and the contemporary presence of Christ: Where a disciple speaks, Christ speaks; where Christ speaks, he is present; where the word is, Christ is wholly there.[10] This explains why Bonhoeffer aims at encounter over interpretation, and it is fitting that there is no consistent interpretive method to be found across his exegetical writings. What I have done in the latter chapters of this study is demonstrate how Bonhoeffer pursues the presence of Christ in various exegetical contexts. While there are certain commonalities among them, it is clear that he does not adopt a one-size-fits-all approach.

When lecturing on homiletics, Bonhoeffer identifies three distinct but related spheres of biblical encounter: the pulpit, the study and the kneeler.[11] This threefold distinction offers a useful framework for considering Bonhoeffer's exegesis. The *pulpit* is the sphere of proclamation, and it denotes Scripture's 'most essential use'.[12] If, as Bonhoeffer believes, the incarnate Christ really is present in the 'scandalous form'[13] of preaching, then what the sermon does for human beings is exactly what Christ does for them: accepts sinful humanity upon himself. The purpose of a sermon is not primarily to exhort, educate or edify (although these may well occur); it is to proclaim and to be Christ's presence in the congregation in the form of the preached word. This account of Christ's presence in preaching implicates Bonhoeffer's approach to preparing and delivering sermons, examples of which can be found in CHAPTERS 5, 6 and 8.

The *study* is the sphere of knowledge and teaching. Not that these are absent from the pulpit and prayer, but we approach Scripture in the study in order to come to renewed understanding. There is no true knowing of God's word that occurs apart from the presence of that same word. The motivation for study, Bonhoeffer clarifies, is not to increase in knowledge and scholarship but to increase in humility and love. Study is for the sake of the church. Pastors especially need to study regularly in order to pray rightly, to support their theological claims, to bring to mind passages for the needy under their care. This is not about mastering Scripture, but being mastered by it. The teaching of the church – doctrine – arises from the study, although it is always tempered by the pulpit and prayer in and for the church-community. Bonhoeffer's reflections on the faith– works problem, as well as baptism, ecclesiology, justification and sanctification mark *Discipleship* as a profoundly doctrinal book. But the doctrines emerge by grappling with the biblical text and, more importantly, with the presence of the one who encounters us in this text (see CHAPTER 9). Discipleship and Christian ethics cannot be reduced to propositional content: discipleship means following

---

10. DBWE 14, 516; DBW 14, 509.
11. DBWE 14, 516; DBW 14, 510. Note that Bonhoeffer is specifically addressing pastors in this context, but these points apply *mutatis mutandis* to laypersons.
12. DBWE 14, 517; DBW 14, 510.
13. DBWE 12, 313; DBW 12, 295.

a living person; ethics means living in accordance with reality itself. Even Bonhoeffer's later ethical writings are grounded in his theology of revelation-as-*Christus-praesens* and are far more scripturally grounded than has often been recognized (see CHAPTER 10).

The *kneeler* is the sphere of prayer. It is no surprise that the Psalter takes pride of place in Bonhoeffer's reflections here. His call to ground prayer in the words of Scripture reminds us that we do not know how to pray as we ought, and that we depend on God's own word even in the words we offer to God in prayer. The encounter with Christ in prayer is his presence as the Mediator. We pray not in our own name, but Christ's. The Psalms, as the prayer book of the Bible, are the words God has given us to give back to him, and because Christ has made these words his own, we pray them in his name by his Spirit. I demonstrated this at length in CHAPTER 6. Moreover, as we pray the words of Scripture, we are transformed into the image of the word. All of Scripture is suitable for this task. Prayerful meditation on the word is how we posture ourselves to receive it humbly and openly. I explored this in CHAPTER 7.

Even a brief summary such as this makes it clear that the exegetical implications of a bibliology grounded in *Christus praesens* can take many forms. Perhaps the best way to generalize Bonhoeffer's approach is by way of the exegetical 'who' question, which I sketched in CHAPTER 5. Framing Bonhoeffer's exegesis as the pursuit of a question rather than the application of a method accounts for the varieties of approaches he employs. This same question can be brought into the pulpit, the study and the kneeler: Who is speaking to us here? Moreover, because this is the *Christological* question, it demands a Christological answer, and the only answer is Christ himself. We are not dealing with the sort of enquiry that can be satisfied with newfound knowledge. With the exegetical 'who' question, we dare to encounter the Logos of God, the counter-Logos who puts to death all ways of human knowledge. This question, this singular interrogative, must be asked in myriad ways, ways that arise from our various contexts, vocations, responsibilities and relationships; and its answer, when it comes, will not be the sort that puts the question to rest, but rather the sort that opens into deeper mystery and invites our return to this question again and again.

The exegetical 'who' question resists the movement towards theological calcification. Bonhoeffer's bibliology emphasizes the present-tense character of revelation, thereby drawing attention both to what God is saying today and to how we might faithfully testify to his word today. Exegesis aims at a present-tense act of hearing and telling the truth about Scripture (as I argued in CHAPTER 8). The way to acknowledge and evaluate Bonhoeffer's contributions to biblical exegesis is to recognize that he does not aim to produce definitive interpretations of biblical texts, but rather to ask, 'what is God saying to us here?'[14] The inexhaustible richness of the scriptural witness should give rise to a polyphonic reading of Scripture, as I proposed in CHAPTER 11.

---

14. DBWE 14, 168; DBW 14, 146.

Reading Scripture with Bonhoeffer

A sacramental reading of Scripture

Bonhoeffer's reading of Scripture for the real presence of Christ is not a twentieth-century innovation. As Hans Boersma has shown, 'Scripture as real presence' can be identified as a common interest in Patristic exegesis.[15] This 'sacramental' reading of Scripture takes seriously the Christian conviction that God's word really comes to human beings in and through this collection of writings, and that the word which comes is Jesus Christ himself. Therefore, Bonhoeffer's reading of Scripture for the real presence of Christ should be recognized as a *ressourcement*.

As Boersma's study shows, the treatment of Scripture as real presence manifests itself in sometimes vastly different readings of biblical texts, but he keys in on four distinct features of patristic 'sacramental' reading.[16] And each of these features can be discerned in Bonhoeffer's exegesis. (1) Sacramental reading does not concern itself with the one true meaning, but with endlessly unfolding the revelation of God as disclosed in Christ. This, as I have shown, is a hallmark of Bonhoeffer's exegesis, especially his Christological reading of the Old Testament. (2) Patristic exegesis assumes that spiritual transformation is both a prerequisite and a result of reading Scripture well. For Bonhoeffer, the presence of Christ is transformational, which comes through most strongly in his 'Meditation on Psalm 119' and his writings on scriptural meditation. (3) The church fathers believed that it was possible to progress to greater levels of maturity and greater levels of scriptural understanding. This, too, Bonhoeffer affirmed. The notion of formation as an ongoing process is integral to his *Discipleship*, 'Meditation on Psalm 119' and *Ethics*. He also acknowledges 'degrees of cognition' in his prison writings.[17] (4) God was understood to be providentially active in guiding history, especially the salvation history narrated in the Old and New Testaments. Again, Bonhoeffer would agree. As was the case for the church fathers, his allegorical reading of Old Testament texts is grounded in his belief that God's ways with his people do not change, and that what God has fulfilled in Christ sheds light on all of his ways with his people.

Is such a *ressourcement* possible? Boersma points to a gulf that has emerged in the humanities between the *study* of a discipline and the study of the *history* of that discipline.[18] The historicist outlook treats every historical development as nothing but a link in the chain that has brought their discipline to where it

---

15. Hans Boersma, *Scripture as Real Presence: Sacramental Exegesis in the Early Church* (Grand Rapids: Baker Academic, 2017).
16. Ibid., 17–25.
17. DBWE 8, 373; DBW 8, 415.
18. Boersma, *Scripture as Real Presence*, 275. He is drawing on Andrew Louth, *Discerning the Mystery: An Essay on the Nature of Theology* (Oxford: Clarendon, 1983).

is today. Often, this results in a kind of 'chronological snobbery',[19] which tacitly assumes that previous developments are, by definition, outdated, and therefore not worth pursuing today. So, the historicist might assume, ancient exegetes might be interesting links in the chain of scriptural interpretation, but we certainly shouldn't try to imitate them! Against this view, Boersma calls for the recovery of sacramental exegesis.

What might this recovery entail? Bonhoeffer himself acknowledges that we cannot simply go on as if historical-criticism had never happened. He asks, 'What is a theological interpretation … after the conclusion of historical theology?'[20] Hans Frei and Robert Jenson, both born a generation after Bonhoeffer, offer some promising ways to carry on his exegetical project. Jenson's proposed creedal critical theory bolsters Bonhoeffer's Christological reading of the Old Testament, and Frei's concentration on the narrative identity of Christ follows naturally from Bonhoeffer's Christology and complements the exegetical 'who' question.

A creedal reading of Scripture

Robert Jenson's later writings are characterized by an increasing interest in scriptural interpretation.[21] In 2009, he delivered the Burns Lectures at the University of Otago on the subject of Scripture and creed, which he later revised and expanded as *Canon and Creed*.[22] His Burns Lectures aimed to address some of the issues of biblical interpretation that his recent work had raised.[23] Specifically, he sought to explore the relationship between the church's Scriptures and the church's creeds, and he offers an interesting proposal that has potential to round out the exegetical conclusions I have drawn from Bonhoeffer's writings.

The main thrust of Jenson's argument is fairly straightforward: canon and creed belong together. It was only by the mutual emergence and interdependence of canon and creed that the early church was able to endure from the first apostles' preaching into future generations, up to and including our own. The fundamental problem was this: if the church was to survive, as it in fact did, it needed to deal with the problem of maintaining its communal identity across time. Its identity was constituted by its message, and its message, Jenson argues (in that most Jensonian of phrases), was 'that the God of Israel has raised his servant Jesus from the dead'.[24]

---

19. I borrow the expression from C. S. Lewis, *Surprised by Joy: The Shape of My Early Life* (London: HarperCollins, 2002), 240.
20. DBWE 14, 390; DBW 14, 374.
21. His writings on these topics, the vast majority of which were written after the publication of his *Systematic Theology*, have helpfully been compiled in Robert W. Jenson, *The Triune Story*, ed. Brad East (Oxford: Oxford University Press, 2019).
22. Jenson, *Canon and Creed*.
23. Robert W. Jenson, *Song of Songs*, Interpretation (Louisville, KY: Westminster John Knox, 2005); Robert W. Jenson, *Ezekiel*, Brazos Theological Commentary on the Bible (Grand Rapids: Brazos, 2009).
24. Jenson, *Canon and Creed*, 3.

Various challenges imposed themselves on the early church, not least of which was one that plagues all multi-generational and multi-regional communities, namely, the 'telephone-game' problem. How can we be sure that the message proclaimed by the first generation of the church is the same one we proclaim today? Does the message not become increasingly garbled through the process of transmission?

The apostolic message had thus far been preserved by two main streams of tradition: the apostles themselves and the *regula fidei*, the Rule of Faith. Neither of these in their origins were 'texts'. The apostolic preaching was just that: the proclamation of the gospel message by Jesus's followers. It was quickly supplemented by the apostolic writings (which included writings associated with their followers), but these writings were not 'Scripture' in any sense until some time later. The *regula fidei* was not a written set of doctrines, but rather 'a sort of communal linguistic awareness of the faith delivered to the apostles'.[25] The Rule of Faith was not recited because it was not fixed in a particular text; it could be adduced in and for particular situations, and there was considerable freedom in its exact wording. The only Scripture that the church had in its infancy was Israel's, and indeed it needed no other Scripture for the continuity of its message.[26] However, the telephone-game problem, exacerbated by early conflicts with heresy and division, compelled the church to depend more and more on a standardized set of documents and formulas that could be considered reliably apostolic. And so, the witness of the apostles was eventually gathered into a standard set of documents we now know as the New Testament, while the *regula fidei* and baptismal creedal formulations took on fixed, textual form.

In light of the way canon and creed have functioned together to sustain the church – and Jenson is careful to credit the success of this work to the Holy Spirit – the Scriptures and the creeds must be recognized as mutually interpretive. Accordingly, if the church ignores the ways in which canon and creed fit together as 'conversely notched puzzle pieces',[27] it does so at its own peril. How, then, should the church acknowledge the interdependence of canon and creed in practice? Jenson proposes that the creed can function as the 'critical theory for Scripture'.[28] A critical theory arises from the suspicious hermeneutical eye, which, because texts cannot be trusted to mean what they appear to mean, must peer beneath the text's appearance to determine what it is 'really' about. A critical theory amounts to a 'set of instructions' to unmask the text's hidden agenda, and it aims to answer the question, 'Who is up to what with this text?'[29] A creedal critical theory for

---

25. Ibid., 15.
26. As Jenson puts it, it is not 'as if the church somehow "took over" or "accepted" old Israel's Scripture. On the contrary, Israel's Scripture accepted – or did not accept – the church' (ibid., 20).
27. Ibid., 41.
28. Ibid., 79.
29. Ibid., 80.

12. Conclusion

Scripture will answer that it is the Triune God who is up to something with this text, and that God's agenda with this text is none other than Jesus Christ.

In practice, the exegete reading with a creedal critical theory will assume that the plain sense of the text *and* the church's creedal affirmations are both true.[30] So in an example drawn from his own recent work, he examines Ezekiel 1.26, which depicts the appearance of the figure of a man on the heavenly throne. Why, Jenson asks, does the one on the throne, the appearance of God's glory, look like a man? Because, he answers with the tradition, the one on God's throne *is* a man, namely Jesus Christ. Such an answer would be ruled out of court by any standard of historical-critical exegesis, but is required by the creedal critical eye. And this shapes how a creedal critic will read the Old Testament from beginning to end: 'The Lord's appearances throughout the Old Testament, as a persona within the very history of which he is the author, are appearances … "in the person of" the second triune identity, who is Jesus the Christ.'[31]

Like Bonhoeffer, Jenson has little time for a version of inspiration that locates the Spirit's inspiratory work in the past only, and which guarantees Scripture's reliability on the basis of this past event. He makes this point more clearly in other writings, but is an operating assumption behind the whole of *Canon and Creed*.[32] For Jenson, scriptural inspiration is not a one-off transaction between the Spirit and the biblical writer. The inspired words of the prophets are none other than the word himself, whom Christian confession identifies as the Second Person of the Trinity. Thus, for a creedal reading of Scripture it is not because the Old Testament prophets predict events that Christ fulfils that they can be said to testify to him, but rather because 'Christ is the one who spoke by them, testifying to himself'.[33]

Jenson's discussion of the church's Scriptures is focused largely on answering how it is that these particular texts have function and continue to function within the church-community.[34] One of the simplest reasons that canon and creed cannot be separated is because canon and *church* cannot be separated, at least not without surrendering the continuity of the church-community's identity with that of the apostles. In this way, the whole of *Canon and Creed* could be read as a way of expanding on one of Bonhoeffer's earliest statements about theological interpretation: 'Theological exposition takes the Bible as the book of the church and interprets it as such. This is its presupposition and this presupposition

---

30. Anticipating the tendency of hermeneuticians and epistemologists to over-sophisticate what it means for something to be 'true', he clarifies that he is referring to the 'ordinary-language sense of "true"' (ibid., 82).

31. Ibid., 85.

32. See Robert W. Jenson, *Systematic Theology*, 2 vols. (Oxford: Oxford University Press, 1997–9), 2:270–88; Robert W. Jenson, 'A Second Thought about Inspiration', in *The Triune Story*, 121–6; Robert W. Jenson, 'On the Inspiration of Scripture', in *The Triune Story*, 187–219.

33. Jenson, 'A Second Thought about Inspiration', 125.

34. Jenson, *Canon and Creed*, 13–14.

constitutes its method.'³⁵ How does one read Scripture as the book of the church? Jenson's answer is simple: read it in accordance with the church's faith as expressed in the creeds.³⁶

Jenson's proposal supports the kind of Old Testament exegesis that Bonhoeffer – and most Christian interpreters before modernity – practised and furthermore offers some methodological direction for those who might want to follow in the same footsteps. His construal of theological interpretation as a 'creedal critical theory' is an interesting way of framing the church's exegetical task in a way that is fully compatible with Bonhoeffer's approach. But his emphasis on creed and dogma reminds theological exegetes that Christological interpretation should remain polyphonic. Christian doctrine is, at its heart, nothing but gospel commentary. The confession of faith in Jesus as the crucified and risen Lord as witnessed to in Scripture has given rise to the church's creedal and dogmatic confessions and continues to do so. The right kind of Christocentrism has an expansive rather than a reductive effect, and finding Christ in Scripture is always the beginning rather than the end of exegesis.

A narrative reading of Scripture

Hans Frei offers another compelling, complementary exegetical proposal.³⁷ In his book, *The Identity of Jesus Christ*, Frei explores the relation between Jesus's identity and presence. Although he does not cite Bonhoeffer, his approach could hardly be more Bonhoefferian: 'If we begin with the often nagging and worrisome questions of *how* Christ is present to us and *how* we can believe in his presence, we shall get nowhere at all. It is far more important and fruitful to ask first, *Who* is Jesus

---

35. DBWE 3, 22; DBW 3, 22.

36. Jenson's proposal does align better with Bonhoeffer's earlier, ecclesiocentric bibliology, and it suffers from some of the same shortcomings. One looks in vain for an ontology of Scripture in *Canon and Creed*, and the same can be said of his other writings. Fred Sanders has noted this with respect to his *Systematic Theology*: 'All of Jenson's most characteristic conceptual moves ... should be understood as serving the task of saying systematically how we should construe the total content of Scripture. But the actual doctrine about the nature of Scripture, the bibliology, is strikingly thin in Jenson's systematics' ('Holy Scripture under the Auspices of the Holy Trinity: On John Webster's Trinitarian Doctrine of Scripture', *International Journal of Systematic Theology* 21 [2019]: 7–8). Jenson's interest in the doctrine of inspiration was, by his own admission, 'an embarrassingly late development' (Jenson, 'On the Inspiration of Scripture', 187), but the version of inspiration he eventually puts forth turns out to be perfectly compatible with his systematics and, in certain ways, anticipated by it.

37. For a more comprehensive study of Frei and Bonhoeffer, see Tim Boniface, *Jesus, Transcendence, and Generosity: Christology and Transcendence in Hans Frei and Dietrich Bonhoeffer* (Lanham, ML: Lexington/Fortress Academic, 2018).

Christ?'[38] Where Frei goes beyond Bonhoeffer is in his careful study of how Jesus's identity is narratively rendered by the Gospels.

Frei divides the question of Jesus's identity into two formal questions. Firstly, *what is he like?* This is not about comparing him to others but describing his characteristic actions. Here we look at specific events in his life and ask how in this or that action Jesus was being himself. Secondly, *who is he?* This question seeks Jesus's self-continuity across the story of his life. Here we look at his whole story and trace the persistence of his person throughout. These two questions are 'formal' because they deal with the form of things; they do not attempt to dive beneath the narrative to mine out its deeper meaning, but treat things as they present themselves. In this way, the Gospels should be read as 'realistic narrative', which, as Frei explains, means that 'we cannot have what they are about (the "subject matter") without the stories themselves. They are history-like precisely because like history-writing and the traditional novel and unlike myths and allegories they literally mean what they say. There is no gap between the representation and what is represented by it'.[39] The Gospels, whatever else they may be, whatever situations inspired their composition, whatever streams of tradition served as their source material, represent this sort of narrative, realistic narratives that disclose the identity of Jesus. Their narrative form best preserves their message, because their message is not a set of moral guidelines or eternal principles but a singular human life.

How, then, do we grasp Jesus's identity in the story told about him? Where in this story is he most clearly identified? Frei examines the gospel narratives and divides Jesus's life into three distinct stages, through which his identity is progressively brought into sharper focus: the infancy narratives, his Galilean ministry, and his passion and resurrection. The infancy narratives identify Jesus with the people of Israel. Matthew and Luke both begin their Gospels by connecting the birth of Jesus to Israel's whole history, so that Jesus becomes 'a climactic summing-up of that whole story'.[40] The ministry narratives, from his baptism to his passion, identify Jesus in his announcement and enactment of the kingdom of God, through his teachings and miracles. The passion-resurrection narratives identify Jesus most clearly as the one who, unsubstitutably, enacts these events in fulfilment of his mission and thereby manifests himself as the one he is. For Frei, Jesus's identity comes most sharply into focus in the crucifixion and resurrection stories. Indeed, the resurrection is so climactic and integral to the gospel narratives that to conceive of Jesus apart from it would be to misunderstand who it is the Gospels present.

If Jesus is 'the resurrection and the life' (John 11.25), we cannot imagine him as anything but resurrected and alive: 'Jesus defines life, he is life: How can he who constitutes the very definition of life be conceived of as the opposite of what he

---

38. Frei, *The Identity of Jesus Christ*, 4.
39. Ibid., xiv.
40. Ibid., 128.

defines? To think him dead is the equivalent of not thinking of him at all.'[41] This is why we cannot speak of Jesus's identity apart from his presence; the Gospels identify him precisely as the one who is alive and present, so to speak of him as dead or absent is to speak of someone else entirely. Thus, what Frei offers, as the subtitle of his essay suggests, is a hermeneutical basis for dogmatic Christology. His proposal is especially congruent with Bonhoeffer's Christology, which is framed from beginning to end around the 'who' question. Frei provides a biblical hermeneutic that, whether he intended it or not, supports Bonhoeffer's claim that Jesus Christ is by virtue of who he is always the *present* Christ.

Frei's work offers more than this, however. *Identity of Jesus Christ* focuses on the narrative logic of the Gospels, but his broader project in support of 'biblical narrative' bolsters Bonhoeffer's approach in other ways.[42] One of the working assumptions in reading biblical narrative as 'history-like' or 'realistic' is that the story's meaning is not something other than its narrative form. Unlike a myth or an allegory, a realistic narrative simply means what it says. It may give rise to any number interpretations, but none of these could substitute for the narrative itself. As I have engaged with Bonhoeffer in this study, I have likewise concluded that his bibliology encourages (to borrow Webster's expression) 'faithful reading'.[43] As I noted in CHAPTER 8, without wishing to deny the active participation of the reader in the encounter with Scripture, 'faithful reading' connotes a receptive attitude towards the speaking God and an openness to encountering God in the scriptural word. Reading biblical narrative as 'realistic' narrative encourages this posture. If Scripture is the Spirit-breathed story of God's self-revelation in Christ, then a narrative reading of Scripture will direct attention to the form of the text itself and simultaneously to the God who is revealed and encounters us there.

This raises one final question, which, to be sure, has suggested itself at various points throughout this study. How much agency does the interpreter of Scripture actually have? Bonhoeffer's bibliology and exegesis both resist the idea of a repeatable hermeneutical 'method' that can reliably extract the meaning of a biblical text, but does this mean that the reader is entirely passive? Jens Zimmermann has recently argued that Bonhoeffer's hermeneutic theology

---

41. Ibid., 148. Frei grounds this argument not merely on this Johannine text, but primarily on his exegesis of the gospel narratives as a whole. See ibid., 102–52. Paul DeHart explains Frei's logic this way: 'Frei is simply asserting that the resurrection accounts are integral to the stories which render Jesus Christ's identity for the reader'; accordingly, he continues, 'the proper way to deny the resurrection is not to say that Jesus Christ was not raised (since the story of his raising is part of how we know who "Jesus Christ" is), but rather to say that the raised Jesus Christ is a fictional person' (Paul J. DeHart, *The Trial of the Witnesses: The Rise and Decline of Postliberal Theology* [Oxford: Blackwell, 2006], 116 n. 15).

42. On this, see Frei, *The Eclipse of Biblical Narrative*.

43. Webster, *Holy Scripture*, 86.

'encompasses both a childlike posture of directly hearing God speak *and* a profound sense of interpreting the divine word'.[44] He criticizes John Webster in particular for downplaying the active role of the interpreter in Bonhoeffer's theological hermeneutics, as if there is a 'binary choice of *either* a Barthian position of God's revelation as sheer divine self-presentation without the need for theoretical hermeneutic reflection *or* hermeneutic mediation "free from divine action" leading to idolatry'.[45] Bonhoeffer's concept of simple (*einfältig*) obedience denotes not an anti-intellectual fundamentalism, but 'an attitude of self-forgetfulness in complete intentional orientation toward Christ'.[46] And it is precisely from within this single-minded Christ-centredness that the hard work of responding to Christ's call occurs. In this way, Bonhoeffer's theology can be seen in support of the hermeneutical endeavour – not as a way *into* faithfulness (because a hermeneutic on its own cannot place us into truth) but as a way of faithfully responding to the concrete call of God's word.

The necessity of discerning God's command in one's concrete situation requires, as Zimmermann suggests, a combination of unreflective reception and reflective action, of *actus directus* and *actus reflectus*.[47] In the context of biblical interpretation, this would suggest that the exegete must be willing to deploy the full range of critical tools in the interest of reflecting on the text. But the proper order must be maintained. Interpretive strategies, whether the creedal reading endorsed by Jenson or the realistic-narrative reading endorsed by Frei, must not take priority over simple obedience to God's word. (As Bonhoeffer shows in *Discipleship*, hermeneutical sophistication is all too often a way of evading the command.) But neither can 'simple obedience' be played as a kind of hermeneutical trump card, as if there is an obvious one-to-one correspondence between the words of the Bible and God's word for us today. This would simply be another way of objectifying revelation. The only sure 'method' (if it can be called that) is for the reader to recognize in the encounter with Scripture – be it in preaching, prayer, or study – that none other than Jesus Christ himself is there *pro-me* in and as that word. This is the person who can never be objectified, who always comes as the counter-Logos.

Conclusion

I have only just scratched the surface of how Bonhoeffer might inform discussions of theological interpretation of Scripture today. It has been my intention

---

44. Zimmermann, *Bonhoeffer's Christian Humanism*, 149.
45. Ibid., 150.
46. Ibid., 166–7.
47. For another recent treatment on this theme, see Jacob Phillips, *Human Subjectivity 'in Christ' in Dietrich Bonhoeffer's Theology: Integrating Simplicity and Wisdom*, T&T Clark Studies in Systematic Theology 31 (London: T&T Clark, 2020).

throughout to provide a more complete portrait of him as a biblical theologian, not only by exploring his exegesis, but also in expounding his bibliology. What we do with Scripture cannot, after all, be separated from what we believe it is. The relationship is, of course, not purely linear. It is not as if Christians always and necessarily formulate a robust bibliology before venturing into the biblical texts. Nor is it as if one's interpretation is always and necessarily consistent with one's beliefs about what Scripture is. Bonhoeffer's beliefs about the Bible and his reading of it developed in tandem.

Does Bonhoeffer's reading of Scripture help the church to hear the word of God in the words of Scripture today? Does he help us attend to Scripture's present witness to the present Christ? Any answer to this question is necessarily provisional. It may be that what Bonhoeffer discerned as the 'right word' for his day would be the wrong word for ours. In any case, those who want to draw on Bonhoeffer need not appeal to his exegesis as authoritative readings of particular texts. Bonhoeffer's exegesis belongs to the memory of the church, to his particular historical moment in which (if one believes it) God genuinely and concretely addressed human beings. But God's word for the church today is not to be found in Bonhoeffer's time or any other. In this way, Bonhoeffer's bibliology furnishes the most enduring critique against his exegesis: The final judge of all human exegetical efforts is the present Christ himself, and this means that Bonhoeffer's words stand under Christ's judgement and grace. As Bonhoeffer says of systematic theology, so too of scriptural exegesis: 'Because theology turns revelation into something that exists, it may be practised only where the living person of Christ is itself present and can destroy this existing thing or acknowledge it.'[48] This is a warning against placing too much weight on our 'interpretations', because every interpretation, including Bonhoeffer's, is 'something that exists'. Bonhoeffer's biblical exegesis ought to be welcomed, but only insofar as it facilitates the church's hearing of these texts today as God's present witness to his present word.

It is my hope that this study has contributed not only to our understanding of Bonhoeffer's theological project but also to the important, ongoing conversation about what Scripture is and how the church should read it. However, I suspect that Bonhoeffer would caution us against becoming so distracted in the pursuit of methodological sophistication that we forget about the primary task and gift of encountering God's word in Scripture, for it is in this word that the Word himself meets us.

---

48. DBWE 2, 131; DBW 2, 129.

BIBLIOGRAPHY

Primary Sources

Bonhoeffer, Dietrich. *Dietrich Bonhoeffer Werke*. Ed. by Eberhard Bethge. 17 vols. Gütersloh: Chr. Kaiser, 1986–99.
Vol. 1: Bonhoeffer, Dietrich. *Sanctorum Communio: Eine dogmatische Untersuchung zur Soziologie der Kirche*. Ed. by Joachim von Soosten. München: Chr. Kaiser, 1986.
Vol. 2: Bonhoeffer, Dietrich. *Akt und Sein: Transzendentalphilosophie und Ontologie in der systematischen Theologie*. Ed. by Hans-Richard Reuter. München: Chr. Kaiser, 1988.
Vol. 3: Bonhoeffer, Dietrich. *Schöpfung und Fall: Theologische Auslegung von Genesis 1–3*. Ed. by Martin Rüter and Ilse Tödt. München: Chr. Kaiser, 1989.
Vol. 4: Bonhoeffer, Dietrich. *Nachfolge*. Ed. Martin Kuske and Ilse Tödt. Gütersloh: Chr. Kaiser, 1994.
Vol. 5: Bonhoeffer, Dietrich. *Gemeinsames Leben; Das Gebetbuch der Bibel*. Ed. by Gerhard Ludwig Müller and Albrecht Schönherr. Dietrich Bonhoeffer Werke 5. München: Chr. Kaiser, 1987.
Vol. 6: Bonhoeffer, Dietrich. *Ethik*. Ed. by Ilse Tödt et al. München: Chr. Kaiser, 1992.
Vol. 8: Bonhoeffer, Dietrich. *Widerstand und Ergebung*. Ed. by Christian Gremmels et al. Gütersloh: Chr. Kaiser, 1998.
Vol. 9: Bonhoeffer, Dietrich. *Jugend und Studium: 1918–1927*. Ed. by Hans Pfeifer, Clifford Green and Carl-Jürgen Kaltenborn. München: Chr. Kaiser, 1986.
Vol. 10: Bonhoeffer, Dietrich. *Barcelona, Berlin, Amerika: 1928–1931*. Ed. by Reinhard von Hase et al. München: Chr. Kaiser, 1991.
Vol. 11: Bonhoeffer, Dietrich. *Ökumene, Universität, Pfarramt: 1931–1932*. Ed. by Eberhard Amelung and Christoph Strohm. Dietrich Bonhoeffer Werke 11. Gütersloh: Chr. Kaiser, 1994.
Vol. 12: Bonhoeffer, Dietrich. *Berlin: 1932–1933*. Ed. by Carsten Nicolaisen and Ernst-Albert Scharffenorth. Gütersloh: Chr. Kaiser, 1997.
Vol. 13: Bonhoeffer, Dietrich. *London: 1933–1935*. Ed. by Hans Goedeking, Martin Heimbucher and Hans-Walter Schleicher. Gütersloh: Chr. Kaiser, 1994.
Vol. 14: Bonhoeffer, Dietrich. *Illegale Theologen-Ausbildung: Finkenwalde 1935–1937*. Ed. by Otto Dudzus et al. Gütersloh: Chr. Kaiser, 1996.
Vol. 15: Bonhoeffer, Dietrich. *Illegale Theologen-Ausbildung: Sammelvikariate 1937–1940*. Ed. by Dirk Schulz. Gütersloh: Chr. Kaiser, 1998.
Vol. 16: Bonhoeffer, Dietrich. *Konspiration und Haft: 1940–1945*. Ed. by Jørgen Glenthøj, Ulrich Kabitz and Wolf Krötke. Gütersloh: Chr. Kaiser, 1996.
Vol. 17: Bonhoeffer, Dietrich. *Reigister und Ergänzungen*. Ed. by Herbert Anzinger and Hans Pfeifer. Gütersloh: Chr. Kaiser, 1997.
Bonhoeffer, Dietrich. *Dietrich Bonhoeffer Works*. Ed. by Victoria J. Barnett, Wayne Whitson Floyd Jr and Barbara Wojhoski. 17 vols. Minneapolis: Fortress, 1996–2014.
Vol. 1: Bonhoeffer, Dietrich. *Sanctorum Communio: A Theological Study of the Sociology of the Church*. Ed. by Clifford J. Green. Trans. by Reinhard Kraus and Nancy Lukens. Minneapolis: Fortress, 1998.

Vol. 2: Bonhoeffer, Dietrich. *Act and Being: Transcendental Philosophy and Ontology in Systematic Theology*. Ed. by Wayne Whitson Floyd Jr.. Trans. by Martin Rumscheidt. Minneapolis: Fortress, 1996.
Vol. 3: Bonhoeffer, Dietrich. *Creation and Fall: A Theological Exposition of Genesis 1–3*. Ed. by John W. de Gruchy. Trans. by Douglas Stephen Bax. Minneapolis: Fortress, 1997.
Vol. 4: Bonhoeffer, Dietrich. *Discipleship*. Ed. by Geffrey B. Kelly and John D. Godsey. Trans. by Barbara Green and Reinhard Kraus. Minneapolis: Fortress, 2001.
Vol. 5: Bonhoeffer, Dietrich. *Life Together and Prayerbook of the Bible*. Ed. by Geffrey B. Kelly. Trans. by Daniel W. Bloesch and James H. Burtness. Minneapolis: Fortress, 1996.
Vol. 6: Bonhoeffer, Dietrich. *Ethics*. Ed. by Clifford J. Green. Trans. by Reinhard Kraus, Charles C. West and Douglas W. Stott. Minneapolis: Fortress, 2005.
Vol. 8: Bonhoeffer, Dietrich. *Letters and Papers from Prison*. Ed. by John W. de Gruchy. Trans. by Isabel Best et al. Minneapolis: Fortress, 2010.
Vol. 9: Bonhoeffer, Dietrich. *The Young Bonhoeffer: 1918–1927*. Ed. by Paul Duane Matheny, Clifford J. Green and Marshall D. Johnson. Trans. by Mary C. Nebelsick and Douglas W. Stott. Minneapolis: Fortress, 2003.
Vol. 10: Bonhoeffer, Dietrich. *Barcelona, Berlin, New York: 1928–1931*. Ed. by Clifford J. Green. Trans. by Douglas W. Stott. Minneapolis: Fortress, 2008.
Vol. 11: Bonhoeffer, Dietrich. *Ecumenical, Academic, and Pastoral Work: 1931–1932*. Ed. by Victoria J. Barnett, Mark S. Brocker and Michael B. Lukens. Trans. by Anne Schmidt-Lange et al. Minneapolis: Fortress, 2012.
Vol. 12: Bonhoeffer, Dietrich. *Berlin: 1932–1933*. Ed. by Larry L. Rasmussen. Trans. by Isabel Best, David Higgins and Douglas W. Stott. Minneapolis: Fortress, 2009.
Vol. 13: Bonhoeffer, Dietrich. *London: 1933–1935*. Ed. by Keith Clements. Trans. by Isabel Best and Douglas W. Stott. Minneapolis: Fortress, 2007.
Vol. 14: Bonhoeffer, Dietrich. *Theological Education at Finkenwalde: 1935–1937*. Ed. by H. Gaylon Barker and Mark S. Brocker. Trans. by Douglas W. Stott. Minneapolis: Fortress, 2013.
Vol. 15: Bonhoeffer, Dietrich. *Theological Education Underground: 1937–1940*. Ed. by Victoria J. Barnett. Trans. by Victoria J. Barnett et al. Minneapolis: Fortress, 2012.
Vol. 16: Bonhoeffer, Dietrich. *Conspiracy and Imprisonment: 1940–1945*. Ed. by Mark S. Brocker. Trans. by Lisa E. Dahill and Douglas W. Stott. Minneapolis: Fortress, 2006.
Bonhoeffer, Dietrich. *Meditating on the Word*. 1st Rowman & Littlefield ed. Ed. and trans. by David McI. Gracie. Lanham, MD.: Rowman & Littlefield, 2008.
Bonhoeffer, Dietrich. *No Rusty Swords: Letters, Lectures and Notes from the Collected Works*. Ed. by Edwin H. Robertson. Trans. by Edwin H. Robertson and John Bowden. London: Collins, 1965.
Bonhoeffer, Dietrich. *Theologie-Gemeinde; Vorlesungen, Briefe, Gespräche, 1927 bis 1944*. Vol. 3. Munich: Kaiser, 1966.

Secondary sources

Banman, Joel. 'Discipleship as a "Who" Question: Bonhoeffer on Reading Scripture as the Call of the Present Christ'. *Stimulus: The New Zealand Journal of Christian Thought and Practice* 26 (2019): 18–23.
Banman, Joel. 'The Word of the Church to the World: Bonhoeffer's Concept of the Logos and the Bilingual Character of Public Theology'. *The Bonhoeffer Legacy: An International Journal* 5 (2018): 47–62.

Barnett, Victoria J. 'Dietrich Bonhoeffer's Relevance for Post-Holocaust Christian Theology'. *Studies in Jewish–Christian Relations* 2 (2007): 53–67.
Barth, Karl. *Church Dogmatics*. Ed. by Thomas F. Torrance and Geoffrey W. Bromiley. 4 vols. Edinburgh: T&T Clark, 1956–75.
Barth, Karl. *Church Dogmatics* i/1: *The Doctrine of the Word of God*. 2nd ed. Ed. by Geoffrey W. Bromily and Thomas F. Torrance. Trans. by Geoffrey W. Bromily. Edinburgh: T&T Clark, 1975.
Barth, Karl. *Die christliche Dogmatik im Entwurf 1 – Die Lehre vom Worte Gottes: Prolegomena zur christlichen Dogmatik*. Munich: Chr. Kaiser, 1927.
Barth, Karl. *The Epistle to the Romans*. 6th ed. Trans. by Edwin C. Hoskins. London: Oxford University Press, 1933.
Barth, Karl. 'Fate and Idea in Theology'. In *The Way of Theology in Karl Barth: Essays and Comments*. Ed. by Martin Rumscheidt. Trans. by George Hunsinger, 25–61. Eugene, OR: Pickwick, 1986.
Barth, Karl. *Letters 1961–1968*. Trans. by Geoffrey W. Bromiley. Grand Rapids: Eerdmans, 1981.
Barth, Karl. 'The Need and Promise of Christian Proclamation'. In *The Word of God and Theology*. Trans. by Amy Marga, 101–30. London: T&T Clark, 2011.
Barth, Karl. *The Word of God and Theology*. Trans. by Amy Marga. London: T&T Clark, 2011.
Barth, Karl. 'The Word of God as the Task of Theology'. In *The Word of God and Theology*. Trans. by Amy Marga, 171–98. London: T&T Clark, 2011.
Baumgärtel, Friedrich. *Die Kirche ist Eine – die alttestamentlich-jüdische Kirche und die Kirche Jesu Christi? Eine Verwahrung gegen die Preisgabe des Alten Testaments*. Greifswald: Universitätsverlag Ratsbuchhandlung L. Bamberg, 1936.
Beckmann, Joachim, ed. *Kirchliches Jahrbuch für die Evangelische Kirche in Deutschland 1933–1944*. Gütersloh: Bertelsmann, 1948.
Bede. *On Ezra and Nehemiah*. Ed. and trans. by S. DeGregorio. Translated Texts for Historians 47. Liverpool: Liverpool University Press, 2006.
Beintker, Michael. *Die Dialektik in der 'dialektischen Theologie' Karl Barths: Studien zur Entwicklung der Barthschen Theologie und zur Vorgeschichte der 'Kirchlichen Dogmatik'*. Munich: Chr. Kaiser, 1987.
Berger, Peter. 'The Social Character of the Question Concerning Jesus Christ: Sociology and Ecclesiology'. In *The Place of Bonhoeffer*. Ed. by Marty, Martin E., 53–79. London: SCM, 1963.
Bethge, Eberhard. 'The Challenge of Dietrich Bonhoeffer's Life and Theology'. In *World Come of Age: A Symposium on Dietrich Bonhoeffer*. Ed. by Ronald Gregor Smith, 22–88. London: Collins, 1967.
Bethge, Eberhard. *Dietrich Bonhoeffer: A Biography*. Rev. ed. Ed. and trans. by Victoria J. Barnett. Minneapolis: Fortress, 2000.
Boersma, Hans. *Scripture as Real Presence: Sacramental Exegesis in the Early Church*. Grand Rapids: Baker Academic, 2017.
Boniface, Tim. *Jesus, Transcendence, and Generosity: Christology and Transcendence in Hans Frei and Dietrich Bonhoeffer*. Lanham, ML: Lexington/Fortress Academic, 2018.
Brock, Brian. 'Bonhoeffer and the Bible in Christian Ethics: Psalm 119, the Mandates, and Ethics as a "Way"'. *Studies in Christian Ethics* 18 (2005): 7–29.
Brunner, Emil. 'Nature and Grace'. In *Natural Theology*. Trans. by Peter Fraenkel, 15–64. London: Centenary, 1946.

Bultmann, Rudolf. *Faith and Understanding: Collected Essays*. Ed. by Robert W. Funk., Trans. by Louise Pettibone Smith. The Library of Philosophy and Theology. London: SCM, 1969.

Bultmann, Rudolf. 'Liberal Theology and the Latest Theological Movement'. In *Faith and Understanding: Collected Essays*. Ed. by Robert W. Funk., 28–52. London: SCM, 1969.

Bultmann, Rudolf. 'What Does It Mean to Speak of God?' In *Faith and Understanding: Collected Essays*. Ed. by Robert W. Funk., 53–65. London: SCM, 1969.

Busch, Eberhard. *Karl Barth: His Life from Letters and Autobiographical Texts*. Trans. by John Bowden. Grand Rapids: Eerdmans, 1994.

Congdon, David W. *The God Who Saves: A Dogmatic Sketch*. Eugene, OR: Cascade, 2016.

Congdon, David W. *The Mission of Demythologizing: Rudolf Bultmann's Dialectical Theology*. Minneapolis: Fortress, 2015.

DeHart, Paul J. *The Trial of the Witnesses: The Rise and Decline of Postliberal Theology*. Oxford: Blackwell, 2006.

DeJonge, Michael P. *Bonhoeffer's Reception of Luther*. Oxford: Oxford University Press, 2017.

DeJonge, Michael P. *Bonhoeffer's Theological Formation: Berlin, Barth, and Protestant Theology*. Oxford: Oxford University Press, 2012.

Ebeling, Gerhard. *Word and Faith*. Trans. by James W. Leitch. Philadelphia: Fortress, 1960.

Feil, Ernst. *The Theology of Dietrich Bonhoeffer*. Trans. by Martin Rumscheidt. Minneapolis: Fortress, 2007.

Feuerbach, Ludwig. *The Essence of Christianity*. Trans. by George Eliot. New York: Harper & Brothers, 1957.

Floyd, Wayne Whitson, Jr. 'Encounter with an Other: Immanuel Kant and G. W. F. Hegel in the Theology of Dietrich Bonhoeffer'. In *Bonhoeffer's Intellectual Formation*. Ed. by Peter Frick, 83–120. Tübingen: Mohr Siebeck, 2008.

Frei, Hans W. *The Eclipse of Biblical Narrative: A Study in Eighteenth and Nineteenth Century Hermeneutics*. New Haven/London: Yale University Press, 1974.

Frei, Hans W. *The Identity of Jesus Christ: The Hermeneutical Bases of Dogmatic Theology*. Philadelphia: Fortress, 1975.

Frick, Peter, ed. *Bonhoeffer's Intellectual Formation*. Tübingen: Mohr Siebeck, 2008.

Frick, Peter. 'Friedrich Nietzsche's Aphorisms and Dietrich Bonhoeffer's Theology'. In Frick, *Bonhoeffer's Intellectual Formation*. Ed. by Peter Frick, 175–99. Tübingen: Mohr Siebeck, 2008.

Godsey, John D. *The Theology of Dietrich Bonhoeffer*. London: SCM, 1960.

Goethe, Johann Wolfgang von. *Maxims and Reflections*. Trans. by Thomas Bailey Saunders. New York: Macmillan, 1906.

Gogarten, Friedrich. 'Between the Times'. In *The Beginnings of Dialectical Theology*. Trans. by Keith R. Crim and Louis De Grazia, 277–82. Richmond, VA: John Knox, 1968.

Green, Clifford J. *Bonhoeffer: A Theology of Sociality*. 2nd ed. Grand Rapids: Eerdmans, 1999.

Gruchy, John W. de, ed. *The Cambridge Companion to Dietrich Bonhoeffer*. Cambridge: Cambridge University Press, 1999.

Hamilton, Nadine. *Dietrich Bonhoeffers Hermeneutik der Responsivität: Ein Kapitel Schriftlehre im Anschluss an Schöpfung und Fall*. Forschungen zur systematischen und ökumenischen Theologie 155. Göttingen: Vandenhoeck & Ruprecht, 2016.

Harnack, Adolf von. *What Is Christianity?* 2nd ed. Trans. by Thomas Bailey Saunders. New York: G. P. Putnam's Sons, 1903.

Harrelson, Walter. 'Bonhoeffer and the Bible'. In Marty, *The Place of Bonhoeffer*, 115–42.

Hart, Trevor. 'Revelation'. In *The Cambridge Companion to Karl Barth*, Ed. by John Webster, 37–56. Cambridge: Cambridge University Press, 2000.
Harvey, Barry. *Taking Hold of the Real: Dietrich Bonhoeffer and the Profound Worldliness of Christianity*. Cambridge: James Clarke & Co., 2015.
Haynes, Stephen R. 'Bonhoeffer, the Jewish People and Post-Holocaust Theology: Eight Perspectives; Eight Theses'. *Studies in Jewish-Christian Relations* 2 (2007): 36–52.
Hohmann, Martin. *Die Korrelation von Altem und Neuem Bund (Innerbiblische Korrelation statt Kontrastkorrelation)*. Berlin: Evangelische Verlagsanstalt, 1978.
Holmes, Christopher R. J. 'Beyond Bonhoeffer in Loyalty to Bonhoeffer: Reconsidering Bonhoeffer's Christological Aversion to Theological Metaphysics'. In Mawson and Ziegler, *Christ, Church and World*, 29–43. London: Bloomsbury T&T Clark, 2016.
Holmes, Christopher R. J. 'Bonhoeffer and Reformed Christology: Towards a Trinitarian Supplement'. *Theology Today* 71 (2014): 28–42.
Holmes, Christopher R. J. *Ethics in the Presence of Christ*. London: T&T Clark, 2012.
Hunsinger, George. 'The Harnack/Barth Correspondence: A Paraphrase with Comments'. In *Disruptive Grace: Studies in the Theology of Karl Barth*. Ed. by George Hunsinger, 319–37. Grand Rapids: Eerdmans, 2000.
Hütter, Reinhard. *Bound for Beatitude: A Thomistic Study in Eschatology and Ethics*. Washington, DC: The Catholic University of America Press, 2019.
Igrec, Marie Theres. 'Bonhoeffer's "Theological Interpretation" of the Biblical Narrative of the "Creation and Fall" of Man'. In Wüstenberg and Zimmermann, *God Speaks to Us*, 141–67. Frankfurt am Main: Peter Lang, 2013.
Jenson, Robert W. *Canon and Creed*. Interpretation. Louisville, KY: Westminster John Knox, 2010.
Jenson, Robert W. *Ezekiel*. Brazos Theological Commentary on the Bible. Grand Rapids: Brazos, 2009.
Jenson, Robert W. 'On the Inspiration of Scripture'. In *The Triune Story*. Ed. by Brad East, 187–219. Oxford: Oxford University Press, 2019.
Jenson, Robert W. 'A Second Thought about Inspiration'. In *The Triune Story*, 121–6.
Jenson, Robert W. *Song of Songs*. Interpretation. Louisville, KY: Westminster John Knox, 2005.
Jenson, Robert W. *Systematic Theology*. 2 vols. Oxford: Oxford University Press, 1997–9.
Jenson, Robert W. *The Triune Story*. Ed. by Brad East. Oxford: Oxford University Press, 2019.
Johnson, Keith L., ed. *Bonhoeffer, Christ and Culture*. Downers Grove, IL: IVP Academic, 2013.
Jowett, Benjamin. 'On the Interpretation of Scripture'. In *Essays and Reviews*, 10th ed. London: Longman, Green, Longman/Roberts, 1862.
Jüngel, Eberhard. *God's Being Is in Becoming: The Trinitarian Being of God in the Theology of Karl Barth*. Trans. by John Webster. Edinburgh: T&T Clark, 2001.
Kähler, Martin. *The So-Called Historical Jesus and the Historic Biblical Christ*. Ed. and trans. by Carl E. Braaten. Philadelphia: Fortress, 1964.
Kelsey, David H. *The Uses of Scripture in Recent Theology*. London: SCM, 1975.
Kempis, Thomas à. *The Imitation of Christ*. Ed. by Harold C. Gardiner. Trans. by Richard Whitford. New York: Doubleday, 2009.
Kolb, Robert and Timothy J. Wengert, eds. *The Book of Concord*. Minneapolis: Fortress, 2000.
Krötke, Wolf. 'Dietrich Bonhoeffer's Exegesis of the Psalms'. In *Barth and Bonhoeffer*, 177–89. Grand Rapids: Baker Academic, 2019.

Krötke, Wolf. *Karl Barth and Dietrich Bonhoeffer: Theologians for a Post-Christian World*. Trans. by John P. Burgess. Grand Rapids: Baker Academic, 2019.
Krötke, Wolf. 'The Meaning of God's Mystery for Dietrich Bonhoeffer's Understanding of the Religions and "Religionlessness"'. In *Barth and Bonhoeffer*, 135–49. Grand Rapids: Baker Academic, 2019.
Kuske, Martin. *The Old Testament as the Book of Christ: An Appraisal of Bonhoeffer's Interpretation*. Trans. by S. T. Kimbrough Jr. Philadelphia: Westminster, 1976.
Lange, Frits de. *Waiting for the Word: Dietrich Bonhoeffer on Speaking about God*. Trans. by Martin N. Walton. Grand Rapids: Eerdmans, 2000.
Lessing, Gotthold E. *Lessing's Theological Writings*. Ed. and trans. by Henry Chadwick. Stanford, CA: Stanford University Press, 1957.
Lewis, C. S. *Surprised by Joy: The Shape of My Early Life*. London: HarperCollins, 2002.
Louth, Andrew. *Discerning the Mystery: An Essay on the Nature of Theology*. Oxford: Clarendon, 1983.
Luther, Martin. *First Lectures on the Psalms II: Psalms 76–126*. Ed. by Hilton C. Oswald. Trans. by Herbert J. A. Bouman. Luther's Works 11. St Louis: Concordia, 1976.
Luther, Martin. *Luther's Works*. American ed. Ed. by Jaroslav Pelikan and Helmut T. Lehman. 55 vols. St Louis and Philadelphia: Concordia/Fortress, 1955–76.
Luther, Martin. *Word and Sacrament I*. Ed. by E. Theodore Bachmann. Trans. by E. Theodore Bachmann et al. Luther's Works 35. Philadelphia: Fortress, 1960.
Marsh, Charles. *Reclaiming Dietrich Bonhoeffer: The Promise of His Theology*. New York: Oxford University Press, 1994.
Marty, Martin E., ed. *The Place of Bonhoeffer: Problems and Possibilities in His Thought*. London: SCM, 1963.
Mawson, Michael. *Christ Existing as Community: Bonhoeffer's Ecclesiology*. Oxford: Oxford University Press, 2018.
Mawson, Michael and Philip G. Ziegler, eds. *Christ, Church and World: New Studies in Bonhoeffer's Theology and Ethics*. London: Bloomsbury T&T Clark, 2016.
Mawson, Michael and Philip G. Ziegler, eds. *The Oxford Handbook of Dietrich Bonhoeffer*. Oxford: Oxford University Press, 2019.
McCormack, Bruce L. *Karl Barth's Critically Realistic Dialectical Theology: Its Genesis and Development 1909–1936*. Oxford: Clarendon, 1995.
McGarry, Joseph. 'Con-formed to Christ: Dietrich Bonhoeffer and Christian Formation'. *Journal of Spiritual Formation & Soul Care* 5 (2012): 226–42.
Pangritz, Andreas. *Karl Barth in the Theology of Dietrich Bonhoeffer*. Trans. by Barbara Rumscheidt and Martin Rumscheidt. Grand Rapids: Eerdmans, 2000.
Pangritz, Andreas. *Polyphonie des Lebens: Zu Dietrich Bonhoeffers 'Theologie der Musik'*. Berlin: Alektor, 1994.
Pannenberg, Wolfhart. *Jesus: God and Man*. Philadelphia: Westminster, 1968.
Phillips, Jacob. *Human Subjectivity 'in Christ' in Dietrich Bonhoeffer's Theology: Integrating Simplicity and Wisdom*. T & T Clark Studies in Systematic Theology 31. London: T&T Clark, 2020.
Phillips, John A. *The Form of Christ in the World: A Study of Bonhoeffer's Christology*. London: Collins, 1967.
Pieper, Josef. *Die Wirklichkeit und das Gute*. Leipzig: Jakob Hegner, 1935.
Pieper, Josef. *The Four Cardinal Virtues: Prudence, Justice, Fortitude, Temperance*. Trans. by Daniel F. Coogan et al. New York: Harcourt, Brace, & World, 1965.
Pieper, Josef. *Living the Truth*. Trans. by Lothar Krauth and Stella Lange. San Francisco: Ignatius, 1989.

Plant, Stephen J. *Taking Stock of Bonhoeffer: Studies in Biblical Interpretation and Ethics.* Surrey: Ashgate, 2014.
Plant, Stephen J. 'Uses of the Bible in the "Ethics" of Dietrich Bonhoeffer'. PhD thesis, University of Cambridge, 1993.
Pribbenow, Brad. *Prayerbook of Christ: Dietrich Bonhoeffer's Christological Interpretation of the Psalms.* Lanham, MD: Lexington Books/Fortress Academic, 2018.
Rad, Gerhard von. *Fragen der Schriftauslegung im Alten Testament.* Leipzig: Deichertsche, 1938.
Rad, Gerhard von. 'Sensus Scripturae Sacrae duplex? Ein Erwiderung'. *Theologische Blätter*, 1936, 30-4.
Rumscheidt, Martin. 'The Significance of Adolf von Harnack and Reinhold Seeberg for Dietrich Bonhoeffer'. In Frick, *Bonhoeffer's Intellectual Formation*, 201-24. Tübingen: Mohr Siebeck, 2008.
Sanders, Fred. 'Holy Scripture under the Auspices of the Holy Trinity: On John Webster's Trinitarian Doctrine of Scripture'. *International Journal of Systematic Theology* 21 (2019): 4-23.
Schlingensiepen, Ferdinand. *Dietrich Bonhoeffer 1906-1945: Martyr, Thinker, Man of Resistance.* Trans. by Isabel Best. London: T&T Clark, 2010.
Seeberg, Reinhold. *Die Kirche Deutschands im neunzehnten Jahrhundert: eine Einführung in die religiösen, theologischen und kirchlichen Fragen der Gegenwart.* 3rd ed. Leipzig: Deichert, 1910.
Slot, Edward van 't. 'The Freedom of Scripture: Bonhoeffer's Changing View of Biblical Canonicity'. In Wüstenberg and Zimmermann, *God Speaks to Us*, 101-22.
Slot, Edward van 't. *Negativism of Revelation?: Bonhoeffer and Barth on Faith and Actualism.* Dogmatik in der Moderne12. Tübingen: Mohr Siebeck, 2015.
Stanley, Timothy. 'Bonhoeffer's Anti-Judaism'. *Political Theology* 17 (2016): 297-305.
Steinmetz, David C. 'The Superiority of Pre-Critical Exegesis'. *Theology Today*, 1980, 27-38.
Taylor, Charles. *A Secular Age.* Cambridge, MA: Harvard University Press, 2007.
Thurneysen, Eduard, ed. *Karl Barth-Eduard Thurneysen: Briefwechsel, 1921-1930.* Zurich: TVZ, 1974.
Thurneysen, Eduard. 'Schrift und Offenbarung'. In *Das Wort Gottes und die Kirche: Aufsätze und Vorträge.* Ed. by Ernst Wolf, 35-64. Theologishe Bücherei: Neudrucke und Berichte aus dem 20. Jahrhundert 44. München: Chr. Kaiser, 1971.
Tietz, Christiane. 'Bonhoeffer on the Ontological Structure of the Church'. In *Ontology and Ethics: Bonhoeffer and Contemporary Scholarship.* Ed. by Adam C. Clark and Michael Mawson, 32-46. Eugene, OR: Pickwick, 2013.
Torrance, Alan J. *Persons in Communion: Trinitarian Description and Human Participation.* Edinburgh: T&T Clark, 1996.
Torrance, Thomas F. *Karl Barth: An Introduction to His Early Theology, 1910-1931.* London: SCM, 1962.
Troeltsch, Ernst. *The Absoluteness of Christianity and the History of Religions.* Trans. by David Reid. London: SCM, 1972.
Wannenwetsch, Bernd. 'The Whole Christ and the Whole Human Being: Dietrich Bonhoeffer's Inspiration for the "Christology and Ethics" Discourse'. In *Christology and Ethics.* Ed. by F. LeRon Shults and Brent Waters, 75-98. Grand Rapids: Eerdmans, 2010.
Webster, John. *The Domain of the Word: Scripture and Theological Reason.* London: T&T Clark, 2012.

Webster, John. *Holy Scripture: A Dogmatic Sketch*. Cambridge: Cambridge University Press, 2003.
Webster, John. *Word and Church: Essays in Christian Dogmatics*. Edinburgh: T&T Clark, 2001.
Wendel, Ernst Georg. *Studien zur Homiletik Dietrich Bonhoeffers: Predigt – Hermeneutik – Sprache*. Hermeneutische Untersuchungen zur Theologie 21. Tübingen: J. C. B. Mohr, 1985.
Williams, Rowan. *Christ the Heart of Creation*. London: Bloomsbury Continuum, 2018.
Wolf, Ernst, ed. *Theologische Aufsätze: Karl Barth zum 50. Geburtstag*. Munich: Chr. Kaiser, 1936.
Wüstenberg, Ralf K. 'Religion and Secularity'. In Mawson and Ziegler, *The Oxford Handbook of Dietrich Bonhoeffer*, 321–30. Oxford: Oxford University Press, 2019.
Wüstenberg, Ralf K. *A Theology of Life: Dietrich Bonhoeffer's Religionless Christianity*. Trans. by Douglas W. Stott. Grand Rapids: Eerdmans, 1998.
Wüstenberg, Ralf K. and Jens Zimmermann, eds. *God Speaks to Us: Dietrich Bonhoeffer's Biblical Hermeneutics*. International Bonhoeffer Interpretations 5. Frankfurt am Main: Peter Lang, 2013.
Ziegler, Philip G. 'Christ for Us Today: Promeity in the Christologies of Bonhoeffer and Kierkegaard'. *International Journal of Systematic Theology* 15 (2013): 25–41.
Ziegler, Philip G. '"Completely within God's Doing": Soteriology as Meta-ethics in the Theology of Dietrich Bonhoeffer'. In Mawson and Ziegler, *Christ, Church and World*, 101–19.
Ziegler, Philip G. 'Dietrich Bonhoeffer: A Theologian of the Word of God'. In *Bonhoeffer, Christ and Culture*. Ed. by Keith L. Johnson, 17–37. Downers Grove, IL: IVP Academic, 2013.
Zimmermann, Jens. *Dietrich Bonhoeffer's Christian Humanism*. Oxford: Oxford University Press, 2019.

INDEX

aporia 39, 55, 62
arcane discipline 188–9
aseity 43, 59

baptism 66, 161–3, 190–1. *See also* sacraments
Barmen Declaration 144, 174
Barth, Karl 6, 8, 19–26, 30–2, 34–6, 38, 44–5, 50, 57 n. 15, 69–70, 78 n. 30, 140, 166, 202, 205. *See also* dialectical theology
  Bonhoeffer's critique of 10, 28–9, 39–42, 187–8, 198 n. 62
  Epistle to the Romans 16, 31 n. 85, 187, 196
  threefold form of God's word, *see under* revelation
Baumgärtel, Friedrich 127, 132–5, 139–46
beatitudes 158–60
belief. *See* faith
Bethge, Eberhard 3, 21, 23 n. 44, 36, 55, 103, 127, 135–6, 139, 145, 157, 184, 190, 194, 199
Bible. *See* Scripture
biblicism 31, 87, 203 n. 6
bibliology
  Bonhoeffer's 26–31, 83–9, 203–7
  definition 5–6
  historicist 203
  occasionalist 48–51, 203
Boersma, Hans 10, 208–9
Bonhoeffer, Julie 103–5
Brunner, Emil 20–3, 25, 32
Bultmann, Rudolf 20, 22–5, 45

casuistry 176–7
Christ
  being in 37, 44, 117
  as collective person 37, 43–4
  as counter-Logos 56–7, 64, 118, 150, 207, 215
  cross of 107–8, 150, 157–60, 190, 193–4
  divine and human natures 40 n. 30, 56, 60–2, 76 n. 23
  indivisibility 60–3, 118, 161. *See also totus Christus*
  as Logos 60, 64–5, 84, 118, 204–5
  as Lord 153–4, 157, 159
  mediation 94–5, 109, 152
  promeity 58–60, 63, 65, 76, 89, 189
  real presence 11, 59, 87, 97 n. 20, 118, 162, 195–6, 208. *See also* presence of Christ
  speech of 73, 84, 86–7, 99, 156, 206–7
  suffering 157–8, 160, 190, 193–4, 196, 198–9
  transcendence 56–7, 64
Christology
  Chalcedonian definition 61 n. 34, 199 n. 68
  'from above' vs. 'from below' 60
  'how' vs. 'who' question 56–7, 79, 86–9
Christus praesens 45, 60, 69, 72–3, 79, 140, 185, 190, 201, 204. *See also* presence of Christ; *under* revelation
church. *See* ecclesiology
Confessing Church 127–8, 131, 133–4, 142–4, 174, 198
confessional theology 144, 188
  Lutheran confessions 28 n. 71, 75, 175
conscience 160, 168, 170, 178
creator–creature distinction 35–6
crucifixion. *See* Christ – cross of

David. *See* King David
DeJonge, Michael 23 n. 47, 28 n. 71, 38
Deus dixit 20, 32. *See also* God – speech of; God – word of
Deutsche Christen 77, 82
dialectical theology 20–6, 40 n. 31, 202
didache 68, 84, 88

discipleship 121, 149–63, 193, 206–7,
doctrinal theology 172, 174–7, 180, 183, 188–9

ecclesiology 33–8, 72
   'Christ existing as community' 8, 34, 42–5, 49, 62–3, 69
   continuity with Israel 129, 132–3, 141
   and God's word 49, 68
   Roman Catholic 35 n. 12
   and sociology 34–7, 43 n. 45
election 81, 84, 99, 106–7, 130, 203–4
epistemology 38–9
ethics 154, 165–84
exegesis
   allegorical, 130, 146, 199–200, 208
   contemporizing (*Vergegenwärtigung*) 76–83
   'faithful reading' 88, 145, 214
   historical-critical 27, 81–2, 88, 132–5, 155
   method 80, 109, 145, 152, 156, 200, 202, 207
   narrative 212–15
   nonreligious 195–6
   objectivity 53–4
   for preaching 80, 100–1
   spiritual 27, 30
   theological 53, 134, 139
extra ecclesiam 127

faith 41, 65, 75, 116, 130, 158, 187–90, 194, 204
   justification by 24, 83 n. 48
   and obedience 150, 152–3, 158, 163, 175
   and works 114, 149, 151
fall, the 170, 177–80
Feuerbach, Ludwig 17
finitum incapax infiniti 40
formation 124–5
Frei, Hans 10, 212–15

God
   freedom of 24, 39–40, 44. *See also* revelation – freedom of God in
   objectivity/non-objectivity 39, 43, 47, 51, 62, 87, 202
   simplicity 62
   speech 24, 155, *see also Deus dixit*
   word of, *see* word of God
Gogarten, Friedrich 21
good, the 166–71, 176–8
gospel. *See* law–gospel
grace 67, 114, 116, 131, 184
   cheap vs. costly, 149–54, 158, 188
Grisebach, Eberhard 21

Harnack, Adolf von 18–19, 26 n. 59, 27 n. 68, 31, 77 n. 27, 78
Harrelson, Walter 2, 95, 201
Hellenization thesis 18
heresy 72
historical criticism. *See* exegesis – historical-critical
history-of-religions school 17, 35, 76–7, 154, 187
Hohmann, Martin 96–8
Holy Spirit 41, 100, 109, 116, 125, 144, 171–2, 210
   and God's word, 20, 67–9, 79, 84–5, 88, 172, 196, 204
   and interpretation, 31, 85, 141
homiletics 71–6. *See also* preaching
human subject 41–2

interpretation. *See* exegesis

Jenson, Robert 10, 209–12
Jewish struggle 103–5
Jowett, Benjamin 1
joy 115, 124
Jüngel, Eberhard 45

Kant, Immanuel 17, 180, 181 n. 76
King David 95–100, 106–7, 130
koinonia 68, 84
Kuske, Martin 96–8, 135–6, 141

law. *See under* word of God; law–gospel
law–gospel 114, 153
liberal theology 16–20, 78, 187. *See also under* religion
Logos. *See under* Christ
Lord's Supper. *See* sacraments
Luther, Martin 16 n. 3, 28 n. 71, 29, 101, 114–15
Luther Bible 82–3

Mawson, Michael 36 n. 17, 38 n. 23, 47 n. 62, 172 n. 35
McCormack, Bruce 23 n. 47, 40 n. 30, 60 n. 30, 78 n. 30
meditation, scriptural 85, 117–23
Middle Ages 85

New Testament 5 n. 20, 18, 77–8, 96, 106, 154, 161, 180, 210. *See also* Scripture – relation of Old and New Testament

obedience. *See under* faith. *See also* simple obedience
Old Testament 5, 54 n. 5, 96–9, 130, 132–6, 142, 191–6, 198–200, 208–9, 211–12. *See also* Scripture – relation of Old and New Testament

Pentecost 67–8
perspicuity 65
petitio principii. *See under* revelation
Pieper, Josef 166–71
pneumatology. *See* Holy Spirit
polyphony 196–200, 212
'positivism of revelation' 187–8, 192, 198 n. 62
prayer 94–5, 101–2. *See also* meditation, scriptural
preaching 20, 44, 80–1, 119. *See also* homiletics
  application, 79–80, 88
  as *Christus praesens*, 72–4, 206
  funerals 103–5
  as God's word 50
  office of 75–6
  as witness 72–3, 86
presence of Christ 8, 44, 58–60, 63, 66, 73–4, 78–80, 86–9, 94, 118, 124–5, 137–9, 145–6, 150, 154, 161, 176, 196, 198, 206. *See also Christus praesens*; ecclesiology – 'Christ existing as community'
pro-me. *See* Christ – promeity
proclamation. *See* preaching
promeity. *See under* Christ
prudence 168
Psalms 93–109, 111–26, 130, 207

reality 34, 137–8, 166–73, 176–8, 182–4
reason 77, 170–1
religion
  in Bonhoeffer's prison letters 186–200
  in dialectical theology 19
  in liberal theology 17–18
  religious *a priori* 187
  and revelation, *see under* revelation
religionlessness 185–91, 195–7
responsibility 138, 171, 173, 175–6, 183–4
Reuter, Fritz 112
revelation 6, 39–45
  being of 39–40, 43
  as *Christus praesens* 11, 33, 43, 45, 49, 69, 73, 109, 111, 136, 139, 143, 149–51, 176, 185, 196, 207
  and ecclesiology 34–8, 34 n. 2, 43
  freedom of God in 39–40, 43, 81, *see also* God – freedom of
  and history 19, 27, 30, 36, 38, 46, 139–40
  knowledge of 41–2, 44–5, 172
  objectivity 19, 39, 43, 55, 62, 87, 174
  as *petitio prinipii* 8, 24, 109, 201
  present-tense character 82, 98, 135–9
  and religion 17, 19–20, 25, 187–8
  and Scripture 30, 84
  and theology 25, 32
'threefold form' 46–8, 50, 63
Rule of Faith (*regula fidei*) 27, 29, 210

sacrament 65–7, 74, 169 n. 17
Scripture. *See also* New Testament; Old Testament
  'book of the church' 53–4
  canon 28–9
  as *Christus praesens* 84–6, 88, 156, 195
  as God's word 49, 85–6, 203–4, *see also* revelation – and Scripture
  and history 98, 132–41, 146–7
  as human book 27
  infallibility 30
  inspiration 29–30, 81, 84, *see also* word of God – inspiration
  ontology of 51, 55, 71, 85, 201–4
  as physical object 85–6
  and preaching 48–51
  relation of Old and New Testament 5 n. 20, 67 n. 70, 96, 97 n. 20, 99, 134–5, 192–5, 198

and revelation, *see under* revelation
scriptural evidence 174–6, 180, 182–4
substance (*Sache*) 77–80, 78 n. 30
translation 82
verbal inspiration 29, 48–9, 51, 82, 96–8, 107, 203
as witness 30, 46, 80, 139, 153
Seeberg, Reinhold 26–7, 26 n. 59
sermon. *See* preaching
Sermon on the Mount 149–63
silence 118–19, 194
simple obedience 131, 150–2, 156, 215
singing 102, 120
solitude 119–21
stillness 121–3
supersessionism 142

Taylor, Charles 186 n. 2
theologia crucis 157. *See also* Christ – cross of
theological anthropology 41–2, 44, 117, 187
'heavenly double' 42, 44
theology of the word 63–9
Thurneysen, Eduard 20–1
totus Christus. *See* Christ – indivisibility

Trinity 40 n. 30, 45, 57 n. 15, 99, 205
Troeltsch, Ernst 17, 27 n. 68, 77 n. 27, 78, 187
truth 65, 137–9, 167–8, 174–5, 182–4, 204–5

vicarious-representative action 37
von Rad, Gerhard 97–8, 136

Webster, John 3, 145–6, 202, 214
Wendel, Ernst Georg 5, 135
word of God. *See also* revelation; Scripture
  – as God's word; theology of the word; Christ – as Logos
as address 65, 67, 83, 94
as command 144, 152–9, 165 n. 1, 183
embodiment 65–7
inspiration 67, *see also* Scripture – inspiration
intelligibility 64–5
as law 113–15, 129
as way 112–13, 124
worldliness 192–200

Ziegler, Philip 8 n. 26, 32 n. 90, 65, 176 n. 57
Zimmermann, Jens 214–15

www.ingramcontent.com/pod-product-compliance
Lightning Source LLC
Chambersburg PA
CBHW072108010526
44111CB00037B/2028